New Directions in Urban–Rural Migration

The Population Turnaround in Rural America

STUDIES IN POPULATION

Under the Editorship of: H. H. WINSBOROUGH

Department of Sociology
University of Wisconsin
Madison, Wisconsin

Samuel H. Preston, Nathan Keyfitz, and Robert Schoen. Causes of Death: *Life Tables for National Populations.*

Otis Dudley Duncan, David L. Featherman, and Beverly Duncan. Socioeconomic Background and Achievement.

James A. Sweet. Women in the Labor Force.

Tertius Chandler and Gerald Fox. 3000 Years of Urban Growth.

William H. Sewell and Robert M. Hauser. Education, Occupation, and Earnings: *Achievement in the Early Career.*

Otis Dudley Duncan. Introduction to Structural Equation Models.

William H. Sewell, Robert M. Hauser, and David L. Featherman (Eds.). Schooling and Achievement in American Society.

Henry Shryock, Jacob S. Siegel, and Associates. The Methods and Materials of Demography. *Condensed Edition by Edward Stockwell.*

Samuel H. Preston. Mortality Patterns in National Populations: *With Special Reference to Recorded Causes of Death.*

Robert M. Hauser and David L. Featherman. The Process of Stratification: *Trends and Analyses.*

Ronald R. Rindfuss and James A. Sweet. Postwar Fertility Trends and Differentials in the United States.

David L. Featherman and Robert M. Hauser. Opportunity and Change.

Karl E. Taeuber, Larry L. Bumpass, and James A. Sweet (Eds.). Social Demography.

Thomas J. Espenshade and William J. Serow (Eds.). The Economic Consequences of Slowing Population Growth.

Frank D. Bean and W. Parker Frisbie (Eds.). The Demography of Racial and Ethnic Groups.

Joseph A. McFalls, Jr. Psychopathology and Subfecundity.

Franklin D. Wilson. Residential Consumption, Economic Opportunity, and Race.

Maris A. Vinovskis (Ed.). Studies in American Historical Demography.

Clifford C. Clogg. Measuring Underemployment: Demographic Indicators for the United States.

David L. Brown and John M. Wardwell (Eds.). New Directions in Urban–Rural Migration: *The Population Turnaround in Rural America.*

A. J. Jaffe, Ruth M. Cullen, and Thomas D. Boswell. The Changing Demography of Spanish Americans

Robert Alan Johnson. Religious Assortative Marriage in the United States.

New Directions in Urban–Rural Migration

The Population Turnaround in Rural America

Edited by

David L. Brown

Economics, Statistics, and Cooperatives Service
U.S. Department of Agriculture
Washington, D.C.

John M. Wardwell

Center for Social Data Analysis
Montana State University
Bozeman, Montana

and

Departments of Sociology and
Rural Sociology
Washington State University
Pullman, Washington

ACADEMIC PRESS

A Subsidiary of Harcourt Brace Jovanovich, Publishers

New York   London   Toronto   Sydney   San Francisco

ACADEMIC PRESS, INC.
111 Fifth Avenue, New York, New York 10003

United Kingdom Edition published by
ACADEMIC PRESS, INC. (LONDON) LTD.
24/28 Oval Road, London NW1 7DX

Library of Congress Cataloging in Publication Data
Main entry under title:

New directions in urban–rural migration.

    (Studies in population series)
    Includes bibliographies and index.
    1. Migration, Internal––United States––Addresses,
essays, lectures. 2. United States––Population Rural––
Addresses, essays, lectures. I. Brown, David L.
II. Wardwell, John M. III. Series: Studies in population.
HB2385.N48   307'.2   80–23021
ISBN 0–12–136380–5

PRINTED IN THE UNITED STATES OF AMERICA

80 81 82 83   9 8 7 6 5 4 3 2 1

Contents

I
URBAN–RURAL MIGRATION IN THE 1970s

1
Population Redistribution in the United States during the 1970s

JOHN M. WARDWELL AND DAVID L. BROWN

2
The Changing Nature of Rural Employment

CALVIN L. BEALE

3

The Rural Population Turnaround: Research and National Public Policy   51

KENNETH L. DEAVERS AND DAVID L. BROWN

II

EXPLANATIONS FOR THE URBAN–RURAL TURNAROUND

4

Toward a Theory of Urban–Rural Migration in the Developed World   71

JOHN M. WARDWELL

5

The Demand for Public Goods as a Factor in the Nonmetropolitan Migration Turnaround   115

JOE B. STEVENS

6

The Effect of Trends in Economic Structures on Population Change in Rural Areas   137

LLOYD D. BENDER

7

Residential Preferences in Migration Theory   163

JAMES J. ZUICHES

8

Migration Decision Making among Nonmetropolitan-Bound Migrants   189

JAMES D. WILLIAMS AND DAVID BYRON McMILLEN

9

Retention of Metropolitan-to-Nonmetropolitan Labor-Force Migrants   213

EDWIN H. CARPENTER

III
MIGRATION TRENDS AND CONSEQUENCES IN RAPIDLY GROWING AREAS

10

The Ozark–Ouachita Uplands: Growth and Consequences   233

GEORGE H. DAILEY, JR. AND REX R. CAMPBELL

11

Migration and Energy Developments: Implications for Rural Areas in the Great Plains   267

STEVE H. MURDOCK, F. LARRY LEISTRITZ, AND ELDON C. SCHRINER

12

Effects of Turnaround Migration on Community Structure in Maine 291

LOUIS A. PLOCH

13

Migrant–Native Differences in Social Background and Community Satisfaction in Nonmetropolitan Utah Communities 313

WILLIAM F. STINNER AND MICHAEL B. TONEY

14

Industrial Dispersal and Labor-Force Migration: Employment Dimensions of the Population Turnaround in Michigan 333

JAMES J. ZUICHES AND MICHAEL L. PRICE

IV
DATA RESOURCES FOR
POPULATION DISTRIBUTION RESEARCH

List of Contributors

Numbers in parentheses indicate the pages on which authors' contributions begin.

CELIA A. ALLARD (383), Center for Social Data Analysis, Montana State University, Bozeman, Montana 59717

CALVIN L. BEALE (37), Economics, Statistics, and Cooperatives Service, U.S. Department of Agriculture, Washington, D.C. 20250

LLOYD D. BENDER* (137), Economics, Statistics, and Cooperatives Service, U.S. Department of Agriculture, Washington, D.C. 20250

DAVID L. BROWN† (5, 51), Economics, Statistics, and Cooperatives Service, U.S. Department of Agriculture, Washington, D.C. 20250

REX R. CAMPBELL (233), Department of Rural Sociology, University of Missouri, Columbia, Missouri 65211

EDWIN H. CARPENTER (213), Department of Agricultural Economics, University of Arizona, Tucson, Arizona 85721

GEORGE H. DAILEY, JR. (233), Office of Research and Economic Development, City of Oklahoma City, Oklahoma City, Oklahoma 73102

KENNETH L. DEAVERS (51), Economics, Statistics, and Cooperatives Service, U.S. Department of Agriculture, Washington, D.C. 20250

C. JACK GILCHRIST (383), Center for Social Data Analysis, Montana State University, Bozeman, Montana 59717

*Present address: Departments of Agricultural Economics and Economics, Montana State University, Bozeman, Montana 59717

†Present address: Science and Education Administration, U.S. Department of Agriculture, Washington, D.C. 20250

F. LARRY LEISTRITZ (267), Department of Agricultural Economics, North Dakota State University, Fargo, North Dakota 58102

DAVID BYRON McMILLEN (189), Bureau of the Census, U.S. Department of Commerce, Washington, D.C. 20230

STEVE H. MURDOCK (267), Department of Rural Sociology, Texas A&M University, College Station, Texas 77843

LOUIS A. PLOCH (291), Department of Agricultural and Resource Economics, University of Maine, Orono, Maine 04473

MICHAEL L. PRICE (333), Department of Sociology, Michigan State University, East Lansing, Michigan 48824

VERNON RENSHAW (365), Bureau of Economic Analysis, U.S. Department of Commerce, Washington, D.C. 20230

ELDON C. SCHRINER (267), Department of Sociology and Anthropology, North Dakota State University, Fargo, North Dakota 58102

JOE B. STEVENS (115), Department of Agricultural and Resource Economics, Oregon State University, Corvallis, Oregon 97331

WILLIAM F. STINNER (313), Population Research Laboratory and Department of Sociology, Utah State University, Logan, Utah 84321

MICHAEL B. TONEY (313), Population Research Laboratory and Department of Sociology, Utah State University, Logan, Utah 84321

JOHN M. WARDWELL (5, 71), Center for Social Data Analysis, Montana State University, Bozeman, Montana 59717 and Departments of Sociology and Rural Sociology, Washington State University, Pullman, Washington 99164

JAMES D. WILLIAMS (189), Department of Sociology and Anthropology, New Mexico State University, Las Cruces, New Mexico 88003

JAMES J. ZUICHES* (163, 333), Department of Sociology, Michigan State University, East Lansing, Michigan 48824

*Present address: Sociology Program, National Science Foundation, Washington, D.C. 20550

Foreword

Regional Research and
the Study of Migration

Migration has been a major factor in the development of American society. From the early years of the sixteenth century there have been flows and counterflows of people from Europe to the colonies and the states and out across the continent. There have been great migrations from the East to the West; from the South to the North; from the country to the cities and metropolitan areas; from the cities to the suburbs; from the North to the South and West; and most recently, the movement from metropolitan areas to the nonmetropolitan hinterlands. These migrations have left their mark on the cities, the countryside, and the society as a whole. We are a people in search of our roots and an understanding of what the last—and the next—move may bring.

This volume explores what has come to be called the population turnaround in rural America: the reversal of what only a few years ago was thought of as the inevitable flow of people from small towns and rural areas to the cities and metropolitan centers. The "new direction in urban–rural migration" is this turnaround. Urban–rural migration during the 1970s is described and characterized. Explanations of the turnaround are explored. Consequences, particularly those in rapidly growing areas, are examined. Potentials and pitfalls in the use of data resources for population distribution research are reviewed, as are some strategies for processing large data files.

Migration research has a long and distinguished history in the cooperative research system that has emerged out of federal–state partnership between the Department of Agriculture, the land grant universities, and the state agricultural experiment stations. From their founding in 1887, the research stations were acutely aware of the effects that a rapidly changing pattern of population distribution would have on agriculture and the rural community. This emphasis was reasserted in the 1930s and 1940s by the Department of Agriculture's creation of a Division of Farm Population and Rural Life within the Department's Bureau of Agricultural Economics. Monitoring and explaining changes in the demographic makeup and distribution of population were seen as basic to an understanding not only of the people of the nation as a whole and of its rural areas but of the problems and prospects of agriculture and the demand for and consumption of food and fiber.

Much of the research reported in this book was originally reported at a U.S.D.A. sponsored migration research conference held in Snowbird, Utah, in October, 1978, and was done through cooperative regional projects in the North Central states, the Northeast, and the West. One-quarter of federal fund appropriations from the Hatch Act must be used by state agricultural experiment stations for regional research activities. A cooperative regional project is one initiated by scientists who are located in different states but who are interested in a common problem, such as migration. With the cooperation and assistance of the regional association of state agricultural experiment station directors, they jointly develop a project outline and request funding. The project is reviewed by peers in the state experiment stations and by a scientist in the Cooperative Research Unit of the Science and Education Administration of the U.S. Department of Agriculture. It is also reviewed by a group of nine research directors who recommend approval and funding. Following approval, the researchers form a regional technical committee through which they plan and coordinate their work. Regional projects are usually approved for a period of between 3 and 5 years.

The first regional population project (commonly referred to as NC–18) was undertaken in the North Central states. The project was started in 1951 under the title "Population Dynamics." Losses of farm and rural population appeared to be escalating in all of the North Central states and were changing the character of small towns and rural areas. Cities and suburbs were growing rapidly. The initial work of the project focused on establishing net migration rates for the counties. Standardized procedures were developed so that individual state data could be cumulated into a regional total. The first regional bulletin identified the areas of growth and decline in the region.[1]

From 1951 to 1963 researchers under NC–18 produced some 214 publications of various types—journal articles, dissertations, station bulletins,

---

[1]Jehlik, P. M., & Wakely, R. E. *Population Change and Net Migration in the North Central States, 1940–1950* (North Central Regional Publication 56). Ames: Iowa Agricultural Experiment Station, 1955.

extension pamphlets, and mimeographed reports. Population research initiated under this first project was continued under such titles as "Community Adjustment to Social Change in the North Central Region," "The Relationship of Population to Social Changes in the North Central Region," and "Population Redistribution in the North Central Region—Pre and Post 1970." The latter study documented the population turnaround in the North Central states through the 1970s. Case studies of particular communities in the region indicate that the reversal of long-term trends of population loss has had a significant impact on land use patterns, utilization of resources, tax bases, and demands for community services. The work suggests that the consequences of population change for a community may vary with the type of migrant or source of change; with the rate of change; and with the long-term patterns of change.

Another project entitled "Population Redistribution in the Nonmetropolitan Areas of the North Central Region" has been approved for 3 years, effective January 1, 1980. This project has three major objectives: (a) to document population trends through the 1980 Census; (b) to delineate impacts of and interaction between population changes and measures of community vitality; and (c) to develop a typology of growing and declining communities on the basis of function and location.

It is significant that the cooperative research system and the North Central region have done regional population research continuously for some 30 years. Three factors seem to account for the achievement. First, there has been a continuing group of interested researchers. Second, these workers have had the support of the cooperative research system. Third, research productivity has validated requests for continuing financial support. The work has been widely applied by planners and decision makers in the various states in helping to assess change and to manage its consequences.

Population research in other areas of the country does not have the long history and continuity of that in the North Central region. In the Northeast, a regional project was initiated in July 1954 under the number and title NE–17, "Rural Population Dynamics." The project was terminated June 30, 1955 because of difficulties in getting it underway and in maintaining some appreciation of its potential value. The individual states continued to do some demographic research, but there was no regional project until October 1, 1977, when NE–119, entitled "Impact of In and Out Migration and Population Redistribution in the Northeast," began. Researchers in this region have developed an innovative project design which uses multiple documentary data sources integrated with primary data collected explicitly for the project.

Regional population research in the West began on July 1, 1971. The title of the first project suggests the focus: "Economic and Social Significance of Human Migration for the Western Region." This project (W–118) was continued October 1, 1976, with a September 30, 1981 termination date. The continuation project is explicitly concerned with the causes and consequences of the nonmetropolitan migration turnaround.

A search of the regional project records shows no regional project that focused specifically on population in the South. However, population data seem to have made up an important component of a number of regional projects. The existence of the Southern Regional Demographic Group, which brings together Land Grant and non-Land-Grant researchers, has served at least some of the functions of a regional technical committee.

One way of interpreting and gaining perspective on the work done under the regional projects is to look at some of their major emphases. I see four such emphases:

1. *Analyzing and characterizing changes in population.* The various projects have analyzed and characterized changes in population with emphases on migration but with some attention, particularly in the North Central region, to fertility and mortality. All such changes have been interpreted in relation to national patterns and trends.
2. *Examining the consequences of changes in population.* There are a number of studies on the consequences of migration for migrating individuals and families and for the sending and receiving communities, counties, substate areas, and states. Although some significant work has been done, this is now and will continue to be an area of great need.
3. *Determinants of population change.* Some significant but limited work has been done on attitudinal and other factors that influence decisions to migrate. Some beginning theoretical and explanatory work has been done—and more is now underway—to get at the causal factors in the revival of nonmetropolitan population growth.
4. *Policy implications and alternatives.* Some attempts have been made to examine policy implications and alternatives as guides to local, state, and federal decision makers. Much more work needs to be done on impact and policy questions.

New Directions in Urban–Rural Migration encompasses all four of these areas of research and includes original articles by researchers from all three regional population projects.

The book is divided into four parts. In the first part, three chapters document the population turnaround. The next part, containing six chapters, examines the complex set of conditions that have contributed to this turnaround. The focus is mainly on the United States, but attention is also given to the fact that similar trends are evident in most developed and highly urbanized countries. The third part explores the impacts and implications of recent changes in migration patterns in rapidly growing sections of the United States. The five chapters in this part identify and discuss changes in quality of life, employment conditions, living and working situations, and community satisfaction that result from the population turnaround. The final part, consisting of two chapters, discusses strategies for research on migration.

Collectively, these chapters provide a wide-ranging and timely treatment of urban–rural migration and population growth in contemporary America. The book explores the causes and consequences of a demographic event that must be ranked with the baby boom and subsequent fertility decline and the continuing suburbanization of urban populations as one of the three most significant demographic changes of the twentieth century.

EDWARD O. MOE
U.S. Department of Agriculture

Acknowledgments

This book was made possible by salary and operational support from the state–federal cooperative research program. Accordingly, we wish to thank the three Regional Associations of State Agricultural Experiment Station Directors who approved this use of resources and personnel. Grants in support of this effort were received from the Farm Foundation and the Western Rural Development Center. Support was also provided by the Economic Development Division, Economics, Statistics, and Cooperatives Service, U.S. Department of Agriculture, and by the Center for Social Data Analysis at Montana State University. We wish to thank R. J. Hildreth, Russell Youmans, Kenneth L. Deavers, and C. Jack Gilchrist, respectively, directors of these agencies, for their enthusiastic and persistent encouragement of this endeavor.

Edward O. Moe, Cooperative Research, Science and Education Administration, U.S. Department of Agriculture, has provided continuing encouragement and personal support through all phases of this project. We wish particularly to thank Peter A. Morrison of the Rand Corporation for his helpful evaluation of the entire manuscript and for his detailed comments and suggestions on several chapters. The staff of Academic Press has been enthusiastically cooperative throughout the preparation of the book.

We wish to thank the authors of the chapters, without whom there would be no book. In the sometimes difficult task of editing a collection such as this, they have been unfailingly cooperative in preparing successive revisions of their work and have in all ways contributed to the progress of this effort.

Finally, we wish to thank Micki Weimerskirch for her conscientiousness and skill in typing and proofreading the entire manuscript.

URBAN–RURAL MIGRATION IN THE 1970s

For the first time in this century, population and economic growth in nonmetropolitan America is exceeding metropolitan growth. Growth is occurring in remote and completely rural counties as well as in counties that are partly urban or dominated by nearby metropolitan centers. The new growth trends are evident in most major regions; they began in the Ozark–Ouachita uplands in the mid-1960s and extended to most other regions by the early 1970s.

In most regions, the new growth is entirely due to changes in net migration. Movement of people from metropolitan to nonmetropolitan areas since 1970 has exceeded the counterflow into metropolitan centers. Low and convergent rates of natural increase have provided a passive background for these migration-induced changes in population distribution. This background has made the population losses through out-migration from the largest Standard Metropolitan Statistical Areas (SMSAs) more visible than would have been the case in periods of higher fertility.

The migration reversal is as pervasive across sociodemographic characteristics of movers as it is across regions. However, these aggregate patterns should not be seen as statistically unitary. They mask a number of complex conditions that are shaping the form and function of rural and nonmetropolitan America in the last third of this century.

The Chapters in this part of the book focus on the complexity of change. They document this diversity and examine the implications of the turnaround for national public policy.

Wardwell and Brown (Chapter 1) present a comprehensive analysis of

1

national and regional changes in internal migration and population distribution. They note that the growth of nonmetropolitan areas is taking place in the context of two other shifts in population distribution: regional redistribution from the North to the South and West, and continuing suburbanization. All three of these trends act to move people and economic activities from higher-density areas to more sparsely populated locales.

The dynamics of the nonmetropolitan migration turnaround are detailed in terms of its component changes in gross in-migration and out-migration and in terms of prevalence across migrant characteristics.

Wardwell and Brown provide insight into the process through which the turnaround was discovered and documented. They indicate that early skepticism about the reality and duration of the change gradually gave way to intensive analyses of the causes and consequences of the new distribution trend. They conclude their chapter with speculations on the effects of higher energy costs on future patterns of population concentration and deconcentration.

The structure of nonmetropolitan employment has become increasingly diverse and decreasingly agricultural. Beale (Chapter 2) provides a picture of the regional diversity and complexity of economic structure in modern-day rural America. This complexity suggests that there is no simple explanation of the role of employment in the nonmetropolitan migration turnaround. The migration effect of economic change is examined from various perspectives in Chapters 4, 5, 6, 7, 9, and 14.

Beale's discussion of employment change in nonmetropolitan America focuses on such other issues as female labor-force participation, part-time farming, and commuting to metropolitan jobs. Beale discusses the size distribution of economic establishments, pointing out that nonmetropolitan areas have many large establishments—employers that would be large even in a metropolitan context.

The nonmetropolitan migration turnaround has tended to be uncritically viewed as a success story. The problems attendant on rapid unanticipated growth have been eclipsed by the pervasiveness of the view that growth is indicative of rising social and economic welfare.

Deavers and Brown (Chapter 3) examine some of the reasons for the gap, or lag, between changed conditions and unchanged policy. The very geographic diversity of nonmetropolitan America, noted in Chapters 1 and 2, contributes to the low political salience of the problems of growth. Attention has remained focused on those nonmetropolitan areas that are not participating in renewed growth—those that are experiencing stagnant economic conditions and stable or declining population. Because population decline was the rule for most of rural America for 30 years, public policies and programs were formulated primarily to meet the problem of lack of growth.

Deavers and Brown point out that the problems of growth are neither uniform nor appropriately addressed by traditional programs aimed at rural poverty and economic distress. They do not suggest abandoning existing programs, for much rural poverty and unequal access to institutions and services remain. Rather, they call for additional attention to the new problems of adaptation to growth-induced changes. The demographic composition of growing areas, for example, is markedly different from that of stable and declining areas. These differences call for a different mix of services and facilities. Low settlement density and relative physical isolation remain the dominant ecological parameters for many nonmetropolitan areas that are faced with rising service needs and changed service mixes. These parameters create unique problems in satisfying the needs brought about by new and largely unanticipated growth. The limited capacity for institutional adaptation to population and economic growth in impacted areas was part of the population problem in nonmetropolitan America in the 1970s.

1

Population Redistribution in the United States during the 1970s[1]

JOHN M. WARDWELL
DAVID L. BROWN

Introduction

The reversal of relative growth rates between metropolitan and non-metropolitan areas is associated with change in the relative importance of natural increase and net migration. Historically, local differences in population growth rates were primarily dependent on variations in natural increase, supplemented by net migration. For example, rural areas and central cities of large metropolitan areas have shown population stability or slow growth in spite of massive out-migration because the excess of births over deaths was great enough to offset the migration loss. Today, net migration has taken over, in most areas, as the prime determinant of local population change (Goldstein, 1976; Long and Hansen, 1977).

Rural out-migration has declined while urban out-migration has increased sharply; convergent and low levels of natural increase have caused population growth rates to be more responsive to variations in migration. High fertility no longer masks the population decline associated with net out-migration, and net in-migration is now the primary component of growth, not a supplement to natural increase.

Aside from being a principal component of population growth and decline, migration is a symptom of basic social and economic change. Migration is a necessary part of normal population adjustment and

[1] The research reported herein has been supported by the Economic Development Division, Economics, Statistics, and Cooperatives Service, U.S. Department of Agriculture, and by the Center for Social Data Analysis, Montana State University.

5

equilibrium and an instrument of cultural diffusion and social integration (Bogue, 1959). Hence, it is ironic that demographers have focused less attention on migration than on fertility and mortality (Goldstein, 1976).

Relative Lack of Interest in Migration

In part, the relative lack of emphasis on migration reflects the traditional sparseness of high-quality data on population movement, particularly for cities, counties, and other small geographic areas. However, it is more likely that the lack of data reflects a relative lack of interest. The development of accurate birth and death registration systems in the first third of this century reflected a great interest in fertility and mortality. This interest was sustained by the still high but rapidly declining death rates and widely fluctuating birth rates of the time.

Death rates continued to decline but soon stabilized, whereas birth rates varied even more widely through the middle third of the century. Scientists concerned with population change devoted most of their attention to the change from Depression-era lows to post–World War II highs in birth levels in the United States and in other countries. Sustained high fertility throughout the 1950s and 1960s continued this emphasis, particularly as high world-population growth rates captured the interest and concerns of demographers and biological scientists.

The effect of sustained high fertility on local population growth was immediate and obvious, and it demanded response from federal, state, and local institutions. In contrast, internal migration seemed to be a much less pressing problem. The relative lack of attention to migration continued into the early 1970s, when low and stable birth rates finally began to create a space within which the importance of migration could become manifest. With the increasing similarity of birth and death rates between regional and rural–urban parts of the country (U.S. Bureau of the Census, 1975b), migration has become the primary engine driving local variations in population growth and composition.

Renewed Interest in Migration

Renewed interest in migration as a component of local population growth and as the primary component of variations in population distribution, coincided with a change in patterns of population movement that is already being called one of the most significant demographic events of this century: the reversal of relative growth rates between metropolitan and nonmetropolitan areas. Like most forms of demographic change, this turnaround reflects other changes in society and the economy, and the turnaround itself initiates additional changes. The redistribution of population among regional and rural–urban areas of the United States is the subject of this chapter and of this book.

The concentration of the population into large cities has been one of the most dependable population distribution trends of the twentieth century. Migration from rural areas to urban places outnumbered the reverse flow in every decade from 1900 to 1970. Changes in the structure of agriculture were prime determinants of this cityward migration. Mechanization of farming and the resultant migration of farm people to the cities reduced the populations of hundreds of counties in the United States. From 1940 to 1970, about 900 of the nation's 3100 counties showed a decline in population in each successive decade. The vast majority declined because the loss of farms was not offset by other forms of employment. In about 400 counties, the maximum population was reached as early as 1900 because they were oversettled to begin with or because deteriorating productivity induced loss of farm people even before the advent of the tractor.

In the Great Plains and western Corn Belt regions, stretching over about 700,000 square miles from Iowa to Montana and from North Dakota to Texas, the total rural population (farm and nonfarm) fell 27% in 1940–1970. In the old Cotton Belt of the coastal southern plain, from South Carolina to east Texas, rural population fell by 36% during the same period. These declines resulted almost entirely from a drop in labor requirements in counties that depended heavily on farming and lacked compensating increases in nonagricultural activity. At the same time, rural population was increasing steadily in the Southern Piedmont textile belt, the industrialized and suburbanizing rural areas of the Lower Great Lakes region and the Northeastern Coast, the Florida Peninsula recreation and retirement communities, and areas of the far West and Southwest. As a result, the distribution of rural people shifted. The national level of rural population changed little, for these regional changes compensated for each other. But in the agricultural regions, hundreds of towns declined in population, hundreds of thousands of former farm homes were demolished or abandoned, and many businesses closed. The volume of agricultural output grew, but the proportion of rural people engaged in agriculture fell, either directly or indirectly.

Nonmetropolitan population loss through out-migration accelerated sharply following World War II. From 1950 to 1960, 3.0 million people left nonmetropolitan counties for metropolitan destinations. The loss continued from 1960 to 1970, although the amount declined to a net of 2.2

million persons for the decade. This apparently inexorable trend was suddenly reversed about 1970. Nonmetropolitan counties grew by 9.1% compared with 5.4% in metropolitan counties (4.9 million and 8.1 million persons, respectively) between 1970 and 1977 (USDA, 1979). Entirely rural counties and counties remote from any metropolitan territory also showed reversals from the pattern of decades-long population loss to that of population gain. Nearly three-fourths of all nonmetropolitan counties in the United States have gained population during the 1970s. Although over 400 nonmetropolitan counties are still experiencing population declines, many of these show reduced rates of loss. Still-declining counties are located primarily in the Great Plains and the Mississippi Delta.

Three Patterns of Redistribution

This chapter examines the metropolitan–nonmetropolitan population reversal in the context of two other major trends that are shaping the patterns of population distribution in the last quarter of this century: continuing suburbanization and redistribution among regions. All three of these trends act to move population and economic activity from high-density areas into areas that are less densely settled (Long, J., 1980). The pervasiveness of the migration reversal, both across migrant characteristics and across regional and other classifications of counties, are examined in the context of the many explanations that have been advanced to account for the phenomenon. These explanations are contrasted with explanations that had sought to explain the continuing concentration of the national population.

SUBURBANIZATION

Suburbanization is not a new phenomenon in the American settlement experience. Adna Weber (1899) wrote that an outward shift of residential population around certain larger cities occurred during the last quarter of the nineteenth century, and Leo Schnore (1959) demonstrated that 10 American cities with 100,000 or more population in 1950 were already deconcentrating before 1900. New York City had begun by 1850. By the beginning of the 1920s, the majority of U.S. cities had begun to experience lower rates of population growth than their surrounding suburbs (Hawley, 1971).

The growth of suburban areas proceeds both through outward movement of population from the central area and through in-migration to the urban periphery from nonmetropolitan and other metropolitan areas. Centrifugal movement of central population was facilitated by innovations in short-distance transportation and communication. The reduction of costs associated with distance allowed central city workers to move their residences further away from their principal workplaces. Horsedrawn, steam, and electric streetcars; the telephone; and later, the private automobile were principal innovations that permitted this outward movement, which was also impelled by rising land values in the more centrally accessible locations. Peripheral development first occurred along major transportation arteries, and later in the rural interstices between such routes. The reasons for suburbanization are many and varied, but the availability of large tracts of relatively cheap land on which to locate residential developments has been of crucial importance.

This is not to deny the importance of individual motivations among suburban movers. Congestion, crime, pollution, noise, and other urban disamenities acted as push factors, while residential space for children and access to open space acted as pull factors. Both sets of factors contributed to the suburban trend throughout this century.

Suburban growth continued apace during the decade of the 1970s. Peripheral areas grew at an average annual rate of 1.6% between 1970 and 1977 (Table 1.1). This compares with an annualized rate of growth of

TABLE 1.1

Average Annual Percentage Population Change for Central and Suburban Counties by Region, 1970–1977

Area	United States	Region			
		Northeast	North Central	South	West
Metro total	.6	.4	.1	1.4	1.6
Central cities [a]	− .7	−1.6	−1.5	− .2	1.0
Outside central cities	1.6	.5	1.4	2.9	2.1
Metro areas of 1 million or more	.5	− .5	.3	1.7	1.3
Central cities	−1.1	−1.7	−1.4	− .9	.3
Outside central cities	1.6	.4	1.4	3.3	1.9
Metro areas of less than 1 million	.8	[b] ---	− .1	1.2	2.3
Central cities	− .2	−1.0	−1.6	.1	2.2
Outside central cities	1.7	.6	1.3	2.5	2.5

Source: U.S. Bureau of the Census, 1978b, Current Population Reports, Special Studies Series P–23, No. 75. "Social and Economic Characteristics of the Metropolitan and Nonmetropolitan Population 1977 and 1970." Washington, D.C., USGPO.
[a] Metropolitan status as of 1970.
[b] Less than .05%.

less than 1% (.9%) for the total U.S. population. In contrast, central-city portions of SMSAs declined by .7% per year during the period. This decline was mainly in central cities of SMSAs with a million or more population—the largest metropolitan areas. Central cities of small SMSAs declined much less rapidly.

There was little if any central-city growth in any region of the country, except in the West, and here appreciable growth only occurred in smaller SMSAs. In contrast, suburban areas grew in all of the regions, although their rate of growth in the Northeast was slight. Suburban growth was especially great in the South and West regardless of metropolitan area size. The suburbs surrounding large SMSAs in the South grew at an average annual rate of 3.3% during the 1970s—a rate comparable to that being experienced by many underdeveloped countries.

Indications are that rapid suburban growth and slow growth or decline of central cities will continue into the twenty-first century (Morrison, 1976). It is projected that the number of inhabitants of what is now defined as the suburban fringe will increase by 62% to 75% by the year 2000. Central-city residents are expected to increase in number only slightly (12%) or to decline by about 4%. As a consequence, the suburban land that surrounds existing metropolitan cities may have to accommodate as many as 135 million persons in the year 2000, or 58 million more than in 1970.

This continuing suburbanization of the metropolitan population has contributed a part of the growth in counties classified as nonmetropolitan, as is discussed more fully below. As the radius of the metropolitan periphery grows, it extends settlement into territory that remains classified as nonmetropolitan, either because the reclassification procedures lag behind the population movements or because the affected counties still fail to qualify as metropolitan despite the influx of new growth. Thus, for example, nonmetropolitan counties that are adjacent to metropolitan areas account for more than one-half of the total nonmetropolitan growth. Much of this growth in adjacent nonmetropolitan counties is widely assumed to represent the effects of continued suburbanization.

REGIONAL REDISTRIBUTION

The South gained over 5 million persons between 1970 and 1975. This growth exceeded that of all other regions combined. The West grew by 2.9 million persons, slightly less than in the 1960s but nonetheless a continuation of past trends. In contrast, the North Central states and the Northeast grew only slightly, by 1 million and 400,000 persons, respectively. This is radically different than in previous decades (U.S.

Bureau of the Census, 1975a). Internal migration is the basic determinant of regional variations in population growth. This is increasingly so because natural increase, births minus deaths, is at a low point and thus contributes very little to regional variations in population change.

In the South, recent population growth and in-migration contrasts sharply with previous history (Long, 1978). Traditionally, the South has been an exporter of population. Strong motivations for leaving the region have included poverty, economic underdevelopment, and a labor surplus in agriculture. Among blacks, additional motivations have been prejudice, discrimination, and the abandonment of sharecropping. Migration from the South reached its peak during World War II and in the following decade—during the 1940s the region had a net loss of over 2 million persons. However, the South began to industrialize and modernize in the late 1950s and early 1960s, and the flow of jobs and people began to reverse their traditional course. Low taxes, other investment incentives, cheap land and labor, and a relative lack of unionization were among the factors responsible for this reversal. Both increased in-migration and decreased loss of persons to other regions figured importantly in the South's shift to net in-migration (Long and Hansen, 1975). However, it should be noted that in-migration to the South was selective of specific areas during the 1960s—Florida accounted for a large proportion of growth. In fact, had it not been for Florida, the region would have continued to show a net migration loss (U.S. Bureau of the Census, 1975a).

In-migration to the South accelerated during the 1970s. More importantly, in-migration was characteristic of numerous areas throughout the region. Texas, the mid-South uplands (Tennessee, Kentucky, northern Alabama and Georgia) and the Ozark–Ouachita plateau (Arkansas and Oklahoma) had substantial growth (Roseman, 1977). Similarly, California's dominance of in-migration to the West ended during the 1970s. Between 1965 and 1970, California was the destination of almost 70% of all migrants to the West. In contrast, during the first 5 years of the 1970s, that state's share declined to under one-third (U.S. Bureau of the Census, 1975a).

The primary streams of interregional migration are from the North Central and Northeast regions to the South and West (Table 1.2). The volume of migration between the North and South has increased markedly since 1965–1970, while the North-to-West stream has remained relatively stable. Also, the South to West movement has been reversed. Thus, regardless of which region we specify, the South is no longer a net exporter of population. To the contrary, it is a major locus of economic and population growth for the nation.

TABLE 1.2
Streams of Migration among Regions

Direction of net migration	1965–70	1970–75
Between		
Northeast and		
North Central	− 53	− 67
South	−438	−964
West	−224	−311
North Central and		
Northeast	+ 53	+ 67
South	−275	−790
West	−415	−472
South and		
Northeast	+438	+964
North Central	+275	+790
West	− 57	+ 75
West and		
Northeast	+224	+311
North Central	+415	+472
South	+ 57	− 75

Source: U.S. Bureau of the Census, 1973, U.S. Census of Population, 1970. Subject Reports Mobility for States and the Nation PC(2)–2B, Washington, D.C.: USGPO. 1975 Current Population Reports, Series P–20, No. 285, "Mobility of the Population of the United States, March 1970 to March 1975."

NONMETROPOLITAN POPULATION TURNAROUND

Past notions of metropolitan concentration and of decline or abandonment of small towns and rural areas can no longer serve as guides for understanding population distribution in the United States. In fact, from 1970 to 1977, 2.6 million more people moved into nonmetropolitan counties than moved out of them. By contrast, during the 1960s these same counties lost 3 million persons through out-migration (Table 1.3). Consequently, for the first time in the twentieth century, the rate of population growth in nonmetropolitan America (9.1%) exceeded that in metropolitan areas (5.4%) (USDA, 1979). This turnaround affects most regions of the country and remote and completely rural areas as well as those that are partly urbanized and dominated by large metropolitan cities. The reasons for the turnaround are complex, but three interrelated factors appear to be at the root: economic decentralization, preference for rural living, and modernization of rural life.

TABLE 1.3
Population Change by Metropolitan Status, 1960–1977

Area	Population Number(000s) 1977	Population Number(000s) 1970	Population Number(000s) 1960	Percentage change 1970–1977	Percentage change 1960–1970	Net migration [a] 1970–1977 Number(000s)	Net migration [a] 1970–1977 Rate(%)	Net migration [a] 1960–1970 Number(000s)	Net migration [a] 1960–1970 Rate(%)
Total United States	216,350	203,301	179,323	6.4	13.4	3,210	1.8	3,001	1.7
Metropolitan counties [b]	156,984	148,877	127,191	5.4	17.0	617	.5	5,959	4.7
Nonmetropolitan counties	59,366	54,424	52,132	9.1	4.4	2,593	5.0	−2,958	−5.7
Adjacent counties [c]	30,775	28,033	26,116	9.8	7.3	1,504	5.8	−705	−2.7
Nonadjacent counties	28,591	26,391	26,016	8.3	1.4	1,089	4.2	−2,253	−3.7

Source: U.S. Census of Population, 1970 and Current Population Reports, Bureau of the Census.
[a] Net migration expressed as a percentage of the population at beginning of specified period.
[b] Metropolitan status as of 1974.
[c] Nonmetropolitan counties adjacent to Standard Metropolitan Statistical Areas.

1. *Economic Decentralization.* There has been a decentralization of employment opportunities from metropolitan to nonmetropolitan areas (Beale, 1978a; 1978b). Between 1970 and 1977, nonfarm wage and salary employment increased by 22% in nonmetropolitan areas. In addition, the character of nonmetropolitan employment has changed: Service-performing jobs have taken the lead in recent growth. Mining and energy extraction are new sources of employment growth in some areas such as the northern Great Plains. People are not being displaced from rural areas by diminishing employment in extractive industries to the extent that they were during the 1950s and 1960s. Commuting from nonmetropolitan to metropolitan areas brings additional jobs within the reach of rural residents.

2. *Preference for Rural Living.* National surveys have repeatedly found a decided preference for living in the country and in small towns, particularly within commuting range of a metropolitan central city (Fuguitt and Zuiches, 1975; Zuiches and Carpenter, 1978). This preference for rural living becomes increasingly important as the employment constraints to living in rural areas are lessened (Zelinsky, 1977).

3. *Modernization of Rural Life:* All-weather roads, controlled access highways, cable television, telephone service, and centralized water and sewer systems have helped to modernize rural living. And because of these advances the stereotype that rural areas are isolated and backward has become increasingly inappropriate.

However, it should be pointed out that nonmetropolitan America is extremely heterogeneous. The factors that bring about growth in one area may be of little consequence in another. In the midst of this population turnaround, there are still about 400 nonmetropolitan counties in the Great Plains and the Mississippi Delta that continue to experience outmigration and population decline.

REGIONAL AND METROPOLITAN–NONMETROPOLITAN INTERACTION

The interaction between interregional and metropolitan–nonmetropolitan migration streams since 1970 is difficult to specify. Current Population Survey data do not permit a decomposition of migration streams by region and residence of origin and destination. However, it is possible to analyze interregional labor-force mobility by metropolitan–nonmetropolitan place of work, using the Continuous Work History Sample (CWHS) of Social Security records. Labor-force mobility and population mobility are different phenomena, but there is

evidence that CWHS labor-migration streams bear a significant resemblance to trends and patterns of general population mobility shown
in other data (Wardwell and Gilchrist, 1979b).

CWHS data show that the sources of nonmetropolitan labor force
migration differ among the four census regions (Table 1.4). In the
Northeast, in-migrants were mainly from metropolitan counties within
the region. In contrast, most of the net gain experienced by nonmetropolitan counties in the South came from metropolitan areas outside of
the region. Migration to the nonmetropolitan West was much less specific. These counties gained in-migrating workers from metropolitan
areas inside and outside of the West, and from nonmetropolitan counties in other regions. Nonmetropolitan areas in the North Central region
experienced a net loss of 68,000 workers—almost all to counties outside
of the region, both metropolitan and nonmetropolitan (Brown, 1980).

Thus, the population distribution trends of the 1970s are new in several ways: Migration has largely taken the place of variations in natural
increase as the primary force behind local population change. All three
of the distribution trends bring people and activities into lower-density
places and areas. Two of these trends, regional redistribution and nonmetropolitan growth, are breaks with the past and were largely unanticipated. As a consequence, there is an increasing awareness that

TABLE 1.4
*Nonmetropolitan Net Worker Migration by Region and Metropolitan-
Nonmetropolitan Place of Work, 1970–1975*

Origin of migrants	Net migration (000s)			
	Northeast	North Central	South	West
From all areas	39	−68	88	114
From metropolitan areas within the region	43	5	3	52
From metropolitan areas outside the region	−6	−51	78	44
From nonmetropolitan areas outside of the region	2	−22	7	16

Source: Continuous Work History Sample (CWHS); adapted from
Brown (1980).

migration-induced population change merits the kind of systematic demographic attention historically given changes induced by fertility and
mortality.

Discovery and Documentation of the Turnaround

The first signs of a change in the patterns of nonmetropolitan and
rural depopulation were detected nearly a decade before the turnaround
became an accepted demographic fact. The time lag can be attributed to
two factors present in the period during which this change took place.
The first factor was a pervasive skepticism based on the stability of
historical trends of population concentration in metropolitan areas and
on the economic and demographic models developed to explain that
concentration. The second factor was the nature of the data available to
study population distribution between 1965 and 1975.

Early Skepticism

Throughout the 1960s and into the early 1970s, new models of population distribution were presented, and a number of authoritative projections based upon the extrapolation of past trends were developed.
None of these models or projections accurately forecasted the patterns
that were then unfolding.

The most fully elaborated models of the urban growth and development process were presented by Berry (1972) and Thompson (1965,
1968). Thompson argued that population size and growth rates insured
future growth through the diversity and depth of the modern metropolis. Large urban centers provided the locus of new technological
and industrial growth, and the diverse infrastructures of these centers
provided the ability to weather recessions and shifts in production and
consumption that could severely inhibit the growth of smaller, more
industry-specific communities. Thus, for example, the severe impact of
the decline in aerospace industries on the growth of Seattle or of the
decline in tourism and copper extraction on the growth of Tucson was
attributed to the lack of depth associated with those cities' relatively
small sizes. It was argued that impacts of comparable magnitude could
be absorbed by a city the size of Cleveland, Chicago or Detroit without
severe effects on city size or growth rates. Very large cities were held to
contain an internal growth dynamic insulating them from economic recessions and other cyclic phenomena.

Berry focused on the effects of changes in short-distance and long-distance transportation and on the diffusion of modern electronic communication. These explained both the geographic spread within urban systems of ever-increasing physical size, and the continued organization and distributional dominance and centrality of these large urban centers in the national system of cities.

Models of this type dominated the demographic context within which national and international projections of urban growth and population distribution were made for the closing decades of the twentieth century. In 1969, for example, the United Nations released a study of world urban and rural population growth, 1920–2000, in which the urban patterns described above were projected for all of the most developed (and also most urban) nations in the world (United Nations, 1969). Similarly, in the United States, the Water Resources Council developed the OBERS projections (U.S. Water Resources Council, 1974) of population growth and distribution in the United States. Separate projections to the year 2000 of SMSA and non-SMSA portions of the individual Bureau of Economic Analysis (BEA) economic areas were prepared, as well as projections of total SMSA and non-SMSA growth for the United States (U.S. Water Resources Council, 1974, Volume I, pp. 108–133, Tables, 20 and 23). Both the UN and the OBERS projections concluded that metropolitan agglomeration and nonmetropolitan decline would continue through the remainder of the twentieth century.

Documentation and Eventual Acceptance

Vining and Kontuly's (1978) documentation of net migration patterns in the large urban regions of other developed countries has shown that the UN projections were already in error by the time they were released. Similarly, population redistribution patterns in the United States during the 1960s and 1970s were rendering the OBERS population projections obsolete at the very time they were in preparation.

As early as 1968, the census estimates of county growth from 1960 to 1966 showed reversals from population decline to gain for some rural and nonmetropolitan parts of the country and a distinct slowdown in the rate of population loss for other areas. The first public presentation of this evidence was in congressional testimony by Calvin Beale in the summer of 1969 (Beale, 1969). At that time, neither Beale nor anyone else anticipated that within a few years the nonmetropolitan category as a whole would begin to reverse its historical pattern of population decline and exceed the metropolitan category in rates of net migration and population growth. Nonmetropolitan population decline was forecasted by all official projections made during the 1960s.

Early evidence of a resurgence in rural and nonmetropolitan areas was not limited to population data. Employment data also showed a rural growth advantage. At approximately the same time that the results of the 1966 county population estimates were being reported, data from County Business Patterns showed complementary changes in the more rapid growth of manufacturing activity in nonmetropolitan counties. Moreover, this renewed employment growth was in many of the same areas that were showing the change from population loss to gain. However, these preliminary indications were overshadowed by the results of the 1970 Census, which did not evidence the new trends. Numerous rural counties showed a lower population in 1970 than they had in the estimates for 1966. On the basis of the 1970 Census results, then, the 1966 estimates appeared to have been in error, and national substantiation of renewed rural growth was not forthcoming.

But the change from decline to gain showed up again in the 1973 county population estimates, and by that time the change was apparent across the nation (Long, L., 1980). Beale (1974) presented these findings at a conference of small-town newspaper publishers in the Fall of 1973. The national turnaround in relative growth and net migration rates between metropolitan–nonmetropolitan areas was first discussed in this paper, and in a subsequent U.S. Department of Agriculture (USDA) Bulletin (Beale, 1975). Moreover, the *New York Times* (King, 1973) and the *Washington Post* (Chapman, 1973) developed extensive feature articles on the turnaround. Information about the turnaround was widely circulated through congressional testimony and newspaper wire services well before it found dissemination in professional forums and scientific journals.

Professional skepticism remained strong through the mid-1970s. The findings were, after all, based on population estimates, and there was much reluctance to forget past trends and to give up models that had projected these trends indefinitely into the future. But in 1975 the data situation improved markedly with the release of the 1970–1975 Current Population Survey (CPS) of mobility patterns (U.S. Bureau of the Census, 1975a). (A national survey of 78,000 households, the CPS provides accurate annual information on the size, distribution, and composition of the U.S. population.) Tucker (1976) confirmed with these CPS data that approximately 1.5 million more people moved from metropolitan to nonmetropolitan counties in this period than had made the more traditional opposite move.

At about the same time, Vining and Kontuly (1977) documented a comparable reversal in net migration patterns of large urban regions in some of the other more developed countries. Annual net migration statistics for core urban regions in France, West Germany, East Germany, and the Netherlands showed diminishing rates of gain and eventual losses in the 1960s. The 1970s witnessed similar reversals in Japan, Sweden, Norway, Italy, Denmark, New Zealand, and Belgium. Urban growth rates had slowed relative to natural increase rates in Australia, Israel, the United Kingdom, and Canada (Wardwell, 1977). Growth of rural areas proximate to urban regions was also evident in the United Kingdom (Drewett *et al.*, 1976), Canada (Beaujot, 1978), and Australia (Bourne and Logan, 1976). A total of 16 developed and highly urbanized countries showed some degree of slowing in large urban growth rates and of increasing in growth rates in proximate or remote rural areas.

Frisbie and Poston (1975, 1976) laid the groundwork for an understanding of the pre-1970 structural changes in nonmetropolitan counties that formed part of the basis for new population and economic growth. They identified the diversifying employment structure of growing counties and showed how diversity, or complexity, of sustenance organization was related to growth. Technological change helped to diversify the nonmetropolitan economy, giving impetus to rising productivity. This productivity functioned both to attract and to retain population.

Thus by 1977, skepticism began to give way to a gradual acceptance. Annual county net migration estimates continued to evidence the change, County Business Patterns data continued to document the deconcentration of manufacturing and other activities, and subsequent CPS mobility surveys continued to show more metropolitan to nonmetropolitan moves than the reverse. By that time, additional data sets were able to shed further light on the phenomenon. Brown (1978) and Wardwell and Gilchrist (1978) used longitudinal data from the CWHS on workers who were covered for social security to demonstrate that patterns of change in county location of employment closely paralleled the patterns of change in residential mobility. These data also showed that nonmetropolitan counties were gaining workers at the expense of the largest metropolitan counties, that nonmetropolitan counties that were not adjacent to any SMSAs evidenced a more rapid rate of change than did the adjacent counties, and that the employment turnaround was manifest in all four census regions of the country.

Long (1978) used 1970–1975 revenue sharing estimates for population change in size categories of incorporated places to demonstrate that deconcentration was characteristic of even the small towns and cities in nonmetropolitan counties. In all regions of the country, growth rates in the open country outside of places with a population of 2500 or greater were more rapid than any other category.

By 1978, a number of intensive, primary-data-gathering efforts were underway in many states and regions (Williams and Sofranko, 1979; Zelinsky, 1975). The reasons for the turnaround offered in Beale's original articles (1974, 1975) were evaluated and supported through these efforts and through other research. Attention shifted from documenting and explaining the new trends to the tasks of hazarding new, short-term projections (Fuguitt and Beale, 1977, Table 1.9) and exploring the consequences of unanticipated rural growth. Skeptics remained (Engels and Healy, 1979; Thompson, 1977), but most seemed to be waiting in the wings for the results of the 1980 Census to provide a definitive assessment of change during the 1970–1980 decade. Another, more unfortunate manifestation of this waiting with suspended judgment was the continued use by some Federal agencies of the OBERS projections, which by this time had become thoroughly unreliable as a guide to contemporary and projected population redistribution (see, for example, Environmental Protection Agency, 1978).

Perhaps the most difficult task in demographic practice is to detect the difference between a fluctuation and a new trend when the departure from old and heretofore reliable trends has just begun. That task has been as difficult in assessing the nonmetropolitan turnaround as it had been in determining how long the low fertility levels of the 1970s will persist or as it has been in judging how long the baby boom would continue. But regardless of duration, the new migration patterns have already gone on long enough to leave a lasting impact on the social, economic, and demographic structures of nonmetropolitan and metropolitan places. Factors such as increasing costs and decreasing flexibility of transportation systems (because of rising real costs and uncertain supplies of energy resources) could reverse the reversal within the next decade. However, even if this happens, it would take much more than 10 years to modify the changes in infrastructure that are both causes and results of the migration turnaround.

Dynamics of Migration Change

Changing patterns of net migration result from alterations in the gross migration streams that constitute the net. In the case of the metropolitan–nonmetropolitan reversal, both in-migration and out-migration streams contributed to the turnaround—migration from metropolitan to nonmetropolitan areas increased, and migration from nonmetropolitan to metropolitan areas decreased between 1965 and 1975. These changes are evident in the three major data sources that can be used to trace gross migration in this period: the Current Population Survey, the CWHS, and the census.

Tucker (1976) used mobility data from the 1970 Census and from the March 1975 Current Population Survey to demonstrate that metropolitan out-migration increased and nonmetropolitan out-migration decreased between these two periods. He showed that a 12% decrease in nonmetropolitan out-migration was of almost equal importance to the 23% increase in metropolitan out-migration.

Data from the CWHS permits a more disaggregated analysis of metropolitan–nonmetropolitan migration. Using these data, Wardwell and Gilchrist (1978) demonstrated that the importance of nonmetropolitan retention (decreasing nonmetropolitan out-migration) varied both with adjacency to an SMSA and with the size of the SMSA to and from which migration streams are compared. In general, they showed that the greater the size difference between categories being compared, the greater the importance of nonmetropolitan retention in accounting for the nonmetropolitan reversal. That is, movement from nonadjacent nonmetropolitan counties to the largest SMSAs declined more than did movement from adjacent or nonadjacent nonmetropolitan counties to the smallest size category of SMSAs (Table 1.5).

The data in Table 1.5 show that work force migration from nonadjacent nonmetropolitan counties to large SMSAs declined by 19.7% from 1965 to 1975, while the reverse flow increased by 47.8%. Similarly, migration from adjacent nonmetropolitan counties to large SMSAs declined by 11.4%, compared with a 26% increase in the reverse flow. Migration from nonadjacent nonmetropolitan counties to the smallest SMSAs declined only marginally (.6%), and migration from adjacent nonmetropolitan counties to small SMSAs actually increased slightly during the period (5.5%). Thus, in this comparison, the increased migration from small SMSAs to both nonmetropolitan categories (11.2% and 13.9%, respectively) accounts for the entire net exchange between the categories. Insofar as these CWHS county employment data can be used to make inferences about population deconcentration, changes in the patterns of movement between the largest SMSAs and nonmetropolitan counties account for the bulk of the nonmetropolitan turnaround. It is evident that the smallest SMSAs are also participating in the overall pattern of deconcentration—their growth experience is much more like that of the nonmetropolitan categories than it is like that of the other two metropolitan categories. Both of these findings from the CWHS data parallel the patterns of change presented in other work by Fuguitt and Beale (1977) on general nonmetropolitan population growth.

In summary, Current Population Survey data on general population

TABLE 1.5
Migration Streams between Metropolitan and Nonmetropolitan Counties, 1965-1975

Direction of migration	1965-1970		1970-1975		Change in rates (%)
	Number	Rate (%) [a]	Number	Rate (%) [a]	
Large metropolitan to					
medium metropolitan	8,856	47.3	10,631	56.2	+18.8
small metropolitan	2,619	14.0	3,477	18.4	+30.5
adjacent nonmetropolitan	3,383	18.1	4,323	22.8	+26.0
nonadjacent nonmetropolitan	2,116	11.3	3,166	16.7	+47.8
Medium metropolitan to					
large metropolitan	9,301	97.9	8,990	91.6	- 6.4
small metropolitan	1,928	20.3	2,292	23.4	+15.3
adjacent nonmetropolitan	3,079	32.4	3,679	37.5	+15.7
nonadjacent nonmetropolitan	1,697	17.9	2,052	20.9	+16.8
Small metropolitan to					
large metropolitan	3,215	99.9	2,775	83.1	-16.8
medium metropolitan	2,224	69.1	2,273	68.0	- 1.6
adjacent nonmetropolitan	1,378	42.8	1,589	47.6	+11.2
nonadjacent nonmetropolitan	953	29.6	1,125	33.7	+13.9
Adjacent nonmetropolitan to					
large metropolitan	3,969	89.1	3,574	78.9	-11.4
medium metropolitan	3,703	83.1	3,637	80.3	- 3.4
small metropolitan	1,621	36.4	1,740	38.4	+ 5.5
nonadjacent nonmetropolitan	1,728	38.8	2,006	44.3	+14.2
Nonadjacent nonmetropolitan to					
large metropolitan	3,009	81.7	2,458	65.6	-19.7
medium metropolitan	2,127	57.7	2,057	54.9	- 4.9
small metropolitan	1,216	33.0	1,227	32.8	- 0.6
adjacent nonmetropolitan	1,944	52.8	1,964	52.4	- 0.8

Source: Continuous Work History Sample; adapted from Wardwell and Gilchrist, 1980, Table 2.
a Per thousand.

mobility and Continuous Work History Sample data on labor-force mobility show similar patterns of change in gross migration. Both declining nonmetropolitan out-migration and increasing nonmetropolitan in-migration are responsible for the new pattern of nonmetropolitan population growth. The remaining component of differential population growth, of course, is natural increase. Its contribution to the turnaround in growth rates has been passive in most areas, defining the context or setting the stage for population change that is primarily due to migration (Morrison, 1975). Current levels of natural increase in the United States are quite low, and the historical metropolitan–nonmetropolitan differentials in levels of natural increase have converged on these low levels in most areas. Consequently, variations in population growth are largely attributable to variations in net migration. In the case of the largest metropolitan centers, the very low levels of natural increase made the actual population declines, which were the result of substantial net out-migration, much more evident than they would otherwise have been.

Pervasiveness of the Rural Turnaround

The pervasiveness of the nonmetropolitan turnaround is striking. The ubiquitous nature of the change has been noted by most researchers pursuing the causes and consequences of the new patterns of population movement (Beale, 1975; Beale and Fuguitt, 1978; Bowles, 1978; Fuguitt and Zuiches, 1975; Long, J., 1980; Morrison and Wheeler, 1976; Tucker, 1976; Wardwell, 1977; Zelinsky, 1978; Zuiches and Brown, 1978). The pattern of deconcentration has been observed at all size levels of urban places and in virtually all of the subregions of the nation. It is characteristic of most age cohorts, occupational classes, and industry groupings. Metropolitan–nonmetropolitan migration includes persons of all labor-force statuses: employed, unemployed, and out of the work force. The ubiquity of the changed pattern is one more indication that the phenomenon is real and not illusory and enduring rather than ephemeral—a new trend rather than a minor and temporary fluctuation in the historical concentration of population and economic activity.

Geographic Patterns of Migration Change

Overall comparisons of the relative migration rates between metropolitan and nonmetropolitan areas mask important differences within the categories (Figure 1.1). Metropolitan out-migration arises primarily in

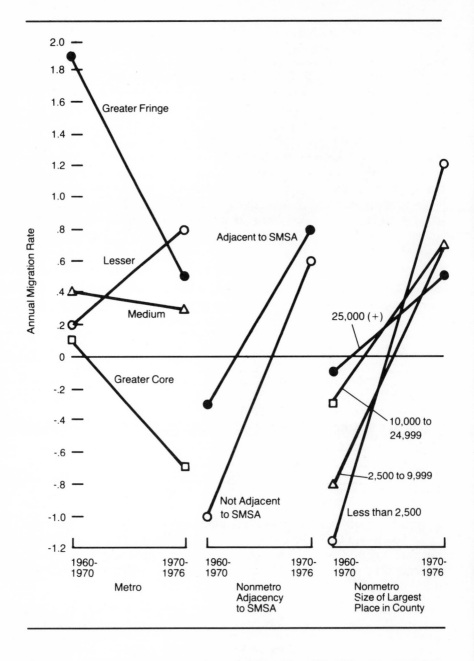

Figure 1.1. Change in average annual net migration rates, 1960–1970 versus 1970–1976, by type of county. (Source: U.S. Bureau of the Census.)

the core counties of the largest SMSAs. Annual net migration rates between 1960 and 1976 declined from a gain of .1% to a loss of .6% in these counties. In-migration to fringe counties of these large metropolitan areas also declined, but from a very high rate of 1.9% per year during the 1960s to .8% per year in 1970–1976, still one of the highest rates of net in-migraton for any type of county.[2] Medium sized SMSAs remained stable during the 16 years, gaining in-migrants at a rate of .4% per year during the 1960s and .3% per year in 1970–1976. The net migration rate of the group of smallest metropolitan counties increased markedly during the period from .2% per year in 1960–1970 to .6% per year in the 1970s.

All categories of nonmetropolitan counties shifted from net out-migration to net in-migration, but the magnitude of the shift differed among county types. In particular, there appears to be an inverse relationship between the magnitude of the migration turnaround and the level of urbanization of nonmetropolitan counties. Totally rural nonmetropolitan counties reversed from a loss of 1.1% a year in the 1960s to an increase of 1.1% a year in the 1970s. In comparison, the reversal in highly urbanized counties (with a place of at least 25,000 population) was from −.1% to .4% per year. Similarly, the magnitude of the migration reversal was greater in nonmetropolitan counties that were physically separated from SMSAs compared with contiguous nonmetropolitan areas (−.9 to .5 and −.3 to .8, respectively).

Data presented earlier in this chapter indicated that the Northeast and North Central regions were exporters of population to the South and West during 1970–1975. In contrast, nonmetropolitan counties within these regions showed net migration gains. In fact, with the exception of two economic subregions, the Mississippi Delta and the central Corn Belt, nonmetropolitan counties in all areas of the country gained in-migrants (Figure 1.2).[3] The explanations for the migration vary by subregion. Industrial decentralization is of primary importance in the Ozarks, southern Piedmont, and northern Great Plains; energy extraction is primary in Appalachia, the northern Great Plains, and the Rocky

---

[2]The average annual rate of net migration to fringe counties declined during this period because fringe counties no longer captured all of the central-city out-migrants nor those from nonmetropolitan counties. In fact, labor-force migration data from the CWHS show that the nonmetropolitan to fringe migration stream reversed in favor of nonmetropolitan areas in the years after 1970 (Brown, 1980).

[3]The analysis here uses a delineation of 26 subregions developed by Calvin L. Beale (Beale and Fuguitt, 1978). State Economic Areas were combined into reasonably homogeneous units based on information on economic activities, physical setting, settlement patterns, and culture.

Mountains; and recreation and retirement are of most importance in the Upper Great Lakes, the Ozark–Ouachita uplands, northern New England, Florida, northern Pacific Coast and the Southwest (see McCarthy and Morrison, 1979, for a fuller description of these trends).

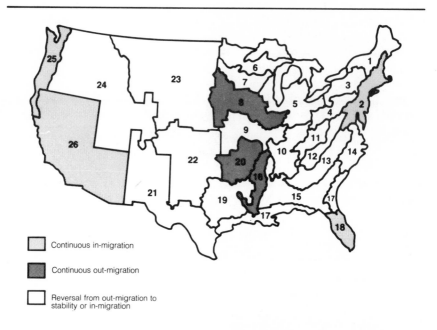

Continuous in-migration

Continuous out-migration

Reversal from out-migration to stability or in-migration

1. Northern New England - St. Lawrence	**14.** Coastal Plain Tobacco and Peanut Belt
2. Northeastern Metropolitan Belt	**15.** Old Coastal Plain Cotton Belt
3. Mohawk Valley and New York - Pennsylvania Border	**16.** Mississippi Delta
4. Northern Appalachian Coal Fields	**17.** Gulf of Mexico and South Atlantic Coast
5. Lower Great Lakes Industrial	**18.** Florida Peninsula
6. Upper Great Lakes	**19.** East Texas and Adjoining Coastal Plain
7. Dairy Belt	**20.** Ozark - Ouachita Uplands
8. Central Corn Belt	**21.** Rio Grande
9. Southern Corn Belt	**22.** Southern Great Plains
10. Southern Interior Uplands	**23.** Northern Great Plains
11. Southern Appalachian Coal Fields	**24.** Rocky Mountains, Idaho-Utah Valleys, and Columbia Basin
12. Blue Ridge, Great Smokies, and Great Valley	**25.** North Pacific Coast (including Alaska)
13. Southern Piedmont	**26.** The Southwest (including Hawaii)

Figure 1.2. Nonmetropolitan net migration by economic subregion, 1960–1976. (Source: U.S. Bureau of the Census.)

Compositional Pervasiveness of the Turnaround

To what extent have various segments of the population participated in recent migration to nonmetropolitan areas? How does this migration compare with the metropolitan–nonmetropolitan migration experience that would have occurred if previous rates of migration had persisted into the 1970s? The data in Table 1.6 show that the turnaround is almost totally accounted for by changes in the movement patterns of the white population. Black out-migration from nonmetropolitan areas is similar in direction to what would have been expected based on their metropolitan–nonmetropolitan migration experience of the 1965–1970 period, although it is 32.5% lower than expected. However, this decline does not compare to the dramatic change from an expected loss of 97,000 whites to a gain of 1,734,000.

TABLE 1.6
Expected and Actual Net Migration to Nonmetropolitan Areas by Selected Population Characteristics, 1970–1975

	Net migration, 1970–1975	
Characteristics	Actual (000s)	Expected (000s)
Sex/race		
White	1,734	− 97
Black	−137	−203
Male	836	− 40
Female	761	−260
Age		
5 to 14 years	719	36
20 to 29 years	−335	−665
30 to 64 years	917	241
65 + years	284	89
Educational attainment		
High school graduate	519	60
1 or more years of college	177	1
Occupation (males)		
White collar	− 3	−151
Blue collar	205	−267
Total	1,597	−300

Source: Adapted from Zuiches and Brown, 1978.

All age groups except 20–29 contributed to the rural turnaround. Net migration was especially great in the under-20 group and in the groups between 30 and 64. Older persons comprised only 17% of the net migration to nonmetropolitan areas, but this figure is substantially greater than their proportion of the general population (12% in 1975). Actual net migration to nonmetropolitan areas exceeded expected migration at all ages, including 20–29 years. The latter category experienced a nonmetropolitan net migration loss during 1970–1975, but it was approximately 50% smaller than the loss that would have been expected had previous age-specific metropolitan–nonmetropolitan migration rates persisted.

Almost half (45%; 696 of 1597 net migration) of the nonmetropolitan net migration consisted of persons with at least a high school education. Had the education-specific migration rates of the 1960s persisted into the 1970s, nonmetropolitan counties would have experienced a net loss of persons with this degree of education. While a substantial amount of the migration to nonmetropolitan areas was among persons who had not completed 12 years of formal schooling, the average educational attainment of the nonmetropolitan population has risen through the recent net in-migration.

A net loss of workers in all occupational categories of employment was forecasted by the occupation-specific migration rates of the 1960s. In fact, only for the professional and managerial categories did a net loss occur (Zuiches and Brown, 1978). All other occupations experienced net gains in nonmetropolitan areas, and the bulk of the net migration was among blue-collar workers (205,000). The net loss of professionals had a negligible effect on the occupational composition of the nonmetropolitan population, accounting for the small loss of 3000 white-collar workers shown in Table 1.6. The overall occupational status of the in-migration stream was much higher than that of longer-term nonmetropolitan residents (Bowles, 1978).

A recent study by Lichter et al. (1979) produced somewhat different conclusions concerning the selectivity of migration between metropolitan and nonmetropolitan areas. Their data (Public Use Sample for 1960 and 1970 and Current Population Survey for 1975) agreed that both migration streams were disproportionately comprised of higher socioeconomic status groups and were more similar to each other than to their respective origins. However, they also showed that the nonmetropolitan to metropolitan stream was of differentially higher status than the stream operating in the opposite direction. Hence they concluded, "What changes in interchange and selectivity are occurring tend to be to the advantage of metropolitan areas [Lichter et al., 1979:664]."

Discussion

The nonmetropolitan migration turnaround is a real and ongoing trend. Contrary to the reports of some critics that the phenomenon is largely an artifact of fluctuations that took place only in the early 1970s (Engels and Healy, 1979), the latest available data at the time of this writing indicate that during the period from March 1975 through March 1978, 5,321,000 people moved from metropolitan areas to nonmetropolitan counties, while 4,220,000 moved in the opposite direction for a net gain of 1,101,000 persons to the nonmetropolitan category (U.S. Bureau of the Census, 1978a). Unlike the findings shown by the 1970 Census, the 1980 Census cannot fail to show significant nonmetropolitan population and economic growth throughout the decade.

Substantive theory in demography has long been less effective at forecasting the population outcomes of social and economic change than at identifying the mathematical interrelationships of fertility and mortality. This ineffectiveness is particularly acute in forecasting changes in migration and population distribution. All of the changes identified below as contributing causes of the nonmetropolitan migration turnaround were well known as they were occurring. It was only their implications for rural–urban migration that were not foreseen. The failure to anticipate change, or even to recognize change as it was taking place, reflects the absence of models that take all of these factors into account in dynamic, interactive ways.

Rural depopulation from the 1930s to the late 1960s almost exhausted the pool of potential rural–urban migrants. Both in terms of metropolitan growth rates and of absolute numbers, the "people left behind" could contribute little to metropolitan expansion or to rural decline. Farm-to-city migration has now stabilized at low levels, and farm migration contributes little to rural–urban migration (Banks, 1978). As the declines in fertility in rural areas in the late 1960s and the 1970s converged on national levels, the pool of rural–urban migrants was further diminished.

At the same time, rural areas were rapidly losing their historic characteristic of backwardness. This modernization of rural America has produced a convergence between urban and rural life-styles. It is no longer necessary to be a resident of a large urban place to enjoy the amenities of electrification, modern water and sewage systems, telecommunications, access to good roads, good schools, and recreation. Increasing affluence has increased the purchasing power of rural residents for most goods and services.

Another factor contributing to population growth in some nonmetropolitan counties was the location of community colleges and state universities. As those persons born during the peak fertility years of the baby boom entered college in the late 1960s and early 1970s, enrollment swelled dramatically and brought a new source of growth to college communities and counties. However, this source will diminish in the 1980s and will soon cease to be a major factor in the growth of nonmetropolitan areas.

Trends toward metropolitan–nonmetropolitan convergence also began to appear in the late 1960s and early 1970s in employment opportunities and in declining real income differentials. The development of small-scale and some large-scale manufacturing activities in both adjacent and nonadjacent nonmetropolitan counties has led to greater nonmetropolitan growth rates in these industries. The deconcentration of manufacturing activity expanded the employment base of nonmetropolitan counties, as did the development of retail and service industries. Labor-force participation rates of women rose in many nonmetropolitan areas, further diminishing the already declining metropolitan–nonmetropolitan differentials in median family income.

The growth of affluence in the nation, the earlier age of retirement, the relatively slow rise in the cost of gasoline relative to other household expenditures, and the boom in outdoor recreation contributed to the economic and population growth of nonmetropolitan counties that were rich in natural amenities. Amenities drew more than recreation-based growth. Retirement-related migration overwhelmingly favored these same counties and contributed to their growth. The combination of the high birth rates in the 1910s and 1920s and the retirement benefits of social programs of the 1930s and 1940s swelled the ranks of the retirement population and greatly increased their mobility because it increased their financial independence and locational flexibility.

The factor of residential preference has been implicit in the discussions of retirement-related migration and of the changing character of rural and nonmetropolitan areas. With growing economic convergence, preferences for living in lower-density areas have become increasingly important in guiding migration flows to small towns and the countryside.

Finally, the increasing awareness of energy scarcities and rising costs and the many uncertainties about the traditional sources of energy have made extractive activities economically feasible in areas that were formerly underdeveloped or abandoned. Although increasing employment in extractive industries probably has done no more than offset the low but continuing employment declines in agriculture, the expansion of mineral-related industries has brought an infusion of new capital into many nonmetropolitan counties. In some cases, renewed expansion of extractive industries has greatly expanded the revenue base for the provision of local services. Funds for impact mitigation have been made available for community adaptation and development. As the real cost of future energy supplies becomes more apparent, most if not all of these impacts in nonmetropolitan areas can be expected to grow as the extractive industries themselves continue to thrive.

Conversely, consideration of energy impacts also provides the major potential for diminishing the size of present metropolitan out-migration. Aggregate costs of movement across the greater distances associated with working and living in rural areas may be no greater than those of metropolitan areas when improved vehicle performance, lower maintenance costs and lower costs per mile of travel are taken into account. But the greater density of metropolitan settlement, and the greater probability of having access to some mass transit alternative to the private automobile for employment commuting and for procuring essential goods and services are major factors favoring metropolitan areas. The vast majority of nonmetropolitan counties completely lack these alternatives, particularly outside of the larger nonmetropolitan cities.

Continuing increases in transportation costs, as gasoline and diesel fuel prices rise, may be absorbed so long as supplies remain dependable. But undependable supplies in the context of the necessity of traversing distance to reach work and consumption sites may force some degree of reconcentration of the population. Furthermore, the diversion of an increasing proportion of the household budget to transportation expenses undercuts the increasing purchasing power for goods and services that in part was responsible for expanding the employment bases in low-density rural areas. As that purchasing power constricts, the market for goods and services may diminish, and a part of the impetus for growth in the nonmetropolitan economy will disappear.

There are alternatives that can ameliorate the reconcentration forces of increasing energy costs (Wardwell and Gilchrist, 1979a). If these alternatives are brought into play, continuing population and economic deconcentration and the consequent growth of nonmetropolitan and rural areas will not necessarily be affected. But in either event, the structural and demographic changes resulting from a decade of migration reversals will not permit a return to the metropolitan–nonmetropolitan relationships of the 1940s and 1950s, or even of the 1960s. Change in the nonmetropolitan realm has been only partially dependent on low energy and transportation costs. It is cumulative and directional (Hawley, 1971). The course of change will be modified by the future of energy in our society, and patterns of population distribution and internal migration will continue to reflect the course of social and economic change.

Acknowledgment

We wish to thank Calvin L. Beale for his helpful contribution to portions of the chapter.

References

Banks, Vera J.
  1978   "Farm population estimates for 1977." Rural Development Research Report No.
          4. Washington, D.C.: U.S. Department of Agriculture.
Beale, Calvin L.
  1969   "Population trends." Congressional testimony during hearings of the Ad Hoc
          Subcommittee on Urban Growth of the Subcommittee on Housing and Com-
          munity Development of the Committee on Banking and Currency, U.S. House
          of Representatives, June 3 to July 31.
  1974   "Rural development: Population and settlement prospects," *Journal of Soil and
          Water Conservation* 29 (January–February): 23–27.
  1975   "The revival of population growth in nonmetropolitan America." Economic Re-
          search Service, U.S. Department of Agriculture, ERS–605.
  1978a   "Making a living in rural and smalltown America." *Rural Development Perspec-
          tives* 1 (November):1–5.
  1978b   "People on the land." Chapter 3 in Thomas R. Ford (ed.), *Rural USA: Persistence
          and Change.* Ames: Iowa State University Press.
Beale, Calvin L. and Glenn V. Fuguitt
  1978   "The new pattern of nonmetropolitan population change." Pp. 157–177 in Karl
          E. Taeuber, Larry L. Bumpass, and James J. Sweet (eds.), *Social Demography.*
          New York: Academic Press.
Beaujot, Roderic P.
  1978   "Canada's population: Growth and dualism." *Population Bulletin* 33(2), April.
          Washington, D.C.: Population Reference Bureau, Inc.
Berry, Brian, J. L.
  1972   "Population growth in the daily urban systems of the United States, 1980–2000."
          In *U.S. Commission on Population   Growth and the American Future.* Population
          Distribution and Policy, edited by Sara Mills Mazie, vol. 5. Washington, D.C.:
          U.S. Government Printing Office.
Bogue, Donald J.
  1959   "Internal migration," Pp. 486–509 in Philip M. Hauser and Otis Dudley Duncan
          (eds.), *The Study of Population.* Chicago: University of Chicago Press.
Bourne, L. S. and M. I. Logan
  1976   "Changing urbanization patterns at the margin: The examples of Australia and
          Canada." Pp. 111–143 In Brian J. L. Berry (ed.), *Urbanization and Counterurbaniza-
          tion.* Urban Affairs Annual Reviews, vol. II. Beverly Hills, Calif.: Sage Publica-
          tions, Inc.
Bowles, Gladys K.
  1978   "Contributions to recent metro-nonmetro migrants to the nonmetro population
          and labor force." *Agricultural Economics Research* 30 (October):15–22.

Brown, David L.
  1978   "Some spatial aspects of work force migration in the United States, 1965–1975."
          Paper presented at the Population Association of America Annual Meeting,
          April, Atlanta.
  1980   "Some spatial aspects of post-1970 work force migration in the United States."
          Growth and Change, in press.
Chapman, William
  1973   "Cities' growth rate sharply slowed." *Washington Post*, September 26.
Drewett, Roy, John Goddard, and Nigel Spence
  1976   "Urban Britain: Beyond containment." Pp. 43–79 In Brian J. L. Berry (ed.), *Ur-
          banization and Counterurbanization*. Urban Affairs Annual Reviews, vol. II. Beverly
          Hills, Calif: Sage Publications, Inc.
Engels, Richard and Mary Kay Healy
  1979   "Rural renaissance reconsidered." *American Demographics* 1(5), May:16–21.
Environmental Protection Agency
  1978   "Draft environmental impact statement for San Antonio wastewater treatment
          system." Dallas Texas: U.S. Environmental Protection Agency (April).
Frisbie, W. Parker and Dudley L. Poston, Jr.
  1975   "Components of sustenance organization and nonmetropolitan population
          change: A human ecological investigation." *American Sociological Review* 40
          (December):773–784.
  1976   "The structure of sustenance organization and population change in nonmet-
          ropolitan America." *Rural Sociology* 41 (Fall): 354–370.
Fuguitt, Glenn V. and Calvin L. Beale
  1977   "Recent trends in city population growth and distribution." Pp. 13–27 In Her-
          rington J. Bryce (ed.), *Small Cities in Transition*. Cambridge: Ballinger Publishing
          Company.
Fuguitt, Glenn V. and James J. Zuiches
  1975   "Residential preferences and population distribution." *Demography* 12
          (August):491–504.
Goldstein, Sidney
  1976   "Facets of redistribution: Research challenges and opportunities." *Demography*
          13 (November):423–434.
Hawley, Amos H.
  1971   *Urban Society: An Ecological Approach*. New York: The Ronald Press Company.
King, Wayne
  1973   "Dying American small towns showing vitality and popularity" and "The small
          towns: They didn't disappear after all." *Washington Post*, November 6 and
          November 11.
Lichter, Daniel, Tim B. Heaton, and Glenn V. Fuguitt
  1979   "Trends in selectivity of migration between metropolitan and nonmetropolitan
          areas: 1955–1975." *Rural Sociology* 44(4) Winter:645–667.
Long, John
  1978   "The deconcentration of nonmetropolitan migration." Paper presented at the
          annual meeting of the Population Association of America, April, Atlanta.
  1980   *Population Deconcentration in the United States*. U.S. Bureau of the Census Mono-
          graph. Washington, D.C.: U.S. Government Printing Office.
Long, Larry H.
  1980   "Back to the countryside and back to the city in the same decade." Chapter in
          Shirley Laska and Daphne Spain (eds.), *Back to the City: Issues in Neighborhood
          Renovation*. Elmsford, New York: Pergamon Press.

Long, Larry H. and Kristin A. Hansen
   1975   "Trends in return migration to the South." *Demography* 12 (November):601–614.
   1977   "Migration trends in the United States." U.S. Bureau of the Census. Unpublished.
McCarthy, Kevin F. and Peter A. Morrison
   1979   *The Changing Demographic and Economic Structure of Nonmetropolitan Areas in the United States.* Santa Monica: The Rand Corporation, R–2399–EDA.
Morrison, Peter A.
   1975   "The current demographic context of national growth and development." Santa Monica: The Rand Corporation, P–5514.
   1976   "The demographic context of educational policy planning." Santa Monica: The Rand Corporation, P–5592.
Morrison, Peter A. and J. Wheeler
   1976   "Rural renaissance in America?" Population Bulletin 31 (October). Washington, D.C.: Population Reference Bureau.
Roseman, Curtis C.
   1977   *Changing Migration Patterns Within the United States.* Resource Paper for College Geography No. 77-2. Washington, D.C.: Association of American Geographers.
Schnore, Leo F.
   1959   *The Urban Scene.* New York: Free Press.
Thompson, Wilbur R.
   1965   *A Preface to Urban Economics.* Baltimore: The Johns Hopkins University Press.
   1968   "Internal and external factors in the development of urban economies." Pp. 43–62 In Harvey S. Perloff and Lowdon Wingo, Jr. (eds.), *Issues in Urban Economics.* Baltimore: The Johns Hopkins University Press.
   1977   "The urban development process." Pp. 95–112 In Herrington J. Bryce (ed.), *Small Cities in Transition.* Cambridge, Mass.: Ballinger Publishing Company.
Tucker, C. Jack
   1976   "Changing patterns of migration between metropolitan and nonmetropolitan areas in the United States: Recent evidence." *Demography* 13 (November):435–443.
United Nations
   1969   *Growth of the world's urban and rural population, 1920–2000.* New York: United Nations.
U.S. Bureau of the Census
   1973   "Mobility for metropolitan areas: 1970." Subject Reports, Final Report PC(2)–2C. Washington, D.C.: U.S. Government Printing Office.
   1975a   *Mobility of the Population of the United States, March 1970 to March 1975.* Current Population Reports, Series P–20, No. 285. Washington, D.C.: U.S. Government Printing Office.
   1975b   *Social and Economic Characteristics of the Metropolitan and Nonmetropolitan Population: 1970 and 1974.* Current Population Reports, Special Studies, Series P–23, No. 55. Washington, D.C.: U.S. Government Printing Office.
   1978a   *Geographical Mobility: March 1975 to March 1978.* Current Population Reports, Series P–20, No. 331. Washington, D.C.: U.S. Government Printing Office.
   1978b   *Social and Economic Characteristics of the Metropolitan and Nonmetropolitan Population 1977 and 1970.* Current Population Reports P–23, No. 75. Washington, D.C.: U.S. Government Printing Office.
U.S. Department of Agriculture
   1979   Unpublished tabulation from Population Studies Program, ESCS–EDD.
U.S. Water Resources Council
   1974   *1972 OBERS Projections: Regional Economic Activity in the U.S.* Washington, D.C.

Vining, Daniel R., Jr. and Thomas Kontuly
  1977   "Population dispersal from major metropolitan regions: An international comparison." Regional Science Research Institute Discussion Paper No. 100 (September), Philadelphia.
  1978   "Population dispersal from major metropolitan regions: An international comparison." *International Regional Science Review* 3(1):49–73.
Wardwell, John M.
  1977   "Equilibrium and change in nonmetropolitan growth." *Rural Sociology* 42 (Summer):156–179.
Wardwell, John M. and C. Jack Gilchrist
  1978   "Metropolitan change and nonmetropolitan growth." Paper presented at the Population Association of America Annual Meeting, April, Atlanta.
  1979a   "The distribution of population and energy." Paper presented at the Rural Sociological Society Meetings, August, Burlington, Vermont.
  1979b   "Improving the utility of the CWHS for analysis of worker mobility: The case of metropolitan employment deconcentration." *Review of Public Data Use* 7 (Fall): 54–61.
  1980   "Employment deconcentration in the nonmetropolitan migration turnaround." *Demography* 17 (May): 145–158.
Weber, Adna F.
  1899   *The Growth of Cities in the Nineteenth Century.* New York: Macmillan.
Williams, James D. and Andrew J. Sofranko
  1979   "Motivations for the inmigration component of the population turnaround in nonmetropolitan areas." *Demography* 16 (May):239–255.
Zelinsky, Wilbur
  1975   "Nonmetropolitan Pennsylvania: A demographic revolution in the making?" *Earth and Mineral Sciences* 45 (October):1–4.
  1977   "Coping with the migration turnaround: The theoretical challenge." *International Regional Science Review* 2 (Winter): 175–178.
  1978   "Is nonmetropolitan America being repopulated?" *Demography* 15 (February): 12–39.
Zuiches, James J. and David L. Brown
  1978   "The changing character of the nonmetropolitan population, 1950–75." Chapter 4 In Thomas R. Ford (ed.), *Rural Society in the United States–Current Trends and Issues.* Ames: Iowa State University Press.
Zuiches, James J. and Edwin H. Carpenter
  1978   "Residential preferences and rural development policy." *Rural Development Perspectives* 1 (November):12–17.

2

The Changing Nature of Rural Employment

CALVIN L. BEALE

Introduction

The need to generalize about issues and the tendency of the mind to lag in acquiring and accepting new information often lead to over-simplified or outmoded conceptions of conditions and trends. It is well to remember this when drawing conclusions about rural life, for diversity and change are as characteristic of rural and small-town society as they are of any other aspect of American life. *Rural* and *urban* are meaningful concepts, but they are not discrete. People live in a vareity of situations that grade subtly from rural to urban. A family on a Corn Belt farm or a western ranch represents the essence of rurality in the public mind. But just as validly rural are the millions of residents of the open country and of small towns who are not directly involved in agriculture. Some of these people work in local industries and services, others commute to cities for employment, and a growing number are retired persons who do not work at all.

Change in Dependence on Farming

In 1820, when nation-wide census data on occupations first became available, three-fourths of all employed rural residents worked in farming. As late as 1930, the proportion so employed was still slightly above one half, despite the greater commercialization of agriculture; the growth of the mining, transportation, and manufacturing industries;

37

*New Directions in
Urban–Rural Migration*

ISBN 0–12–136380–5

and the increase in commuting to cities. In the writer's experience, it was very common into the mid-1960s for people requesting information of the Department of Agriculture to use the terms *farm* and *rural* interchangeably and to express surprise and puzzlement on learning of the existence of a large rural population that did not live on farms. Dramatic changes in the place of residence and nature of employment of rural people had taken place but were not widely understood. Especially after 1940, millions of people left farms, as the national economy revived and as the rapid development and adoption of new farm technology made it possible for increased agricultural output to be produced by far fewer people. From 1940 to 1970, the total number of people working solely or primarily in agriculture (whether living on farms or not) dropped from 8.4 million to 2.5 million, as counted in the censuses of those years. We actually had as few people working directly in farming in 1970 as we had 150 years earlier; however, they were providing food for a population 20 times larger.

Despite the loss of 70% of farm employment in just 30 years, the total rural and small-town population did not decline, whether measured by the census concept of *rural* (which refers to people in open country and in places of fewer than 2500 residents) or by the concept *nonmetropolitan* (which refers to the populations of counties that lack an urban center of 50,000 people and that are not in the commuting zone of a metropolitan area). To be sure, some of the drop in farm employment was offset by increases in farm-related rural jobs in businesses that provide farmers with goods and services. Such businesses include government agricultural offices, farm machinery production and distribution, tax and computer services, irrigation projects and equipment, greater local processing of raw farm products, or production of fertilizers, seeds, and pesticides. The precise amount of employment in these agribusinesses is difficult to identify, but it is not the major source of nonfarm rural growth. Other kinds of work have been more important, such as manufacturing of nonagricultural products, mining, health and other professional services, recreation and related businesses, defense activities, and service and trade employment generated by resident commuters. One effect of the diversification in employment has been to provide many more opportunities for rural women to work.

Off-Farm Work

A substantial number of people work in agriculture and hold off-farm jobs as well. We know comparatively little about such people, for data on multiple-job holding are not collected in the Census of Population.

However, there is an annual sample survey on the subject. According to this source, of all people who held two or more jobs in May 1978 about 900,000 held at least one job in agriculture. The number has not changed much in recent years. In the early 1960s it reached 1,070,000, and it has drifted downward since then. By far the greatest proportion of these people have their principal work off the farm (three-fourths), with farming (or occasionally farm labor) as their secondary work (as measured by time spent on the job). Although the number of people combining farming with other work has declined somewhat, it has not fallen as rapidly as total agricultural employment. Thus, the proportion of farmers whose operations are secondary to nonagricultural work has gradually increased (from 20% in May 1965 to 25% in May 1976). Secondary farming is most common among men who work as craftsmen, truck drivers, factory operatives, and laborers.

Women are not as likely as men to hold more than one job, and comparatively few of those who do so have farm work as one of their activities. What has changed for farm women is the proportion who are employed (including unpaid family workers) and the degree to which they work at off-farm jobs. In 1960, only 29% of farm women reported themselves as working or looking for work. By 1978, the percentage had risen to 43. This growth went entirely into off-farm work. In the same period of time, the percentage of employed farm women who worked in agriculture (again, including unpaid family workers) dropped from 44% to 30%. Thus, many more farm families are partly supported by off-farm income today even if the operator is fully employed on the farm.

Labor-Force Participation of Rural Women

The growth in employment of farm women is part of the larger trend of increased entry into the labor force of women in general and rural women in particular. In the past, rural women were much less likely than urban women to work outside the home. In 1950, when the current trend was already underway, the labor-force participation rate of rural women was less than two-thirds that of urban women (20% versus 31.7%). By 1970, the rural rate had advanced to 34.1% and was only one-sixth below the urban rate of 44.2%. Several factors may explain the low rural rate of the past; for example, greater rural family responsibilities (larger numbers of children), smaller percentages of unmarried women requiring self-support, farm responsibilities (even if not reported as employment), scarcity of off-farm work, inaccessibility to employment centers, lower material expectations, and general rural social conservatism. All of these factors have been modified in recent decades.

Numerically, the biggest increases in employment of rural women have come in professional services and manufacturing. The growth in professional services largely reflects the rapid expansion of health services and schools—a trend not unique to rural areas. Factory employment has come as part of the general trend in manufacturing toward decentralization, accompanied by a broadened rural product mix. The use of rural and small-town women employees in business and repair services had the highest percentage rate of growth from 1960–1970 of all major industry groups. However in actual numbers more women have been employed in professional services and manufacturing.

It seems unlikely that there will be a full convergence of rural and urban female labor-force participation rates—at least at any time soon—because the inhibiting factors mentioned above continue to operate to some extent. However, the change that has occurred is of major dimensions and represents another way in which the aspirations and life patterns of rural people are now closer to those of urban residents.

Employment Mix

To look at the most recent data on employment of rural and small-town people, we have to shift the concept used from *rural* to *nonmetropolitan*, inasmuch as rural data per se are collected only in the decennial censuses and thus do not yet exist for years after 1970. In March 1975, 21.6 million nonmetropolitan residents were employed (Table 2.1). By major industry group, the largest number of these (5 million) worked in manufacturing, followed by 4.2 million in wholesale and retail trade and 3.8 million in professional services such as health, education, business and repair services. Only 2 million worked solely or primarily in agriculture (including forestry and fishing). Thus, just 9% were in agriculture, compared with 23% in manufacturing. And the disparity is growing.

The well-publicized movement of people into rural and small-town communities in the 1970s is a factor in the growing dominance of nonagricultural pursuits. Although there are some "back-to-the-landers" among the new residents, they are comparatively few in number. Only 5% of the employed people who had moved into nonmetropolitan areas between 1970 and 1975 were working in agriculture in 1975. This is just half the percent of longer-term residents working in agriculture (Figure 2.1). The largest groups of newcomers were supplying professional services (23%); working in trade (21%) or employed in manufacturing (18%). Note that the order of employment in the three leading categories

TABLE 2.1
Employed Civilian Nonmetropolitan Population by Major Industry, 1975

Industry	Persons employed	
	Number(000s)	Percent
Total	21,586	100.0
Agriculture [a]	2,039	9.4
Mining	428	2.0
Construction	1,388	6.4
Manufacturing	5,042	23.4
Durable goods	2,745	12.7
Nondurables	2,297	10.7
Transportation, communication, and public utilities	1,256	5.8
Trade	4,217	19.5
Finance, insurance and real estate	753	3.5
Professional services	3,819	17.7
Other services	1,615	7.5
Public administration	1,032	4.8

Source: Bowles, (1978).
[a] Includes forestry and fisheries.

for recent in-migrants is the reverse of the order for these same categories among all nonmetropolitan workers. The newcomers are less likely to go into manufacturing and more likely to be involved in professional services.

Regional Differences

The national numbers mask a great deal of regional diversity. Agriculture continues to be the dominant industry in many counties. In 1970, there were 331 counties in which 30% or more of all employment was directly in agriculture (Table 2.2). In such counties most of the remaining employment was closely related to or supported by farming. One can probably argue that counties with 20% to 29% agricultural employment (of which there were 372) are also likely to be more dependent on farming than on anything else, even though some other industries are present. These two classes of counties are concentrated in the Great Plains, the central and western Corn Belt, the Mississippi Delta, and selected areas in the Pacific Northwest. But they tend to be thinly populated, averaging about 10,000 population each.

On the other hand, there are more than 1000 nonmetropolitan counties in which less than 10% of employment is in agriculture. Some of

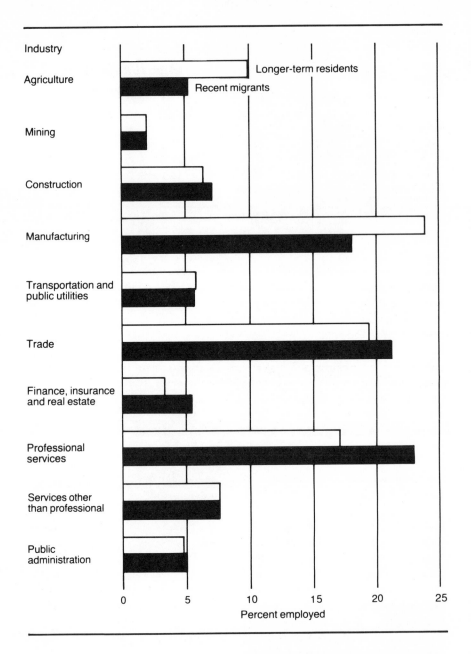

Figure 2.1. Industrial composition of nonmetropolitan workers by length of residence, 1975. Longer-term residents were nonmetropolitan in both 1970 and 1975. Recent migrants lived in metropolitan areas in 1970. (Source: U.S. Bureau of the Census.)

TABLE 2.2
Population of Nonmetropolitan Counties by Employment in Agriculture, 1970

Percent of employment in agriculture	Counties	Total population	
		Number	Percent
All nonmetro counties [a]	2,469	54,425,000	100.0
30 percent and over	331	2,059,000	3.8
20–29 percent	372	4,664,000	8.6
10–19 percent	724	13,295,000	24.4
Under 10 percent	1,042	34,407,000	63.2

Source: 1970 Census of Population.
[a] Nonmetropolitan as of 1974.

these counties have a prosperous agriculture in which most of the land is used for farming; others are entirely unsuited for agriculture. But in either case nonagricultural industries are overwhelmingly dominant, and agricultural trends leave the great majority of the population untouched. These counties average 35,000 people each—generally they contain small urban centers—and they have 64% of the total U.S. nonmetropolitan population. This percentage contrasts strongly with the 12% of the nonmetropolitan population who live in counties where agriculture can be considered the primary industry. The nonagricultural rural and small-town areas are found particularly in the Northeast, the industrial belt from Pittsburgh to Chicago, the upland areas of the South (both east and west of the Mississippi River), the northwoods country of the upper Great Lakes, and the mountainous, desert, or timbered areas of the West (Figure 2.2).

Large Scale Manufacturing

Nonmetropolitan areas, this writer believes, have many more large industrial plants and other establishments than is widely realized. Consider, for example, the number and kinds of nongovernmental establishments that employ at least 500 workers in a given location. Employers of this size would be regarded as large even in metropolitan areas. As of 1975, over 1800 such establishments were located in nonmetropolitan counties, and about a fourth of them hired more than 1000 employees. The total employment figure for these places is not available, but we can estimate it to be at least 1.67 million. Eighty percent of these large establishments prove to be manufacturing plants. By comparison, in metropolitan areas only 45% of employers this size are manufacturers. It is much easier for a rural and small-town community to acquire

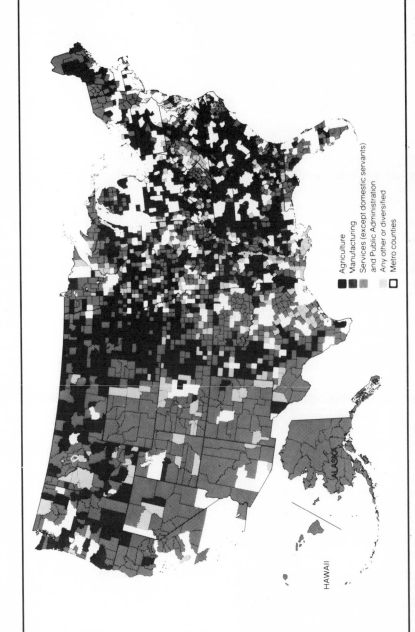

Figure 2.2. Principal industry of employment in nonmetropolitan counties, 1970. The principal industry is one with the largest employment and at least 25% of total employment. Counties with no industry employing 25% or more were coded diversified. (Source: U.S. Bureau of the Census.)

Agriculture
Manufacturing
Services (except domestic servants) and Public Administration
Any other or diversified
Metro counties

HAWAII

ALASKA

large-scale employment through manufacturing than in any other way. Most manufacturing is for export to other areas, and the number of workers can be large if the market is big, if considerable labor is needed in the manufacturing process, and if there are no obstacles to the large-scale assembly of materials or the distribution of products. Trade and service employment, however, tends to be more for local patronage or to require numerous small units. In metropolitan areas, manufacturing plants constitute a lower proportion of all large employers because the numbers and density of people in such centers permits the growth of large-scale employment in department stores, utilities, transportation, hospitals, wholesale trade, and other functions. Thus, rural areas' greatest opportunity for adding measurably to their economic base is in acquiring manufacturers. However, these areas also may find their fate tied more closely to just one employer or one industry.

The most common large nonmetropolitan manufacturing plants are textile mills and factories that make clothing or other fabricated textile products. A majority of all large textile mills in the United States are located in nonmetropolitan communities. In that sense, textile manufacturing is a basically rural industry, just as farming, logging, and mining are. The overwhelming majority of the large plants in this industry are located in the Southeast (North Carolina, South Carolina, Georgia); many of the clothing makers are dispersed into the East South Central States (Alabama, Mississippi, Tennessee).

Other industries in which most large employers are nonmetropolitan are pulp, paper and paperboard mills; logging and wood products (exclusive of furniture); coal and metal mining; primary aluminum plants; and poultry processing. These activities tend to locate near rural-based raw material sites or (in the case of aluminum) at locations with large quantities of water and power. Industries with a disproportionate nonmetropolitan location of large plants (even though a majority are in metropolitan areas) including clothing and other fabricated textiles, farm machinery, meat packing, canned and frozen foods, oil and gas extraction, inorganic industrial chemicals, man-made fibers, and plastic products. In addition, hundreds of plants in nonmetropolitan areas produce machinery and other metal products, exclusive of farm equipment. Metal producers and fabricators are still disproportionately situated in metropolitan areas overall, but their collective employment in nonmetropolitan areas is second only to the textile industries. They produce a wide variety of primary metals, automotive equipment, industrial machines and tools, hardware, heating and refrigerating equipment, electronic products, and consumer goods. Such plants are especially important in rural and small-town communities of the mid-Atlantic and lower Great Lakes regions, but also have a wide distribution in the upper South.

Mining, Services, and Public Administration

Although mining is a predominantly rural industry and one that is recurrently in the news with each energy crisis, it accounts for only 2% of all nonmetropolitan employment. In 1920, there were about twice as many workers in mining nationally as there were 50 years later (1.2 million versus .6 million). Loss of work in coal mining was the basic reason for the decline. Since 1970, employment in coal mining has revived and oil and gas activities have increased also. However, the industry still employs fewer people than it did at its peak.

New growth in mining since 1970 has affected primarily the coal fields of the southern Appalachians—a fairly compact area focused on eastern Kentucky and southern West Virginia—and widely scattered locations in the High Plains and the West. In the latter areas, mining is often a new activity or it induces a high rate of population change on a comparatively small base. These circumstances, coupled with significant environmental impact, have led to much discussion, research, and publicity about the detrimental effects of actual or potential boom town development. This public concern may well reflect the real fears of affected people, but it may also have led to exaggerated notions of the demographic effects to date of renewed mineral development. Only a comparative handful of western counties are having outright mining booms, and the overall contribution to nonmetropolitan employment and population growth has been minor. As of 1976, only nine western counties had more than 30% of their employment in mining. This could change if coal gasification plants, shale oil development, and other alternative energy measures become a substantive reality.

Public administration and the provision of services are generally not thought of as "export" industries. However, they often function as such in the rural and small-town economy if the services are provided to an imported clientele or the facility or resource to be administered is of a national or state-wide nature (such as a national forest, a military base, or a prison). To some extent, historical events or past political decisions have determined the existence of these industries in numbers greater than would be required to serve their local communities. The placement of military bases, state colleges, mental hospitals, and prisons in single counties scattered here and there has had a real if localized effect on rural employment.

However, there are also much larger districts and even regions that are affected systematically by a high dependence on services and public administration. Recreation and retirement areas have such a pattern. With general economic prosperity, ease of transportation, and the popularity of second homes and rural-based sports such as skiing, employment in recreation services has grown. Complementing the growth of recreation-based jobs is the inmovement of retired people. In the period 1970–1975, .4 million people of age 55 and over moved into nonmetropolitan areas, with another such movement expected in the last half of the decade. This is roughly twice the inflow of predominantly retired people in the 1960s. The influx stimulates trade, services, and construction, especially in the increasing number of counties where concentrations of older in-migrants are occurring. It also adds to the number of areas where transfer payments comprise the largest single source of income or of income growth. Hundreds of nonmetropolitan counties are now in one or both of these situations, and social security payments usually are the leading type of transfer. Counties heavily dependent on transfer income rarely have high per capita income. Indeed, many of them are affected by higher than average incidence of poverty. However, the increased role of such income reduces the vulnerability of these areas to economic cycles and provides a measure of income stability.

In many parts of the West, and especially the Southwest, neither agriculture nor manufacturing is commonly the major source of rural and small-town work. In some places mining is such a source. More commonly, however, public administration and professional services in combination constitute the leading nonmetropolitan work mode. The nature of this work is not uniform, but seems to result from the combined effect of several factors. The high proportion of public lands requires an enlarged government presence in the management of forests, grasslands, parks, monuments, dams, and reservoirs. There are also a number of military and atomic installations. The large reservation-based Indian population adds notably to requirements for government and professional service employment. An abundance of children resulting from a relatively high birth rate heightens the need for educational workers in all of the predominantly Indian, Mexican American, and Mormon areas of the West, as well as in those characterized by young families such as the mining or military communities. Similarly, the need for social, medical, and welfare service employment is high in the Indian and Mexican American populations, which are characterized by greater than average incidence of poverty and health problems. As a result of these various factors, over much of the West employment in professional services amounted to 20% of all nonmetropolitan jobs in 1970, and public administration accounted for about 8% additional. By contrast, in most of the rest of the country these industries did not involve more than 16% and 4%, respectively, of nonmetropolitan workers.

Commuting to Metropolitan Jobs

Information has been lacking in the past on the number and characteristics of people who live in nonmetropolitan communities and commute to jobs in metropolitan areas. Data for some individual states show that in 1970 the proportion of employed nonmetropolitan people who did so ranged from essentially none in Wyoming to one-third in New Jersey. Special tabulations from the Annual Housing Survey of the United States now reveal that 9% of all employed nonmetropolitan household heads who have a fixed place of work commuted to metropolitan jobs in 1975. (The comparable figure for other household members is not known but is definitely lower.) The number of people involved in commuting to metropolitan jobs is sizeable (1 million household heads), but it is the writer's view that the proportion is lower than commonly has been thought (Bowles and Beale, 1980).

More than 91% of nonmetropolitan workers are still employed within their own or nearby rural areas and small towns, despite recent trends that foster commuting. Such trends include the improved network of multi-lane and limited access roads, the shift of metropolitan job sites away from the central cities and out to the metropolitan periphery, and the movement into rural areas and small towns in recent years of people who have metropolitan work ties. Among household heads who had moved into nonmetropolitan communities from metropolitan areas between 1970 and 1975, 18% commuted to metropolitan jobs. This is twice the rate for nonmigrants, although it is still rather low. The vast majority of employed people who leave a metropolitan area to live in a nonmetropolitan community take local work and do not retain their working ties with the big cities and suburbs. Those who commute tend to be somewhat younger and to earn more money than the noncommuters, but they do not appear to be better educated.

Conclusion

In sum, the structure of nonmetropolitan employment has become increasingly diverse and decreasingly agricultural. Regional differences are very pronounced, and the current movement of people and employment into nonmetropolitan territory is accelerating the changes that had already become so noticeable in recent decades. The precise policy implications of these shifts are not self-evident, but it is clear that the increasingly nonagricultural character of the rural economy is at the heart of the population turnaround in recent years and presents a different setting for development and employment policies than would have been presented earlier. Thus, for instance, the rural and small-town labor force is now more directly vulnerable to general economic recession than it was in the past or than it is to agricultural crises. This was demonstrated in 1975 when formal unemployment rates during the heart of the recession were slightly higher among nonmetropolitan people than they were in the cities and suburbs. This is not usually the case in more normal economic times, however, and there seemed to be almost no public awareness during the recession that the relatively more severe loss of employment was occurring in the nonmetropolitan communities.[1]

At present, farm employment is much more stable than it was in the 1950s and 1960s, but it is still decreasing somewhat. Additional build-up of mining employment is likely, and if and when such energy processes as coal gasification become economically competitive, energy-related rural jobs should become even more numerous. All in all, the growth of nonagricultural jobs in nonmetropolitan areas is expected to continue in the foreseeable future, as a result of both the continued relocation of manufacturing and other activities and the growing need to service the further inflow of retired people or commuters.

References

Bowles, Gladys K.
   1978   "Contributions of recent metro/nonmetro migrants to the nonmetro population and labor force." *Agricultural Economics Research* 30(4) October:15–22.
Bowles, Gladys K. and Calvin L. Beale
   1980   "Commuting and migration status in nonmetro areas." *Agricultural Economics Research* 32(3) July:8–20.

[1]Between the first quarters of 1974 and 1975, metropolitan unemployment rose from 5.7% to 9.1%. In the same period, nonmetropolitan unemployment (excluding farm men) went from 5.5% to 9.6%. By the first quarter of 1976, the rates were 8.7% and 8.5% for metropolitan and nonmetropolitan employment, respectively. (All data from *Employment and Earnings*, U.S. Department of Labor.)

The Rural Population Turnaround: Research and National Public Policy

KENNETH L. DEAVERS
DAVID L. BROWN

Introduction

Seldom before has a social phenomenon generated so much popular interest as has the population turnaround in rural America and yet resulted in so little new policy and program development. Beginning in 1973 with extensive stories in the *Washington Post* (Chapman, 1973) and the *New York Times* (King, 1973) and continuing to this day, scores of feature articles in major newspapers and magazines have focused on the turnaround. Paradoxically, this significant social change, rapid and largely unanticipated in most parts of the country, has generated very little legislative discussion or action. This contrasts sharply with the 1960s and early 1970s when continuing rural depopulation and economic decline brought forth significant new agencies and programs such as the Area Redevelopment Administration and its successor, the Economic Development Administration; the Appalachian Regional Commission; and the Rural Development Service (which resulted from passage of the Rural Development Act of 1972). The purpose of this chapter is to analyze the reasons for the gap between changed social and economic conditions in rural America and public policy.

Why Should Public Policy Focus on the Rural Turnaround?

Despite its renewed population growth and economic vitality, rural America continues to have substantial developmental problems. Most

New Directions in
Urban-Rural Migration

ISBN 0-12-136380-5

closely related to the turnaround itself is the problem of institutional capacity to adjust to change.[1]

Adjusting to Demographic Change

Population decline was the rule for most of rural America for 30 years. As a result, we are used to thinking mainly about the problems attendant on rural population decline, and our public policies and programs have been formulated primarily to meet these problems. But rapid growth, particularly if it is unanticipated or breaks with past trends, creates adjustment problems as well. Since the outcomes of growth and decline are different, different adjustments are likely to be required of local institutions; thus, different public policies and programs may be appropriate.

Three aspects of population change—size, composition, and geographic distribution—must be considered in order to understand its impact. All three have direct implications for community structure and function. Moreover, alterations in the rate of change can also cause social and economic dislocations and necessitate institutional adaptations and modifications. Population change bears a potential impact on the delivery of public and private services, fiscal capacity and the tax base, the adequacy of social and political institutions, and the structure of the economy and the labor force. It affects agriculture, land use, water resource use, business and commercial activity, the availability of community facilities and infrastructure, social relations, housing, and access to various types of credit.

Population decline through out-migration in nonmetropolitan counties in the decades preceding 1970 was selective of young adults. It created an imbalance between older persons and persons in the prime working ages. This situation is evident in sparsely populated areas such as the Great Plains, where sustained losses have led to very distorted age structures. For example, the percent of people over 65 years of age is twice as high in completely rural nonmetropolitan counties of the Great Plains as it is in metropolitan counties of the same region (Fuguitt, 1978).

Fertility and mortality, of course, also affect a community's age composition. Historically, birth rates in rural and nonmetropolitan areas have far exceeded the level necessary for population replacement. Thus, the nonmetropolitan population generally has had a broad base of children and young adults. Ironically, the periods of highest fertility in nonmetropolitan America have coincided with periods of contraction in

---

[1]In this chapter, the terms *rural* and *nonmetropolitan* are used interchangeably.

the labor-force needs of agriculture, mining, and other traditionally rural industries. Consequently, heavy and sustained out-migration helped to adjust the imbalance between younger and older age groups.

It is against this background that one must consider the significant demographic changes that are affecting rural communities today. The level of childbearing in nonmetropolitan America has declined from previous levels and is less of a force in local population growth or in the determination of age structure. Migration is now the main determinant of changes in the size and composition of the nonmetropolitan population. However, the nature of this migration is extremely variable. In some areas out-migration persists from earlier decades, further reducing the size of the local population base and aging its composition. In the majority of nonmetropolitan counties, net in-migration is the case, but the composition of migration streams differ. In some areas, inmigration is heavily concentrated in the older age groups while in others young families make up the bulk of newcomers. Consequently, the demographic situation in nonmetropolitan America is much more complex than it was in the past, when high fertility and outmigration characterized most areas.

Changes in population size and composition have a direct bearing on the demand and need for services, facilities, and economic opportunities. Figure 3.1 demonstrates that varying demographic trends place distinctly different pressures on the community. Migration is selective by age. Over 50% of post-1970 nonmetropolitan net migration was composed of persons between the ages of 35 and 64, 33% of persons under 35, and 17% of the elderly (Bowles, 1978; Zuiches and Brown, 1978). The corresponding percentages of these age groups in the general nonmetropolitan population in 1977 were 30%, 57%, and 12%, respectively (U.S. Bureau of the Census, 1978). Although the elderly made up only 17% of nonmetropolitan net migration, they are often much more prominent in rapid growth areas such as Florida, the Southwest, the Ozarks, and the Upper Midwest. Migration of the young and elderly exerts very direct demands on the community for social, economic, and institutional support.

Communities experiencing net in-migration can expect to receive a larger number of school-age persons; younger working-age persons; and, in some instances, retired persons. Conversely, communities experiencing net out-migration can expect to lose younger households and, with them, numerous school-age and working-age persons. They can expect their populations to become relatively older and to be composed of relatively smaller households. In most instances, out-migration does not reduce the number of households but merely diminishes their size.

INCREASED NEED FOR:

	Age Composition	Households	Labor Force
INCREASED NEED FOR:	• Educational resources and facilities • Day care facilities • Pediatric and obstetrical medical care • Recreation and other services oriented to individuals	• New housing units • Water, sewer, utilities, trash collection, fire protection • Residential roads • Sidewalks	• Economic expansion and/or commuting to outside jobs • Investments in community infrastructure • Commercial credit • Potential volunteer workers to help the elderly
Growth Through In-migration a. Young adults and children b. Elderly	Becomes Younger Becomes older	More, Larger More, smaller	More Works, More Potential Workers No Direct Impact
Population Change	Age Composition	Households	Labor Force
Decline Through Out-migration Young adults and children	Becomes Older	Fewer or Constant Number Smaller	Fewer Workers Fewer Potential Workers
	INCREASED NEED FOR: • Geriatric medical services • Public transportation • Nursing homes • Feeding services • Social programs	REDUCED NEED FOR: • Large houses INCREASED NEED FOR: • Smaller housing units and/or apartments CONSTANT NEED FOR: • Water, sewer, utilities, trash collection, fire protection	NEED TO: • Contract economic activity • Train local workers • Import outside workers Excess plant capacity and/or underutilized public infrastructure may occur

Figure 3.1. Some alternative outcomes of in-migration and out-migration.

Thus, household-oriented service needs may remain constant in such communities.

As a consequence, communities experiencing inmigration will be pressed to increase their support of educational resources and to provide more and larger housing units, water, sewers, utilities and other services associated with housing. They will also need to expand their economic base to provide more jobs and allied manpower services for in-migrating workers (and for such workers' children, who will join them in the labor force in the years to come).

On the other hand, communities that are losing population will have a reduced need for educational services, new housing units and new jobs.[2] However, as their populations age, communities may be pressed to supply other types of services that may not have been previously needed. The demand for health care is likely to grow, as is the need for public transportation, since older persons are less apt to drive their own automobiles. The nature of existing housing may become inappropriate; smaller units, apartments, and institutional housing may take on new importance. Job training and retraining may be necessary to prepare older workers, or persons previously outside of the labor force, for jobs in local businesses that are experiencing a labor deficit because some of their workers have moved away.

Adjustments to population change are not automatic. The decisions to provide more schoolrooms and teachers, more miles of sewer pipe, or more industrial parks do not flow automatically from the mere presence of more school-age children, households, or working-age persons in the community. Moreover, the timing of adjustments to population change may vary among impacted communities. Consequently, evaluating the adjustments of revenue needs and revenue flows to support needed services and facilities requires an examination of the time path with which each grows (or declines) (Fox and Sullivan, 1979).

The impacts of population change are mediated by local institutions and social structure. In fact, the same demographic changes may lead to distinctly different outcomes in various communities because of differences in values and in the organization and nature of decision making. There is great variation in the capacity, and sometimes the will, of local governments to adjust to social, economic, and demographic change. The result may be an imbalance between the supply and demand of services, facilities, and opportunities in such areas. The vast

---

[2]Communities often lose population because of insufficient employment opportunities. After a period of decline, ironically, they often find themselves with excess capacity vis-á-vis their current labor force.

majority of rural governments serve very small communities; they receive a disproportionately small share of government revenues; they
generally lack strong elected officials and hired professional managers;
and their political and administrative styles generally emphasize a maintenance of the status quo. Consequently, rural governments are probably less likely to become involved in activities to bring about or accommodate change. Hence, institutional capacity to anticipate and adjust to
change is an important part of the population problem in rural America.

Adjusting to a new regime of population change should be considered
in the context of several sociodemographic problems that have beset
rural America for decades and that have not been alleviated by renewed
population growth and economic vitality. A disproportionate share of
the nation's poor population and a dispersed settlement structure that
reduces access to essential facilities, services, and economic opportunities are foremost among these lingering problems.

Rural Poverty

A disproportionate share of the nation's poor live in nonmetropolitan
areas (35% of the poor population in 1976 compared with 27% of the
total population) (U.S. Bureau of the Census, 1978). Moreover, all of the
persistently low-income counties in the nation (those that have been in
the lowest 20% by income rank in each decade since 1950) are located
outside of SMSAs (Davis, 1979). Poverty is not uniformly distributed in
rural America. Because of the residence patterns of rural minorities and
historic U.S. economic development patterns, rural poverty is heavily
concentrated in the South (Figure 3.2). Nearly two-thirds of the rural
poor live in this region. Moreover, there is a close relationship between
areas in which there is both a concentration of poverty and a residential
dominance of minority populations—principally blacks, Hispanics, and
American Indians.[3]

The occupational and industrial structure of many rural economies is
such that a substantial proportion of the rural work force earns very low
wages. One quarter of poor rural families are headed by a full-time
worker, and almost one-third have two or more workers. In contrast,
only 16% of urban poor families have two or more workers, and almost
half have no workers at all. Thus, rural poverty reflects the relatively low
wage level or the part-time nature of many of the jobs available in rural
labor markets.

---

[3]The exception to this is the Southern Appalachian Cumberland Plateau, which is almost exclusively white but has a long history of economic disadvantage.

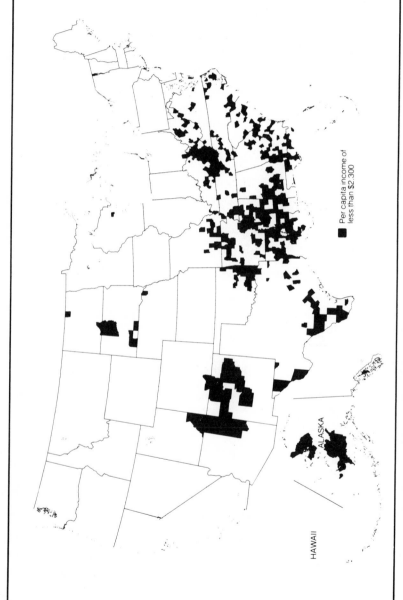

HAWAII

ALASKA

■ Per capita income of less than $2,300

Figure 3.2. Nonmetropolitan low income counties. (Source: U.S. Bureau of the Census.)

The personal and area characteristics of the rural poor make it difficult for federal welfare and development programs to reach them effectively. Poor people in rural America suffer many forms of disadvantage—poor housing, low education attainment, few marketable vocational skills, poor health, and physical isolation. The incidence of rural disadvantage is highest in areas that lack enough local resources to support needed facilities and services. Communities in these areas chronically underinvest in human capital—inadequate educational opportunity and poor health conditions are continuing problems.

Inadequate Access to Essential Services

By their very nature, dispersed rural populations are not as close to urban services as are city people. About 600 nonmetropolitan counties, with a population of over 6 million, lack a sizable settlement (at least 10,000 population) and are not readily and inexpensively accessible to either the larger rural cities or to metropolitan centers. Most of these predominantly rural and remote counties are in the West (Figure 3.3). At the extreme of this group are a number of sparsely settled areas in the Great Plains, the Great Basin, and Alaska, which lie more than 160 km (100 miles) from the nearest place of 10,000 population.

Small rural places often lack the fiscal capacity to support a wide range of urban-type services. In 1972, the level of per capita government spending in metropolitan counties was 1.5 that of their nonmetropolitan counterparts, and within the nonmetropolitan sector spending was significantly greater in larger place ($106 per capita in places with less than 2500 population compared with $224 in places with 10–20,000 people) (U.S. Bureau of the Census, 1974). Thus, urban–rural differences in government expenditures and higher per-unit costs of providing services in rural areas imply a more limited range and quality of services available in rural communities.

Overcoming the disadvantages of physical isolation and low population density may require new forms of institutional organization and the application of modern forms of technology. Transportation, communication, and telecommunications can contribute to alleviating conditions of isolation. Innovative forms of intergovernmental cooperation can help to break down the fiscal barriers to services and facilities.

Why Has Public Policy Not Focused on the Turnaround?

Public policy responses to a social issue can take several forms, ranging from no action or relatively simple change in the rules and procedures of

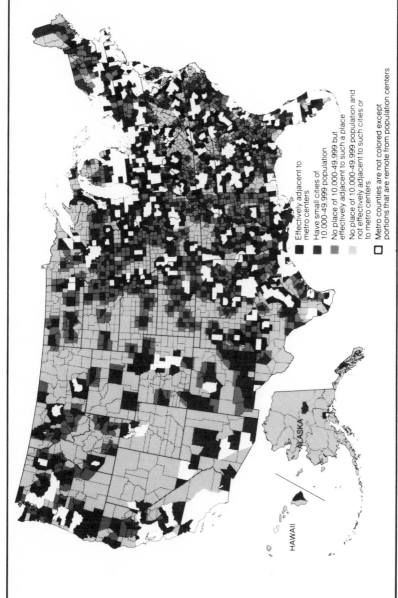

Figure 3.3. Nonmetropolitan areas by accessibility to metropolitan centers and small cities. Metropolitan status as of 1974. Small city population as of 1975. (Source: U.S. Bureau of the Census.)

Effectively adjacent to metro centers

Have small cities of 10,000–49,999 population

No place of 10,000–49,999 but effectively adjacent to such a place

No place of 10,000–49,999 population and not effectively adjacent to such cities or to metro centers

Metro counties are not colored except portions that are remote from population centers

ALASKA

HAWAII

current programs to legislative initiatives that create new agencies and programs. One can argue that the level of policy response will (and should) be related to the perceived political and substantive importance of the issue. In addition, there is an essential time dimension. Clearly, one reason public policy has not yet responded to the rural population turnaround with new legislation and programs is its relative newness. This newness affects both the perceived political salience of the turnaround and understanding of the substantive issues it raises.

The relative lack of political salience is attributable to many factors. Most important, perhaps, is that the turnaround is not uniform or universal for rural areas. The map of rural population change since 1970 shows nearly 350 counties that grew by one-sixth or more from 1970–1976. This is fully three times the growth rate of the United States as a whole—nearly 2.5% annually compounded. The reasons for this rapid growth differ among areas: Retirement and recreation are of central importance in some areas, and industrial deconcentration or renewed vitality in mining are prominent in others (Figure 3.4).

At the opposite end of the distribution, more than 500 rural counties are declining in population because of net out-migration. Most of these counties are not declining as rapidly as in the past, but the setting is one of concentration and adjustment to limited opportunities. As with growing areas, the conditions of decline differ greatly. For example, declining counties in the Great Plains are *not* poor in per-capita income terms, but they have a high proportion of older persons (one-sixth or more). This circumstance is associated with special needs and difficulties in providing services for the elderly. Most other declining rural areas are characterized by underdevelopment and poverty.

For well over a decade most rural communities have had to adjust to population decline. In some cases they have consolidated services and economic activities; in others they have eliminated services altogether. Federal rural policy has focused attention on the problems of decline and created rural developmental institutions and programs mandated to deal with such areas. Until new resources, institutions, and programs are provided, attention to growth-related problems will come largely at the expense of attention to other rural problems. Such redirection of effort is politically difficult, since existing programs have established constituencies who may be adversely affected by any redirection. Moreover, as was shown earlier, poverty and disadvantage continue to be serious problems in rural America. Hence, a redirection of effort away from rural poverty would not be wise from the point of view of overall rural policy.

The lack of a rural policy also results from the fact that in the 1970s

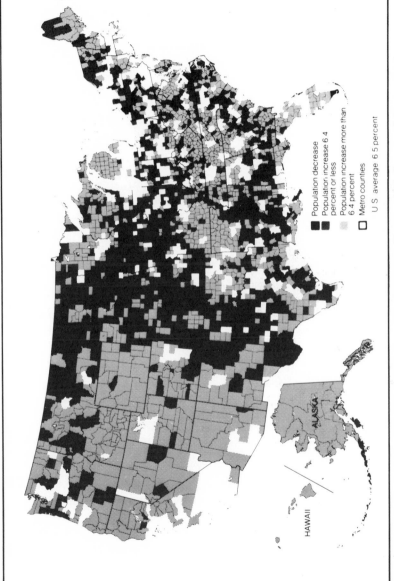

Legend:
- Population decrease
- Population increase 6.4 percent or less
- Population increase more than 6.4 percent
- Metro counties
- U.S. average 6.5 percent

HAWAII

ALASKA

Figure 3.4. Population change for nonmetropolitan counties, 1970–1977. (Source: U.S. Bureau of the Census.)

federal programs have been dominated by *urban* concerns. With nearly 73% of the nation's population living in metropolitan areas and over 40% in areas with a population of 1 million or more, urban centers are sufficiently large that their problems attract federal attention *individually*, as well as collectively. However, the concerns of 59 million people in rural America, scattered across the countryside in smaller settlements, do not receive much individual recognition. Also, because of their geographic dispersion and diversity, rural people do not represent a well-organized rural constituency. Thus they lack effective ways of making their common problems known and of influencing federal polices that affect them.

Most people have a positive feeling about the rural turnaround. Rural growth, which is seen as an indicator of a revitalized rural America, is consistent with deeply held values of the importance of rural life in the national scheme of things. Numerous state and national studies show a preference for rural living, especially if the rural area is close to a metropolitan city (Fuguitt and Zuiches, 1975). This general positive view of rural growth complicates the political problem of developing policies. It is difficult to mobilize political will to deal with a situation that is widely viewed as a success story: "Growth is good." It is in this context that rural social science research has the most to contribute to policy formulation and that current research is subject to the most criticism.

To date, most research has monitored population trends and attempted to explain the determinants of population change (Beale, 1976; McCarthy and Morrison, 1978). Only passing interest has been paid to the potential implications of these trends. Thus it is difficult for policymakers to judge the costs and benefits of the turnaround or to anticipate its impact in different areas and for different population groups. Moreover, very little research has focused on the process through which population change impacts on community structure. Questions about the specific institutions involved, the timing of impacts vis-à-vis the initial population growth, and the way impacts are distributed throughout the community can give the turnaround political salience as an issue.

There is, of course, no guarantee that the results of such research will be influential in shaping policy. The relationship between research and policy is tenuous. Often, policymakers do not understand how to use the results of research. Equally often, researchers are naive about the policymaking process. Hence, important policy-relevant research goes unutilized. It is our judgment that the burden for improving this situation falls primarily on researchers.

Researchers need to learn how, where, and when one gains entry to the policy process. They need to understand that many groups are involved—the White House, executive branch agencies, Congress, governors and mayors, and private interest groups. As a consequence, there are many options for building bridges between their work and the policymaking process. In addition, research results need to be disseminated to policymakers in a useful and *understandable* way. Without effective communication there is little chance that the knowledge gained from rural research will impact the policy process.

Conclusions

Adjusting to the impacts of rapid unanticipated population change is the population problem most closely associated with the post-1970 rural turnaround. However, it is a mistake to consider the turnaround a policy issue in and of itself. The turnaround should be considered in the context of overall rural development policy.

The economic well-being of rural people should be a primary focus of such a policy. Governmental actions to alleviate poverty and disadvantage must recognize that rural poverty differs from that in urban areas in some very fundamental ways. At the community level, rural poverty is often located in environments that lack adequate human and community facilities, are isolated from other areas with such facilities, and lack a wide range of employment opportunities. In these environments, institutional capacity—particularly governmental—is unable or unwilling to provide support. Furthermore, years of out-migration have complicated the problem of designing programs to assist many such areas, since the age structure and other characteristics of the local population may make public or private development efforts appear to be a very high risk activity.

At the individual or family level, policy must recognize that the low-income position of many rural people does not result from unemployment. Rather, it results from the types of jobs available in rural labor markets, a lack of appropriate skills and training for better jobs, a lack of transportation access to take advantage of opportunities, and chronically poor health. Governmental activity designed to assist the rural working poor must be more than income support.

All of the welfare reform proposals considered in recent years would have established national minimum payment standards. They would also have made numerous changes in asset qualification requirements—assumptions about family status and labor market status that would have benefited rural residents. Thus, for many of the rural poor, especially in chronically disadvantaged areas of the South, welfare reform is a key element of federal rural policy. No other single policy action would have as immediate and obvious consequences for their well-being, in terms of their ability to obtain the goods and services essential to a decent level of living.

But rural policy must focus more widely. It must be concerned with the provision of essential services in areas of spatial isolation and low population density; the capacity of local institutions to anticipate, plan for, and adjust to change; and the activities of the federal government in rural areas and its relation to state governments and local institutions.

The political feasibility of such a comprehensive policy is not high, but certain actions could be taken to increase the understanding of rural issues and their priority on the National policy agenda. Better communication of research results to policymakers, along with more thoughtful selection of rural research topics to ensure that important policy-relevant questions are addressed, would be a major first step. This would help to ensure that rural stereotypes are diminished, that accurate descriptions of trends and conditions in rural America are available, and that implications of these trends are known to the policymaking community.

Policymakers are unlikely to propose new programs to ameliorate rural growth problems unless the costs and benefits of the turnaround are quantified. While there will never be unaimous agreement as to whether the population turnaround is "good" or "bad," research can identify some important social and economic consequences of recent trends. Who is impacted by renewed growth and in what ways? What does a community have to provide to accomodate new growth and to maintain the quality of life and the physical, social, and institutional environment? How willing is the community to provide the necessary services and facilities and how can the latter be financed?

Faced with serious gaps in substantive knowledge and the limited political salience of rural issues, the Carter administration has still managed considerable policy innovation. The administration's efforts have been concentrated on a series of reforms that seek to make federal programs more responsive to the rural situation. These reforms have focused on such critical rural issues as health care, water and sewer facilities, communication, and transportation. Such "rural initiatives" do not imply a redistribution of resources from outside of rural-oriented programs or substantial new spending. And from most reports, these changes have been well received by rural citizens, politicians, and interest groups.

Recently, the Administration announced a rural development policy as a counterpart to its earlier urban policy (White House, 1979). This overall statement of rural goals and objectives provides a useful framework within which to research the social and economic changes affecting rural America, and to evaluate the impacts of Federal programs. The announced policy focuses action primarily on further efforts to make Federal programs more sensitive to the unique problems of rural people. Like the preceding rural initiatives, there are no major new commitments to spending. However, the Administration's rural policy does highlight the substantive and political importance of the population turnaround. Because it recognizes that this "success story" can pose significant problems for areas impacted by renewed growth, it may lead to some redistribution of spending among rural areas.

References

Beale, Calvin L.
   1976   "A further look at nonmetropolitan population growth since 1970." *American Journal of Agricultural Economics* 58(5): 953–958.
Bowles, Gladys K.
   1978   "Contribution of recent metro/nonmetro migrants to the nonmetro population and labor force." *Agricultural Economics Research* 30(4): 15–22.
Chapman, William
   1973   "Cities' growth rate sharply slowed." *Washington Post,* September 26.
Davis, Thomas F.
   1979   *Persistent Low-Income Counties in Nonmetro America.* Rural Development Research Report No. 12. Washington, D.C.: U.S. Department of Agriculture.
Fox, William and Patrick Sullivan
   1979   "Revenue needs in growing and declining areas." In *Revenue Administration, 1979.* Proceedings of the 47th Annual Meeting of the National Association of Tax Administrators. Chicago: Federation of Tax Administrators.
Fuguitt, Glenn V.
   1978   "Population trends in sparsely settled areas of the United States: The Case of the Great Plains." Paper presented at United States/Australia Joint Seminar on Settlement in Sparsely Populated Regions, Adelaide, Australia.
Fuguitt, Glenn V. and James J. Zuiches
   1975   "Residential preferences and population distribution." *Demography,* 12(3): 491–504.
King, Wayne
   1973   "They didn't disappear after all." *New York Times,* November 11, p. 8.
McCarthy, Kevin F. and Peter A. Morrison
   1978   *The Changing Demographic and Economic Structure of Nonmetropolitan Areas in the United States.* R–2399–EDA. Santa Monica, Calif.: The Rand Corporation.
U.S. Bureau of Census
   1974   *Census of Governments 1972.* Vol. 4, *Government Finances.* Washington, D.C.: U.S. Government Printing Office.
U.S. Bureau of the Census
   1978   *Social and Economic Characteristics of the Metropolitan and Nonmetropolitan Popula-*

tion: 1977 and 1970. Special Studies P-23, No. 75. Washington, D.C.: Bureau of the Census.

White House
  1979   *The Carter Administration Small Community and Rural Development Policy.* Washington, D.C.: The White House.

Zuiches, James J. and David L. Brown
  1978   "The changing character of the nonmetropolitan population, 1970-75." Chapter 4 In Thomas R. Ford (ed.), *Rural USA: Persistence and Change.* Ames: Iowa State University Press.

EXPLANATIONS FOR THE URBAN–RURAL TURNAROUND

Population change of any form usually reflects other changes that have taken place in the social and economic relationships that constitute the society and in the individual values and beliefs of the people. When millions of people change their mobility patterns in the short span of a decade, we have a reliable indicator that the conditions governing population distribution have been modified. Morrison has commented that this change can be characterized as a shift from primarily resource or production-oriented migration to primarily consumption-oriented migration. Economic models of migration that dominated earlier theories of geographic mobility did not anticipate the turnaround. The aims of this part of the book are to explain how and why the turnaround shift has taken place and to identify some of the turnaround's implications for new models of migration.

Wardwell (Chapter 4) notes that a similar urban–rural turnaround has taken place simultaneously in numerous developed societies. He argues that consequently, explanations for the turnaround should include factors that are demonstrably common to these several countries and offers the outlines of a new paradigm. He rejects explanations based solely on the conditions of large urban places or on changing residential preferences. Similarly, explanations based on cyclic economic fluctuations or expansion of natural-resource-based industries are inadequate in themselves to account for the turnaround. Instead, Wardwell argues that both rural growth and stability and decline in large urban centers are a function of international and intranational convergence on common levels of a number of factors. These factors include changes in the technology and use of transportation and communications; growth in personal affluence; shifts in labor force composition; and convergence between rural and urban areas on common lifestyles, employment opportunities, and income levels. Residential preferences have been a passive factor, according to Wardwell, coming into play as residential differences in the traditional determinants of migration have diminished.

Wardwell cites illustrative data to indicate that these changes are common to several turnaround countries. He concludes by emphasizing the key causal role played by declining real transport costs, and speculates that energy prices may contribute to a reconcentration of population and economic activity.

Stevens (Chapter 5) provides an economic framework for the turnaround, distinguishing between access to public goods and to private goods. He argues that people are increasingly willing to sacrifice income to gain access to public goods, which are perceived to be more readily available in nonmetropolitan areas.

Stevens contrasts the theory of hedonic prices with a utility-function approach to account for income sacrifices associated with migration to southern Oregon (an environmentally attractive but economically depressed area). The utility-function approach is shown to be superior to the hedonic-price approach in explaining variation in income loss among in-migrants.

Although migrants are consumers as well as suppliers of labor, as Stevens points out, Bender (Chapter 6) is more concerned with the traditional concept of the migrant as labor, and with the structural conditions within and between areas that fix the demand for labor. Bender argues that long-term changes in the economic structure of rural areas are having a cumulative interactive effect on population shifts.

Bender's model consists of five propositions: (1) Basic economic activities are dispersing increasingly into rural areas; (2) services disperse as a result of the growth of basic industries in rural areas; (3) existing labor-force participation rates in combination with new employment opportunities determine the degree to which labor conditions induce new migration; (4) wage growth induces both higher labor-force participation and new migration; and (5) increasing transport costs encourage further decentralization and encourage the substitution of labor for energy.

Each element in the model influences population independently, but the key effect is the interactive nature of the separate elements. These dynamic linkages tie rural areas more intimately into the national economy and increase the sensitivity of rural areas to fluctuations in national economic conditions. Hence, rural areas no longer are a buffer for metropolitan centers during national economic recessions.

More than any other approach, the residential-preference explanation of the migration turnaround views the migrant as a pure consumer. Zuiches (Chapter 7) reviews 15 major studies of residential preferences in order to examine the links between preferences and expected and actual mobility behavior. He further examines the association between preferences and the process of destination selection, anticipating the focus of Williams and McMillen's research. Zuiches's discussion of the duration of residence following movement also anticipates Carpenter's research in Chapter 9.

Like Stevens and Williams and McMillen, Zuiches distinguishes between "productive" and "consumptive" moves and emphasizes the necessity to word questions carefully in order to separate preferences from behavioral expectations. He is concerned with the theoretical integration of preference explanations and with changes in the structural conditions that govern people's abilities to implement their residential preferences in actual moves. He focuses on the association between these two factors and the relationship between individual characteristics and preferences for nonmetropolitan destinations.

Williams and McMillen (Chapter 8) stress that migration decision making is a complex process that must be separated into at least two steps: deciding to leave a place, and selecting a destination. Their research, in rapidly growing nonmetropolitan counties in the Midwest, identified these decisions separately and thus permitted them to examine the propensity to give similar and different reasons for leaving an origin and selecting a destination. They found that economic factors predominate in the reasons given for leaving a place, whereas social factors predominate in destination selection. For approximately 35% of the migrants, the destination selection process is fully determined by the reason for leaving (e.g., returning to one's hometown). The remainder, almost two-thirds of the migrants, made two decisions. For example, nearly one-half of migrants who gave employment-related reasons for leaving gave some other reason for their destination selection (personal and social ties, environmental considerations, etc.).

Williams and McMillen find the concept of location-specific capital useful in understanding the migration decision-making process, particularly of migrants who are motivated by retirement and environmental considerations. As we have noted, such migrants are prominent in the growth of remote and rural nonmetropolitan countries.

Retention of new in-migrants from metropolitan areas is an important factor in the dynamics of population growth in nonmetropolitan America. Carpenter's (Chapter 9) cohort analysis captures a subtle but significant difference in these growth dynamics. Nonmetropolitan growth could occur in two ways. A pattern that combined successively larger waves of metropolitan out-migrants with very short duration of residence and return migration might actually mask the high turnover and low residential stability that this pattern would necessarily produce. Conversely, a longer retention pattern suggests greater aggregate growth as additional new arrivals are added to, rather than merely replace, prior migrants. Turnover would be lower with greater retention, and growth would be more stable.

Turnover rates also have important implications for rural development, including community infrastructure, political participation of new migrants, and the stability or conflict of assimilation of new migrants.

Carpenter constructs seven cohorts according to whether their constituents moved to a nonmetropolitan area between 1965 and 1968 or between 1969 and 1972. Using data from the Continuous Work History Sample, he demonstrates an increasing propensity to remain in the nonmetropolitan destination for more than 3 years. He attributes part of the growth of nonmetropolitan counties to this tendency toward increased retention.

The six chapters in this part, therefore, juxtapose alternative but complementary explanations of the migration turnaround. In combination, they respond to a call for a more holistic approach to migration theory and research. Taken together, these six chapters emphasize change in structural (social, economic, and demographic) conditions in nonmetropolitan America, the change in individual values regarding preferred work and residence location, and the process by which people make migration decisions.

Toward a Theory of Urban–Rural Migration in the Developed World[1]

JOHN M. WARDWELL

Introduction

The nonmetropolitan migration turnaround with which this book is concerned is not confined to the United States. It has appeared in one stage or another in at least 11 other countries: Japan, Sweden, Norway, Italy, Denmark, New Zealand, Belgium, France, West Germany, East Germany, and the Netherlands (Vining and Kontuly, 1978). Each of these countries has experienced either a reversal in the direction or a drastic reduction in the levels of net population flows from rural to core urban regions. The phenomenon appeared in France, West Germany, East Germany, and the Netherlands in the 1960s but only became evident in the other countries in the early 1970s.

Geographically large countries with remote rural regions—such as the United States, Norway, and Sweden—exhibit two distinct patterns of deconcentration: the repopulation of remote rural regions, and the continued deconcentration of large urban cores into adjacent territory of lower settlement density. The aggregation of metropolitan growth statistics confounds these two patterns. Urban decentralization has been going on throughout the twentieth century (Long, 1980), and it is the

[1]This is a revised and expanded version of a paper presented at the International Union for the Scientific Study of Population, Congress on Economic and Demographic Issues for the 1980s, Helsinki, Finland, August–September, 1978. Support has been provided by the Center for Social Data Anaalysis, Montana State University and Washington State University. The present chapter is Scientific Paper No. 5574, Project 0354, College of Agriculture Research Center, Washington State University.

New Directions in
Urban–Rural Migration

only form of the migration turnaround that can be observed within the national boundaries of small nations, such as the Netherlands and Belgium. This form of resettlement of low-density peripheral areas is also taking place in Great Britain (Drewett *et al.*, 1976), Canada (Beaujot, 1978), and Australia (Bourne and Logan, 1976). Repopulation of remote rural territory is more prevalent in the larger countries. Vining and Kontuly (1978) demonstrated that rural regions that had contributed heavily to urban growth through out-migration are now experiencing either net in-migration or greatly reduced rates of migration loss. Their analysis gains credibility from the fact that they conservatively over-bounded urban regions in geographically large countries in order to control for urban deconcentration into adjacent territory.

The similarity in recent migration patterns in these countries is striking. It extends beyond the near-simultaneity of its appearance, although that fact alone is sufficiently arresting to demand explanation. Annual net migration into the large urban cores of Japan, Sweden, Italy, and the United States shows remarkable similarity in the pattern of increasing net in-migration rates in the late 1960s, followed by an abrupt cessation in the 1970s (Figure 4.1). These similarities, in the context of similar social and economic conditions, suggest that the search for explanations of the migration turnaround should be concentrated in factors common to the several countries that are experiencing the change. They also suggest that the two separate questions "Why?" and "Why now?" be given equal emphasis.

This chapter seeks to identify underlying causes of change in the patterns of net migration between urban regions and nonmetropolitan areas that are common to most, if not all, of the developed countries listed above. A pervasive urbanization of the total society is the foremost of these causes. The process of urbanization is here conceived of as a form of the social organization of space, not as the mere concentration of people in space. In these terms, the phrase "highly urbanized society" means a society in which urban forms of social organization have so extended themselves in space as to make the old distinctions between center and hinterland, urban and rural less meaningful than they had been (Hawley, 1971). Concomitantly, rural areas have become more thoroughly integrated in the network of urban activities. They have become more like urban places in some ways, while remaining quite unlike them in other ways. Convergence between urban and rural areas is now as important in guiding migration flows as are the residual differences between them.

This chapter begins a theory that integrates several causes into a single model of the socioeconomic development of advanced societies.

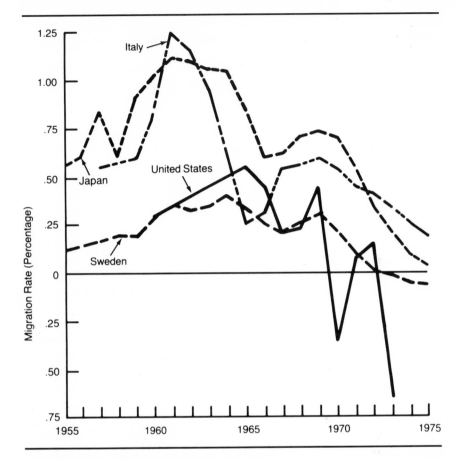

Figure 4.1. Annual net domestic migration rates into metropolitan regions of four developed countries. (Source: Italy, Japan, and Sweden from Vining & Kontuly, 1977; United States from Continuous Work History Sample.)

Changes in social and economic factors that are closely related to migration are the elements of the model. The model is thus only an abstraction from the total process of social change. It is a model that takes a developmental or evolutionary view of the growth and change of large urban centers and their rural hinterlands. The model is no more than an elaboration of the mechanisms of the process of urbanization. The mechanisms by which urban forms of social organization extend themselves in space constitute the main elements of the model. It is a perspective that addresses the question "Why now?" by assuming that certain outcomes are not possible until all of the necessary elements for those outcomes are in place. The particular constellation of elements that has produced the nonmetropolitan migration turnaround is characteristic of a stage of societal evolution. That stage has been attained at approximately the same time in a range of societies in which new patterns of population distribution are as strongly influenced by similarities as by differences.

This approach to the problem minimizes the risk of developing 12 theories to account for the appearance of the phenomenon in 12 countries. Instead, this approach maximizes the opposite risk: that of brushing too lightly over differences within and between countries. It errs in the direction of assuming that statistically comparable changes in the direction and volume of net migration flows to large urban regions represent substantively similar behaviors. It is those statistical similarities, or aggregate patterns, that the model seeks to explain. Differences between countries may account for the variations in timing, scope, or volume of the aggregate patterns, but they cannot account for the similarities in net migration shifts. These similarities demand examination of the fundamental reasons for large urban growth and rural-to-urban migration and an examination of changes in the structure, composition, and activities of both urban and rural regions.

These reasons will be elaborated, first, in a review of explanations for cessation or diminishing of large urban growth, and for the turnaround in patterns of rural–urban migration. Included are diseconomies and disamenities of urban scale, cyclic recession theories, expansion of demand for labor in rural locations, and the changing role of residential preferences. The review of each will consist of a statement of how the explanation seeks to account for the phenomenon, a consideration of the major counterarguments, and a review of empirical evidence. Elements from these several explanations will then be considered with other factors known to have significant relationships with population distribution. These factors can be shown to be logically interrelated in a model of the changing relationships between urban centers and rural hinterlands.

Limits to Urban Growth

The concept of limits on continued growth of large urban areas is one rationale for the new patterns of growth and migration. National urban growth has followed a logistic pattern (Figure 4.2). In such a pattern, growth rates slow down and stabilize or even reverse as the asymptote, or upper limit, is approached. The theoretical task is to identify the

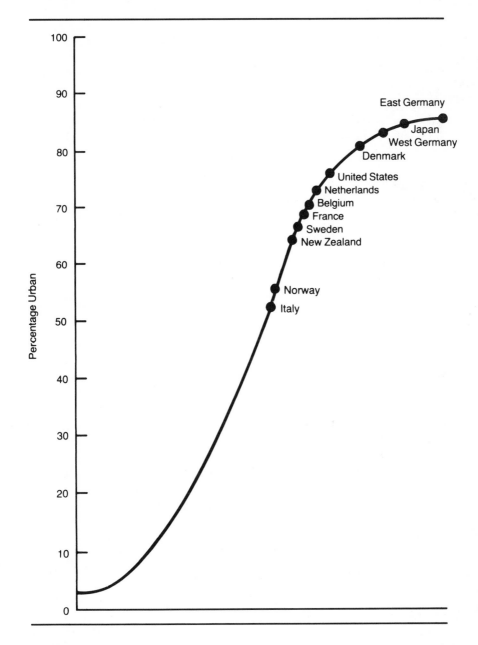

Figure 4.2. Logistic model of urban growth and percentage urban by national definition, 12 turnaround countries, 1970.

forces that manifest themselves in this limit. Limits on large urban growth must manifest themselves in one of two forms: external constraints on the sources of urban growth, or internal constraints, in the form of conditions arising within large urban centers, that impede continued growth.

In the turnaround nations, growth of large urban areas at rates in excess of the national rate of population change is dependent upon net inmigration. Natural increase of the urban population has diminished because of precipitously declining birth rates in all of these countries (Table 4.1). Crude birth rates are below 15 per thousand in all but two of these countries, and the crude rate of natural increase ranges from a low of −3.5 per thousand per year to a high of only 10.8 per thousand. Consequently, the slowing down of urban growth must be explained by factors that have either reduced urban in-migration or increased out-migration.

External Constraints on the Sources of Urban Growth

External constraints may change the conditions that regulate the release of labor from agriculture and other extractive industries. If increases in labor productivity slow down, or if expansion of such industries takes place, a society may reach a point where continuing urban growth is forced to wait upon further change in the extractive sector as this traditional source of growth is removed.

It is unlikely that employment opportunities in the extractive industries are responsible for the reversal or equilibrium in net urban–rural migration. The diminution of the rural migrant pool, as employment in agricultural industries nears a minimum (in the current state of the agricultural arts), has played a role in reducing the rural–urban migration stream. However, farm-to-city migration has made a progressively smaller contribution in total rural–urban population movements in these countries. More importantly, the proportions of the labor force actively engaged in agriculture and other extractive industries has continued to decline in countries that are experiencing rural or nonmetropolitan growth at the expense of large metropolitan areas.

Table 4.1 demonstrates the wide variety of proportions in agriculture and mining found in this group of turnaround countries. The uniformity of decline in the absolute numbers of laborers employed in these industries is also shown. Belgium, the German Democratic Republic, and the United States have less than 7% of their labor forces in agricultural and extractive industries. But Italy and Japan also manifest the turnaround

TABLE 4.1
Demographic and Labor Force Indicators, Turnaround Countries, 1960-1975

Country	Crude birth rates				Crude rate of natural increase				Labor force in extractive industries [a]	
	1960	1965	1970	1975	1960	1965	1970	1975	Percent of labor force 1975	Percent of decline 1966-1975
Belgium	16.9	16.4	14.7	12.2	4.5	4.3	2.3	0	6.2	[b] 21.8
Denmark	16.6	18.0	14.4	14.2	7.1	7.9	4.6	4.2	9.9	[c] stable
France	17.9	17.8	16.7	14.1	6.5	6.7	6.1	3.5	15.4	29.6
Germany, D.R.	17.0	16.5	13.9	10.8	3.7	3.1	- 0.2	- 3.5	4.1	stable
Germany, F.R.	17.5	17.7	13.4	9.7	6.1	6.5	1.4	- 2.8	9.9	34.7
Italy	18.1	19.1	16.8	14.8	8.4	9.1	7.1	4.9	20.9	35.4
Japan	17.4	18.8	18.8	17.2	9.8	11.7	11.9	10.8	17.8	36.2
Netherlands	20.8	19.9	18.3	13.0	13.1	11.9	9.9	4.7	7.7	[d] 11.8
New Zealand	26.5	22.9	22.1	18.5	17.7	14.2	13.3	10.3	---	---
Norway	17.3	17.8	16.6	14.1	8.2	8.7	6.8	4.1	12.8	[c] 14.4
Sweden	13.7	15.9	13.7	12.6	3.7	5.8	3.8	1.8	8.7	30.0
United States	23.6	19.4	18.3	14.8	14.0	10.0	8.9	5.9	5.2	15.1
Coefficient of variation	.185	.103	.158	.177	.512	.394	.385	.120	---	---

Source: Birth rates and natural increase from United Nations, 1976; labor force from International Labor Organization, 1976.
 [a] Agriculture, forestry, fisheries, mining, and quarrying.
 [b] 1970-1975.
 [c] 1972-1975.
 [d] 1969-1975.

77

with approximately 20% of their labor forces so employed. The decline in absolute numbers employed in these industries in the countries experiencing the population turnaround is about 25% from 1966 to 1975.

The correlation of annual data on numbers of people employed in extractive industries with net metropolitan migration for the 1967–1975 period for Japan, Finland, the two Germanies, Hungary, Italy, Norway and Sweden fails to show the consistently negative association that would support the hypothesis of urban loss due to expanded employment in these sectors. Only in Norway, during the 1966–1970 period, and in West Germany does one find a moderately high and negative correlation between net metropolitan migration and numbers of workers employed in extractive industries.

Finally, Beale (1978a) has shown that the expansion of extractive industries can be expected to do no more than offset the continuing decline in agricultural employment. Thus, external constraints on continued metropolitanization arising in the agricultural–extractive sectors must be tentatively set aside as an explanation for the observed patterns of large urban loss in these several countries. Of course, it remains a contributing factor in some countries.

Another external constraint on continued large urban growth may be a decline in the rate of new industry formation in large urban areas. According to Thompson (1965, 1968) new, innovative industries with high information and part-time skill requirements originate in the thoroughly modern milieu of the large, diverse metropolis. At the same time, maturing industries continue to depart large metropolises. As firm growth stabilizes, ability to sustain full-time employment no longer requires location near a large pool of highly skilled labor. Skill requirements diminish, and information economies no longer compensate for the higher costs of large metropolitan locations. The relative rates of growth of major cities compared with smaller places thus depend, in part, on how rapidly the dispersion of maturing, urban-originating activities proceeds compared to the initiation of new urban activities (Hoover, 1971). Large urban areas lose population relative to the rest of the system if new industry formation slows down while the dispersion of maturing industries remains constant or accelerates.

Two factors influence these relative rates of change in the necessary direction: economy-wide recession, which disproportionately impacts larger cities through a slowdown in investments in new industries; and changes in the infrastructure of smaller places such that they "receive each successive industry a little earlier in its life cycle [and thus] acquire the industry at a point in time when it still has both substantial job-forming potential and high-skill work [Thompson, 1969:6–9]."

Vining and Kontuly (1978) note that the cyclic recession theory does not fit the data for Norway, which experienced continuing economic growth through the recessions that have occurred in the rest of Europe and in the United States. They also note that this explanation predicts a resurgence of large urban growth in the economic recoveries of Japan and Italy following their recessions. Such a resurgence failed to occur (see Figure 4.1). Similarly, nonmetropolitan growth in the United States has been consistent through the 1970s despite the fluctuations in economic trends that have characterized the decade (U.S. Bureau of the Census, 1975, 1978). Thus in the United States, as in Norway, Japan, and Italy, the timing of the patterns of population movements shows considerable independence from that of economic cycles.

Changes in the infrastructure of smaller places, enabling them to receive industries at earlier points in their life cycles, would permit but not require an acceleration of the dispersion process. Accordingly, the evidence for this will be considered in a later section of this chapter.

Internal Constraints on the Sources of Urban Growth

An examination of internal constraints is appropriate since externally imposed limits on large metropolitan growth do not of themselves account adequately for the cross-national patterns observed. If Thompson's "urban size ratchet"—by which size and growth insure further growth—has stopped or even reversed, has it been because the gains to firms and households located in large urban areas no longer compensate for the costs? Have economies of scale been exhausted, or have diseconomies of scale entered into the calculus of locational decisions? Are such changes the result of the growth of cities to sizes that are neither manageable, economic, nor pleasant? Given either the lack of economic incentive for large urban location or the existence of disincentives, firms and individuals may leave the large urban regions. Moreover, firms or individuals that in the past would have moved to such regions may no longer do so. Higher costs of production and distribution of market goods and services, and the disamenities of congestion, air and water pollution, and noise levels, belong to the class of explanations here called internal constraints on urban growth.

Traditionally, large urban areas have offered economies in transport costs, labor diversity, and volume, as well as the external economies of agglomeration. Firms derive advantages in production, assembly, and distribution costs by virtue of the proximate location of similar and complementary firms (Hoover, 1971). Consumers achieve economies of access and variety. If diseconomies develop, firms and households may consider relocation to more economic locations. The arguments for and against such diseconomies are mixed, and the empirical evidence that follows seems at most to be weighted toward earlier capture of scale economies rather than toward the entrance of diseconomies. Smaller-sized places may now offer many, if not most, of the economies available in larger urban areas. In contrast, there is little evidence supporting the contention that costs rise disproportionately to gains with increasing population size in these large agglomerations. The possibilities of capturing economies at lower points in the urban size hierarchy is discussed more fully later in this chapter.

Examples of major diseconomies include the provision of public sector services such as police and fire protection, education, and refuse disposal, on the one hand, and on the other, the familiar disamenities litany of air and water pollution, noise levels, traffic congestion, increased rates of deviant behavior (most notably crime rates), and mental and physical health (see Barnett, 1968; Crowley, 1977; Gilbert, 1976; Hirsch, 1968; Johnston, 1976).

Proponents of the diseconomy explanation argue that measurable diseconomies in the public sector's provision of urban services are made manifest to producers and to households in higher taxes for schools, fire districts, police protection, and so on, and in higher wages to offset the disamenities of large urban living. The translation of these disamenities into cost calculations is frequently indirect and subjective. This is apparent in the case of such conditions as noise levels, air and water pollution, and congestion. It is less apparent but equally real in the indirect effects of the higher costs of providing public sector services. For example, as quality of service deteriorates, this also becomes a part of the context within which consumers and producers make location decisions.

The counterarguments show continued scale economies and external economies in the increasing ability of large urban areas to withstand industry-specific recessions through their depth and breadth and to call upon the diversity of resources in their public and private sectors to adapt to change (Alonso, 1973; Mera, 1973; Thompson, 1968). Empirical studies of factor productivity in the United States and Japan indicate that the return to factors in the largest metropolitan areas is 8% higher than in smaller cities (Segal, 1976). Moreover, in the United States, each doubling of population size is associated with a 6% increase in labor productivity (Sveikauskas, 1975).

Alonso (1973) and Hoover (1971) argue that the supposed diseconomies accruing to households are largely a function of rising levels of expectation. The larger the city, the more people expect to consume of the goods and services available. Living costs associated with city size thus chiefly reflect differences in consumption levels. When consumption levels are held constant across city size, income gains more than compensate for increased costs. Thus, households do in fact experience net income gains with increasing city size. Consequently, dissatisfaction with the relationship between income and cost of living may merely reflect the propensity for consumption expectations to outpace income gains, as both rise with the increased availability of goods and services in the larger metropolitan areas. The actual increase in money income is more than adequate to purchase the same array of goods and services as is purchased in the smaller place. However, it is worth noting that both analyses of factor productivity and income satisfaction are restricted to market goods and services. For an alternative approach, see Stevens, in Chapter 5.

Finally, both the range of sizes of the largest cities in the turnaround countries and the range of population concentration in these large cities are great. This fact argues against explaining the turnaround on the basis of any simple function of scale diseconomies related to city size. The data in Table 4.2 show the size of the largest urban area in each of the turnaround countries, and three indicators of the concentration of the large urban population. The first measure is simply the city proper population as a percentage of the population of the urbanized area for the largest urbanized area in each country. The second is the proportion of the population living in places of 100,000 or greater that is located in places of 1 million or greater. The third is the four-city index, which measures the ratio of the population in the largest place to the combined populations of the next three largest places. This provides an indicator of the primacy or dominance of the largest city. The index cannot fall below .33. While it has no fixed upper limit, no nation had a value for the ratio larger than 8.00 in 1970 (Davis, 1969).

The size range of the largest urban areas in the nations known to be experiencing the more radical form of the urban turnaround (that is, the repopulation of remote rural regions) extends from well under 1 million (Norway) to just under 12 million (Japan and the United States). Urban areas in the 1 million range are well represented, as are urban areas in the range between 1 million and 12 million. A simple explanation of the relationship between size of urban area, diseconomies of scale, and urban dispersion of population and economic activity must address this marked variation in size of urban areas that are losing population to less urban regions of the respective countries. An argument of interaction between some other facet of society and the size at which diseconomies force deconcentration would be difficult to postulate, given the equivalent levels of socioeconomic development in these countries.

But economic scale is a function of population concentration as well as

TABLE 4.2
Indicators of Urban Concentration, Turnaround Countries, 1970-75

Country	Percent urban by nation's definition	Size of largest urban area (000)	City proper as percent of urban area [a]	Percentage of city population in places of 1,000,000+ [b]	Four-city index
Belgium	68.9	1,075	41.0	44.5	.77
Denmark	80.1	1,328	55.5	77.8	3.50
France	67.9	9,863	23.2	53.0	3.10
Germany, D.R.	84.2	1,095	c	28.7	.77
Germany, F.R.	82.2	2,048	c	65.8	1.03
Italy	52.0	2,868	c	45.2	.69
Japan	83.2	11,623	74.3	46.7	1.53
Netherlands	72.2	996	76.7	39.9	.50
New Zealand	66.0	635	69.6	48.1	1.10
Norway	55.0	645	72.1	59.7	1.48
Sweden	66.1	1,354	49.6	51.1	1.14
United States	75.2	11,572	66.1	64.4	.77

Source: United Nations, 1975; Four-City Index from Davis, 1969.
[a] City population is population in places of 100,000 or more.
[b] Or in largest place if no place larger than 1,000,000.
[c] Reported urban area population is for city proper.

of population size. The city-proper population as a percentage of the population of the urbanized area may chiefly reflect local and national variations in the definition of city and urban boundaries. But the range of concentration among the urban turnaround countries is so great that the indicator, which ranges from 23.2% to 76.7% will not discriminate turnaround countries from non-turnaround countries. However, in combination with other factors, the size distribution of cities may contribute to the timing, volume, and distribution of the turnaround migration pattern.

Similarly, the range of the second concentration measure (percentage of population in places of 100,000 or greater that resides in places of 1 million or greater) is quite wide (28.7–77.8%). Finally, the four-city index ranges from .50 to 3.50; the value of this index has been declining in each of the turnaround countries since 1950 (as shown in Davis, 1969, Table G: 242–246). Thus, these indicators of urban size and density show a large degree of independence between the fact of the migration turnaround and the national context of urban concentration.

The use of these data in this manner requires the simplifying assumption that the relationships between urban size and economic scale can be compared cross-nationally. Two explanations for an interaction between urban size, scale effects, and population deconcentration that would invalidate these comparisons have been advanced and merit discussion. Catton (1978) has suggested an interactive mechanism that would operate independently of the size of the largest place: shifts in residential preferences toward smaller-sized places (see Zuiches in Chapter 7 for a summary of this perspective and supporting data). The absolute size of the largest place within the country, or the degree of urban concentration of the population, would be irrelevant if the residential search space were restricted to smaller-sized places within that country.

Ultimately, this argument awaits the collection of comparable international survey data on residential preferences. But even with satisfactory comparative attitudinal data, the argument begs the question of why the value shift has taken place at about the same time in so many countries and the question of what changes have permitted a greater degree of implementation of these preferences. Both questions lead back to the underlying economic and technological changes that permit shifts in values and attitudes.

The second argument, advanced by H. ter Hyde (1978), is that economic scale is relative and cannot be compared cross-nationally. Scale is relative, that is, to the composition of consumer demand. Consumer demand is heavily dependent upon reference-group influences. Reference groups are chosen intranationally, and thus cross-national cultural differences preclude the validity of the inferences that have been drawn from Table 4.2.

However, a casual inspection of consumer goods in demand in northern and western Europe, Japan, and the United States shows more similarity than difference. French cosmetics and American jeans are marketed throughout the world, as are Japanese automobiles. McDonald's restaurants are becoming as ubiquitous as Swiss watches, Italian shoes, or French bicycles. Perrier water is marketed to American joggers. American automobiles are manufactured in West Germany, while German automobiles are manufactured in the United States. The marketing of products such as "Le Car" and "Le Machine" demonstrates that national origin is often made a significant point in developing appeal for a product: A similar case is that of the immersion coffee pots used throughout Europe and now developing a head of steam in the United States. All of these, together with an endless list of international influences in the diffusion of popular sports and music, argue against the intranational confinement of reference groups for consumer expenditures and for the increasingly international referents for these expenditures. The proliferation of international communications (chiefly television), lifestyles, goods, brandnames, and credit mechanisms is both responsible for the increasing diffusion of one country's products throughout the other countries and reflective of the increasingly convergent trends in consumer expenditure patterns (discussed at length later in this chapter).

These data and arguments, other empirical research on the economies of city size, and consideration of theoretical models of scale effects, lead away from models that imply limits on further metropolitan growth in the developed countries. But they do not fully address the role of changing residential preferences toward smaller-sized places. The argument that residential preferences are in some measure responsible for the population shifts from large urban to smaller urban and rural places may take two forms (Wardwell, 1977). The first is that the distribution of preferences in a population has itself shifted in favor of rural and small city living. The second is that long-standing and relatively stable preferences have acquired a greater weight when other conditions have changed.

The distribution of size-of-place preferences in a population may change in two ways: First, it may change as a consequence of changing population composition combined with a high association between residential preferences and population characteristics. For example, if preferences for living in smaller-sized places were highly correlated with age, the proportional increases in either the aged or the very young adult population could generate the observed changes in gross population shifts. Second, it may change as a consequence of changes in individual values over time, perhaps due to increasingly disagreeable conditions in large cities.

This latter view belongs in a consideration of internal constraints on continued large urban growth because it is predicated on a model of endogenous change. The conditions of size and growth in large urban places themselves create the conditions that constrain further growth. This view differs from the arguments of diseconomies of scale only in the mechanism by which deconcentration is achieved. It suggests that market or monetary costs have not driven firms and households out of the large cities. Rather, it suggests, living conditions have deteriorated such that deconcentration is achieved through changes in residential location—changes that may even run counter to the direction of pecuniary benefits. This view is widely held in the United States (Zelinsky, 1978) in combination with the view that monetary factors no longer enjoy the explanatory power in accounting for internal migration patterns that they once did (Goldstein, 1976). But this explanation fails to take into account the questions "Why *now?*" and "If now, how can this hypothesized change in values be demonstrated?"

The paucity of data on residential preferences predating the migration turnaround in the United States makes a hypothesized change in individual values difficult to demonstrate (Dillman, 1973). Hence, it is difficult to show that the hypothesized independent variable, city-size preference, has changed over time. This leaves the proponents of the argument in the uncomfortable position of inferring the cause from the very behavior the argument seeks to explain. Some limited data have become available. Zuiches and Rieger (1978) found that preference for living in rural areas has increased over time both within and across cohorts of rural youth from Michigan's upper peninsula.

The question of timing also lacks adequate answers. If values have changed, why has the timing of change been so similar across the varying urban conditions of Japan, northern and western Europe, New Zealand, and the United States? Change of preferences in response to worsening urban conditions seems unlikely in view of the available documentation that negative externalities of cities such as density, congestion, substandard housing, and financial instabilities have been decreasing rather than increasing in recent decades (Banfield, 1973; Hawley, 1972; Thomlinson, 1969; Thompson, 1965). Moreover, there is little evidence of an association between size of city and the severity of these negative externalities (Hawley, 1972; Hoover, 1971).

Finally, there is little evidence to indicate that preferences are closely correlated with the population characteristics that are increasing as a function of independent sociodemographic processes. Little relationship is found between the preference for residence in smaller-sized places and age, sex, number and age of children; income; or education (Dillman, 1973; Dillman and Dobash, 1972; Fuguitt and Zuiches, 1975).

In summary, it is more conservative to assume that preferences of large urban residents for living in smaller cities and rural regions have remained relatively constant through the period immediately preceding the turnaround in migration patterns. The changes accounting for the turnaround are then to be found in the structural conditions that determine the abilities of large urban residents to implement their pre-existing residential preferences.

Convergent Socioeconomic Change: A Paradigm for the Turnaround

Three propositions emerge from the review of explanations of the turnaround:

1. Changes in the infrastructure of smaller places encourage industries to expand into them or move to them at earlier points in their life cycles, thus hastening the process by which economic growth takes place in smaller places.
2. Economies of scale and agglomeration may be captured at lower levels in the city-size continuum, thus reducing the relative gains available in large cities and reducing the costs incurred through location in smaller cities.
3. Pre-existing nonpecuniary preferences of firms and households for relocation away from large cities are now being realized to a greater extent in actual moves.

These propositions define major aspects of a process of convergent change among places of widely varying size and density in urbanized society. Urban transformation of rural regions diminishes the differences that once inhibited urban-to-rural migration and impelled rural-to-urban migration. The migration turnaround has taken place largely because of the convergent similarities between urban and rural areas. The propositions express consequences of the extension of urban organizational forms into formerly rural space. The mechanisms by which these changes in urban and rural places are coming about are the focus of the remainder of this chapter.

A Paradigm of the Nonmetropolitan Turnaround

The changing role of distance in determining the social organization of space is the key element in this paradigm. Distance has long been the prime ordering element in theories of location, but these theories were formulated primarily to explain the location of manufacturing activities that were strongly influenced by transport costs (Alonso, 1972). The constraint of distance has been loosened by a number of factors: (*a*) lowered transport costs and substitution of communication for physical movement; (*b*) increases in personal affluence that have generated a shift in the composition of consumer demand toward goods and services that are less dependent on transport costs; (*c*) increases in personal affluence that have increased the time and other resources available for more frequent and longer-distance personal travel; (*d*) changes in the occupational composition of manufacturing employment, again toward a mix of activities less subject to the constraints imposed by costs of transport; and (*e*) simultaneous and related changes in the conditions of living in low-density areas that have more thoroughly integrated rural areas into the network of urban activities. Rural areas have become more like urban places in important respects, but they have remained quite unlike them in other respects.

This paradigm is summarized in Figure 4.3. The change process in this model begins with three exogenous variables: transportation and com-

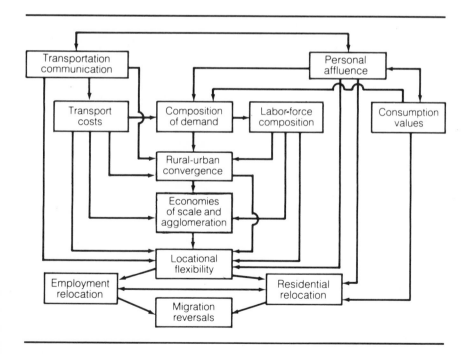

Figure 4.3. A paradigm of the nonmetropolitan migration turnaround.

munication technologies; personal affluence; and a set of consumption values. The change process in turnaround countries has been taking place at varying rates, leading to convergence among nations to common levels of the variables specified in the model. The process accounts for the near-simultaneity of the appearance of shifts in rural–urban population distribution and net migration patterns. For example, similarities in levels of transportation and communication usage have produced a state of rural–urban integration that permits freer movement. Similar patterns of consumer expenditure across societies have reduced the economic gains of large urban places and permitted a wider dispersion of production and marketing activities. The model represents a process of convergence that has generated the dispersion of urban populations into rural regions that were formerly remote and isolated, as well as into rural regions that are proximate to the large metropolitan centers.

Summary of the Paradigm

Transportation and communication facilities determine the transport costs of materials, goods, and services within and between urban areas and between urban areas and their hinterlands. These facilities influence the lifestyles available in cities and in rural areas. Hence they influence the extent to which households may choose locations in either area without sacrificing their selected lifestyles.

Declining transport cost has four effects. It influences the composition of demand, as the transport component of the cost of goods and services declines. It makes goods and services available in all areas so that populations can converge upon a common quality of life. It enables firms to achieve economies of scale and agglomeration at lower points in the city-size continuum. And it increases the array of locational choices by lowering the costs of reaching remote locations.

Rapid growth in affluence in developed societies has been accompanied by a change in the composition of demand (as a function of income elasticities of demand). Convergent value structures interact with increasing affluence to determine the composition of demand for goods and services and to expand the array of choices available to households in selecting residential locations.

Changing composition of demand is one of many influences on the industrial and occupational composition of the labor force, most of which are left unspecified in this model. A diverse industry mix in rural and urban areas expands the array of employment opportunities in rural areas, contributes to the capturing of scale and agglomeration economies, and expands the array of locational choices.

Rural–urban convergence, scale and agglomeration economies, and increasing locational flexibility constitute the heart of this model. Convergence contributes directly to locational flexibility, as the array of consumption opportunities available in large urban areas also becomes increasingly available in lower-density areas. It contributes indirectly through its contribution to the capturing of economies of scale and agglomeration.

The concept of locational flexibility summarizes the process by which economic, technological, and other structural changes have expanded the array of choices within which firms and households make their locational decisions. The removal or weakening of constraints, which in the past dictated large urban locations for a wide range of production and consumption activities, means that firms and households can select from a wider range of city sizes without incurring increased production costs, reduced marketing gains, or fewer life-style options. Employment deconcentration is made possible by the expansion or relocation of these firms. Residential deconcentration, in combination with consumption values that influence the residential preferences of the population, is facilitated by employment deconcentration. The combination of these two deconcentration processes has produced the shifts in internal migration patterns that have brought about a resurgence of growth in remote rural regions, a continuation of growth in regions of low settlement density that are adjacent to deconcentrating urban centers, and a decline or reversal in the rates of growth of large urban areas.

The Model in Greater Detail

Not all parts of the model can be tested, or even illustrated with available data. However, in the following sections, each of the major components will be more fully discussed. Where possible, empirical data bearing on the hypothesized relationships will be presented and summarized.

TRANSPORTATION AND COMMUNICATION TECHNOLOGIES

Changes that reduce the time and cost of transportation, facilitate the substitution of communication for transportation, or extend the flexibility of modern transportation and communication technologies to a greater proportion of the population affect the relationships among scale and production economies. Transportation improvements facilitate the ability of increasingly distant communities to "borrow scale" from proximate large urban centers (Alonso, 1973). Population potential becomes a more appropriate indicator of economic scale than population size or density. It indicates how many people can reach a given location within a given travel time rather than how many people reside or work in the given location. Increased frequency and length of consumer travel thus reduces the minimum efficient community size for businesses serving local rather than export markets. Hence, changes in transportation costs and facilities enable businesses in relatively small places to serve a larger market than before.

Several indicators demonstrate that transportation and communication facilities are experiencing increasing use in the turnaround societies. These include the diffusion of telephones and television, the rapid increase in ownership of personal transportation equipment, use of railways and aircraft and, as a summary measure, the growth in average annual expenditures on transportation and communication in relation to growth in gross domestic product. These data are presented in Table 4.3.

Two important qualifications should be noted. First, all indicators are analogous to the computation of crude migration rates; they represent the number of occurrences per 1000 inhabitants. For example, they do not control for multiple ownership or usage of transport facilities. Second, a satisfactory time series is not available that discriminates usage by rural and urban residence. Hence, these data cannot be used to demonstrate convergence between residential sectors within a society, but only to demonstrate convergence across societies.

Table 4.3 presents data only for the known turnaround countries. These data cannot be used to demonstrate that the turnaround countries differ from countries that have not experienced a reversal in urban–rural migration patterns. That demonstration must await the collation of comparable data for a much wider array of countries.

The pattern of change in private automobile ownership over the past two decades has been the single most influential force in increasing the flexibility and ease of access to rural regions. Dramatic increases are evident in levels of personal motor vehicle usage and in rates of increase between 1960 and 1975 (Table 4.3). Compact nations such as Belgium and the Netherlands have experienced threefold–fivefold increases in levels of ownership. The index numbers show a strong relationship between level at the start of the period and rate of change over the period. The lower the level in 1960, the greater the rate of change from 1960 to 1975 (across all nations, starting level and rate of change are correlated at −.47). Given this inverse relationship, the convergent trends noted in the coefficients of variation at the bottom of Table 4.3 show declining differences between nations over time in this key aspect of transportation.

Conversely, railroad usage remains relatively stable in most countries.

TABLE 4.3
Change in Personal Motor Vehicle Use and Railroad Use, Turnaround Countries, 1960-1975

Country	Personal motor vehicles in use per thousand inhabitants				Rate of increase indexed to 1960 level			Railroad usage indexed to 1960 level		
	1960	1965	1970	1975	1965	1970	1975	1965	1970	1975
Belgium	82.3	141.6	213.2	266.7	172	259	324	105	96	96
Denmark	89.1	156.2	218.8	256.9	175	246	288	96	103	102
France	121.4	196.9	254.0	289.8	162	209	238	121	130	161
Germany, D.R.	18.5	41.5	67.9	111.6	224	367	603	82	83	100
Germany, F.R.	81.5	158.5	222.5	289.4	194	273	355	100	99	98
Italy	40.1	106.0	189.7	257.9	264	473	643	94	106	117
Japan	4.8	22.3	84.6	154.5	464	1,762	3,218	139	159	179
Netherlands	45.5	103.5	173.2	249.0	227	381	547	99	102	109
New Zealand	217.8	272.0	317.1	380.3	125	145	175	94	78	74
Norway	62.8	125.0	192.6	237.8	199	307	378	96	88	109
Sweden	159.6	232.0	284.7	336.9	145	178	211	102	91	113
United States	341.6	384.9	433.6	499.7	113	127	146	82	50	46
Coefficient of variation	.906	.619	.443	.409	---	---	---	.744	.680	.553
Zero-order correlation, 1960 level and 1975 index	-.47						+.62			

Source: United Nations, 1970, 1976.

Marked increases in usage are found only in France and Japan and even in these cases, the rate of change in railroad usage is a small fraction of the rate of increase in personal motor vehicles. The correlation between level of usage in 1960 and rate of change from 1960 to 1975 is positive ($r = .62$). There is a moderately strong negative correlation between motor vehicle usage and railroad usage ($r = -.67$).

Data in Table 4.4 summarize similar patterns of change in the diffusion of telephones and television, the use of commercial aviation, and the ratio of average annual growth in transportation and communication expenditures to the average annual growth of domestic product. Differences in geographic size, population and geographic dispersion, and political system have relatively little impact on the convergent trends in communications. This is indicated by the declining coefficients of variation and by the inverse correlations between level at the start of the period and rate of change across the period ($r = -.56$ for telephone and $r = -.53$ for television receivers in use or licenses issued). As was the case with personal motor vehicles, turnaround countries are becoming more alike in the use of communications. Convergence is less evident in the case of air travel, where size of country and isolation from other developed countries play a large role. Of these 12 countries, 10 experienced a disproportionate growth in overall expenditures on transportation and communication relative to the growth of gross domestic product in one or both of the time periods shown in Table 4.4.

A monotonic decline in the coefficient of variation is evident in the annual data on transportation and communication (Figure 4.4). This pattern provides the single strongest argument in support of convergence on common forms and levels of transportation and communication in developed societies. This similarity extends even to patterns of railroad usage. Despite the excellent service, well-maintained roadbeds, and comfortable coaches of northern and western European and Japanese railroads, there is evidence in these data of declining usage comparable to, though not so marked as, the pattern in the United States.

These similarities indicate the extension in space of urban forms of transportation and communication. Developed societies are linked in common modes of and facilities for interaction. Societies that have not yet experienced a reduction in or reversal of rural–urban migration are also undergoing rapid and revolutionary change in their transportation and communications facilities. However, in these societies the change processes tend still to be urban-centered and have not yet attained the levels indicated for the turnaround countries.

The integration of urban and rural sectors within societies is only a

TABLE 4.4
Growth in Transportation and Communication, Turnaround Countries, 1965-1975

Country	Telephones (1960=100)			Television receivers in use or licenses issued		Commercial aviation passenger miles (1960=100)			Ratio of average annual growth in transportation/ communication to average annual growth in gross domestic product	
	1965	1970	1975	1970	1975	1965	1970	1975	1969-70	1970-75
Belgium	133	170	229	133	156	129	194	300	1.04	.65
Denmark	122	149	194	117	136	142	268	390	1.09	1.63
France	131	180	275	162	202	144	260	445	.89	1.43
Germany, D.R.	130	158	190	147	173	---	---	---	.82	.69
Germany, F.R.	138	200	282	141	159	295	643	1,062	.91	1.09
Italy	149	220	333	155	182	296	627	806	.96	1.31
Japan	241	425	683	120	128	437	1,563	2,860	2.04	1.59
Netherlands	136	185	262	---	151	126	216	386	.96	1.00
New Zealand	131	141	160	---	---	169	319	772	1.38	---
Norway	121	152	173	168	195	163	285	420	1.56	.78
Sweden	124	158	187	116	130	147	242	359	.97	1.80
United States	117	147	169	114	158	177	336	419	1.28	1.80
Coefficient of variation	.567	.492	.415	.406	.312	2.707	2.607	2.402	.306	.478
Zero-order correlation, 1960 level and 1975 index			-.56		-.53			-.09		

93

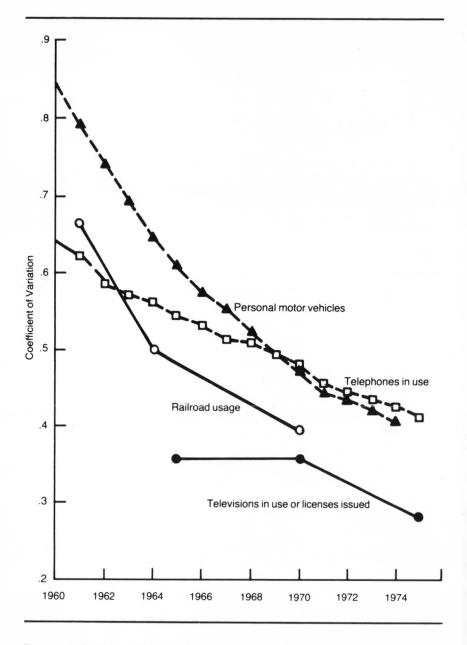

Figure 4.4. Declining differences between turnaround countries in use of transportation and communication technology. (Source: United Nations, 1970, 1976.)

part of the process of urban transformation. However, it is the part that effectively paves the way to rural areas. It provides the urban populace with the freedom to relocate in rural places and yet to maintain ready access to urban centers of their own societies through transportation facilities and to the urban milieu of many other socieites through modern telecommunications.

PERSONAL AFFLUENCE

Growth in personal affluence is another factor that opens societal processes to previously bypassed rural regions. It directly influences locational flexibility and residential relocation, and it also changes the composition of consumer demand (Figure 4.3). Aggregate demand changes because different goods and services have different income elasticities of demand. Activities that have very high elasticities such as housing (Muth, 1968), personal transportation and leisure (Hoover, 1971), and outdoor recreation (Simmons, 1975) expand relative to activities with lower elasticities. More of the growth in added purchasing power is directed into those activities with high elasticities than into those with lower elasticities.

Affluence contributes to the outward drift of economic activities into areas well beyond the peripheries of large urban centers. With more disposable income to spend on leisure activities, more time to spend on the travel costs of getting to the leisure place, and more time and money to spend on outdoor activities once there, consumers stimulate the growth of the industries providing these services. Many of these activities, by their very nature, are nonurban. They tend to be activities in which the traditional locational concepts of transport costs are less applicable. The activities involve the consumers of the services in transit. The transit itself becomes defined as part of the recreational activity. Thus to a large extent the traditional constraints based on transport costs of goods give way to such considerations as the suitability of the location for the desired activity. Factors determining the availability of time to reach the location, and the recreational amenities found at the location are also involved. Increasingly, these considerations favor low-density rural areas over more congested and frequently more expensive urban areas.

Affluence interacts with changes in transportation that reduce the costs and time required for personal transit. The latter makes more sites accessible, while the former makes more resources available for personal transportation. The interaction of these two forces, both of which have themselves been growing at rapid rates, has generated an extremely rapid acceleration in the drift of consumer expenditures and activities outward from the urban core.

The firms servicing activities removed from the large urban complex initiate external economies which facilitate the subsequent relocation of other services and small retail establishments. The emergence of exurban shopping centers at transportation intersections in areas of low settlement density brings variety and ease of access to rural areas that heretofore was only available in large urban centers (Berry and Kasarda, 1977; Hoover, 1971). With increasing population shifts to and beyond the periphery of the large urban center, consumer-serving activities are forced to follow population, adding their own external economies to facilitate the relocation of later arrivals. Lower land costs beyond the metropolitan periphery serve to make the deconcentration process economically more attractive to firms and households.

The growth of consumer purchasing power and the drift in composition of demand are indicated in Figures 4.5 and 4.6 and in Table 4.5. Again, these data are only presented for turnaround countries. A satisfactory time series of economic indicators can be constructed for only 7 of the 12 turnaround countries: Belgium, France, Italy, the Netherlands, Norway, Sweden, and the United States. Figure 4.5 demonstrates the growth from 1960 to 1975 in per capita disposable income and in private final consumption in the domestic market (in constant values). Figure 4.6 presents growth trends in three areas of consumer expenditure: recreation; restaurants, cafes, and hotels; and personal transportation equipment. Each has been calculated in constant prices. The graphs for these indicators present average levels for the seven countries. The coefficients of variation in Table 4.5 show the increasing validity of the averaging process: Low and declining coefficients indicate narrowing dispersion about the mean values presented in these two figures.

Because of changing bases for calculating national accounts in three of the seven countries during the 1960s (Italy, 1963; Norway, 1963; Sweden, 1968), 1970 rather than 1960 has been taken as the base year for construction of the indices in Figures 4.5 and 4.6. The use of the 1970 base artifically exaggerates the tendency toward convergence; consequently the use of these figures is restricted to the demonstration of growth trends. The table of coefficients of variation and the inverse correlation coefficients between 1960 level and 1975 index are used to demonstrate convergence.

The index of growth in per capita disposable income increases from 46 to 209.5 (Figure 4.5). Private final consumption in the domestic market has grown in index values from 68 to 121. Correlations between 1960 level and 1975 index are $-.54$ and $-.55$, respectively. Figure 4.6 demon-

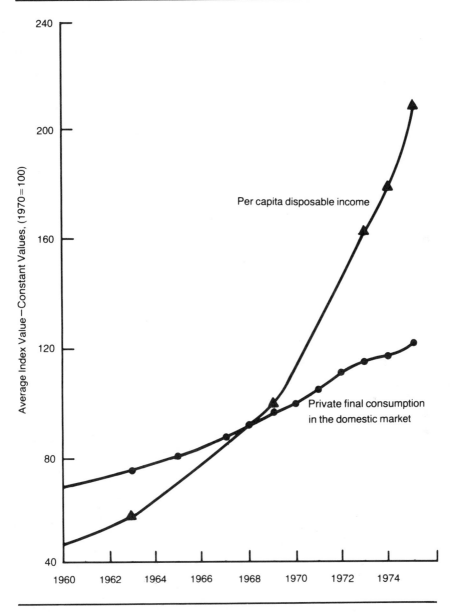

Figure 4.5. Growth in per capita disposable income and private final consumption in the domestic market, seven turnaround countries, 1960–1975. The seven countries include Belgium, France, Italy, Netherlands, Sweden, Norway, and the United States. (Source: United Nations, 1976.)

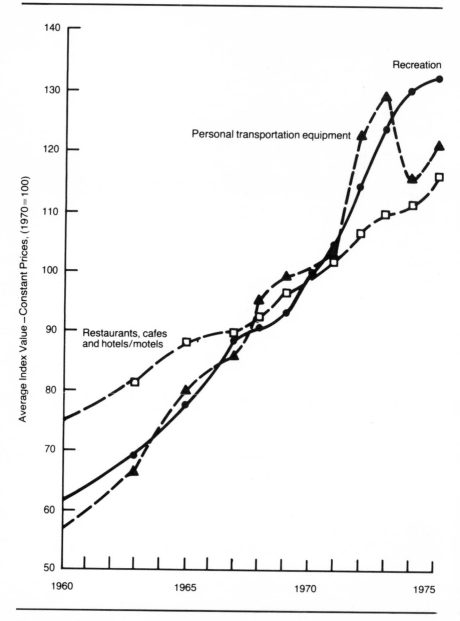

Figure 4.6. Growth in expenditures for recreation, restaurants, cafes and hotels–motels, and personal transportation equipment in seven turnaround countries, 1960–1975. Seven countries include Belgium, France, Italy, Netherlands, Norway, Sweden, and the United States. (Source: United Nations, 1976.)

TABLE 4.5

Coefficients of Variation and Indicators of Growth in Selected Categories of Consumption, Seven Turnaround Countries, 1960-1975

	1960	1963	1965	1967	1970	1973	1975
Indicator							
1. Private final consumption in the domestic market	.949	.957	.706	.712	.481	.442	.442
2. Recreation expenditures	1.028	.969	.718	.717	.497	.444	.453
3. Expenditures on restaurants, cafes and hotels/motels	1.249	1.261	1.259	1.275	.971	.442	.442
4. Expenditures on personal transportation equipment	1.001	.990	.734	.728	.552	.464	.466
Rate of growth ratios relative to growth in private final consumption							
5. Recreation	.945	.939	.686	.685	.444	.444	.450
6. Restaurants, etc.	1.256	1.254	1.247	.936	.441	.443	.445
7. Personal transportation equipment	1.028	.959	.707	.688	.470	.461	.448

Note: The seven countries are Belgium, France, Italy, Netherlands, Norway, Sweden, and the United States.

strates a high rate of growth in recreation, restaurants/hotels, and personal transportation expenditures. Recreation expenditures have increased from a level of 62 to 132.5; expenditures in restuarants, cafes and hotels from 74 to 114; personal transportation expenditures from 56.5 to 121.0. The correlations between 1960 levels and 1975 indices for these three indicators are −.69, −.40, and −.48, respectively.

The coefficients of variation are low and declining for all seven of these indicators (Table 4.5). This indicates increasing similarity among the seven countries in consumption growth and in distribution of that consumption growth. The drift in patterns of expenditure that tends to accompany income growth, and that tends to favor the outward drift of population and economic activity is shown in Figure 4.6 and in Table 4.5. Firms providing high-elasticity goods and services enjoy a relative freedom from locational constraints, or are forced to follow the population and activities favoring low population-density areas.

These convergent consumption patterns indicate similar and/or convergent value structures in the turnaround countries. High elasticities of demand for such goods and services as recreational activities, food and lodging outside the home, and personal transportation equipment indicate a preference for spending increasing proportions of real income growth on these goods and services. Income growth thus acts in concert with consumption values and changes in transportation and communication technologies to facilitate progressive relocation down the settlement scale, from large metropolitan centers to smaller cities and rural territory. Declining transport costs and changing composition of demand modify the scale and agglomeration economies formerly enjoyed primarily by the larger cities. They permit economic operation of a wider range of goods and services in smaller-sized places. Access to remote rural areas and the diversity and volume of goods and services available in these areas increases. The differences that had in the past inhibited population and economic deconcentration diminish. Urban and rural parts of the country converge upon a common employment structure, real income level, and style of living.

LABOR-FORCE COMPOSITION

The role of distance and of costs of transportation in location decisions is further reduced by three other changes. The shift in the distribution of the labor force from goods-producing activities to service-producing activities generates employment growth in rural areas. A greater reliance on communication for the conduct of business activities increases locational flexibility, as does a greater reliance on the personal transport cost borne by the consumer of goods and services with increasing number and distance of shopping trips. The combination of these changes shifts the economy from a high degree of dependence on the transport of goods. More industries in modern society are increasingly foot-loose (Alonso, 1972; Hoover, 1971). The rapid growth of administrative and other information-processing industries, and the growth of industries responding to changes in the composition of consumer demand, are taking place in the context of the changes in transportation technologies and growth of affluence that have been discussed above. These shifts contribute further impetus to the decreased dependence of firms on economies of scale and agglomeration and, by virtue of their growing presence in nonurban locations, increase the employment opportunities and reduce the employment–income differentials that have long been associated with rural–urban location.

Comparable longitudinal data on the changing composition of the labor force are even more fragmentary than are national accounts statistics. Table 4.6 presents some indications of the shifts just discussed: changes in the proportion of the civilian labor force engaged in services, and changes in the proportion of the economically active population engaged in professional, technical, and related occupations. These data indicate that the trend is from goods-producing to information-processing industries and occupations.

By 1975, in 9 of these 10 turnaround countries 50% or more of workers were engaged in service industries. In most cases, the change in this proportion was accounted for largely by the growth of community, social, and personal services. The second panel in Table 4.6 indicates the generally increasing proportion engaged in professional, technical, and related occupations. These are occupations in which processing of information and providing of other services constitute the whole of the work activity. These data indicate convergent change across the countries in the table. The correlation between level at the start of the period and rate of change across the period is negative (−.49 for the proportion of the labor force in services).

Another indication of these trends is the proportion of the manufacturing work force that is engaged in administrative, technical, and clerical activities. Between 1964 and 1975, this proportion increased from 22.5% to 27.2% in Denmark; form 19.6% to 27.6% in Norway; from 27% to 33.1% in Japan; and from 25.6% to 28.8% in the United States.

While only illustrative, these data further indicate that a significant proportion of the labor force is engaged in activities that do not inherently require location in or on the peripheries of the largest urban centers. The consumer orientation of these activities requires that they follow the population redistribution trends. These shifts also contribute

TABLE 4.6
Changing Composition of the Labor Force in Turnaround Countries, 1960-1975

County	Percent of total civilian employment engaged in services (community, social and personal services in parentheses) [a]					Percent of total economically active population in professional, technical, and related occupations		
	1964	1967	1970	1973	1975	1960-1962	1970-1971	1974-1976
Belgium	45.9 (22.2)	48.7 (22.0)	52.0 (22.7)	54.7 (23.6)	56.1 (24.8)	8.0	11.1	---
Denmark	45.8 [b]	49.5	50.7	56.2 (28.2)	58.2 (30.5)	7.8	9.5	12.2
France	42.1 (18.1)	44.6 (19.4)	46.3 (20.2)	48.4 (21.2)	50.1 (22.1)	9.1	11.4	---
Germany, F.R.	39.7 (15.8)	42.0 (16.7)	42.9 (17.5)	45.0 (19.4)	46.7 (20.9)	7.6	9.8	---
Italy	33.2 (15.0)	34.7 (15.9)	36.6 (17.6)	38.6 (18.9)	40.1 (20.6)	5.2	7.3	---
Japan	43.3	45.1 (17.2)	46.8 (17.9)	49.1 (19.1)	51.4 (20.1)	4.9	6.6	7.8
Netherlands [c]	49.7 (25.8)	52.3 (27.7)	54.2 (29.5)	57.1 (31.5)	58.6 (33.9)	---	13.3	---
Norway	45.5 (17.2)	45.9 (18.2)	47.8 (20.2)	54.7 (24.5)	55.5 (26.5)	8.0	12.3	15.8
Sweden	45.9	48.8 (21.6)	53.4 (27.1)	56.0 (29.7)	57.1 (30.7)	12.9	19.2	22.4
United States	60.6	61.0	63.3	64.3	67.0	10.8	13.8	13.9

Source: International Labor Organization, 1976.
[a] Services include wholesale and retail trade, restaurants and hotels; transport, storage and communication; finance, insurance and real estate; and community, social and personal services.
[b] 1965.
[c] Figures in parentheses includes finance, insurance, and real estate.

102

to the facility with which the work force can participate in the deconcentration trends that are evident in population net migration statistics.

RURAL-URBAN CONVERGENCE

There are few typologies in the social sciences so enduring as those based on size of place of residence. The rural–urban continuum survives, despite a continuing barrage of evidence testifying to its low explanatory utility (Dewey, 1960) and despite the emergence of alternative models. These models argue for the diminishing of locational differences, and they are designed to undertake the empirical demonstration of regional and other locational convergence in values, attitudes, and behavior. The continuum survives in part because these alternative models have not been sufficiently explicated to provide a definite test of the hypothesis of rural–urban differences (Fischer, 1975c), and in part because of inability to demonstrate the greater predictive utility of other variables consistently (Lowe and Peek, 1974).

Fischer (1972, 1975b) advanced a "subcultural theory of urbanism" to account for the covariation of diverse sociocultural behaviors with size of place of residence that was postulated in Wirth's (1938) original formulation. Fischer argues that "cities are the sites for many diverse and flourishing subcultures, and it is that character which generates some urban–rural differences" through "subcultural intensification and cultural diffusion [1972:220–221]." Because urban centers always have the temporal advantage on innovation, lags in the diffusion process will maintain differences at any given point in time. In Fischer's model, rural–urban differences are synchronic manifestations of a diachronic process of cultural diffusion. He argues that the residual variation, however slight, is essential to a theoretical understanding of this process. The formal identity between Fischer's model and Thompson's explanation of why new industries originate in the large city and then filter down through smaller cities is evident.

The opposing argument, that urban–rural differences are transitional and diminishing over time, can be drawn from a variety of interpretations of the dominant social changes taking place in contemporary society (Hawley, 1971; Sjoberg, 1964; Wirth, 1969). Historically, "to know where a person resided was to know what he did for a living, the pattern of his values, and his normal interaction situations [Bealer, Willits, and Kuvlesky, 1965:256]." Now, "being highly rural in regard to one component does not imply a high degree of 'rurality' in regard to other components," so that "the use of various meanings of 'rurality' no longer necessarily leads to the designation of the same person [Willits and Bealer, 1967:10]." Hawley would add that the various meanings of rurality no longer lead to the designation of the same places. The increasingly independent variation of the ecological, occupational, and cultural dimensions of rurality "have made such notions as we have about rural–urban differences and likenesses obsolete [Wirth, 1969]," because "social and economic space no longer coincide with residence [Stewart, 1958]."

Four changes are argued to have brought about the increasing independence of social and physical space (Fuguitt, 1963): changes in transportation and communication that have decreased rural isolation (Firey, Loomis, and Beegle, 1957); increasingly integrated trade, institutional, and social relationships (Hawley, 1971; Spaulding, 1959; Warren, 1972); changing occupational composition and diversity (Steward, 1958); and transformation of the population composition of rural areas with the decline of agriculture and the progressive urbanization of open country-side (Beale, 1979; Carroll and Wheeler, 1966; Zuiches and Brown, 1978).

The composite effects of these changes have diminished urban–rural differences and have contributed to the turnaround in metropolitan–nonmetropolitan migration patterns. At the same time, that very reversal in migration patterns and growth rates has kept the rural–urban continuum hypothesis alive. The current inverse association between size of place and rate of growth breathes new vigor into the old argument. The long-standing tradition of this hypothesis implicitly forms part of the theoretical background within which some of the contemporary research on residential preferences is being conducted. That research is oriented toward identifying the differences between rural and urban places that can account for the preference toward smaller-sized places and away from large cities. This approach tends to deemphasize structural convergence between urban and rural places. But this convergence permitted residential preferences for smaller-sized places and for community attributes associated with those places to be implemented in actual mobility behavior. Fischer's hypothesis of a necessary temporal lag in cultural diffusion fails to take account of two corollaries of the changes identified by Fuguitt. The first of these is the possibility of changing rates of diffusion over time. If the media of modern telecommunications have made the diffusion process virtually instantaneous, no temporal lag need remain to produce rural–urban differences at any given point in time. The second is concerned with the paths or vectors along which change diffuses. One such vector of course is physical space. Fischer's argument may be restated as the familiar ecological principle of time representing the friction encountered in crossing physical space (Hawley, 1971). It is apparent that there are other vectors along which change diffuses, and other forms of friction that can cause temporal lags in the diffusion process. Diffusion of urban-originating change may be virtually instantaneous across physical space and still be impeded or filtered by the friction of social space. There may be as many such paths as there are linkages between the individual and the larger society, particularly the urban centers of society. Three linkage mechanisms that form vectors for diffusion are the educational and occupational subsystems and the age structure of society. The friction encountered in crossing educational levels may be compared to that of crossing space. Similar educational and occupational linkages may so facilitate the transmission of innovation as to make the residual friction of space negligible.

Sjoberg (1964) cites the failure "to analyze rural and urban communities—both of them partial systems—within the context of the broader social order in which they are embedded [130]." Hawley's approach to the process of urbanization seeks to incorporate that broader social order and to conceptualize change in terms of process. "Urbanization is a process of bringing a multiregional territory under a single organization integrated and administered from a set of urban centers [1971:310–311]." The term *urban* is not limited to describing the densely settled place. It embraces the whole of an organization that is based on a center of settlement and involves virtually all of the activities of a widely dispersed population (1971). Accordingly to Hawley, "urbanization . . . has taken such possession of the entire country that . . . differences in mode of life are rapidly disappearing. Social–economic rather than place-of-residence differences become the most important in accounting for unequal access to urban institutions and cultural opportunities [1971:239]."

The phrase, "highly urbanized society," takes on a new meaning with convergent change between places classified as rural and urban. Change in socioeconomic composition and diversity, change in demographic composition and diversity, change in access through telecommunications and improved transportation systems to urban-originating innovation, all indicate a society in which urban forms of social organization have fully extended themselves in space.

Rural–urban convergence refers to the ways in which urban and rural places are becoming more alike. To the consumer or resident household, convergence means that important rural–urban differentials are diminishing—differentials in employment opportunities, real income levels, and amenities. Declining differentials in combination with changes in transportation and communications facilities mean that rural residents can remain fully in touch with urban forms and changes but often without the necessity of residence or even work in the physical urban form, the large city.

Rural–urban convergence has thus simultaneously reduced the cost of an urban-to-rural move and reduced the gain of a rural-to-urban move. This convergence is associated both with increasing rates of large metropolitan out-migration and with decreasing nonmetropolitan out-migration. *Convergence is the basis for the statement that similarities between urban and rural places are guiding contemporary internal migration flows as much as differences between these places are.* This statement runs directly contrary to the assumptions that underlie most explanations based on residential preferences.

This contradiction can be resolved by distinguishing between the motivational bases of location decisions and the structural changes that set the context for these decisions. It is apparent that migrants perceive real and meaningful differences between alternative metropolitan and nonmetropolitan locations. Williams and McMillen (Chapter 8) articulate this decision-making process and Carpenter (1977), DeJong (1977), Dillman (1978), Fuguitt and Zuiches (1975) have documented the quality of life differentials that are increasingly significant in the mobility process. But the fact of a choice derives more from structural (including economic) convergence between metropolitan and nonmetropolitan areas than from either residual or emergent differences.

Historically, income and other differentials between rural and urban places have been among our most reliable predictors of migration. Perhaps the most significant change of the past two decades in highly urbanized societies has been in this area. If this is the case, the arguments regarding the diminishing explanatory utility of income–pecuniary models of migration have to be modified slightly. The explanatory power of these models has declined in large part because the very economic differentials between places on which these models are based have declined.

Just as the existence of a choice must be included in the process of explaining the direction chosen, so must the increasing availability of employment opportunities, competitive real incomes and urban lifestyles be taken into account in explaining the new growth of nonmetropolitan areas. Structural convergence has been a necessary condition for increased population retention in nonmetropolitan areas and for increased metropolitan to nonmetropolitan migration. Once necessary structural conditions are achieved, the existence of residential preferences for small places may constitute a sufficient condition to change migration behavior. It may even constitute a sufficiently strong force to tip the net direction of migration streams against the net direction of pecuniary benefits, (Long and Hansen, 1977).

These conditions taken together generate the observed shifts in population distribution during the 1970s. However, variations in their relative strength may account for the fact that structural convergence has apparently not led to convergence in the composition of the gross migration streams between metropolitan and nonmetropolitan areas. For example, research by Lichter *et al.* (1979) indicates that in the United States, the two migration streams have actually become more dissimilar since 1955 with respect to age, education, and occupation.

CONSUMPTION VALUES

To summarize the arguments to this point: Three exogenous variables—changes in transportation and communication, growth of personal affluence, and changing consumption values that determine elasticities of demand—have altered the costs of transport, the composition of demand, and the degree of rural–urban convergence very considerably. These changes, in turn, have greatly diminished the friction of space, the differences in socioeconomic and demographic composition of urban and rural areas, and the city size at which economies of scale and agglomeration are operable. These forces act in concert to initiate population and economic growth in smaller places and in less densely settled territory than had previously been thought capable of sustaining increases in such activity. In the context of reduced levels of natural increase through declining fertility, such growth must come from migration from large urban centers (Goldstein, 1976; Morrison, 1975).

The removal or weakening of economic constraints on small city or rural location has permitted firms and individuals to make their location decisions on other than strictly economic criteria. The amenities associated with convergence in rural–urban facilities and life styles and the disamenities associated with large city size play a significant role in urban deconcentration. Given greater market flexibility as to size of place of location, more attention can be paid to the climate, available residential space, cleanliness of air and water, lower risk of personal injury, and other aspects of the social and physical environment desirable to households and firms. An increasingly large number are left with the question "Why locate in a large urban place?"

A clear implication of this process of change is that increasing locational flexibility has allowed consumption values, or residential preferences, to play a larger role than they previously could in guiding the volume and direction of migration streams. It does not suggest that economic and other structural determinants of migration have weakened but rather that the differentials between urban and rural places on these dimensions have diminished. Diminishing of the stronger determinants of migration patterns has allowed the weaker, more proximate determinants to enter the causal picture with a greater impact than they displayed before.

Conclusion

Berry and Kasarda (1977) argue that places of residence and places of work are both responding more to social than to traditional economic dynamics. If this is so, it can only be because the principles of traditional location theory have been tempered by technological process, not because we have been freed from these principles (Bogue, 1968:413).

The nonmetropolitan migration turnaround in the United States and in the developed world caught nearly everyone by surprise. Projections of internal population distribution for the developed countries appearing in the late 1960s and the early 1970s were unanimous in forecasting the continued concentration of national populations in metropolitan agglomerations of ever-increasing size. The physical expansion of the megalopolis was of course observed and its continuing sprawl accurately foreseen. Declining densities in large urban centers were not inconsistent with continued population growth because of this peripheral expansion. But the repopulation of rural regions, remote from any large urban center, was not foreseen.

That fact is as significant to the student of population distribution as the migration turnaround itself. Any explanatory model that purports to account for these changes must be humbled by the failure of all population distribution theories to predict the present when it was still the future. The present paradigm was developed after the resurgence in rural and nonmetropolitan growth appeared: It did not anticipate that change.

Yet there is a need to make projections for the future. Urban and rural policy analysts and program administrators need information to anticipate and adjust to future growth, stability, cr decline. Demographic theorists need predictions to test the models that account for change: A model that does not lend itself to such tests is worse than useless, for its validity cannot be assessed. Despite the past record of demographic theories in failing to anticipate such major demographic events as the baby boom, the rapidity and extent of declining birth rates, and now these new trends in population distribution, some use of the paradigm to project further migration patterns must be made.

Three numerical aspects of the post-1970 migration turnaround provide an important perspective. A comparison of the rates of net metropolitan out-migration with the proportion of national populations residing in these metropolitan centers shows that there is no danger of depopulation of larger urban places. A decade of population redistribution at present rates produces only miniscule changes in the percentage of the population residing in metropolitan places (Fuguitt and Beale, 1977; Vining and Kontuly, 1978). Many decades would have to elapse before significant reductions in metropolitan populations could result from current trends.

The second observation is the converse of this proposition. Small net shifts out of large urban populations generate large numbers of migrants. When those migrants are added to the much smaller population bases in specific nonmetropolitan destinations, abrupt and substantial growth rates and impacts occur. The consequences of the turnaround are accordingly greater for rural and nonmetropolitan places than for large urban places.

The third observation has to do with the duration of those impacts, as distinct from the duration of the trends that are producing them. Beale (1978b) has drawn a useful comparison with the baby boom to illustrate this point. The sudden rise in birth rates in most developed countries was sustained for only 15–20 years, but the impacts, in the form of distortions in the age structure, will last for several decades. The new migration patterns have now been going on for 10–15 years. The trends toward rural depopulation have halted. The importance of this change derives from the changes in social organization that it reflects. The era in which rural areas were little more than the land to leave in search of employment, higher incomes, and the amenities associated with modern life styles is largely at an end. Social change such as this is cumulative and evolutionary. Whatever the future holds for these rural areas, it does not encompass a return to the sociodemographic conditions of the middle of this century.

Beyond these limited observations, population projections require a more fully specified model. The prime movers in the paradigm presented in this chapter are income growth and low transportation costs in the context of converging differences between rural and urban areas. The future is difficult to forecast because the national income consequences of increasing diversion of income to petroleum imports is not clear. Moreover, we have little information on the population distribution impacts of increasing real costs of transportation because of rising energy prices. The friction of space may be reinstated in two ways through increasing energy costs: rising prices with dependable supplies, and rising prices with periodic and unpredictable supply uncertainties. The latter situation may favor population concentration in metropolitan areas because of the greater availability of many alternative forms of transport, but it is not yet clear whether the former situation favors the lower unit cost of movement across low-density rural space, or the higher unit cost and shorter distances found in more congested metropolitan centers.

Similarly, consumer response to declining real incomes as a function of rising energy prices is not clear. Travel patterns may be maintained, but as energy prices rise faster than do incomes, they may be maintained only at the expense of reducing other areas of household and firm expenditures. Which areas of expenditure will be reduced, to what extent and in what order, are crucial questions to the economic future of nonmetropolitan areas that derive a major portion of their renewed growth from recreation and leisure activities, and from other activities that have high income elasticities of demand and that are significant parts of the economic bases of commercial expansion in the nonmetropolitan sectors of societies.

Until these and related issues can be satisfactorily addressed, it is fruitless to speculate on the distribution consequences of all of the other elements in the paradigm. Thus, we see the truth of Bogue's caution: We have not yet been freed of the principles of traditional location theory. The permanence with which those principles have been relaxed by the technological progress in transportation and communication of the recent past will be witnessed in the next decade.

Acknowledgments

Dorothy Jorgensen, Belinda Rinker, Paul Slaughter, and Teresa Zimmer have been particularly helpful in preparation of the manuscript, collation of the data, and statistical computations.

I wish to thank the colleagues who have had the interest and the patience to read through preliminary drafts of this chapter and to advise me on various parts of the argument. They are Calvin L. Beale, Lloyd D. Bender, David L. Brown, William R. Catton, Jr., Don A. Dillman, Lee G. Faulkner, C. Jack Gilchrist, and D. Stanton Smith. I also wish to thank my discussants at the IUSSP meetings, Sidney Goldstein and H. ter Heide, for calling my attention to dimensions of the phenomenon that I had neglected.

References

Alonso, W.
    1972   "Location theory." Pp. 16–37 in M. Edel and J. Rothenberg (eds.), *Readings in Urban Economics*. New York: Macmillan.
    1973   "Urban zero population growth." *Daedalus* 102(Fall):191–206.
Banfield, Edward C.
    1973   "A critical view of the urban crisis." *Annals of American Academy of Political and Social Sciences* 405(January):7–14.

Barnett, H.
   1968   "Discussion." Pp. 229–234 in H. Perloff and L. Wingo (eds.), *Issues in Urban Economics*. Baltimore: Johns Hopkins University Press.
Beale, Calvin L.
   1975   "The revival of population growth in nonmetropolitan America." *Economic Research Service Publication* ERS-605. Washington, D.C.: U.S. Department of Agriculture.
   1978a   "Making a living in rural and smalltown America." *Rural Development Perspectives* 1(November):1–5.
   1978b   "Population trends in the northeast." Paper presented at the Northeast Agricultural Economics Council Meeting, Durham, New Hampshire, June.
Bealer, Rober C., Fern K. Willits, and William P. Kuvlesky
   1965   "The meaning of rurality in American society." *Rural Sociology* 30(September):255–266.
Beaujot, Roderic P.
   1978   "Canada's population: Growth and dualism." *Population Bulletin* 33(2), April. Washington, D.C.: Population Reference Bureau.
Berry, B. and J. Kasarda
   1977   *Contemporary Urban Ecology.* New York: Macmillan.
Bogue, D.
   1968   "Discussion." P. 418 In H. Perloff and L. Wingo (eds.), *Issues in Urban Economics*. Baltimore: John Hopkins Press.
Bourne, L. S. and M. I. Logan
   1976   "Changing urbanization patterns at the margin: The examples of Australia and Canada." Pp. 111–143 In Brian J. L. Berry (ed.), *Urbanization and Counterurbanization*. Vol. 11: Urban Affairs Annual Reviews. Beverly Hills, Calif: Sage Publications, Inc.
Carpenter, Edwin H.
   1977   "The potential for population dispersal: A closer look at residential preferences." *Rural Sociology* 42 (Fall):352–370.
Carroll, Robert L. and Raymond H. Wheeler
   1966   "Metropolitan influences on the rural nonfarm population." *Rural Sociology* 31 (March):64–73.
Catton, William R.
   1978   Personal Communication.
Crowley, R.
   1977   "Population distribution: Perspectives and policies." Pp. 255–274 In A. Brown and E. Neuberger (eds.), *Internal Migration*. New York: Academic Press.
Davis, K.
   1969   *World urbanization* 1950–1970. Volume 1. Berkeley: University of California Population Monograph Series, No. 4.
DeJong, Gordon F.
   1977   Residential preferences and migration." *Demography* 14 (May):169–178.
Dewey, Richard
   1960   "The Rural–Urban continuum: Real but relatively unimportant." *American Journal of Sociology* 66 (July):60–66.
Dillman, Don A.
   1973   "Population distribution policy and people's attitudes: Current knowledge and needed research." Paper prepared for the Urban Land Institute under a grant from the U.S. Department of Housing and Urban Development.

1978   "Residential preferences, quality of life, and the population turnaround."
        American Journal of Agricultural Economics 61 (December):960–966.
and Russell P. Dobash
    1972   "Preferences for community living and their implication for population redis-
            tribution." Agricultural Experiment Station Bulletin 764. Pullman: Washington
            State University.
Drewett, Roy, John Goddard, and Nigel Spence
    1976   "Urban Britain: beyond containment." Pp. 43–79 In Brian J. L. Berry (ed.), *Ur-
            banization and Counterurbanization*. Vol. 11: Urban Affairs Annual Reviews. Be-
            verly Hills, Calif: Sage Publications, Inc.
Firey, Walter, Charles P. Loomis, and J. Allen Beegle
    1957   "The Fusion of urban and rural," PP. 214–222 In P. K. Hatt and A. J. Reiss, Jr.
            (eds.), *Cities and Society*. New York: Free Press.
Fischer, Claude S.
    1972   "Urbanism as a way of life." A Review and an Agenda. *Sociological Methods and
            Research* 1(2):187–242.
    1975a   "The effect of urban life on traditional values." *Social Forces* 53 (March):420–432.
    1975b   "The study of urban community and personality." *Annual Review of Sociology*
            1:67–89.
    1975c   "Toward a subcultural theory of urbanism." *American Journal of Sociology*
            80(May):1319–1341.
Fuguitt, Glenn V.
    1963   "The city and countryside." *Rural Sociology* 28(3):246–261.
and Calvin L. Beale
    1977   "Recent trends in city population growth and distribution." Pp. 13–27 In Her-
            rington J. Bryce (ed.), *Small Cities in Transition*. Cambridge: Ballinger Publishing
            Company.
and James J. Zuiches
    1975   "Residential preferences and population distribution." *Demography* 12(3):491–
            504.
Gilbert, A.
    1976   "The arguments for very large cities reconsidered." *Urban Studies* 13
            (February):27–34.
Goldstein, Sidney
    1976   "Facets of redistribution: Research challenges and opportunities." *Demography*
            13 (November):423–434.
    1978   "Discussion." International Union for the Scientific Study of Population Special
            Congress on Economic and Demographic Issues for the 1980s. Helsinki, Finland
            (August–September).
Hawley, Amos H.
    1971   *Urban Society: An Ecological Approach*. New York: The Ronald Press Company.
    1972   "Population density and the city," *Demography* 9:521–529.
Hirsch, W.
    1968   "The supply of urban services." Pp. 477–525 In H. Perloff and L. Wingo (eds.),
            Issues in Urban Economics. Baltimore: Johns Hopkins Press.
Hoover, E.
    1971   *An Introduction to Regional Economics*. New York: Alfred A. Knopf.
International Labour Organization
    1976   *Yearbook of Labour Statistics*, Table 3. Geneva, Switzerland.
Johnston, R.
    1976   "Observations on accounting procedures and urban-size policies." Environment
            and Planning A8 (March):327–339.

Lichter, Daniel T., Tim B. Heaton, and Glenn V. Fuguitt
  1979   "Trends in the selectivity of migration between metropolitan and nonmetropoli-
          tan areas: 1955-1975." *Rural Sociology* 44 (Winter):645-666.
Long, John F.
  1980   "Population deconcentration in the United States." Washington, D.C.: U.S.
          Bureau of the Census.
Long, Larry H. and Kristin A. Hansen
  1977   "Migration trends in the United States." Washington, D.C.: U.S. Bureau of the
          Census. Unpublished.
Lowe, George D. and Charles W. Peek
  1974   "Location and lifestyle: The comparative explanatory ability of urbanism and
          rurality." *Rural Sociology* 39(3):392-420.
Mera, K.
  1973   "On the urban agglomeration and economic efficiency." *Economic Development
          and Cultural Change* 21 (January):309-423.
Muth, R.
  1968   "Urban residential land and housing markets." P. 314 In H. Perloff and L.
          Wingo (eds.), *Issues in Urban Economics*. Baltimore: Johns Hopkins Press.
Segal, D.
  1976   "Are there returns to scale in city size?" *Review of Economics and Statistics* 58
          (August):339-350.
Simmons, I.
  1975   *Rural Recreation in the Industrial World*. New York: John Wiley and Sons.
Sjoberg, Gideon
  1964   "The rural-urban dimension in preindustrial, transitional, and industrial
          societies." Pp. 127-159 In Robert E. L. Faris (ed.), *Handbook of Modern Sociology*.
          Chicago: Rand McNally.
Spaulding, Irving A.
  1959   "Change in rural life and the reintegration of a social system." *Rural Sociology*
          24(3):215-225.
Steward, Charles T., Jr.
  1958   "The urban-rural dichotomy: Concepts and uses." *American Journal of Sociology*
          64:152-158.
Sveikauskas, L.
  1975   "The productivity of cities." *Quarterly Journal of Economics* 89 (August):393-413.
ter Hyde, H.
  1978   "Discussion." International Union for the Scientific Study of Population Special
          Congress on Economic and Demographic Issues for the 1980s. Helsinki, Finland
          (August-September).
Thomlinson, Ralph
  1969   *Urban Structure: The Social and Spatial Character of Cities*. New York: Random
          House.
Thompson, Wilbur R.
  1965   *A Preface to Urban Economics*. Baltimore: Johns Hopkins Press.
  1968   "Internal and external factors in the development of urban economies." Pp.
          43-62 in H. Perloff and L. Wingo (eds.), *Issues in Urban Economics*. Baltimore:
          Johns Hopkins Press.
  1969   "The economic base of urban problems," Pp. 6-9 In N. Chamberlain (ed.),
          Contemporary Economic Issues. Homewood, Ill: Richard D. Irwin Press.
United Nations
  1970   *Demographic Yearbook*. New York: United Nations.
  1975   *Demographic Yearbook*. New York: United Nations.

1976   *Yearbook of National Accounts Statistics.* New York: United Nations.

U.S. Bureau of the Census
1975   *Mobility of the Population in the United States: March 1970 to March 1975.* Current Population Reports, Series P–20, No. 285. Washington, D.C.: U.S. Government Printing Office.
1978   *Geographical Mobility: March 1975 to March 1978.* Current Population Reports, Series P–20, No. 331. Washington, D.C.: U.S. Government Printing Office.

Vining, Daniel R., Jr. and Thomas Kontuly
1977   "Population dispersal from major metropolitan regions: An international comparison." Discussion Paper Series No. 100. Philadelphia: Regional Science Research Institute, September.
1978   "Population dispersal from major metropolitan regions: An international comparison." *International Regional Science Review* 3(1):49–73.

Wardwell, John M.
1977   "Equilibrium and change in nonmetropolitan growth." *Rural Sociology* 42 (Summer):156–179.

and C. Jack Gilchrist
1980   "Employment deconcentration in the nonmetropolitan migration turnaround." *Demography* 17 (May):145–158.

Warren, Roland L.
1972   *The Community in America.* New York: Rand McNally.

Willits, Fern K. and Robert C. Bealer
1967   "An evaluation of a composite definition of 'rurality.'" *Rural Sociology* 32 (June):165–177.

Wirth, Louis
1938   "Urbanism as a way of life." *American Journal of Sociology* 44 (July):3–24.
1969   "Rural–Urban differences." Pp. 165–169 In Richard Sennett (ed.), *Classic Essays on the Culture of Cities.* New York: Appleton-Century-Crofts.

Zelinsky, Wilbur
1978   "Is nonmetropolitan America being repopulated?" *Demography* 15:12–39.

Zuiches, James J. and David L. Brown
1978   "The changing character of the nonmetropolitan population, 1950–75." Chapter 4 In Thomas R. Ford (ed.), *Rural Sociology in the United States–Current Trends and Issues.* Ames: Iowa State University Press.

and Michael Price
1978   "The composition of migration streams and equilibrium models: The Michigan experience," Paper presented at the Population Association of America Annual Meeting, Atlanta, April.

and Jon H. Rieger
1978   "Size of place preferences and life cycle migration: A cohort comparison." *Rural Sociology* 43 (Winter):618–633.

The Demand for Public Goods as a Factor in the Nonmetropolitan Migration Turnaround[1]

JOE B. STEVENS

Introduction

For several years, researchers have spent considerable effort in de-mographic analysis of the population turnaround from metropolitan to nonmetropolitan areas. They have gained a fair understanding of the types of areas and communities that are growing most rapidly and of the personal attributes and subjective preferences of the mobile and poten-tially mobile populations. In general, demographers and sociologists have focused on why the turnaround is occurring, while economists have concentrated on the impacts of migration on sending and receiving communities.

I would like to depart from this division of labor by suggesting a revised economic framework for explaining migration decisions by indi-viduals and families. A revision is in order because the existing income-oriented models of migration, including those of human capital theory, have been demonstrated by the population turnaround to be less than adequate to deal with the changing scope of important reasons why people move.[2] That is, economic models have generally viewed the

[1]This chapter is a revised and extended version of Technical Paper No. 5195 from the Oregon Agricultural Experiment Station.

[2]The lure of income gain, actual or expected, still appears to be an important force in the migration decision to many people, as evidenced by DaVanzo's (1978) research with lon-gitudinal data from the Panel Study of Income Dynamics, Survey Research Center, Uni-versity of Michigan. DaVanzo has established that the unemployed are more likely to migrate than are the employed, and that origin unemployment rates do affect out-migra-tion, at least among those most directly affected—the unemployed.

115

New Directions in
Urban-Rural Migration

migrant as either a worker who responds only to spatial wage differentials or an investor who responds only to spatial differences in net present values of future income streams. In effect, we have ignored the fact that the migrant is a consumer as well as a labor supplier and investor. If the set of goods and services that the migrant would like to consume are available at the same prices in alternative locations, an income-oriented model would suffice in explaining the actions of consumption-oriented migrants. That is, migration to obtain a higher income would be synonymous with obtaining a higher level of consumption. On the other hand, if certain goods and services are not equally available or if their prices vary between alternative locations, it is imperative that migration models encompass consumption desires as well as potentials for income generation.

Rather than attempt a full development of the formal logic for such an approach, it is my purpose here to outline the conceptual role of a particular type of consumption good that appears to have been very influential in the population turnaround. This is the public good, or one whose availability (in contrast to private goods) is beyond the direct influence of the individual consumer unless he or she moves to another geographic area.[3] Even with migration, the levels of some public goods may not change; national defense against external aggression may be the same in rural Iowa or downtown Chicago. With other public goods (air quality, for example) substantial differences may exist between metropolitan and nonmetropolitan areas, at least as perceived by nonmetropolitan in-migrants.

It is the basic contention of this paper that differential availability of certain public goods is a key factor in the population turnaround, and that metropolitan-to-nonmetropolitan migration is being increasingly resorted to, often at an income sacrifice, in an attempt to satisfy the demand for these goods.[4] This, of course, is a rather ambitious

[3]Samuelson (1954:387) defined a *pure* public good as one "which all enjoy in common in the sense that each individual's consumption of such a good leads to no subtraction from any other individual's consumption of that good." Everyone in an urban airshed, for example, might be subject to the same level of ambient air quality. This definition has been criticized on the grounds that such goods are rare; inmigration by those seeking clear air, for example, might diminish air quality. At any point in time, however, there remains an element of publicness about air quality (and many of the other goods identified below as public), which makes the concept useful in a heuristic sense. The connotation used here is that there is jointness in supply (as in the Samuelson definition), and the good usually exists because of some type of collective action (or inaction). This does not mean the government provides *only* public goods; much of what government provides can be captured by some individuals to the exclusion of others.

[4]In many respects, this is a variation of the "Tiebout hypothesis" (Tiebout, 1956). Tiebout's focus, however, was on optimality in the provision of public goods, whereas this application is positive rather than normative.

hypothesis that cannot be tested here. My purpose is to establish that the hypothesis is plausible and worthy of evaluation in future research. Accordingly, this chapter will be devoted to identifying and measuring public goods and to evaluating methods for quantifying the degree to which metropolitan-to-nonmetropolitan migrants may be giving up access to private goods (or sacrificing income, as a proxy) in order to obtain greater access to certain public goods.

With respect to both measurement of public goods and measurement of income sacrifices, reference will be made to an ongoing study of migration into two environmentally attractive counties in southern Oregon. These counties (Jackson and Josephine) are popular destinations for middle-class urban refugees from California and were studied for that express reason. In general, these migrants' willingness to sacrifice income to alter their consumption of public goods may not be atypical of in-migrants to nonmetropolitan areas throughout the nation.

Public Goods and the Decision to Migrate

Refinements of economic theory come from logical deduction, but new paradigms arise out of intuition and observation. Accordingly, it appears that what many new in-migrants expect (and perhaps even find) in nonmetropolitan areas is access to some things that money could not buy (or at least, buy easily) in metropolitan areas. In other words, the marginal utility of public goods (or at least some segment of them) is perceived to be high relative to the marginal utility of private goods. This situation, in its most general sense, can be considered in the context of an economic theory of representative government, after Breton (1974).

One of Breton's key building blocks is a demand model on the part of citizen-consumers who are assumed to be maximizing individual utility from consumption of both private goods (X) and public goods (S). In its simplest form, with one of each good, a citizen-consumer's utility function can be expressed as:

$$U^j = U^j(X, S) \tag{5.1}$$

which he attempts to maximize subject to his income (I^j), the market price of the private goods ($\bar{p}_x$), and the tax-price of the public good (q^j). In other words, the budget constraint is:

$$I^j = \bar{p}_x X + q^j S, \tag{5.2}$$

where the consumer exhausts his income on the two goods. Not unexpectedly, equilibrium exists when the marginal utilities of the two goods are equated to their respective prices (tax-prices may vary over individuals but the market price does not).

It follows from the definition of public goods (i.e., jointness in the supply of nonmarket goods) that personal differences in subjective valuations will cause some consumers to be out of equilibrium and, hence, willing to consider actions that would change the level of public good provision. Breton defines this (in a nonpejorative way) as *coercion*. Figure 5.1 shows police protection as an example. At the tax-price of $\bar{q}^j$, our consumer would be in equilibrium at the S^j level of protection, that is, on his D^j demand curve. However, if the level of police protection that is actually provided happens to be only S^*, our consumer feels that the public good is undersupplied. Coercion could be reduced or removed in two ways. First, our consumer's tax-price could be increased to q^* (holding protection at S^*); this would clearly make him worse off. Alternatively, police protection could be expanded from S^* to S^j (holding the tax-price at $\bar{q}^j$), thereby making our consumer better off but oversupplying the public good to thieves and swindlers.

At this point, the question is how, and if, the consumer will adapt to

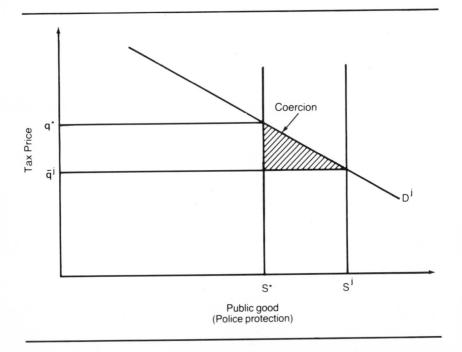

Figure 5.1. An individual's demand for an undersupplied public good.

this coercion or disequilibrium. There may be a threshold for many public goods, short of which little or no action will be taken by the consumer because the personal costs would exceed the personal gains. However, beyond this threshold level we might expect him to exercise one or both of two options: to take political action designed to increase the supply of the public goods, and/or to initiate market transactions to mitigate the incorrect provision of the public good. The real world abounds with both options. People contribute time and money in support of political candidates and issues, they engage in lobbying and join pressure groups, and they also use the market system to ameliorate the under- or overprovision of certain public goods. The provision of education through private schools and the provision of additional personal and property protection through private security firms are two recent major examples; people have long bought locks for their doors, screens for their windows, and extra reading material for their children.

The issue is not who should provide the good or service, but rather how the individual citizen-consumer will react to whatever decisions are made in the public sector. The empirical results may be different in other settings, but my field experience leads me to believe that political activity and *local* markets are increasingly viewed as ineffective in altering the supply of certain public goods in metropolitan areas, and that migration is increasingly resorted to as an alternative for obtaining more suitable provision of these goods. This perception is reinforced by Blackwood and Carpenter's finding (1978) that among "antiurbanists" in an Arizona statewide random sample more than 90% felt the following phrases described nonmetropolitan areas better than metropolitan areas:

> Atmosphere in which to raise children
> Protection of individual freedom and privacy
> Friendliness of people to each other
> Community spirit and pride
> Residents' voice in deciding community affairs
> Residents' general mental health
> Quality of religious life
> Residents' general satisfaction
> Respect for law and order
> Absence of illegal drug use
> Outdoor recreation opportunities

Admittedly, these items are vague, interrelated, and probably influenced by nostalgia, but most appear to be public goods that are inadequately supplied in metropolitan areas, at least in the minds of those who leave such areas. Among these same antiurbanists, a much smaller percentage (48–55%) felt that such things as medical care and entertainment opportunities were better in nonmetropolitan areas. It is not surprising that these are predominantly private goods that can be tailored to personal preferences and budgets through market purchases.

Identification and Measurement of the Relevant Public Goods

It must be recognized that measurement problems associated with public goods are rather complex and are yielding to research efforts in a very stubborn fashion. For example, consider protection from crime and violence. Although numbers of police personnel and vehicles can be easily measured, these are only inputs in the production of personal safety. On the output side, an analyst has the choice of objective measures (such as the violent crime rate in a particular area) or subjective measures (such as the feelings of citizens about their own safety). Ostrom (1977), a leader in this area of research, points out that objective and subjective measures often do not have a high degree of correspondence, and that different measures of output may be useful for different purposes. For the purpose of explaining migration behavior, a strong argument can be made that primary data collection, with emphasis on identifying subjective perceptions of the migrants, is the essential starting point. At the same time, the ultimate usefulness of this approach, in a policy sense, depends on linking objective and subjective measures.

In a particular research setting, the set of relevant public goods is not self-evident. The southern Oregon study, for example, developed a search process that included intuition, literature review, conversations with in-migrants, careful pretesting of a field questionnaire (by phone and in person), and finally, administration of an hour-long revised questionnaire. Blackwood and Carpenter's (1978) work on antiurbanists was a useful starting point. Beyond this, considerable attention was given to Mason et al.'s (1975) *quality of life* (QOL) metric. This scale was used to assess how a random sample of Oregonians felt about their level of well-being in a variety of domains. Respondents in the more urbanized Willamette Valley reported lower QOL levels than did southern Oregonians in five domains—public safety, air quality, transportation, energy, and gasoline availability. The first three in particular appeared to be public goods of relevance to southern Oregon in-migration.

The pretest process focused on whether the QOL in these and several other domains was perceived by in-migrants as different in southern

Oregon, compared to their area of origin, and on whether these differences were significantly related to their decision to migrate. Two domains were excluded.[5] The final field questionnaire elicited ordinal responses on (a) perceived differences in QOL on a better-or-worse basis; and (b) degree of importance (very, somewhat, not at all) in the migration decision. Four QOL domains were somewhat arbitrarily singled out for special attention in the final field questionnaire: These were personal safety from crime and violence, crowding and congestion, air pollution, and family recreation. In addition to asking auxiliary questions in each domain, an adaptation of Cantril's (1965) Self-Anchoring Striving Scale was used to measure satisfaction in southern Oregon and in the area of origin.[6] This scale, used also to measure overall satisfaction with the quality of life in the two locations, ranged from a low of 0 to a high of 10. In Stevens's (1946) typology of measurement levels, this might be viewed as an ordinal scale defined on a more-or-less continuous basis; that is, it has many steps, but the distances between steps are not necessarily equal.

Personal interviews were conducted during September and October 1977 with 222 recent in-migrant household heads who were randomly selected from a sampling frame compiled from power company residential hook-ups and Employment Division job applications. Heads of 165 households were in the labor force (although not necessarily employed); half of these had moved either from southern California or the San Francisco Bay area. Another 49 household heads were retired and 8 were disabled. Both of the latter groups were excluded from the present analysis in order to focus on those who ostensibly would not have had to sacrifice income had they remained in the area of origin.

---

[5]Quality of local government and opportunity to have a voice in local affairs were not included because of lack of salience. Hennigh (1978) found that newcomers to an adjoining southern Oregon county tended to become quite active, however, after moving into the community.

[6]The following is an example:

Looking at the scale again, which one number best represents how safe you feel from crime and violence in this community? The higher the number, the more satisfied you feel as to your own personal safety. The lower the number, the less satisfied you feel. Remembering that 10 means perfect or complete satisfaction, which one number best stands for your present level of satisfaction?

    0   1   2   3   4   5   6   7   8   9   10

In a test of construct validity, Andrews and Crandall (1976) found that 49% of the variance associated with this particular measure was valid variance rather than correlated error or residual variance. Slightly better results (64% valid variance) were obtained with one verbal scale (Delighted—Terrible) and two nonverbal scales (Faces and Circles). Two other scales, the Social Comparison Technique and Ratings by Others, were much less satisfactory in terms of construct validity.

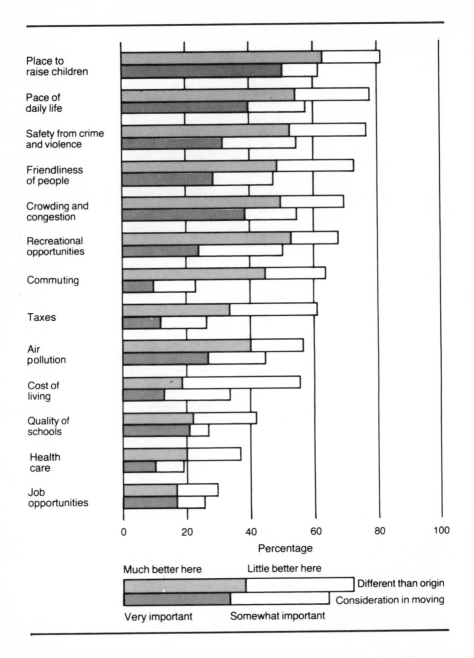

Figure 5.2. Quality of life domains as perceived by in-migrants to Josephine and Jackson Counties, Oregon.

In general, most household heads regarded the quality of life as better in southern Oregon than in their origin areas (Figure 5.2). More important, five of the QOL domains were considered by a majority to be very important or somewhat important factors in the decision to migrate—pace of daily life, a place to raise children, safety from crime and violence, (less) crowding and congestion, and recreational opportunities (open-ended responses indicated that the latter was usually interpreted as referring to public rather than private facilities). Two other domains were regarded as very or somewhat important factors by nearly a majority—friendliness of people and (less) air pollution.

All of the more important domains can be considered public goods. For example, an in-migrant's previous levels of exposure to crime and violence, crowding and congestion, and air pollution are set largely by the economic and political milieu of urban life. Further, these levels may be quite insensitive to either individual political activity or market adjustments in the origin area. To really examine this question, one would have to probe the household's allocations of time and money. One would need to look at expenditures for defensive purposes, such as air filters, locks, and security services; at micro-locational decisions with respect to housing, work, and consumption; and at perceptions of costs and benefits from political participation. No attempt was made to do this in the present study. Instead, it must be assumed that further increases in utility in these domains must have been forthcoming only at substantially higher prices than were actually paid through out-migration and the accompanying income sacrifice.

Quantifying the Degree of Income Sacrifice for Particular Public Goods

One interpretation of the empirical results described in the preceding section is that noneconomic factors may be quite important in some migration decisions. However, my position is that these factors are, in fact, economic commodities in that people are willing to pay for them even though conventional markets do not exist. It is not hard to visualize that people would be willing to give up other things (or to pay money, as a proxy) in order to avoid congestion, crime, and air pollution, to gain convenient access to recreational opportunities, and to enjoy a more relaxed pace of life.

In a very real sense, the migration process itself may serve as a market that allows the purchase of types of goods and services that cannot (easily, if at all) be purchased in the area of origin. Whether or not this market is actually utilized depends on the relative availabilities of public goods in the areas of origin and destination, the willingness of consumers to sacrifice income to gain additional public goods, the effectiveness of additional political and/or market adaptations within the area of origin, and the degree of income sacrifice that is imposed on the in-migrant by the nature of labor markets within the area of destination. If an undersupplied public good could easily be substituted for by local private goods, one would not expect to find use of a migration "market." If this is not the case, however, and if consumers are willing to pay the price of foregoing metropolitan-level incomes, then the migration "market" may be the only way in which they can implement their preferences.

Researchers have not systematically addressed the extent to which household income sacrifice has actually occurred in the population turnaround. Ploch (1978), in one of the few studies to do so, reports that about half of the recent in-migrants to Maine sacrificed income in the migration process. In the southern Oregon study, 50% of households with heads in the labor force reported that they had sacrificed income by moving to Oregon (Figure 5.3). The mean amount of sacrifice (among households reporting a reduction of income) was $6526, or about 45% of average family income prior to migration. Several analytical questions need to be raised regarding self-reported estimates such as these. One is the degree to which they are corroborated by detailed earnings data from past and present employment. Adjustment for differences in costs of living is also necessary. Another consideration is whether migrants view this as a one-time occurrence to be followed by resumption of premigration earnings levels or whether they anticipate some permanent reduction in annual income.

When income sacrifices occur, it should be noted that what is being purchased is a composite commodity. If only one public good varied between origin and destination, one could perhaps attribute the entire income sacrifice to that good. In reality, differences may exist in the perceived availabilities of several public goods. For purposes of economic analysis, it would be desirable if the overall income sacrifice could be partitioned into that attributable to each of the public goods. Ideally, economists would like to establish a price–quantity relationship (demand function) for each public good in order to measure the social benefits from enhanced provision of that good within the area of origin (Freeman, 1979; Peskin and Seskin, 1975). For example, one of the costs of metropolitan area air pollution is the income sacrificed by out-migrants. Conversely, this cost could be used to derive a measure of social benefit from increased pollution abatement.

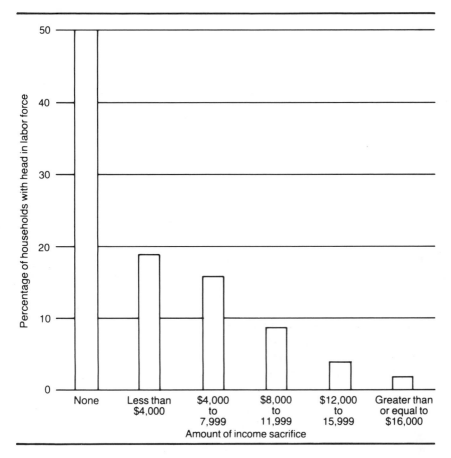

Figure 5.3. Self-perceived income sacrifice among households migrating to Jackson and Josephine Counties, Oregon.

Hedonic Prices of Public Goods

At least two economic models seem appropriate for quantifying the degree of income sacrifice for public goods—the theory of hedonic prices and the utility function approach.[7] The former is based on the hypothesis that goods are valued by consumers because they are made up of attributes or characteristics that yield satisfaction to consumers. As

[7]As used in economics, *hedonism* is an archaic term from early (Benthamite) utility theory that relates to the balancing of pain and pleasure. The primary modern references to this methodology are Lancaster (1966), Griliches (1971), and Rosen (1974); applications to environmental goods include those by Freeman (1974), Kelley (1977), Schefter (1977), Hoch and Drake (1974), and Getz and Huang (1978).

an example, consider a group of single-family dwellings, each described by attributes such as floor area, lot size, number of baths, access to schools, and geographic location. Note that the attributes could include public as well as private goods. A hedonic (or implicit) price function for these houses could be derived by regressing house prices on the set of attributes, using individual homes as the units of observation. This might reveal, for example, that the value of a marginal unit of floor space was $30 per square foot, holding everything else constant, or that location in a certain school district was worth a certain amount. Note that these values, in economists' terms, are derived from reduced-form equations; they do not identify the separate influences of supply and demand. However, it is possible to consider the supply and demand for each attribute separately. Rosen (1974) demonstrated that this approach leads to a theory of product differentiation in competitive markets.

The theory of hedonic prices appears to be amply robust to allow an application to migration decisions. Estimation is facilitated by the fact that the geographically mobile consumer is simultaneously a demander and a supplier of public good attributes. That is, by choosing to migrate with a reduction in income, he supplies himself with a new set of private and public goods. The former are now diminished in total because of reduced earnings, but the latter have been augmented (some public goods may remain better in the area of origin). In this case, the consumer's income sacrifice per unit of time can be viewed as the price of the composite public good that he has purchased (ΔY^j), while the attributes that determine this price are the (objective or subjective) quantities of public goods (ΔS_i^j) that are made available through (or foregone because of) migration. In notation,

$$\Delta Y^j = f(\Delta S_1^j, \Delta S_2^j, \ldots, \Delta S_n^j), \tag{5.3}$$

where the value of an incremental unit of a particular public good, over a set of observations, would be:

$$[\partial(\Delta Y)]/[\partial(\Delta S_i)] \tag{5.4}$$

These equations would identify the (one) marginal value of some public good (e.g., clean air) over a sample of migrants, an analog to the marginal price of a square foot of floor space over a sample of houses. It would be desirable to go beyond this and explain why the marginal values placed on clean air might vary *among* migrants. One could postulate that high-income consumers might be willing to make proportionately larger sacrifices for clean air than would low-income consumers. Capital gains (C) realized from the sale of a previous metropolitan residence might, under some circumstances, permit one to pay more for clean air, especially if there are differentials between regions in housing prices. Age (A), education (E), and family status and needs (F_i) might also explain some of the variation in willingness to pay. All these variables would become explanatory variables in a second-step regression equation, where the dependent variable is the individual's willingness to pay for the public good. That is:

$$\left(\frac{\partial \Delta Y}{\partial \Delta S_i} \right)^j = f(S^j_i, Y^j, C^j, A^j, E^j, F^j_i, \cdots). \tag{5.5}$$

If Eq. (5.5) is successfully estimated, we have demonstrated an inverse demand function for a particular public good as revealed through migration. One complication in estimating (5.5) is that there must be some variation among individuals in willingness to pay. This can be handled by fitting (5.3) as a polynomial or some other nonlinear function.

The usefulness of the hedonic price approach appears to depend on at least four considerations. First, it must be possible to identify the set of public goods that enter into the migration decision. Second, the quantities of these goods must be measurable in some meaningful sense. Third, variations in degree of income sacrifice must be observable among a sample of in-migrants. Fourth, and perhaps most important, the decision processes of migrants must have some resemblance to the theoretical model, which is based on deliberate, purposive, and knowledgeable behavior.

The Utility Function Approach

An alternative method for quantifying the degree of income sacrifice for particular public goods is based on the utility function of the individual. This entails a representation of how changes in private and public goods affect the individual's utility or overall level of subjective well-being. Traditionally, economists have regarded the utility function as an abstraction from which inferences about consumer behavior can be derived and subjected to empirical test. One reason for this approach has been that it appeared impossible to measure utility in any meaningful sense. However, recent research on social indicators in other social science disciplines (e.g., Campbell *et al.*, 1977) has demonstrated the usefulness of the *quality of life* metric in assessing how people feel about their overall level of well-being and the components thereof.

An eclectic approach, then, is to consider that the utility levels for individual migrants can be measured by their responses to the QOL metric concerning overall satisfaction with life in the area of origin and in the area of destination. The difference between the two can be viewed as the change in overall utility arising from migration. The magnitude of this difference can be postulated to depend on two factors. One is the change in access to private goods, represented by the migrant's income sacrifice. The second is the extent of change in each of the individual QOL domains or public goods.

One way of portraying these relationships is to assume that only one public good is relevant and that the ith individual migrant (or household) has a utility function of the following type:

$$\Delta U_i = b_0 (\Delta Y_i)^{b_1}(\Delta S_i)^{b_2} \tag{5.6}$$

where

ΔU_i = change in overall utility;
ΔY_i = income sacrifice;
ΔS_i = objective or subjective change in the public good.

In turn, (5.6) can be used to identify the rate at which the average migrant has sacrificed income to gain an additional unit of the public good. This marginal rate of substitution can be shown as:

$$\frac{\partial(\Delta Y)}{\partial(\Delta S)} = \left[\frac{b_2}{b_1} \right]\left[\frac{(\overline{\Delta Y})}{(\overline{\Delta S})} \right], \tag{5.7}$$

which is the ratio of the two regression coefficients evaluated at the means of the two variables, taken over an entire sample.

In other words, sacrificing money can be expected to decrease utility. Gaining access to public goods can be expected to increase utility. Whether a particular sample of migrants is better off, on balance, than they were prior to migration is another matter. The utility function approach uses *ex post* data and is not necessarily an equilibrium model. If all the migrants plan to return home because of the high income sacrifice, the marginal rates of substitution would overstate their actual willingness to pay. However, the approach may be useful in identifying which of the various public goods are significantly related to changes in overall utility, and identifying the rate at which migrants have in fact sacrificed income for these goods.

An Empirical Application to Data for Southern Oregon

The usefulness of these two models can be illustrated in a specific setting such as the southern Oregon study area. It should be recognized that even if in-migrants to other areas move because of inadequate public goods in their areas of origin, they may be searching for a different set of public goods than those shown in Figure 5.2. However, the research process that identified the latter set should be equally applicable to different empirical settings.

In the southern Oregon case, Table 5.1 shows that the utility function approach has far greater explanatory power than the hedonic price approach. The former approach statistically explains over one-half the variance in the dependent variable (change in overall *quality of life*). Less than 5% the variance in the dependent variable (income sacrifice) is explained by the hedonic model. The data are the same, of course, in both cases; many households have sacrificed income and most have gained greater access to public goods.

It appears that significant factors were excluded from the hedonic analysis. In reality, the extent of income sacrifice was highly dependent

TABLE 5.1
Regression Equations for Alternative Models

Independent variables [a]	Hedonic model: Dependent variable =income sacrifice	Utility function: Dependent variable =change in overall QOL
Income sacrifice[a]		−.0168 (.0099)
Safety from crime and violence	.1426 (.5780)	.1240 (.0650)
Air quality	−.6913 (.3893)	.0284 (.0443)
Crowding and congestion	.8476 (.6328)	.1717 (.0717)
Family recreation	−1.0364 (.6753)	.5076 (.0767)
n	135	135
constant term	4.4156	.0187
R^2	.046	.524
$\bar{R}^2$	.017	.506

Note: Standard errors of the regression coefficients are in parentheses. All variables (except income sacrifice) are expressed as ratios (destination over origin) of responses to the Self-Anchoring Striving Scale. Responses of "2" and "1" at destination and origin, respectively, would have the same ratio as responses of "10" and "5". When converted to natural logarithms, each variable becomes the first difference of the logs.

[a] For consistency, income sacrifice should be measured as the ratio of income at destination to income at origin. These measures are not yet available.

TABLE 5.2
Mean Values for Selected Variables: Households That Did or Did Not Sacrifice Income

Variable	Not different between groups All respondents (n=139)	Different between groups [a] Income sacrifice (n=70)	No income sacrifice (n=69)
DEMOGRAPHIC			
Age of head	33.5 yrs		
Education of head	12.7 yrs		
Married with children	46%		
Population, city of origin	228,000		
HOME OWNERSHIP			
Owned home there	46%		
Sold home after moving [b]	92%		
Equity from previous home	$23,600		
Bought home in southern Oregon	44%		
PREVIOUS EMPLOYMENT			
Skilled occupation [c]	55%		
Unemployed at time of move	9%		
Could have kept previous job [d]	77%		
Financial risk-taker [e]	34%		
Family income	$13,800		
Spouse's hourly wage	$4.07		
Spouse employed [f]		51%	32%
Head's hourly wage		$6.89	$5.62
CURRENT EMPLOYMENT			
Received unemployment compensation	22%		
Spouse employed	34%		
Job waiting in southern Oregon		20%	46%
Weeks to find first job		9.6	4.6
Head's hourly wage		$4.62	$5.77
Misjudged employment prospects [g]		50%	19%
Head unemployed		29%	13%
CHANGE IN QUALITY OF LIFE [h]			
Safety from crime and violence	+2.69		
Crowding and congestion	+1.64		
Overall		+ .94	+2.04
Air quality		-.04	+1.35
Family recreation		+1.84	+2.65

130

TABLE 5.2
(*Continued*)

Variable	Not different between groups All respondents (n=139)	Different between groups [a]	
		Income sacrifice (n=70)	No income sacrifice (n=69)

OUTCOME

Plan to leave southern
Oregon   7%

[a] Univariate "t"-tests for continuous variables; chi-square (against income sacrifice grouping) for discrete variables. $\alpha < .10$ for variables shown as different. An additional 18 households felt they had sacrificed income but could not state a dollar amount, and 8 other households could not answer the question.
[b] If home-owner at origin.
[c] Professional, managers or administrators, or craftsmen.
[d] If employed.
[e] Take financial risks "fairly often" or "once in a while" (compared to "almost never" or "never") as percent of total responses.
[f] If married.
[g] As percent of total responses regarding things respondents may have misjudged or on which they had poor information.
[h] Positive values reflect increased satisfaction, based on a 0 to 10 scale (i.e., differences in responses to the Self-Anchoring Striving Scale).

on whether the household head and/or spouse could find a niche in the local labor market (Table 5.2). For one thing, heads of households who sacrificed income were less likely to have had a job waiting for them in southern Oregon (20% versus 46% for households that did not sacrifice income). Among income sacrificers, those heads who did find jobs earned $2.27 per hour less than they had been earning, and their spouses also had difficulty finding work. Overall, one-half of those with income sacrifice felt they had misjudged local employment prospects, compared with only 19% of those who had no income sacrifice. On the other hand, satisfaction with public goods (particularly personal safety and crowding) was more likely to be the same for both income sacrificers and nonsacrificers. Differences within the family recreation domain may well be due to the role of income in providing access (travel costs) to public recreation facilities within a multicounty area. The reason for the air quality difference remains unclear. Overall satisfaction or utility was higher for those without income sacrifice.

In retrospect, it appears that uncertainty about the degree of income sacrifice was sufficient to invalidate this application of the hedonic price approach. The approach may be more consistent with the data in situations where migrants have better advance knowledge of the price they will have to pay for the new set of public goods. In any event, the lack of success in this case spotlights the need for further study of how, and in what order, decisions are made in migrant households.

In contrast, the utility function approach appears to be a plausible characterization of the manner in which public goods and private goods (i.e., money) affect the utility levels of migrants. Each coefficient has the expected sign and each, except for air quality, is different from zero at or near conventional levels of statistical significance. Increasing the degree of income sacrifice lowers total utility, while increasing satisfaction in the individual QOL domains (and implicitly, increasing objectively measured outputs) adds to total utility.

As noted above, the marginal rates of substitution (MRS) of money for each of the public goods can be calculated from the utility function. These values, shown in column 1 of Table 5.3, are rather large because each of the public goods is measured as a ratio; an additional unit of the public good would be a substantial increase. However, an alternate use of these values would be to apportion the mean income sacrifice among

TABLE 5.3
Implied Values of the Public Goods

Public good	(1) Marginal rate of substitution of money, per unit of public good [a]	(2) Imputed values Per household [b]	(3) Imputed values Total for sample (n=70)
Safety from crime and violence	$ 30,486 (15.4%)	$1,005 (15.4%)	$ 70,350
Crowding and congestion	$ 41,686 (21.0%)	$1,371 (21.0%)	$ 95,970
Family recreation	$126,396 (63.6%)	$4,150 (63.6%)	$290,500
Totals	$198,568 (100.0%)	$6,526 (100.0%)	$456,820

[a] Derived from utility function in Table 5.1; air quality variable not included due to lack of significance. Means of ratios: safety from crime and violence (1.58), crowding and congestion (1.60), family recreation (1.56).

[b] Allocation of mean income sacrifice ($6526) among the various public goods by the percentages in column 1.

the various public goods by using the MRS values as weights (column 2). On this basis, improved access to family-oriented outdoor recreation would be valued at $4150 per household, increased personal safety would be worth $1005, and improvements in crowding and congestion would be worth $1371.

Several reservations about these estimates should be noted. First, analysis has been limited to the continuously measured QOL domains; research is underway to consider simultaneously the domains that were measured on a conventional ordinal basis. Second, the time span of the sacrifice is not clear. Again, the ongoing research may clarify this issue. Finally, some households may enjoy a consumer surplus in that they would have been willing to sacrifice more money than they actually had to sacrifice. This possibility cannot be considered with the method used here. In fact, we have mixed evidence on the real extent of consumer's surplus. On one hand, only 7% of those interviewed planned to move away from southern Oregon in spite of larger-than-anticipated income sacrifices. This indicates that additional income might have been extracted from some of these migrants. On the other hand, almost half of the households in the initial sampling frame could not be located for interviewing even though the sampling frame was quite current. By implication, the income sacrifice may have become intolerably large for many of these households.

In spite of these reservations, the utility function approach appears to be useful. It identifies the relevant set of public goods and approximates the degree to which households are apparently willing to sacrifice income for these goods. This willingness was substantial in the southern Oregon case. A relatively small group of 70 households felt that they had given up nearly .5 million dollars to obtain some goods they could not easily obtain in their metropolitan areas of origin.

Conclusions

Economists, including Alonso (1971) and Hoch (1976), have documented a positive relationship between wage rates (and incomes) and city size. This is due in part to higher land rents, transportation costs, and general increases in the cost of living. This is not to say that the overall well-being of people rises proportionately. On the negative side, increased size and density may generate congestion and pollution; on the positive side, it may allow greater choice in consumption and access to specialized services. Hoch's research (1976) indicates that wage rates rise by 6–9% for every tenfold increase in city population, and that only about one-half to three-quarters of this wage differential can be explained by differences in costs of living (which increase by only 4.5% per tenfold population increase). What, then, about the remainder?

> Because one-quarter to one-half of the wage differential is to be explained, it follows that the costs must outweigh the benefits. The non-market costs include the value of time spent in the journey to work, the value of risks not covered by insurance, and the cost of air pollution, among other items. The benefits include access to specialized activities and services—such as ballet, museums, major league sports, and specialized medical facilities—which become economic at a large enough scale of operation [Hoch, 1976:858].

This does not imply that the "bads" outweigh the "goods" for all urbanites; many could not be coaxed or driven out of the city. For others, it appears that the threshold of action has been reached and that they have opted to migrate to nonmetropolitan areas rather than take political action or make further on-site market purchases. While my research has not tested the hypothesis that this is not happening more frequently than in earlier years, it is consistent with that theme. The extent to which these results can be generalized over space and time is worthy of further study.

Acknowledgments

I am indebted to Irving Hoch and John A. Edwards for advice and critical reviews, and to Rick Cuthbert, Paul Kiesse, Mike Regan, and Tom Ferguson for assistance in collecting and processing the data.

References

Alonso, William
   1971   "Economics of urban size." *Papers and Proceedings of the Regional Science Association*, Vol. 26, 67–83.
Andrews, Frank M. and Rick Crandall
   1976   "The validity of measures of self-reported well-being." *Social Indicators Research* 3 (1):1–19.
Blackwood, Larry G. and Edwin H. Carpenter
   1978   "The importance of anti-urbanism in determining residential preferences and migration patterns." *Rural Sociology* 43 (1):31–47.
Breton, Albert
   1974   *The Economic Theory of Representative Government.* Chicago: Aldine Publishing Company.
Campbell, Angus, Philip E. Converse, and Willard L. Rodgers
   1977   *The Perceived Quality of Life.* New York: Russell Sage Foundation.
Cantril, Hadley
   1965   *The Pattern of Human Concerns.* New Brunswick: Rutgers University Press.

DaVanzo, Julie
    1978   "Does unemployment affect migration? Evidence from micro data." *Review of Economics and Statistics* 60 (4):504–514.
Freeman, A. M. III
    1974   "On estimating air pollution control benefits from land value studies." *Journal of Environmental Economics and Management* 1 (1):74–83.
    1979   *The Benefits of Environmental Improvement.* Baltimore: Johns Hopkins University Press.
Getz, Malcolm and Yuh-ching Huang
    1978   "Consumer revealed preferences for environmental goods." *Review of Economics and Statistics* 60 (3):449–458.
Griliches, Zvi (ed.)
    1971   *Price Indexes and Quality Change.* Cambridge: Harvard University Press.
Hennigh, Lawrence
    1978   "The good life and the taxpayers revolt." *Rural Sociology* 43 (2):178–190.
Hoch, Irving
    1976   "City size effects, trends, and policies." *Science* 193 (September 3):856–863.
Hoch, Irving and Judith Drake
    1974   "Wages, climate, and the quality of life." *Journal of Environmental Economics and Management* 1 (4):268–295.
Kelley, Kevin C.
    1977   "Urban disamenities and the measure of economic welfare." *Journal of Urban Economics* 4:379–388.
Lancaster, Kelvin J.
    1966   "A new approach to consumer theory." *Journal of Political Economy* 74 (2):132–157.
Mason, Robert G., David Faulkenberry, and Alexander Seidler
    1975   *The Quality of Life as Oregonians See It.* Corvallis: Oregon State University.
Ostrom, Elinor
    1977   "Why do we need multiple indicators of public service outputs?" Section 6 in *National Conference on Non-metropolitan Community Services Research*, Paper prepared for the Committee on Agriculture, Nutrition, and Forestry, U.S. Senate. Washington, D.C.: U.S. Government Printing Office.
Peskin, Henry M. and Eugene P. Seskin (eds.)
    1975   *Cost-Benefit Analysis and Water Pollution Policy.* Washington, D.C.: The Urban Institute.
Ploch, Louis A.
    1978   "The reversal in migration patterns—Some rural development consequences." *Rural Sociology* 43 (2):293–303.
Rosen, Sherwin
    1974   "Hedonic prices and implicit markets: Product differentiation in pure competition." *Journal of Political Economy* 82 (1):34–55.
Samuelson, Paul A.
    1954   "The pure theory of public expenditure." *Review of Economics and Statistics* 36 (4):387–389.
Schefter, John E.
    1977   "The demand for and supply of the characteristics of a new residence and the residential location decision." Ph.D. dissertation, Oregon State University.
Stevens, S. S.
    1946   "On the theory of scales of measurement." *Science* 103:677–680.
Tiebout, Charles M.
    1956   "A pure theory of local expenditures." *Journal of Political Economy* 44 (5):416–424.

6

The Effect of Trends in Economic Structures on Population Change in Rural Areas[1]

LLOYD D. BENDER

Introduction

This chapter introduces consideration of the effects of changes in rural economic structures on population change. Employment opportunities, earnings potentials, and living conditions in rural areas are constantly changing. Technological innovations, the organization and optimum size of businesses, the amount and type of capital devoted to public and private enterprise, and the characteristics of communities all change economic and social conditions and thus make locations more or less desirable places in which to live.

The thesis of this chapter is that the structural changes that have been occurring for years in rural economies are among the fundamental determinants of the population patterns observed now and in the past. Economic structure is more than industry composition, size of place, or hierarchy of trade and service relationships among places. Structure implies a set of behavioral relationships in an economy. It includes the willingness of firms and businesses to locate in rural areas, the adjustments of other firms and households to changing economic conditions, and the attractiveness of communities as places in which to live and work.

Aggregate secondary data can be used to describe some aspects of

[1]Research partially sponsored by the Office of Environmental Engineering Technology, the Office of Research and Development, and the U.S. Environmental Protection Agency through the Economic Development Division, the Economics, Statistics, and Cooperatives Service, and the U.S. Department of Agriculture in cooperation with Montana State University.

ISBN 0-12-136380-5

structural change. Expressed in a simple model, these indicators describe how structural changes precipitate population change. A complex structural model would express the behavior of every actor. All the events and conditions affecting behavior would be isolated. This discussion concentrates on a limited number of indicators; thus it is an abstraction and simplification of reality.

The structural indicators of interest are those influencing population change in rural areas. People decide where to work and live, at least partly, on the basis of earnings potentials and living conditions. Preferences, ethical values, and desires need not change for people to become dissatisfied and move. Conditions in the community or potentials in other communities may change. These changes are characterized in the migration literature as push and pull factors.

Opportunities available to people are altered by structural changes in rural economies. Push effects are thought to create dissatisfaction with a place of residence and its potential for income and living conditions. The push effect is relative. Declines in earnings and employment potentials will be push factors only if similar declines have not occurred in other places. If conditions are equally poor elsewhere, the push effect will not operate. Conversely, pull effects due to improved work and living potentials will tend to attract people to a place only if the same improvements have not occurred everywhere else.

Relative declines in economic conditions in a place promote out-migration. Population retention declines. A relative improvement in economic conditions decreases gross out-migration and increases gross in-migration—population retention is said to improve. Numerous empirical studies validate the association between economic conditions on the one hand and net migration and the gross in-migration and out-migration streams on the other, among locations (Bender *et al.*, 1977; Greenwood, 1975; Lowry, 1966; Petto and Bender, 1974).

The classficiation of places into a push or pull dichotomy oversimplifies migration analyses by implying static economic conditions. Rural areas tend to be classified as having low population retention. On the other hand, urban areas are frequently characterized as having high population retention. These general characterizations of rural and urban places disregard changing background conditions, economic structures, and opportunity matrices that affect migration.

The Process of Structural Change: The Farming Example

Farming provides an example of the effect of structural changes on population. The behavioral adaptations to agricultural changes are common enough to be isolated; they may not be analogous, however, to adaptations to changes in other industries.

External Events Affect
the Local Community

The farming revolution was fed by influences originating outside the farm enterprise itself. The same is true for rural economies. External events influence the behavioral relationships and adaptations of those in a community. The farm revolution thrived on increases in product demand, technological developments and innovations, and additions of capital. Farmers adapted to these changing conditions. Similarly, the economies of rural counties, areas, and regions adapt to national and world events.

The adoption of farm technology and capital led to a greater output with less labor. Only 7,806,000 persons (3.6% of the U.S. population) lived on farms in June 1977 (Banks, 1978a). This compares with a farm population of 15,835,000 in 1960 (Banks, 1978b). Farms with sales greater than $40,000 accounted for only 24% of the farm population but 80% of farm receipts (Banks, 1978b). The most direct and visible effect of the decline in the number of farms was the out-migration of farm people. Whether rural communities suffered the same out-migration depended on secondary effects. By the same token, the direct consequence of industries expanding or relocating in rural areas tends to be an expansion of population, conditional upon the availability of local labor. But total in-migration will depend not only on the direct population effect but on other activities induced by industrial expansion.

Changing Farm Structure Affects the
Rural Nonfarm Community

The induced effect on farm communities is the second element in the process of changing farm structure. An increased proportion of inputs was purchased by farmers. In addition, total farm output increased, and in some cases, other industries expanded their operations. The indirect induced effects on rural communities were that supply and marketing businesses expanded their operations even though they served fewer customers. Demand for consumer goods decreased but that was tempered by increases in business supporting agriculture. To be sure, the geographic distribution of such services changed. In the aggregate, however, declines in the farm population were accompanied by an increase in the nonfarm population and by increases in the population of towns other than small villages (Fuguitt and Beale, 1976).

Similarly, the indirect effects of industry on communities are often overlooked. Expansions of industry due to increased product demand can have a pervasive impact. So can changes in technology that enable and encourage nearby suppliers to expand operations. Finally, a simple change in the income of individuals can stimulate the consumer sectors of a local community. In each case, the tendency of the induced effects is to increase employment in locally provided services and to expand population conditioned by the amount of locally available labor.

The proportion of total employment in services on a nationwide basis has increased. In 1940, 46% of total wage and salary employment was in the service sector (Table 6.1). The proportion in 1970 was 61%. Cities are thought to be centers for services, and rural areas (especially sparsely settled areas with little manufacturing) have not been noted for a high proportion of service employment.

The data on service employment presented in Table 6.1 for Montana, Wyoming, North Dakota, and selected sparsely settled counties dramatize the changing proportion of service employment. And this change is occurring despite declining farm employment, lack of manufacturing and urban centers, and an absence of recreational amenities in these areas. The average proportion of employment in services was 63% in Montana and Wyoming and 65% in North Dakota in 1970. These structural changes mean that total employment can increase simultaneously with declining employment in manufacturing and agriculture.

Changes in Farm Structure Affect
Personal Income in Rural Communities

Personal income increased as farms consolidated and as fewer persons derived their living from farming. Low wages in rural communities are partly a function of a low-wage industry mix—farming and service industries often predominate (Nilsen, 1978). General earning levels in nonmetropolitan areas have increased but remain relatively low. They must continue to increase if people are to be attracted to these areas. Conversely, a decrease in wages will probably cause people to out-migrate. An increase in wages tends to decrease out-migration and to increase in-migration. The wage is partly a function of how many underemployed, unemployed, and potentially employable local people are available for work in relation to the demand for labor.

Participation of rural people in the labor force is an extremely important variable affecting rural population change. Consider the following trends. The revolution in farming was accompanied by an increase in the number of farm residents working off the farm. In 1974, about 30% of

TABLE 6.1
Percentage of Service Employment in Selected Areas, 1940-1970

State or county	1940	1950	1960	1970
United States	46	49	55	61
Montana	41	47	56	63
Rosebud	34	33	51	56
Wyoming	44	49	55	63
Campbell	30	35	44	45
North Dakota	37	41	53	65
Mercer	23	30	41	51

Source: Regional Employment by Industry, 1940-1970, U.S. Department Commerce, Bureau of Economic Analysis, no date.
Note: Service employment includes local transportation and utilities; wholesale and retail trade; financial, insurance, and real
estate brokerage; and other business and personal services.

farm operators worked at least 200 days off the farm in contrast with 6%
prior to World War II (Carlin and Ghelfi, 1979). In 1978, 43% of farm
women in nonmetropolitan areas were in the labor force. Moreover,
between 1960 and 1970, 89% of the increase in nonmetropolitan employment was composed of women (Brown and O'Leary, 1979). Off-
farm income contributed 57% of the personal income of the farm population in 1977 (Carlin and Ghelfi, 1979). Total labor-force participation of
farm people had increased to 61.2% by early 1979. The labor-force participation rate of people in nonmetropolitan areas had increased to
60.7% in 1979 compared with 64.2% of those in metropolitan areas
(Bureau of Labor Statistics, 1979).

Job openings in rural areas do not require a net in-migration of people
if they are filled by local people who enter the labor force. Population
can remain stable while employment increases. However, labor-force
participation rates should level off at some point. If they do, then
additional increases in employment will have to be met by in-migration
even if wages are high.

Changes in Farming Affect the
Regional Distribution of Population

The distribution of population among and within regions was affected
by the changes in farming (Brown, 1979). Cattle feeding became common in the West, and irrigation opened new lands. Soybeans expanded
in the Midwest and South in response to increased demand and innova-

tions. In similar ways, changes in technology, product demand, and capital influence the location of most other industries in rural regions.

The distribution of service activities within regions was also altered. The service activities induced by new basic industry may be limited if the community is located near a large urban area. And the nature and extent of induced activities will depend on the type of a new industry and on where the industry purchases supplies. Generally, ease of access to urban areas will decrease the induced effect in rural communities, whereas costly access to urban services will foster services located in rural areas.

A Generalized Model

A model with a chain of five linkages can be generalized from the preceding illustration. The discussion in this section defines a general model. A subsequent section will present aggregate data for nonmetropolitan areas and discuss their implications for population change.

Each linkage in the causal chain is indicative of economic structure. The five linkages are (a) dispersal of basic economic activities into rural areas; (b) the relative amount of service activities associated with basic activities; (c) labor-force participation; (d) wages; and (e) the distribution of service activities among and within regions. These linkages are shown in the second column of Figure 6.1 and are discussed below.

The features of the model are noteworthy for their general population implications. Each linkage summarizes, in aggregate form, a set of behavioral relationships that are a function of the whole economic system, not just the part that is rural. Each linkage by itself influences population in an area. A change in any one linkage alters population in the long run. The causal chain is also multiplicative in that an increase in population due to one linkage is altered even more by each successive linkage. An attempt to predict future population changes in rural areas that concentrates on one linkage alone or ignores long-term trends in each linkage will fail to capture the full change.

The chain of events in the model describes a sequential process of economic adjustments to structural economic change. The linkages are coefficients that change, and it cannot be assumed that the change will be in the same direction or at the same rate as in the past. The heart of the model is composed of long-term trends in these linkages.

Dispersal of Basic Activities

The model of an area's economy is founded on basic economic activities. Long-term growth and cyclical changes in the national economy are

LINKAGE BETWEEN Static Constructs	Structural Trends in Rural Areas		Hypothesized Population and Economic Effects
	Linkages Reflecting Structural Changes	Implications for Rural Areas	
National economic system Basic economic activities in county	• Dispersal of basic activity	• Greater ties to economic system	• County participates in long-term population and economic growth trends
Basic economic activities in county Service activities in county	• Increased demand for services	• Greater mix of services	• Average multiplier greater • Increased local service activities
Employment in county Population	• Higher wages • Higher labor force participation	• More residents enter the labor force • Less excess labor	• Migration is a source of additional labor and population
Population Regional service centers	• Higher energy prices	• Labor substitutes for energy • Fewer shopping trips	• Increased local service employment • Lower rate of agricultural adjustment

Figure 6.1. Summary of regional model, nationwide sturctural trends, and hypothesized effects on rural communities.

reflected in employment in the basic sectors. Basic activities produce exported goods and services—those sold to people who reside outside the area. The activities that are basic to a small local area are difficult to isolate exactly. It is problematic how much gasoline is sold to tourists, what proportion of grocery-store sales are to people in hinterland areas, or how much money is borrowed elsewhere and spent locally. But for an aggregation of rural counties, basic activities are defined as farming, manufacturing, mining, heavy construction, railroads, motor freight, water transportation, and federal activities. An increase in basic-sector employment in turn creates a derived demand for additional services in a locality.

Increased Demand for Services

Local services are those goods and services produced for and sold to firms and people within the area. The rural service sectors include local transportation and utilities; wholesale and retail trade; financial, insurance, and real estate brokerage; and business and personal services. Local service activities live in a symbiotic relationship with the basic activities; each contributes to the well-being of the other. Employment may increase in a county because an expansion in the basic activities leads to additional employment in the service sector. Employment may also increase because of long-term increases in the number and kind of local services that can locate profitably near customers. Moreover, the ratio of service to basic employment can change. Total employment is a function both of basic employment and of changes in the relationships among the basic and service sectors.

Higher Wages and Labor-Force Participation Rates

An increase in demand for labor in an area tends to increase wages. Wages may increase only slightly if little additional labor is needed, if additional local people enter the labor force, or if underemployed and unemployed people accept jobs. Population remains stable as long as local people (and their replacements in old positions) are sufficient to fill new jobs.

In-migration from other areas is required if local residents do not supply sufficient labor. Wage increases stimulate in-migration, and the higher the wage increase the greater the area from which potential migrants are attracted. Thus, long-term trends in labor-force participation and in relative wages among areas influence the geographic location of the nation's working population.

Dispersal of Service Activities

The distribution of service activities within a region is also subject to long-term influences. The location choice of service firms is determined by transportation costs and size economies. Service activities that can operate profitably on a small scale are located near consumers in a dispersed pattern. Changes in technology that make small-sized businesses economic will result in decentralization. Businesses not efficient at small scales of operation locate where the trade-off between cost of production and delivery cost (or access cost to consumers) is most profitable. Increases in delivery or access costs will tend to redistribute service businesses to locations nearer to consumers than before.

A pure service is one that does not endure beyond its production. It is one-on-one consumer-oriented. If consumers have a hard time accessing services, and/or if access costs increase, services adjust quickly by going out of business or moving to consumers.

Generally speaking, a rural (or suburban) area near urban areas will have fewer local service activities than an area with the same-size economy located far from an urban area. Location patterns of service activities tend to change rapidly as their production economies or consumers' transport costs change.

Model Summary

The hypothesized model is summarized in Figure 6.1. The first column describes the sequence of events as national economic conditions bring about changes in the economic base of a small area such as a county. In a static model with fixed linkage coefficients, an increase in manufacturing employment would produce a sequence of changes tending to increase population. The system would then stabilize and remain stable until another change occurred in the economic base of the area.

Changes in the linkage coefficients of the model produced by interactions within the national economic and social systems are summarized in the two middle columns of Figure 6.1. These long-term changes in behavioral relationships can produce employment changes through time (as indicated by each row in Figure 6.1), even though the economic base of an area does not change.

The last column in the figure summarizes the observable effects. Emphasized again is the fact that a change in any one linkage has a population effect that is further magnified in the sequence, even though the economic base may remain the same.

Many of the explanations of employment and population change in

rural areas have isolated alterations in economic base and have neglected modifications in the remaining factors. Manufacturing has had a
rapid rate of increase in rural areas. At the same time, total U.S. manufacturing employment has declined (Beale, 1975; Nilsen, 1979; Petrulis,
1979). Miller's (1980) analysis indicates that expansions of resident manufacturing facilities accounts for much of the employment increase in
that industry, and, contrary to popular notion, relocations play a minor
role. Other basic activities include retirement, recreation, and higher
education (Beale and Fuguitt, 1978; Schwarzweller, 1979). Such discrete
explanations are partial analyses in that they are not meant to account
for growth in services that the added basic activity generates or for
variations in labor-force conditions that precipitate migration. Furthermore, the growth (or the slackening decline) of rural population where the
base is stable is left unexplained, except for changes in residential preferences (Carpenter, 1977; Fuguitt and Zuiches, 1975).

Greater participation in long-term national growth, higher labor-force
participation rates and, in recent years, higher petroleum prices have
tended to stimulate employment growth in rural areas. These stimuli
relate to all basic activities already in an area, not just to those that
increase in some discrete period. Thus, a study of the responses only of
rapid growth areas will intermingle the effects of structural changes and
the effects of change in the economic base. Linkage coefficients derived
from such studies cannot be applied to an incremental change to predict
future employment and population patterns. That would be equivalent
to applying a new labor-force participation rate to in-migrants only
when the rate should also be applied to existing residents.

Analysis of Structural Change

The model identifies five hypotheses (which are not likely to be
exhaustive) that capture economic reasons for change in the population
of rural areas:

1. Participation in the growth of the national economy means that
   rural areas will gain basic activities and will be sensitive to national
   conditions.
2. Increases in service sector jobs relative to total employment imply a
   decentralization of service activities.
3. Wage increases relative to other geographic areas increase labor-
   force participation rates and tend to initiate in-migration.
4. High labor-force participation rates tend to force in-migration to
   supply labor for additional employment.

5. Higher transport costs due to petroleum prices should tend to reduce shopping commutes, encourage decentralization of service activities, and increase employment through substitution of labor for energy.

Data and Analysis

Data concerning the first four hypotheses are to be interpreted here as indicative rather than conclusive because of the data sources and definitions used, and the preliminary nature of the data. The fifth hypothesis is discussed only in speculative and theoretical terms. Employment, earnings, and population data for 1969–1976 have been obtained from the Department of Commerce. Population estimates are those prepared for use in federal revenue-sharing programs by the Bureau of Census. Earnings and employment data have been obtained from the Bureau of Economic Analysis, which compiles these data from various sources and revises them continuously as the sources are made available.

Employment data are classified by location of the economic establishment. The earnings series are by establishment location except that residence adjustments also are reported for totals. Population is estimated for counties from indicators such as school enrollments and automobile registrations, and reflect place of residence rather than location of work. Thus, some data are for county of employment while other data are for county of residence. Counties are classified by urban population size and adjacency to metropolitan areas in order to minimize errors due to reporting, shopping and work commuting patterns. The use of an urban to rural continuum points to variation among rural counties even though this makes the data presentation more complex.

LINKAGE TO THE NATIONAL SYSTEM

Rural counties have become more closely linked to the national economy. They are affected by long-term expansions of the national economy as well as by business cycles. This can be demonstrated by noting changes in employment in basic economic sectors (excluding farmers, who do not respond to the same cyclical pattern). The proportion of counties with more than a 10% change in basic employment is shown in Figure 6.2 for each year from 1969 through 1976. The proportion in each urbanization class increasing more than 10% is shown in the upper part of the graph and the proportion decreasing in the lower frame. Superimposed over the bar graph is the index of U.S. industrial production. Three implications are apparent.

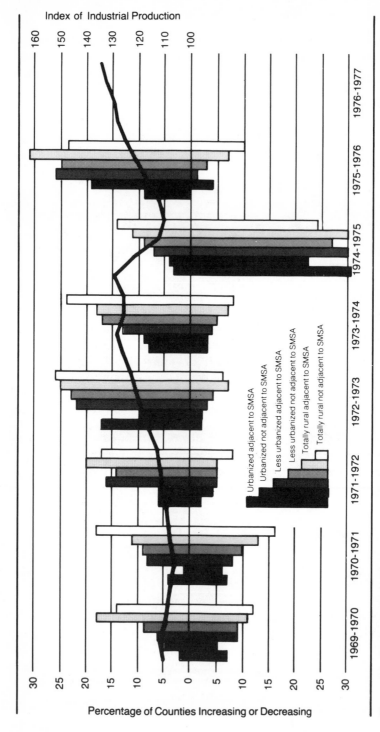

Figure 6.2. Percentage of U.S. rural counties increasing or decreasing by more than 10% in each year in wage and salary employment in basic economic sectors, by type of county. Basic sectors are farm, mining, manufacturing, heavy construction, railroad, motor freight, water transport, and federal employment. 1967 = 100. (Source: Bureau of Economic Analysis and Federal Reserve Bank of St. Louis.)

The first implication is that employment change is common to most nonmetropolitan counties regardless of their size or location. Large proportions of counties exhibit more than a 10% change in basic employment (Figure 6.2). In fact, 34% of adjacent rural counties with urban populations greater than 20,000 did so in 1974–1975: 31% declined and 3% gained more than 10%. The total proportions increasing and decreasing between 1974 and 1975 ranged from 26% of the urban nonadjacent counties to 41% of the counties adjacent to metropolitan centers. Over the whole period, many if not most counties have been subject to rapid changes in basic employment.

Year-to-year variability is a second noteworthy implication. During 1974–1975, 22–31% of rural counties registered decreases greater than 10% in basic employment. The very next year, from 9% to 31% had increases. Much of this short-term variation may be masked if absolute population or migration is used for urban–rural classes of counties, for long periods of time. That is to say, population and mobility are probably more dynamic than revealed by most aggregate-level analyses. The processes of population change through migration should account for short-term changes that accumulate over time to reveal a trend. Not only are changes in basic employment (and, following the model, population) widespread; they also are highly variable from year to year.

Perhaps the most important implication of the data in Figure 6.2 is that rural-area change in basic employment is firmly rooted in the health of the national economy. Gone are the days when the vagaries of agricultural prices and weather dominated rural economies. Periods of national recession are reflected in these data for rural counties. This can be seen by the association between changes in national industrial production and changes in the basic employment of rural counties. Furthermore, the cyclical variations evident in these data may be a part of the process of expansion of newer capacity in less urbanized areas at the expense of removing older and inefficient productive capacity from urban areas. For instance, rural manufacturing tends to be in the nondurable industries that enter recessions at a later time and emerge from recessions earlier than durable industries, such as automobiles and steel. Rural parts of the nation participate in long-term expansions of the national economy through incremental changes precipitated by business cycles. An increase in the comparative advantage of rural areas in basic sectors means more rapid growth in those areas than in the nation as a whole.

THE TREND IN SERVICE EMPLOYMENT

The level of service activity accompanying basic employment in an area is the second critical link in the general model. A change in basic

TABLE 6.2
Percentage of Service Jobs among all Wage and Salary Employment by Urban Class of County, 1969-1976

Population of counties	1969	1970	1971	1972	1973	1974	1975	1976
Metropolitan counties								
Greater than 1,000,000	61	63	64	65	65	65	67	67
250,000 to 999,000	55	56	58	59	59	60	62	62
Less than 250,000	56	57	59	59	60	60	62	62
Adjacent to metropolitan[a] counties								
Greater than 20,000	50	52	53	54	54	54	56	56
2,500 to 19,999	52	53	54	55	54	54	57	56
Less than 2,500	54	55	55	55	55	55	58	57
Not adjacent to metropolitan counties[a]								
Greater than 20,000	52	53	55	55	56	56	58	58
2,500 to 19,999	54	55	56	56	56	56	58	58
Less than 2,500	56	57	57	58	58	58	60	60

Source: Center for Social Data Analysis, Montana State University; Bureau of Economic Analysis, U.S. Department of Commerce data series.
Note: Service sectors include local transportation and utilities; wholesale and retail trade; financial, insurance, and real estate brokerage; and other business and personal services.
[a] Urban population in county.

employment has a magnified effect on total employment. Population (through retention and/or in-migration) is affected directly and, through the employment multiplier, indirectly. A stable multiplier through time means that a change in basic employment increases service employment once and no more. An increasing multiplier over time means that service employment increases even though the economic base is stabilized.

The ratio of service employment to total employment over time provides evidence that the basic-to-service employment mix is changing. The proportion of total employment in the service sectors has continued to increase through the 1970s, regardless of rural–urban residence (Table 6.2). There is no discernible pattern of change among urbanization classes. During this period, all areas show an increase of about the same magnitude. The proportion of service employment is over 50% in all of the urban–rural categories, and it has been increasing. The important point is that it is high in rural areas—that service activities are geographically dispersed much more than in the past.

In the past, service activities have been characterized as uniquely suited to centralized urban locations. Centralization is indicated by the differences in the proportions of service employment in urban centers—67% in urban centers with populations greater than 1 million compared with 56% and 57% in rural areas adjacent to urban centers. These data suggest that the degree to which service employment is centralized in urban places can easily be exaggerated because large differences among rural and urban areas are not evident.

The secular increase in service employment can be explained by income increases, the cost of transportation, service technology and innovations, and the composition and technology of basic industries. The bulk of service activities are in wholesale and retail trade and in professional services, especially health care and education. The demographic composition of the population affects the demands for education and health care.

A provocative fact is that up to 1970 service activities in rural areas increased as real prices of petroleum declined. Theory would have predicted the centralization of services as travel costs declined. Centralized services are thought to capture economies of size as their market areas are enlarged by lower travel costs of people on the fringes. This notion is discussed further in the section on petroleum prices.

THE TREND IN RELATIVE INCOME

Relative income potentials influence labor-force participation of residents, migration, and population change in different locations. Changes in labor-force participation will be treated in the next section. The ten-

TABLE 6.3
Annual Earnings of Wage and Salary Workers in Varying County Classes as a Percentage of Average County Earnings for the United States, 1969-1976

County class	1969	1970	1971	1972	1973	1974	1975	1976
Metropolitan counties								
Greater than 1,000,000	113	113	113	113	113	112	112	112
250,000 to 999,000	98	99	99	99	99	99	99	99
Less than 250,000	91	91	91	92	92	92	92	93
Adjacent to metropolitan counties								
Greater than 20,000 [a]	88	87	87	87	88	88	88	88
2,500 to 19,999	75	75	76	76	76	77	77	78
Less than 2,500	69	70	70	70	70	71	72	73
Not adjacent to metropolitan counties								
Greater than 20,000 [a]	83	83	84	84	85	85	86	86
2,500 to 19,999	74	74	74	74	74	75	76	77
Less than 2,500	67	66	67	67	67	68	69	69
Total all U.S counties	100	100	100	100	100	100	100	100

Source: Center for Social Data Analysis, Montana State University; Bureau of Economic Analysis, U.S. Department of Commerce data series.

Note: Weighted county averages by place of work.
[a] Urban population in county.

dency for out-migration to decrease and in-migration to increase in places with higher incomes is the major focus of this section.

Both average earnings and per capita personal income tend to be increasing more rapidly in rural parts of the nation than in urban areas. Furthermore, the patterns of change are approximately the same except that net farm income (after inventory adjustments) leaped 79% from 1972 to 1973, and then by 1976, returned to 1972 levels. Hence the farming entry distorts the rural income data. Average earnings of wage and salary workers are used to illustrate the decline in income differentials among rural and urban parts of the nation. The use of earnings data for wage and salary workers adjusts for the farm income anomaly.

Annual earnings of workers increased 64% between 1969–1976 in the most rural counties of the nation, from $4330 to $7109. The corresponding increase in large metropolitan centers was 58%, from $7299 to $11,521. The differential between these two extremes remains wide. In part, it may reflect cost of living and quality of life. But the differential is slowly closing (Table 6.3).

A relative increase in earnings per rural worker would tend to attract those people who would be more satisfied in rural areas. The relative earnings increase in rural areas may be due to changes in the industry mix of employment, productivity of workers, or the supply of labor. Regardless, earnings increases should tend to reduce out-migration and increase in-migration.

Relative earnings in counties containing no urban center and not adjacent to an urban area were 67% of the national average in 1969 and 69% in 1976. Earnings in the most rural county groups that were adjacent to an urban center increased four percentage points to 73% of the national average by 1976. Earnings in the largest metropolitan areas declined from 113% to 112% of the national average over the period.

It is noteworthy that personal income per capita in the largest urban areas declined from 117% to 114% of the national average, a larger loss than reflected in earnings. Personal income includes proprietor's income, interest, and transfer payments (Bluestone, 1979). Furthermore, the income differentials adjusted for cost of living would be less than those for earnings (Hoch, 1972a,b). The slow but persistent increase in relative incomes in rural places will tend to hold and attract population.

TRENDS IN LABOR-FORCE PARTICIPATION

Labor-force participation has been increasing in the nation, and rural areas have participated in that trend. Two decades ago, policymakers were concerned about unemployment, the discouraged worker effect, and out-migration from rural areas (Commission on Rural Poverty, 1967).

Rural areas no longer provide such a potential source of labor. An increase in employment opportunities in rural areas will require labor in-migration and a consequent population increase unless the rural labor-force participation rate continues to increase.

Labor-force participation rates for the period 1969–1976 are not available for the county groups considered here (Bureau of Labor Statistics, 1979). Instead, a more general measure is used, which, in many cases, may even be superior to the standard measure. Labor-force participation measures only persons who are currently in the labor force. The more general measure of employment relative to population measures the potential for entry into the labor force of persons who are not currently included in it. The demographic component averages out if aggregates of counties are used. Employment is reported by establishment location; hence commuting to jobs from residences in other counties distorts the ratios to some extent. For that reason, data are reported in Table 6.4 only for urban, adjacent rural, and nonadjacent rural county aggregates. At any rate, a high employment-to-population ratio can be interpreted unambiguously as a measure of high labor-force participation.

Employment per 100 population is high in the nation and has gradually increased (Table 6.4). The increase has been interrupted by periodic recessions. Rural counties not adjacent to urban centers also have high employment ratios. The ratios have tended to increase over the recent period, although the employment ratio slackens in rural counties in periods of recession. The data do not reveal clearly a more rapid increase in the employment ratio in rural counties than in urban areas, as in the past. The major conclusion from these data is that the employment ratio is already high in rural areas and is maintaining a high level.

Further employment increases in rural areas will require an increase in labor-force participation, in-migration, an upgrading of jobs, or a combination of all three. An increase in labor productivity through job upgrading could be an important contribution to rural development and would substitute for in-migration. In any case, earnings increases will accompany higher labor-force participation, in-migration, and job upgrading in rural areas. Rural areas will be competing directly with urban areas for additional labor, especially in the periods when the working age population is not increasing rapidly. It is problematic whether rural or urban areas will have a competitive advantage, and in which industries. The technology of the era, real wage differences among areas, and the predominant mix of industry and employment—given high incomes—all will influence the competition among regions and rural–urban areas of the nation. It is not apparent that rural areas will continue to attract and hold population. Most likely, the process will continue to

TABLE 6.4
Employment per 100 Population in Three Classes of Counties, 1969–1976

County class	1969	1970	1971	1972	1973	1974	1975	1976
Metropolitan counties	44	44	43	44	45	45	44	45
Nonmetropolitan adjacent to metropolitan counties	39	38	38	39	40	40	39	40
Nonmetropolitan not adjacent to metropolitan counties	40	40	40	41	42	42	41	42
Total all counties	43	42	42	43	44	44	43	44

Source: Center for Social Data Analysis, Montana State University; Bureau of Economic Analysis, U.S. Department of Commerce data series.
Note: Employment reported by place of establishment, and population by place of residence.

bring about a reurbanization of population, perhaps in patterns unlike those existing today. Much will depend upon petroleum prices and the cost of the transportation component of production and settlement patterns.

The continued participation of rural areas in the expansion of service industries and manufacturing will depend upon the distribution of economic activities within functional regions—the spatial structure of economic activities and the function of the regional centers. Transportation costs and scale economies are usually identified as the most important determinants of the spatial location of activities. Given a reversal of the trend of low petroleum prices, how will the distribution of economic activities in rural areas be affected? The reversal of each major long-term trend contributing to rural economic activity would be hypothesized only if transportation costs were the dominant and overriding cause of those trends in the first place. The question is whether high petroleum prices will cause basic sectors to shift to urban areas and service activities to centralize in urban places.

Rather than postulate a single variate causation such as higher transportation costs due to petroleum prices, one might summarize the numerous tradeoffs among variables affecting economic activities. The background trends in rural areas take on added meaning in view of the increase in energy prices during the past decade.

The fundamentals of aggregate energy economics in the national system, after all tradeoffs have been accounted for, are that labor substitutes for energy; that the rate of capital formation declines; and that labor productivity declines as energy prices increase (Berndt and Wood, 1979; Özatalay et al., 1979). An obvious case of labor substituting directly for energy is the 55-mile speed limit that requires truck and automobile drivers to take much more time traveling a given distance in order to conserve fuel. However, specific cases can be misleading because the net energy change in the aggregate system is what is summarized by the elasticities of substitution cited above. Capital and energy, on the other hand, are complements; thus where capital is used, energy also is used. Heating and cooling of buildings is an example, as is the transportation that must accompany the assembly of raw materials and distribution of finished products of manufacturing. As energy prices increase, less energy is used, and the rate of new capital formation declines. Finally, the combination of less capital and energy with labor implies a lower labor productivity than would otherwise be the case.

Whether these same effects will be felt in rural economies, which are only a subset of the aggregate national system, is a subject of speculation at this time. In the farm sector, these effects could imply a slower adoption of energy-consuming technology, and thus a slower release of labor from farming than in the past. This process would tend to stabilize employment in a basic economic sector. The food manufacturing sector should be affected in much the same way, and it is a uniquely rural industry. Processing, preparation, and transportation of food products consume the greatest amounts of energy expended in the farm-to-consumer chain. Volume trains with special negotiated rates can substitute for piggyback and truck transportation in shipping produce. Labor and the management of inventories can also substitute for refrigerated warehousing in the food industry.

The effect on manufacturing could be mixed. One of the original reasons manufacturers located in rural areas was that their transportation costs were relatively unimportant. These plants tended to be footloose in that they were not limited by spatial constraints, so higher gasoline costs may not affect the location matrix greatly. On the other hand, the industrialized regions of the nation have the highest process-energy costs. High process-energy costs could very well hasten the relocation of manufacturing to areas with less expensive energy, principally to areas with coal reserves that enable on-site generation of electricity. Thus, high energy costs could lead to a regional redistribution of some industries.

Possibly the greatest effect on the structure of the rural economy will be felt in the service sectors. Increased gasoline costs should reduce the number and length of shopping commutes by rural people. The resulting increase in demand for services locally would complement the long-term trend of increasing service activities in rural parts of the nation at the expense of regional service centers. A greater dependence on wholesaling and volume warehousing would contribute further to that effect. If so, the major function of regional service centers would be to provide enough excess capacity to absorb the variable service sector demands of its hinterland.

Finally, access by urban residents to distant recreation experiences has become much more expensive. This fact, in combination with a relatively high income elasticity for outdoor recreation, could hasten the migration of some recreation enthusiasts to amenity-rich areas. But, to the extent that urban places provide amenities, there could be a counterflow of rural residents to places nearer urban centers. It remains to be seen on balance what residential patterns will evolve.

Summary and Discussion

The objective of this chapter is to assess effects of changes in economic structure in rural areas on past and future population trends. Behavioral

patterns of businesses and people are the focal points of structural relationships. Economic structure responds to technology, innovation,
natural resource endowments, production alternatives, and income potentials. Selected indicators of structural change were identified in a
causal model to illustrate their effects. Recent population increases in
rural areas are consistent with trends in these indicators, and a continuation of rural structural changes implies further population growth.

A generalized causal model is described in which changes in basic
employment generate symbiotic service employment and population increases. Economic structure is reflected in the linkage coefficients of the
model. Each linkage by itself affects population, and the combined linkages taken together tend to be multiplicative. Past trends in the linkage
coefficients are consistent with population increases in rural areas. The
linkages reflect (a) the dispersal of basic economic activities into rural
areas; (b) the relative number of service activities associated with basic
activities; (c) relative wages; (d) labor-force participation rates; and (e) the
geographic distribution of service activities within rural regions.

A static model that assumes that the behavioral coefficients are constant would produce a change in population to new levels after an initial
"shock" and then a return to stability. The "shock" consists of expansions in basic economic activities in the area. An increase in basic employment such as manufacturing increases service employment, wages,
and the labor-force participation of indigenous people. The geographic
pattern of the service employment mix relative to total employment
changes little if at all. Static models explain only part of the population
increase of past years in rural areas. Rural areas where basic employment has remained relatively stable are also participating in the rural
turnaround.

Trends in the model linkages are reinforcing population increases in
rural areas. An increase in service employment relative to basic employment means employment growth even though the economic base
remains stable. Or if basic employment is increasing, then the multiplied
increase in service employment would be greater than indicated by a
static model. Increases in wages in rural areas relative to the remainder
of the nation mean people will tend to be attracted to rural areas. Increases in labor-force participation tend to aid retention of population.
Finally, service activities are tending to decentralize into sparsely settled
areas.

Aggregate data confirm trends in the key linkages. Basic employment
in rural areas was shown to be closely linked to the national economic
activity. Long-term national growth should continue to be reflected in
rural areas. The proportion of rural employment in the service sectors

has increased at a faster pace than in the nation as a whole. Earnings are increasing in rural areas at a slightly higher rate than in the nation. And, labor-force participation rates, as measured by employment-to-population ratios, are high in rural areas. A leveling off of participation rate increases could mean greater in-migration to rural areas as employment opportunities expand. The increase in gasoline costs should produce fewer and shorter shopping commutes, tending to decentralize service activities even more than at present.

The model has implications for future population changes and for research even though it is only meant to introduce the importance of structural changes. Future population changes in rural areas will depend on whether the same structural changes continue. Furthermore, the rate of change for each is important. Examples illustrate this point. As long as technology fosters the efficient delivery of services by small-size firms, service employment will continue to disperse. If technology favors large firms, centralized location patterns will probably develop. The difference between the two cases is reinforcement of growth in rural areas, or a cessation of that reinforcement effect. Another example is that of labor-force participation. A leveling off of the increase in labor-force participation rates in rural areas would mean that the potential for an indigenous labor supply would no longer exist. Any expansion of employment then would bring in-migration of labor and would change migration streams. Future rural population changes and the sources of people will be affected by the structural changes isolated in this model.

The research perspective implied by the model is broad, and the perspective can be useful to formulate and evaluate research procedures. The narrowest research focuses upon changes in basic employment as the cause of migration to rural areas. This explanation is partial at best because it cannot address population growth in areas that have stable or declining basic employment. Research on residential preferences also is partial because it does not explain how people are enabled to live out their preferences. Further, a study of only those who migrate casts aside the clear fact the largest segment of the population has decided, consciously or unconsciously, not to move.

The study of population distribution requires more than a simple analysis of people who move. Concentrating only on migrants is needlessly constraining. Clearly, population in a place can increase because people do not move; that is, as a result of population retention. The migration decision is only one part of a general and ongoing decision process by individuals. The same decision framework is used to decide whether to change jobs. Whereas migration is often treated as a discrete choice, it is in fact one part of a family of choices made on a continuous basis. The difference in research perspective is very meaningful. Careful choice of a time period for migration analysis is unnecessary if migration is conceived as a unique decision. The choice of a time period is critical if temporary conditions such as a national recession will affect decisions.

A general model that has a broad perspective should be capable of isolating root causes applicable in many different circumstances. Structural relationships should be ubiquitous to individual nations if change is truly rooted in technology, innovation, income, and energy prices. Thus, the migration patterns observed in the United States should also be in evidence in other countries.

Policy analyses require explanations of population distribution. The discussion of the rural population turnaround is a case in point because, first, doubt still exists that the trend of rural population may be permanent and second, if it is of a long-term nature, what actions will influence the outcome. A causal model points to linkages that may be altered inadvertently or purposefully through national policies. And, a causal model can identify the distribution of benefits and costs among participants on which political decisions are made. For example, although school enrollments are declining nationally, some rural areas may experience enrollment increases as population increases. Or school enrollments in urban areas could decline more rapidly than simple trend analyses suggest.

One purpose of this chapter is to foster further development of population distribution research and analyses. The model merely illustrates the effect of broad structural parameters on population distribution, and it is purposely simplistic. Greater utility of both forecasting and policy analyses should follow a synthesis of disciplines in the study of population distribution.

Acknowledgment

The statistical and conceptual aid of Larry Parcels is gratefully acknowledged.

References

Banks, Vera J.
  1978a *Farm Population of the United States: Current Population Reports.* Series P–27 No. 51. Washington, D.C.: U.S. Department of Agriculture, Economics, Statistics, and Cooperatives Service, and the U.S. Bureau of the Census.
  1978b *Farm Population Trends and Farm Characteristics.* Rural Development Research Report No. 3. Washington, D.C.: U.S. Department of Agriculture, Economics, Statistics, and Cooperatives Service.

Beale, Calvin L.
1975   *The Revival of Population Growth in Nonmetropolitan America.* ERS–605. Washington, D.C.: U.S. Department of Agriculture, Economic Research Service.
Beale, Calvin L., and Glenn V. Fuguitt
1978   "The new pattern of nonmetropolitan population change." Pp. 157–177 In Karl E. Taeuber, Larry L. Bumpass, and James A. Sweet (Eds.), *Social Demography.* New York: Academic Press.
Bender, Lloyd D., George S. Temple, and David M. O'Meara
1977   "A method of estimating relationships among migration streams and local economic conditions in the Northern Plains." Staff Paper 77-11. Bozeman: Montana State University, Department of Agricultural Economics and Economics.
Bluestone, Herman
1979   "Income growth in nonmetro America, 1968–75." Rural Development Research Report No. 14. Washington, D.C.: U.S. Department of Agriculture, Economics, Statistics, and Cooperatives Service.
Berndt, Ernst R., and David O. Wood
1979   "Engineering and econometric interpretations of energy–capital complementarity." *The American Economic Review* 69 (3):342–354.
Brown, David L.
1979   "Farm structure and the rural community." Pp. 283–287 In *Structure Issues of American Agriculture.* Agricultural Economics Report 438. Washington, D. C.: U.S. Department of Agriculture, Economics, Statistics, and Cooperatives Service.
Brown, David L., and Jeanne M. O'Leary
1979   *Labor Force Activity of Women in Metropolitan and Nonmetropolitan America.* Rural Development Research Report 15. Washington, D.C.: U.S. Department of Agriculture, Economics, Statistics, and Cooperatives Service.
Bureau of Labor Statistics
1979   *Employment and Earnings.* Vol. 26-28. Washington, D.C.: U.S. Department of Commerce.
Carlin, Thomas A., and Linda M. Ghelfi
1979   "Off-farm employment and the farm sector." Pp. 270–273 In *Structure Issues of American Agriculture.* Agricultural Economics Report 438. Washington, D.C.: U.S. Department of Agriculture, Economics, Statistics, and Cooperatives Service.
Carpenter, Edwin H.
1977   "The potential for population dispersal: A closer look at residential locational preferences." *Rural Sociology* 43 (3):354–370.
Commission on Rural Poverty
1967   *The People Left Behind.* Washington, D.C.: U.S. Government Printing Office.
Fuguitt, Glenn V., and Calvin L. Beale
1976   *Population Change in Nonmetropolitan Cities and Towns.* Agricultural Economics Report 323. Washington, D.C.: U.S. Department of Agriculture, Economic Research Service.
Fuguitt, Glenn V., and James J. Zuiches
1975   "Residential preferences and population distribution." *Demography* 12 (3):491–504.
Greenwood, Michael J.
1975   "Research on internal migration in the United States: A survey." *Journal of Economic Literature* 13 (2):397–433.
Hoch, Irving
1972a   "Income and city size." *Urban Studies* 9 (3):299–328.

1972b "Urban scale and environmental quality." Pp. 235-84 In Ronald G. Ridker (Ed.),
       Commission on Population Growth and the American Future. Research Report of the
       Commission on Population Growth and the American Future. Washington,
       D.C.: U.S. Government Printing Office.
Lowry, Ira S.
  1966   *Migration and Metropolitan Growth.* San Francisco: Chandler.
Miller, James P.
  1980   "Manufacturing and nonmetro job growth: The process of locational change."
         Washington, D.C.: U.S. Department of Agriculture, Economics, Statistics, and
         Cooperatives Service. Unpublished.
Nilsen, Sigurd R.
  1979   "Employment and unemployment statistics for nonmetropolitan areas." Back-
         ground Paper No. 33. Washington, D.C.: National Commission on Employment
         and Unemployment Statistics.
  1978   "How occupational mix inflates regional pay differentials." *Monthly Labor Review*
         101 (2):45-49.
Özatalay, Savas, Steven Grubaugh, and Thomas Veach Long II
  1979   "Energy substitution and national energy policy." *The American Economic Review*
         69 (2):369-371.
Petrulis, M. F.
  1979   *Growth Patterns in Nonmetro-Metro Manufacturing Employment.* Rural Develop-
         ment Research Report 7. Washington, D.C.: U.S. Department of Agriculture,
         Economics, Statistics, and Cooperatives Service.
Petto, Anthony C., and Lloyd D. Bender
  1974   "Outmigration: Responsiveness to local economic conditions in the Ozarks."
         Growth and Change 5 (2):8-12.
Schwarzweller, Harry K.
  1979   "Migration and the changing rural scene." *Rural Sociology* 44 (1):1-7.

7

Residential Preferences in Migration Theory[1]

JAMES J. ZUICHES

Introduction

The literature on migration is filled with theoretical models of move-ment between regions, metropolitan areas, and labor markets. Ritchey (1976) has classified most of these studies as labor mobility studies, dependent on ecologically aggregated statistics. As macroanalytic models, they are part of the tradition of gravity studies, intervening opportunity research, and place-to-place stream analysis. Alternatively, microanalytic models of mobility depend on individual statistics and focus on the compositional selectivities associated with migration. In his review of explanations of migrations, however, Ritchey suggests a third orientation: Its source of data is often a survey of individuals or families, but locational geographic characteristics are included as critical aspects of "the decision-making process of migration and [constitute] a critical determinant of migration and its direction [Ritchey, 1976:397]." It is within this "cognitive behavioral approach" that the rapidly increasing literature on residential preferences, expectations, and migration fits. Searching for the causes and explanations of migration in attitudinal data has not been a traditional or predominant mode of analysis. How-ever, as classic economic constraints to mobility decrease (Carpenter, 1977), the decision-making phase of the migration process takes on new relevance.

[1]This work has been supported by the Michigan Agricultural Experiment Station, (Jour-nal Article No. 9130), Project No. 1160, a contributing project to Western Regional Project W-118, and the College of Social Science, Michigan State University, and the Center for the Study of Metropolitan Problems, NIMH (MH23489-01).

163

New Directions in
Urban-Rural Migration

This chapter will briefly discuss the demographic events that have made the role of preferences in migration a critical issue in mobility analysis. Then a systematic review of the major studies of expected and actual mobility will serve as a link to the body of residential preferences literature that has been developing. The demographic, socioeconomic, and community characteristics associated with moving and with the selection of a preferred destination are examined. Finally, an application of this body of research to the turnaround in rural-to-urban migration trends will provide some clues to future population redistribution.

Changing Demographic Trends and Study Context

The revival of population growth in nonmetropolitan America has contributed to a resurgence of interest in the migration process. The secular decline in fertility rates further increased the importance of migration as a factor in community growth. Alternative explanations for the migration turnaround raised a number of issues, not easily explained by classical cost–benefit models, in which personal preferences for community attributes are postulated to outweigh economic motivations.

"The dominant geographic fact in the demography of the contermin-ous United States in the twentieth century has been metropolitan con-centration (Taeuber, 1972:72)." During the 1940s and 1950s, a seemingly endless stream of migrants left agricultural and rural areas to seek eco-nomic opportunity and a modern way of life in the metropolis. In the 1960s, a net of 2 million people moved to metropolitan counties; by 1970, 148 million people lived there, and the majority within metropoli-tan areas lived outside the central cities, in the suburban ring. Although the decentralization around central cities continued into the 1970s, and surburban areas gained 5.4 million people at the expense of central cities, the long-term trend of concentration had reversed. From March 1970 to March 1976, nonmetropolitan areas enjoyed a net in-migration of just under 2 million people (U.S. Bureau of the Census, 1975, 1977).

In this context, preference explanations for migration have been pro-posed, and the last 8–9 years have seen an extensive outpouring of empirical research. Unfortunately, the breadth and volume of this re-search require setting some limits to this review: topical, geographic, and temporal. Reviewing the crucial theoretical issues in population mobility (Morrison, 1973) and the current state of residential preference research, it became apparent that the problem is best divided into two analytic topics: (*a*) the relationship between expected movement and actual movement, and the attributes associated with these mobility types; and (*b*) the attributes associated with preferences for a specific destination, either metropolitan or nonmetropolitan. The first topic is a social demographic analysis of who moves (migrant selectivity); the second is a model of ecological selectivity according to subjective evaluations of spatial and place attributes.

Using the criteria of data availability on demographic, socioeconomic, and community attachment attributes of individuals who also expressed a preference for a specific location, an expected move, or an actual move meant that many state or local-area mobility studies were excluded. For example, most census-based studies were excluded due to a lack of focus on the intention and actual mobility decision. Similarly, no residential preference study prior to 1971 was found that treated these issues more than superficially (Fuguitt and Zuiches, 1975).

That researchers failed to see the merits of a decision model that includes migration expectations, destination selection, and actual mobility may reflect the influence of data-bound theoretical models. Prior models of migration behavior were guided by a place-to-place focus, an ecological–economic theory of locational imbalances, primarily with respect to sustenance needs, and based on aggregated data from census sources. Even human capital models often failed to measure the social costs and benefits of migration in favor of more easily operationalized economic costs and benefits. However, recent studies by DaVanzo (1976) and Williams and McMillen (1979) have introduced a social variant: location-specific capital with nonpecuniary operational indicators.

Furthermore, while the use of survey methodology to determine residential histories had been successful (Taeuber *et al.*, 1968), its use in eliciting migration preferences, intentions, and later mobility had not been attempted on a large scale until Lansing and Mueller's study in 1967. Since then, a number of national and state surveys have focused on expected or preferred mobility and, in some cases, respondents have been followed-up to determine actual mobility. Another problem within the survey context is that of question construction. While the population was concentrating in metropolitan areas, Gallup polls were showing that 49–56% of people preferred small cities, villages, or rural areas. A single, undifferentiated question on size-of-place preferred was used to capture the complexity of locational behavior. Such a question fails to distinguish a key relational characteristic of places people claim to prefer; that is, the proximity to other places, especially a large central city. The introduction of a distance-qualifier question also redefines the preference into a spatial framework that could be comparable to political or census definitions of geographic space, such as metropolitan versus nonmetropolitan counties. This small shift in conceptualizing locational preferences, coupled with the migration turnaround and a renewed interest in rural communities, contributed to many recent studies.

This review is limited to national or state studies, thus excluding the extensive work with high school students that Hansen (1973: Chapter 4) has reported and all of the work of USDA's Regional Research Project S–81, "Development of Human Resource Potentials of Rural Youth in the South and Their Patterns of Mobility" (Cosby and Howard, 1976), as well as the many community studies of rural sociologists (for examples of small-scale studies that included preferences, plans, and migration, see Bohlen and Wakely, 1950; Cowhig et al., 1960; Rieger et al., 1973; Yoesting and Bohlen, 1968). In general, this review excludes any study that did not report at least five of the basic associations discussed below in either bivariate or multivariate form.

The comparison procedures are basically an evaluation of the consistency in direction of results within longitudinal studies and, comparatively, across all studies. Where there are inconsistencies, the conditions under which results were obtained and mediating conditions may contribute to explaining the variations.

Although this review is not formally testing hypotheses, the evidence of trends across studies and consistency in results will lend additional support to theoretical work that has been done in the past. For example, the almost commonplace inverse association between age and mobility on the one hand, as represented in the relation between life-cycle attachments, and social, economic, and personal links to community, on the other, ought to be upheld by a consistent pattern across studies. Similarly, the relationships between attachment to one's community; satisfaction with its services, facilities, and environment; and duration-of-residence, the operational indicator for this sociological integration, are reasonably predicted to be inversely associated with preferring another location, planning, and moving (see Morrison, 1973; Stueve et al., 1975, for a detailed discussion of these issues).

Finally, a number of problems, inherent in a comparative discussion, are immediately apparent. The definitions of preferences for different size–location combinations are not completely replicated across studies; the metropolitan–nonmetropolitan definition also varies from the Bureau of the Census definition. Furthermore, questions about mobility vary in distinct ways with differing results, and the definition of mobility is often left to the respondent's interpretation, thus occasionally including local movement as well as moves of longer distance. These caveats will be noted when pertinent.

Preferences in Migration Research

Although this chapter is essentially a detailed review of the literature, three questions served as guides in the organization and integration of previous research: First, are preferences, expected mobility, and actual migration related in a systematic way? Second, can this relationship be detected in a comparison of the selectivities and differentials generally associated with mobility? Third, are these differentials in the demographic, socioeconomic, and community-attachment characteristics associated, not just with mover–stayer decisions but, more importantly, with choice of a destination? The third element, the differentials associated with an attraction to either metropolitan or nonmetropolitan destinations, will provide the basis for a discussion of future migration trends.

In what is probably the most comprehensive national study of migration behavior, Lansing and Mueller (1967) accented the inertia effect in relating preferences, expectations, and actual moves, yet a distinct systematic relationship was evident. First, "while 20 percent of families had some desire to move away, only 11 percent had at least some expectation of moving in the coming year, and only five percent actually did make a move in the year following the first interview [Lansing and Mueller, 1967:201]." Those preferring a move were 17 times as likely to plan such a move as were those preferring to stay. Similarly, a preference for a move resulted in four times the likelihood of a move; finally, planning to move resulted in a move for 41% of planners, but only 3% of nonplanners actually moved. It is this consistency that suggests that surveys of attitudes toward moving and particularly toward locational destinations of the move may contribute to modeling migration patterns and population redistribution.

If an association exists between attitudes, behavioral intentions, and behavior, it becomes possible to gain further insight into who the potential migrants might be by studying the socioeconomic, demographic, and other characteristics associated with mover–stayer decisions.

Studies of Mobility Expectations and Mobility

The 15 studies reviewed are well-known and often cited. However, for background purposes a summary of sample design, methods, analytic strategies, number of respondents, spatial and temporal units, and range of variables is provided.

Four of the national studies have their source in the "Five Thousand American Families—Patterns of Economic Progress" project organized under the auspices of the Survey Research Center at the Institute for Social Research, University of Michigan. Each study is treated separately because of differences in time-span covered, geographic units, and analytic distinctions. These studies are cited as Goodman (1974); Roistacher (1974); DaVanzo (1976); and Duncan and Newman (1975). The primary project is a panel study of income dynamics that has collected data and documented the social and economic changes that have occurred to 5000 American families between 1968 and 1975.

Duncan and Newman (1975) report on the mobility expectations of panel families in 1970, with a national sample of 3994 respondents. Using multiple classification analysis (MCA), these investigators evaluated the determinants of mobility expectations. Based on information gathered in the 1971–1972–1973 interviews, they determined actual mobility and, in a multivariate analysis, test the association between respondent attributes and the fulfillment of mobility expectations. These researchers developed a very useful typology of expected and actual mobility: (a) productive moves, or those "intended to change the future earnings stream of the family"; and (b) consumptive moves, or those "motivated by housing or locational considerations," such as neighborhood or community environments. All moves are voluntary because involuntary movers were excluded from the study. Duncan and Newman reported that only 4% expected to move for productive reasons and 18% for consumptive reasons. Only 12% actually moved, and the probability of a productively motivated move was slightly lower than that of a consumptive move. The design included the standard variables of age, sex, race, family size, persons per room, education, income, homeownership, duration in job, community satisfaction, and size of place, as well as changes in many of these variables.

Roistacher (1974) reported the association between planned and actual moves between 1968–1972 for the national sample ($N = 5060$). Within the first year, 20% of the families moved; by the fifth year this had increased to 35% and, by the sixth year, to 37%. The multivariate analysis (MCA) of actual mobility was conducted separately for both total moves and voluntary moves. Roistacher also used the productive–consumptive distinction for mobility but did not relate respondent attributes to these types. For the 5 years, she reported that consumptive moves outnumbered productive moves by three to one.

In a variation on the mobility analysis, Goodman (1974) focused on the local mobility of 4165 respondents during the period 1969–1971 and compared the characteristics of movers and stayers (using MCA). The inclusion here of Goodman's analysis provides a test of the patterns over a variety of mobility types.

DaVanzo (1976) reanalyzed the Income Dynamics Panel data but used only the 1605 white, married family units in which both spouses were present to evaluate human capital models of mobility. DaVanzo included both the decision to migrate and the choice of destination for 1971–1972 in a series of ordinary least-squares equations.

Two other national surveys were taken of U.S. families in 1971 and reported by Mazie and Rawlings in 1972 and Newman in 1974. Mazie and Rawlings presented the results of the survey sponsored by the Commission on Population Growth and the American Future. Their method of analysis, using a national sample of 1708 respondents, was presentation of marginal frequencies or bivariate tables. Newman, on the other hand, used MCA in analyzing the desire-to-move questions included in the national Quality of Life study ($N=2137$). Duration of residence was a crucial determinant of desired mobility that formed the core of her comparison.

The studies discussed so far were addressing the issue of expected and actual mobility. Approaching the problem from another perspective, Morgan (1978) and Zuiches and Fuguitt (1976) examined the preferences for another residential location and, by implication, expected mobility. Morgan directly asked about the desire to live elsewhere and then addressed the issue of preference for region and size of place. His analysis is based on waves of interviews in 1973–1974 collected by National Opinion Research Corporation (NORC) for the Continuous National Survey Program. The weighted sample size was 8562; the actual size was 3979. The principal mode of analysis was bivariate cross-tabulation of characteristics and desired mobility.

Zuiches and Fuguitt (1976) reported on the relationship between preferences and expected mobility based on a national survey in 1974, the NORC General Social Survey, to which they added questions. The multivariate analysis reported here is based on 1476 respondents and ignores preferences for specific location by using expectation of moving from one's current community in the next 3 years as the dependent variable.

Finally, for purposes of comparison, the pattern of bivariate relationships between mobility and sociodemographic characteristics is included for the United States, as reported by the Bureau of the Census (1975) in the Current Population Reports series for mobility during the period 1970–1975.

Preference Studies

The recent growth in research interest in residential preferences is a case of simultaneous activity from two different perspectives. Dillman and Dobash (1972), Carpenter (1975), and a number of others approached the question of preferences and migration from a community perspective. The issue was not only where do people want to live but also what are the services, facilities, and community characteristics that contribute to a high quality of community living. Zuiches and Fuguitt (1972) initiated their studies from a demographic perspective, trying to explain the discrepancy between previous popular survey results on residential preferences and the historical migration patterns. As Dillman (1973) has pointed out, both research perspectives have generated a body of internally consistent results, but differences between the results of each perspective need resolution since they vary dramatically, depending on question wording. Regardless of this discrepancy, the preferences literature provides a key new component in migration analysis. No longer is the respondent the neutral mover contrasted to the stayer; now, by choosing a preferred destination, the respondent has an origin and a potential destination. Comparisons of differentials between streams to selected destinations are now possible. For the comparisons discussed below, those preference studies that evaluated differentials between metropolitan and nonmetropolitan streams have been retained. Four state-wide surveys and one national survey provide the examples.

Dillman and Dobash (1972) conducted a mail survey of 3137 respondents in the state of Washington. The analysis treated size and regional community (essentially county) preferred, the characteristics of respondents preferring metropolitan versus nonmetropolitan communities, and public support for population redistribution policies. Carpenter (1975) replicated this study in Arizona with a comparable mail survey (N=1416), and analysis of socioeconomic characteristics of potential movers and nonmovers with metropolitan and nonmetropolitan preferences.

Zuiches and Fuguitt (1972) conducted their survey in the state of Wisconsin with face-to-face interviews of 906 respondents. Although their preferences question differed from Dillman and his colleagues, like the latter researcher(s) they directed their analysis at the characteristics of those preferring one or the other area. DeJong and Sell (1975) have reported on a preferences survey in Pennsylvania (N=1096), where a follow-up survey determined the ability of respondents actually to move to a preferred location. This study was also organized along a metropolitan–nonmetropolitan distinction. Finally, Zuiches and Fuguitt (1976) conducted a second national survey that combined preferences with mobility expectations, as discussed earlier.

Preferences, Expectations, and Mobility

The discussion of the association between individual characteristics and mobility expectations, actual behavior, and preferences for metropolitan or nonmetropolitan areas is based on the summary of the 15 studies in Tables 7.1 and 7.2. In these tables, the association between the characteristics and mobility is recorded as positive (+), negative (−), neutral—indicating lack of any relationship—(O), or curvilinear (U). A blank indicates that the association was not reported. Also, for the sake of brevity, single associations, that is, reports on a specific variable by only one study, were ignored.

The bottom line of Table 7.1 shows the percentages expecting to move (right panel) and actually moving (left panel). Two of the major U.S. studies, one in 1971 (Mazie and Rawlings, 1972) and the other in 1973–1974 (Morgan, 1978), asked the question: "If you could live anywhere you wanted, would you prefer to live here or elsewhere?" In these studies, 37% and 36%, respectively, responded, "elsewhere." In the 1974 national survey (Zuiches and Fuguitt, 1976), 35% also preferred a specific location other than their current location; however, only 21% expected actually to move in the near future. Similarly, the national surveys of expectation to move reported by Newman (1974) and Duncan and Newman (1975) found between 22–28% expecting a move.

The difference in question wording yields quite different results, primarily as a result of defining the issue more as a behavioral intention than simply as an attitude toward moving. Specifically, "prefer to live elsewhere" questions show about 35–37% responding positively, but "expect to move" questions show only 21–28% responding positively. (One might note that Lansing and Mueller phrased their question "like to move" and found 20% agreed.) My interpretation of these differences is that they are a consequence of a differential response to the questions focusing on a potential behavior, in this case, mobility, and an attitude toward mobility.

Examining the actual percentage of people who move also shows wide variations. Duncan and Newman (1975) reinterviewed their 1970 sample and found that from 1970 to 1973 only 12% (40% of expected movers) had actually moved and that two out of three of these moves were

TABLE 7.1
Associations Between Mobility, Expected Mobility, and Respondent Characteristics, United States

Respondent characteristics	Actual mobility					Expected mobility				
	1969–1971	1968–1972	1970–1973	1971–1972	1970–1975	1970	1971	1971	1973–1974	1974
Demographic										
Age	−	−[a]	+[c]	−[d]	−	−	−	−	−	−
Sex (male)	−	0[b]	0	0	+	0	+	0	+	0
Race (white)	−	0	0	0			−	−	+	0
Marital status (married)			−	−	+	−		−	−	−
Family size	+	+	−	−	−	+	+	+	+	
Persons/room		+	+	+	+	0				+
Socioeconomic										
Education	−	0	0	0	+	+	+	+	+	0
Income		−	0	0	+	0	+	+	+	
Employed (yes)	−	0	+	−		−	+	+	+	
Home ownership		−	−	−	−				−	−
Community										
Duration in residence or in job	−		0	0						−
Community satisfaction			−	−		0	u	+	+	−
Size of residence		0				0				0

Percent moving or
expecting a move   21   35   30   3.3   8.6   21   41   22   37   28   36   21

Sources: 1969-1971; Goodman (1974), Table 3.7.
1968-1972; Roistacher (1974), Tables 2.5, 2.13, 2.16.
1970, and 1970-1973; Duncan and Newman (1975), Tables 9.1, 9.3, 9.12.
1971-72; DaVanzo (1976), Table 3.
1970-1975; U.S. Bureau of the Census (1975).
1971; Mazie and Rawlings (1972), Table 6 (bivariate relations).
1971; Newman (1974), Appendix F, Table 3.
1973-1974; Morgan (1977), Table 14 (bivariate relations).
1974; Zuiches, unpublished multivariate analysis, NORC General Social Survey.

Definition of Symbols: 0 = no relationship
       + = positive relationship
       - = negative relationship
       U = curvilinear relationship
   Blank = not included by author(s)

[a]Total mobility
[b]Voluntary mobility
[c]Productive mobility
[d]Consumptive mobility

motivated by consumptive, that is, housing and locational, reasons. Goodman (1974) also followed a portion of the 5000-family sample and reported that from 1969 to 1971, 21% had made a local move. DaVanzo (1976) reported that 21% of married couples moved in the 1971–1972 period. The major report on the 5000-family study by Roistacher (1974) found that 35% of the original sample moved at least once in 5 years and 30% of these moves were listed as voluntary. Although the years covered are not identical, both Roistacher and the U.S. Bureau of the Census (1975) report for a recent 5-year period that over a third of American families have moved at least once.

Research has shown significant demographic and socioeconomic differentials in migration, and we would expect the same to be associated with preferences. In the remainder of this section, we review the association of individual attributes, first, with expected and actual mobility, and then with destination preferences.

First, the classic pattern of an inverse association between age and mobility was reported in 11 out of 12 studies. Only in the case of movers who sought to improve their financial well-being was age positively related to mobility. However, as Duncan and Newman pointed out, this result was not statistically significant.

The relationship between sex of respondent (or head of household) and mobility shows no consistent pattern. In most of the studies that perform a multivariate analysis, the relationship was essentially zero. In Morgan's analysis, males were more likely to expect to move but this relationship was reported without any controls for age, education, and so on. Duncan and Newman reported that female-headed (single-parent) families were more likely to move for productive reasons and male-headed for consumptive reasons, but the former was not statistically significant. The other studies using the same data set reported no relationship, so that Duncan and Newman's finding may be a consequence of their mobility typology. The pattern by race shows no consistency for either expected or actual mobility.

Two family indicators have a clear and consistent pattern. Unmarried, divorced, or widowed persons are more likely to expect to move or move than are married respondents. Similarly, the larger the family, the less likely it is to move. Counterbalancing this size-of-family relationship is a fairly consistent positive association of mobility with housing inadequacy on a persons-per-room basis.

Summarizing the demographic variables, the traditional life-cycle effects are apparent: (a) being young, an unmarried person, or a small family is associated with both expecting to move and actually moving; and (b) the mobility is often induced by changing family size affecting housing needs.

Within the category of socioeconomic indicators of mobility, educational attainment seems to be positively associated with mobility expectations, and in the Current Population Report, it was positively associated with actual mobility. However, in studies that perform multivariate analyses, the effect of education becomes questionable. Moreover, income levels seem another poor predictor of either expected or actual mobility. Unfortunately, employment status was reported in only six studies. The pattern revealed in those studies, however, shows an interesting reversal: employed were more likely to expect to move but the unemployed experienced higher actual mobility. Only the characteristic of home-ownership is consistently negatively associated with both expected and actual mobility.

Theories of residential attachment and stability and mover–stayer models of migration have emphasized the importance of duration or length of residence as a variable in migration analysis. Five out of seven studies that report length of residence or duration of job found an inverse association between either or both of these variables and mobility. The other community-attachment indicator often reported is level of satisfaction with the community. Whether the questions asked about general levels of satisfaction or satisfaction with specific aspects of the community, neighborhood, or services, those less satisfied are more likely to prefer a move and actually to move (again, in five out of six studies).

Do mobility rates vary by size of place? The pattern is mixed. In my own work, I have reported that mobility expectations increase with city size, as did Morgan (1978) and Mazie and Rawlings (1972); however, the multivariate analyses generally show no relationship between mobility expectations, mobility, and size of place. Newman (1974) reported a positive association between mobility and urbanicity, but the operationalization of this variable was very unclear.

Besides the life-cycle indicators, stayers do seem to be differentiated from movers by three community-attachment indicators: investment in a home, long-term residency in the community, and a degree of satisfaction with the community. Moreover, these are not simply surrogates for one another. In three of the studies all three variables contributed an independent degree of explanation, and in the other two studies that incorporated these same variables at least two did so.

Preferences for
Metropolitan—Nonmetropolitan Destination

The overview of compositional differences between movers, persons who expected to move, and nonmovers generates a number of hypotheses. However, accounting for the locational preferences of movers requires more than simply ascribing the above compositional differences to all migrant streams. Dillman and Dobash (1972) have argued that preferences for a major change in residential location (moving from metropolitan to nonmetropolitan locations or the reverse) increases as the amount of experience in the destination environment increases. Furthermore, the preference literature is unanimous in demonstrating that the single most preferred location is one's current location. Additionally, previous experience, with either childhood residence or prior mobility or travel, often provides a basis for judgment about the qualities and desirability of a specific community or type of community.

The contribution of socioeconomic status to explaining preferred location rests on a discussion of consumption patterns and job opportunities and on an assumption that the urbane values of higher-status respondents require large-city locations. Thus, people with higher socioeconomic status prefer to move to metropolitan areas. The nonmetropolitan migrant is sometimes assumed to be a return migrant and to be of lower status than the metropolitan origin population.

Life-cycle predictions also follow: Metropolitan preferences should be expressed by the young and nonmetropolitan by older ages. A corollary of this age relationship is that young families and unmarried individuals also can be expected to prefer the job and social opportunities of the larger cities.

Finally, "people are less likely to want to move to another community if they have a great deal invested in their present community"; that is, if they own their homes, are long-term residents, and have established social, occupational, and organizational ties to the community (Dillman and Dobash, 1972:15). It is this condition of location-specific capital that could operate both to impede migration and to facilitate it. In Chapter 8 of this book, multiple links and ties to the rural community through prior residence, family, and friends are identified as extremely important in the selection of a destination.

The patterns of relationships found in five preference surveys for those preferring but not residing in one or the other destinations are summarized in Table 7.2. These destinations are defined broadly as metropolitan and nonmetropolitan. Although no study claims to be perfectly congruent with census definitions of these areas, all imply a size and proximity to a large "central city" pattern of population distribution that approximates the statistical distinction.

Beginning with the demographic variable of age, a consistent inverse relationship held between age and preference for a metropolitan location. In all five studies, nonmetropolitan respondents who prefer a met-

TABLE 7.2
Associations Between Preferences for Mobility and Respondent Characteristics by Preferred Destination

	Preferred destination									
	Metropolitan					Nonmetropolitan				
Respondent characteristics	ARIZ. 1973	WASH. 1971	WISC. 1971	PENN. 1975	U.S. 1974	ARIZ. 1973	WASH. 1971	WISC. 1971	PENN. 1975	U.S. 1974
Demographic										
Age	−	−		−	−		0		−	−
Family size	−	+	−	+		+	+	+	−	
Socioeconomic										
Education	+	+	+	+	+	+	−	−	+	+
Income	−	+	−	−	−	+	−	+	+	+
Employed (yes)	−	−	−		−	+	+	+	+	
Home ownership	−	−	−	−		−	−		+	
Occupational status	+	+	+	+	+			−	+	+
Community										
Duration in residence	−	−		−	−		−		−	−
Community satisfaction	−	−		−	−		−		−	−
Size of prior residential experience	+	+	+	0	+	+	+	+	+	+

Sources: Arizona, 1973; Carpenter (1975), Table 10 recalculated.
Washington, 1971; Dillman and Dobash (1972), Tables 15,16,17.
Wisconsin, 1971; Zuiches and Fuguitt (1972), Tables 3,4,5.
Pennsylvania, 1975; DeJong and Sell (1975), Tables 10,11,12.
U.S., 1974; calculated by author from 1974 NORC General Social Survey.

ropolitan area are younger than those who prefer their current nonmetropolitan residence. The potential stream from metropolitan to nonmetropolitan areas, however, is mixed; two studies show those preferring a nonmetropolitan destination to be older, two show them as younger, and one shows no difference in comparison with those preferring not to move.

Similarly, the relationship between family size and destination is mixed across the three studies that incorporated this variable of family size. An interesting pattern appears that involves socioeconomic status. Those preferring a metropolitan move are better educated, have higher occupational status, but in general (four out of five) have a lower current income level than those preferring no move. However, the neatness of this result is not duplicated for nonmetropolitan destination preferences. Educational attainment and occupational status have mixed results, and in four out of five surveys, income level is positively associated with a nonmetropolitan preference.

The differentials in income for comparable education and occupational attainment between the two sectors might provide an explanation for this anomaly. Another explanation might be that none of these studies used more than a bivariate analysis. Multivariate analysis might have cast doubt on one or more of these variables. DeJong and Sell (1975) have performed some multivariate analyses, but the comparisons and variables do not match those used here.

Employment status—that is, whether employed or unemployed—was reported in three studies. Nonmetropolitan unemployed preferred a metropolitan move more than the employed, but the pattern seems to reverse for metropolitan residents preferring a more distant location. However, only three studies detailed this information and I am not prepared to make much of it. Similarly, home-ownership status, a powerful variable in migration analysis, has not been commonly reported by preference researchers.

The most consistent and probably most important set of relationships is found in community attachment and experience. In every study for both metropolitan and nonmetropolitan destinations, long-term residency and high levels of community satisfaction are inversely associated with preferences for a residential relocation. Also, in seven out of eight tests, prior residential experience in an area is postively associated with a preference for mobility to the area. The one anomaly is perhaps a result of comparing broad groups of city sizes: I suspect the study by DeJong and Sell (1975), would have shown a positive relationship if they had used smaller city-size classes.

An obvious criticism of all the preferences research is that it has not subsequently reinterviewed respondents to determine their success at achieving preferences. DeJong and Sell's work (1977) is the exception. In a follow-up interview 1 year after their preference survey, DeJong and Sell found that 3% of their sample had moved to a nonmetropolitan setting. Comparing the nonmetropolitan-direction movers, with the nonmovers, these researchers found the nonmetropolitan movers were younger, better educated, in higher occupational statuses, and in higher income classes. Although these movers were nuclear families, they tended to be smaller than nonmover families, as one might expect from the age structure of the movers. With the exception of family size of movers, the other characteristics were predictable from DeJong's earlier preference studies in Pennsylvania.

Two other studies have described compositional differences of both metropolitan and nonmetropolitan streams in some detail. These studies, by DeJong and Humphrey (1976) and Zuiches and Brown (1978), use census sources, so not all variables of Table 7.2 are replicated. However, we can at least examine the sociodemographic characteristics of each stream to resolve some of the ambiguities of Table 7.2.

In their analysis of population redistribution in Pennsylvania during the period 1965–1970, DeJong and Humphrey (1976) reported that migrants to metropolitan areas were younger, better educated, had a larger family size, and were more likely to be employed and to be white-collar workers than nonmetropolitan nonmovers. Income differences were nonexistent. Migrants to nonmetropolitan areas displayed the same differentials except for family size, which was not significantly different from metropolitan nonmovers. These researchers noted that this selectivity also applied to the stream comparisons, with the metropolitan-to-nonmetropolitan migrant stream being younger and of a higher socioeconomic status than the metropolitan-directed stream.

A comparable pattern has been shown nationally for 1970–1975 by Zuiches and Brown (1978) and by Wardwell (1977). Migrants to nonmetropolitan areas tended to be younger, better educated families rather than single individuals, and to be in white-collar occupations when compared with either origin or destination nonmover populations. Income differences again were negligible.

Comparing these analyses with the patterns derived from Table 7.2, it is clear that the inverse association between age and mobility pertains for each destination and that some of the positive relationships between age and nonmetropolitan preferences need to be re-evaluated. Perhaps there are specific factors in Wisconsin and Arizona that can help explain the positive relationships. Both states have experienced extensive retirement migration, which may dominate the expected stream of nonmetropolitan migrants. With respect to income differences, the preference surveys were mixed. Actual mobility showed no real differences, except in the Pennsylvania longitudinal study. However, educational and occupational status were consistently positively associated with mobility in both directions. Again, the preference surveys revealed this pattern for metropolitan migration, but not for nonmetropolitan migration. This lack of congruence could mean that nonmetropolitan preferences may not be as intensive and well-formed as metropolitan preferences.

Since these census-based replications do not include duration in residence, community satisfaction, or prior residential experience—three of the more important predicators of preferences and mobility—use of such studies as a test for comparing stream composition of preferred and actual mobility is difficult. However, on the basis of sociodemographic attributes, using surveys to predict the composition of metropolitan streams seems justified.

This review of the literature on preferences, migration expectations, migration, and the compositional characteristics associated with each attitude and activity can be summarized

1. Demographic (age, family size, and persons per room) and community-attachment (satisfaction and duration in residence) characteristics were systematically related to expected and actual mobility, but socioeconomic variables were not. Home ownership clearly lessens the expectations for and probability of moving, and educational attainment is generally positively associated with mobility. However, income and employment status show mixed results.
2. Demographic, particularly age, socioeconomic indicators, and community attributes were consistently (across all studies) associated with preferring a metropolitan location, but only the community-attachment attributes were consistent for nonmetropolitan preferences.
3. In a limited comparison of compositional association with recent migration statistics for the United States and Pennsylvania, preference surveys do seem to provide some clues to who will migrate to nonmetropolitan areas.

This partial resolution with respect to nonmetropolitan areas makes me uneasy about predicting future migration patterns based solely on preferences. But linking the preference-based explanations with the changing structural conditions in nonmetropolitan areas as Beale (1975), Wardwell (1977), and Carpenter (1977) have done strengthens the argument. The decentralization of industry, increased transportation accessibility, rising recreational opportunities and the growth in service jobs, increased disposable income, and improved retirement benefits have all contributed to the realization of locational preferences. Whenever structural changes lessen the economic and life-style differentials between areas and permit greater locational flexibility, the preferences of mobile segments of the population are more likely to be achieved. Just as in the explanations of migration in developing countries, "economic factors are necessary conditions for migration (to occur) while sociological and life style factors are sufficient conditions regulating migration incidence [Findlay, 1977:14]."

Preference surveys suggest that there is a sizable reservoir of potential migrants. However, we need to devote further study to why these nonmovers fail to act on their preferences and to their compositional characteristics.

The act of moving makes it easier to move again, especially if the differences between expected conditions and reality are great. For example, Zuiches and Fuguitt (1976) showed that half of those who preferred nonmetropolitan areas would give up their preference when potential income declines were a condition of the move. Similarly, in Arizona, although a majority (52%) preferred living in a community of fewer than 50,000 people, only 3% were interested in moving if it involved loss of income or lengthy commuting (Carpenter, 1977). If recent movers to nonmetropolitan areas discover inadequacies of income, services, and social, recreational, and job opportunities, subsequent remigration to the metropolitan areas is distinctly possible (see Chapter 9).

This expectation is borne out in Table 7.3, based on the 1974 NORC national survey. When respondents are classified by mobility status, duration of residence, and current residence, recent migrants to the large cities and to the small cities and rural areas over 30 miles from a large city (essentially nonmetropolitan areas) are more likely than long-term residents to prefer another major relocation. These differences are even more dramatic when we look at the percentage expecting a move from their current community in the next 3 years. In contrast to long-term residents, recent in-migrants to nonmetropolitan areas are twice as likely to expect to move again. Large city in-migrants are also expecting substantially greater mobility than nonmovers, but those living in suburban locations show only minor differences.

According to the Bureau of the Census, 6.7 million people moved into nonmetropolitan areas during 1970–1975. Have these recent movers satisfied their preferences or might we expect additional mobility, a counterstream of metropolitan return migration? The implication of

TABLE 7.3
Preferences and Expected Mobility by Actual Residence and Mobility Status, 1970–1974

Mobility status	Actual residence, 1974		
	Large cities (50,000+ Population)	Small cities, rural (within 30 miles of large city)	Small cities, rural (over 30 miles to large city)
Percentage preferring location other than current residence:			
Recent in-migrants[a]	66	13	37
	(132)[b]	(161)	(68)
Nonmovers	52	19	26
	(483)	(393)	(239)
Percentage expecting to move from current location in next 3 years			
Recent in-migrants[a]	43	27	44
Nonmovers	16	21	22

Source: 1974 NORC General Social Survey, with additional preference and mobility questions.
[a] 1970–1974.
[b] Number in parentheses.

Table 7.3 is that among many recent migrants there is still a lack of congruence between preferences and actual residence, particularly in the large cities and nonmetropolitan areas. This potential for further mobility does not discount the structural changes that have made the turnaround a reality. The point is made simply to demonstrate the complexity of applying preference data to migration analysis.

One might further distinguish between recent in-migrants with no prior experience in the destination and return migrants. DaVanzo (1976) has noted that families, even those with a history of mobility who finally move to a place they have lived in before, are less likely to move (again) than families who have never moved. Since this result occurred at the level of interdivisional migration, its substantiation for nonmetropolitan areas suggests a high retention of return migrants.

Finally, while nonmetropolitan areas have been able to attract in-migrants, and recent surveys indicate that these areas remain highly preferred, retention of longer-term residents is also a crucial component of the turnaround. While the preference surveys all show a desire for life in the country or small towns, the single most preferred location remains one's current location. Rural residents strongly desire to stay where they are living.

Since the structural and preference factors affecting nonmetropolitan growth have not changed, we might expect continued slow growth in these areas, but it will be a growth accompanied by large flows of population. It is the analysis of population composition—who these movers are—that provides further insight into the causes and impacts of this mobility. This review has shown some of the continuities in empirical migration research; unfortunately, the gaps remain.

Discussion

Ritchey (1976) suggests future theoretical development on migration requires an integration of areal structural variables, the status characteristics of individuals, and the values or attitudes of individuals. It is the social psychological attributes that "are rarely considered empirically in migration research [Ritchey, 1976:399]." The surge of research interest in residential preferences has now provided an empirical base with respect to the interrelationships of preferences, expectations, and mobility. However, as noted above, preferences for specific destinations are associated with particular sociodemographic characteristics of potential migrants. Further conceptual and empirical work needs to be done.

The next steps in conceptual development should focus on what preferences for a size–location characteristic of place really mean. Insofar as size–location is a surrogate for other attitudes, there may be better measures of the attitudinal configuration affecting mobility. What are the qualities in a community that people expect, and are these expectations realistic? It is necessary to evaluate attitudes, both before and after migration occurs, to understand the effect of changes in location on attitudes. How are preferences related to satisfaction with one's community? Does satisfaction or preference change over time, as one experiences different locations? How do preferences relate to stages of the life cycle?

One conceptual development is the incorporation of preferences, moving plans, and migration into a research design that captures the elements of the cognitive–behavioral model. In such a model, the decision to move is analytically divided, first, into a phase of evaluation of one's current residence, in which a threshold of dissatisfaction may be reached, bringing the household to consider the possibility of a move. The second stage involves the search-and-selection procedures and includes a comparative evaluation of alternative sites. It is at this stage that locational preferences play a role in the selection process and that, finally, a decision to move is made (see Speare *et al.*, 1974, for an elaborate discussion of this model in intraurban mobility). The migration literature shows that expectations for mobility are associated with higher probabilities for future mobility, in contrast to a lower probability of a move for those not expecting one. Similarly, one might argue that a preference to live elsewhere than one's current residence would be associated with expectations to move and future actual mobility. In classic syllogistic form, preferences for residential relocation ought to be associated with future mobility.

Such a model has been tested in two recent papers. Preference status, that is, a discrepancy between current and preferred size–location characteristics of residential location, was shown to play an important role in the migration decision-making process (Heaton *et al.*, 1979). This role is additional to the effect of satisfaction with one's community and the usual selectivities associated with migration expectations: age, length of residence, home ownership, educational attainment, and size of current residence (Frederickson *et al.*, 1980). Although satisfaction with one's residence and preference status are highly interrelated, each has an independent effect on intentions to move.

Unfortunately, without additional post-migration follow-up studies such as DeJong and Sell (1977) and Zuiches and Rieger (1978) have completed, there remains an uncertainty about the ability of respondents to achieve a preferred destination. Residential redistribution was shown to be associated with preferences in the longitudinal study of rural youth in Michigan, but attitudes were often modified in the wake of one's residential experiences. Similarly, in the Pennsylvania study, although 79% of the intercommunity movers went in the direction of their preferences, so much intraurban mobility occurred that overall only 14% of the total sample achieved their preferences (Fredrickson *et al.*, 1979, data provided by DeJong). The less than total success at predicting direction of movers' preferences suggests a further disaggregation of nonmovers and movers to determine the historical as well as more proximate causes of moves. The discovery of cohort and life-cycle effects on preferences similarly argues for such disaggregation. Methodologically, the study of migration at the microanalytical level requires longitudinal studies that extend the work of these early surveys. A standardization of questions and a systematic evaluation of the reliability and validity of the questions currently used is also required. Decomposing the migration streams into return movers, new movers, and retained nonmovers means using survey questions appropriate to the conditions of the respondent.

The organization of a research program that complements the studies of the Current Population Survey and other census studies would provide the basis for integrating individual and aggregate analysis. Complementing large-scale national and state surveys with in-depth, small-area case studies would provide a valuable counterpoint, as both national estimates of mobility trends and theoretical insight would be possible. A first step in this direction would be the incorporation of a carefully designed set of preference questions in the Annual Housing Surveys. As the importance of migration increases in redistributing the population, the gaps in theoretical understanding and empirical information need attention at both national and local levels.

Acknowledgments

I appreciate the suggestions and comments of Bernard Finifter, William Frey, and Peter Rossi.

References

Beale, Calvin L.
    1975   "The revival of population growth in nonmetropolitan America." Washington, D.C.: U.S. Department of Agriculture, Economic Research Service, ERS–605.
Bohlen, Joe M. and Ray L. Wakeley
    1950   "Intentions to migrate and actual migration of rural high school graduates." *Rural Sociology* 15 (December):328–334.

Carpenter, Edwin H.
1975   *Residential Preference and Community Size: Implications for Population Redistribution in Arizona.* Research Report No. 7. Tucson: University of Arizona, Department of Agricultural Economics.
1977   "The potential for population dispersal: A closer look at residential locational preferences." *Rural Sociology* 42 (Fall):352–370.
Cosby, Arthur G. and William G. Howard
1976   *Residential Preferences in America: The Growing Desire for Rural Life.* Rural Development Seminar Series. Washington, D.C.: U.S. Department of Agriculture Extension Service.
Cowhig, James, Jay Artis, J. Allan Beegle, and Harold Goldsmith
1960   *Orientations toward Occupation and Residence: A Study of High School Seniors in Four Rural Counties of Michigan.* East Lansing: Michigan State University Agricultural Experiment Station, Bulletin 428.
DaVanzo, Julie
1976   "Why families move: A model of the geographic mobility of married couples." Santa Monica: The Rand Corporation, R–1972–DOL.
DeJong, Gordon F. and Craig Humphrey
1976   "Selected characteristics of metropolitan to nonmetropolitan area migrants: A study of population redistribution in Pennsylvania." *Rural Sociology* 41 (4):526–538.
DeJong, Gordon F. and Ralph R. Sell
1975   "Residential preferences and migration behavior." Chapter in *Population Change and Redistribution in Nonmetropolitan Pennsylvania 1940–1970.* A Report Submitted to NIH, HEW. University Park, Pennsylvania: Population Issues Research Office.
1977   "Population redistribution, migration, and residential preferences." *Annals,* 429:130–144.
Dillman, Don A. and Russell P. Dobash
1972   *Preferences for Community Living and Their Implications for Population Redistribution.* Pullman: Washington State University, Agricultural Experiment Station, Bulletin 764.
1973   "Population distribution policy and people's attitudes: Current knowledge and needed research." Paper prepared for the Urban Land Institute under a grant from U.S. Department of Housing and Urban Development.
Duncan, Greg J. and Sandra Newman
1975   "People as planners: The fulfillment of residential mobility expectations." Chapter 9 In Greg J. Duncan and James N. Morgan (eds.), *Five Thousand American Families—Patterns of Economic Progress.* Vol. III. Ann Arbor: University of Michigan, Institute for Social Research.
Findlay, Sally
1977   *Planning for Internal Migration: A Review of Issues and Policies in Developing Societies.* U.S. Bureau of the Census, ISP–RD–4. Washington, D.C.: U.S. Government Printing Office.
Fredrickson, Carl, Tim Heaton, Glenn V. Fuguitt, and James J. Zuiches
1980   "Residential preferences in a model of migration intentions." *Population and Environment: Behavioral and Social Issues* (in press).
Fuguitt, Glenn V. and James J. Zuiches
1975   "Residential preferences and population distribution." *Demography* 12 (3):491–504.

Goodman, John
  1974   "Local residential mobility and family housing adjustment." Chapter 3 In James
          N. Morgan (ed.), *Five Thousand American Families–Patterns of Economic Progress.*
          Vol. II. Ann Arbor: University of Michigan, Institute for Social Research.
Hansen, Niles M.
  1973   *Location Preferences, Migration and Regional Growth.* New York: Praeger.
Heaton, Tim, Carl Fredrickson, Glenn V. Fuguitt, and James J. Zuiches
  1979   "Residential preferences, community satisfaction, and the intention to move."
          Demography, 16 (4):565–573.
Lansing, John B. and Eva Mueller
  1967   *The Geographic Mobility of Labor.* Ann Arbor: University of Michigan, Institute for
          Social Research.
Mazie, Sara Mills and Steve Rawlings
  1972   "Public attitude toward population distribution issues." U.S. Commission on
          Population Growth and the American Future. Pp. 599–616 In Sara Mills Mazie
          (ed.), *Population Distribution and Policy.* Vol. V, Commission Research Reports.
          Washington, D.C.: U.S. Government Printing Office.
Morgan, David
  1978   "Patterns of population distribution: A residential preference model and its
          dynamic." Research Paper No. 176. Chicago: University of Chicago, Department
          of Geography.
Morrison, Peter A.
  1973   "Theoretical issues in the design of population mobility models." *Environment
          and Planning* 5:125–134.
Newman, Sandra
  1974   *The Residential Environment and the Desire to Move.* Ann Arbor: University of
          Michigan, Institute for Social Research.
Rieger, Jon H., J. Allan Beegle, and Philip N. Fulton
  1973   *Profiles of Rural Youth: A Decade of Migration and Social Mobility.* Research Report
          178. East Lansing: Michigan State University Agricultural Experiment Station.
Ritchey, P. Neal
  1976   "Explanations of migration." Pp. 363–404 In Alex Inkeles (ed.), *Annual Review of
          Sociology.* Vol. 2. Palo Alto: Annual Reviews, Inc.
Roistacher, Elizabeth
  1974   "Residential mobility." Chapter 2 In James N. Morgan (ed.), *Five Thousand
          American Families—Patterns of Economic Progress.* Vol. II. Ann Arbor: University of
          Michigan, Institute for Social Research.
Speare, Alden, Jr., Sidney Goldstein, and William Frey
  1974   *Residential Mobility, Migration and Metropolitan Change.* Cambridge, Mas-
          sachusetts: Ballinger Press.
Stueve, Ann, K. Gerson, and Claude S. Fischer
  1975   "The structures and determinants of attachment to place." Paper presented at
          the annual meetings of the American Sociological Association, San Francisco,
          August.
Taeuber, Irene B.
  1972   "The changing distribution of the population in the United States in the twen-
          tieth century." U.S. Commission on Population Growth and the American Fu-
          ture. Pp. 31–107 In S. M. Mazie (ed.), *Population Distribution and Policy.* Vol. V.
          Washington, D.C.: U.S. Government Printing Office.

Taeuber, Karl E., Leonard Chiazze, Jr., and William Haenszel
  1968   *Migration in The United States: An Analysis of Residence Histories.* Public Health Monograph No. 77. Washington, D.C.: Public Health Service.
U.S. Bureau of the Census
  1975   *Mobility of the population of the United States, March 1970 to March 1975.* Current Population Reports, P–20, No. 285. Washington, D.C.: U.S. Government Printing Office.
  1977   *Geographical mobility: March 1975 to March 1976.* Current Population Reports, P–20, No. 305. Washington, D.C.: U.S. Government Printing Office.
Wardwell, John M.
  1977   "Equilibrium and change in nonmetropolitan growth." *Rural Sociology* 42 (Summer):156–179.
Williams, James D. and David B. McMillen
  1979   "The utilization of location-specific capital in migration decision making." Paper presented at the Annual Meetings of the Population Association of America, Philadelphia, April.
Yoesting, Dean R. and Joe M. Bohlen
  1968   "A longitudinal study of migration expectations and performance of young adults." *Journal of Human Resources* 3 (Fall):485–498.
Zuiches, James J. and Glenn V. Fuguitt
  1972   "Residential preferences: Implications for population redistribution in nonmetropolitan areas." U.S. Commission on Population Growth and the American Future. In Sara Mills Mazie (ed.), *Population Distribution and Policy.* Vol. V, Commission Research Reports. Washington, D.C.: U.S. Government Printing Office.
  1976   "Residential preferences and mobility expectations." Paper presented at the annual meetings of the American Sociological Association, New York, August.
Zuiches, James J., Glenn V. Fuguitt, and David L. Brown
  1978   "The changing character of the nonmetropolitan population, 1950–1975." Chapter 4 In Thomas R. Ford (ed.), *Rural USA: Persistence and Change.* Ames: Iowa State University Press.
Zuiches, James J., Glenn V. Fuguitt, David L. Brown, and Jon H. Reiger
  1978   "Size of place preferences and life cycle migration: A cohort comparison." *Rural Sociology* 43 (4):618–633.

8

Migration Decision Making among Nonmetropolitan-Bound Migrants[1]

JAMES D. WILLIAMS
DAVID BYRON McMILLEN

Introduction

The concept of a single decision to move is artificial. Migration decision making is a complex process involving numerous decisions. At the least, we find migration models that separate deciding to leave (out-migration) from the process of *destination selection* (in-migration). The complex conceptualization of the migration decision-making process is not a new idea in migration literature. However, in survey research the separate measurement of the evaluative bases for multiple decisions is by no means standard practice. Our concern is with the substantive misinterpretations that can result from inferring migration causes from simplistic "reason for moving" survey questions. Our analysis uses *separate operationalizations* of bases for *in-migration* and *out-migration* and demonstrates their usefulness in providing a more complete view of individual-level causes of migration.

We will argue that there is a heightened need to improve upon the "why did you move" approach when surveying migrants who are likely to have moved for nontraditional reasons, although our suggestions are generally applicable to any survey including "reason for moving" questions. Nontraditional migrants are particularly important "when we confront those hundreds of remote, thinly settled, and emphatically bucolic counties for whose recent demographic resurgence there is no halfway plausible economic rationale [Zelinsky, 1977: 176]."

[1]This chapter is a revised version of Illinois Agricultural Economics Staff Paper 78–S7, dated December 1978.

189

Although we intend to demonstrate the utility of our approach with particular reference to nonmetropolitan amenity-area in-migrants, it may be noted that our suggestions could prove important in the future for surveys of all migrants. Indeed, if future national flows increasingly come to reflect nontraditional evaluative bases for migration behavior, then national surveys would benefit from the greater specificity we propose for operationalizing migration motivations.

Micro-Perspectives on Migration Motivations

To date there has been little systematic concern with the wording of questions designed to elicit the evaluative dimensions of migration decision making. However, it is clear that some scholars, and geographers in particular, view migration decision making as involving more than one decision. If more than one decision is involved, then more than one behavior must be explained, and the causes of each behavior need not be the same. Reason structures obtained from respondents for different migration-related decisions may themselves differ. Divergent distributions of reasons reflect the differing bases of causation for the different behaviors involved.

For intraurban mobility in particular, Brown and Moore (1970) have suggested that migration involves, for a significant number of migrants, at least two decisions: (a) the decision to leave an area of origin; and (b) the decision of where to move (see also Roseman, 1977). The causal bases of the first help explain out-migration while the causal bases of the second decision help explain in-migration when evaluated at point of origin and point of destination, respectively. Brown and Moore are not alone in their efforts; we find the distinction between leaving and destination selection, for local migrants, in the work of Speare et al. (1974); Quigley and Weinberg (1977); and Rossi (1955). The work of Speare et al. (1974) also exemplifies successful empirical use of the separation of decisions for moving relatively short distances.

At the individual level of analysis, and for long-distance migration, the most extensive conceptualization of the migration decision-making process is found in Wolpert's (1965) work. The concept of *place utility* (satisfaction with an area) is central to this approach, and Wolpert's theoretical statements explicitly suggest three decisions in the process. If place utility is sufficient at a current location, the individual implicitly decides not to consider migration. But, if place utility is relatively low, a person may consider moving and subsequently decide to move. Once this decision is made, destination-selection considerations become paramount. However, we have stated this process in general terms. These decisions are not necessarily made in such perfect succession, and the process is probably not so uniformly rational as the theory might suggest. Unfortunately, most applications and extensions of Wolpert's work have been in the area of intraurban and local migration. Research has shown that the determinants of short-distance moves differ from those of long-distance mobility.

Migration is but one of the possible responses to the disequilibrium that results from dissatisfaction at a place of residence. Alternatively, people may restructure the environment to achieve desired ends, or they may alter their desires and expectations. The stresses that cause an individual to consider migration among alternative behaviors, are, in turn, a function of variables familiar to migration researchers, such as changes associated with career or life-cycle development. The extent to which migration is viewed as a viable option in response to stress is also importantly related to the individual's ability to evaluate alternative residences and thus, to the formation of place utilities. Without an alternative location as a point of comparison, the theory suggests, the individual is not so likely to leave the current location.

However, the primary development of the concept of place utility has been with reference to the process of destination selection. Wolpert, assuming "intendedly rational" behavior wherein individuals engage in an evaluation process that can be flawed, writes that "the utility with respect to . . . alternative sites consists largely of anticipated utility and optimism that lacks reinforcement of past rewards. This is precisely why the stream of information is so important in long distance migration—information about prospects must somehow compensate for the absence of personal experience [1965:162]."

The concept of *search space* describes a subset of places within an *awareness space* (Brown and Longbrake, 1970). Awareness space contains the places about which a potential migrant has some information, no matter how limited. The search space contains only those seriously evaluated, or those for which place utilities are formed. We should expect that information sources can determine the number of places in the ultimate search space by determining the places in the initial awareness space.

Little research has been conducted with the specific goal of understanding the destination selection process as distinct from the decision to leave an origin area. However, information sources, or paths of contact, appear to be a central determinant in focusing a potential migrant's view on possible alternative locations. The role of social ties in analyses of migration has often been noted (for a review, see Shaw, 1975) and with alternative interpretations, depending on the decision being considered.

For example, Goldscheider considers the role of social ties in the context of the decision to leave an area. He suggests that social contacts at a location are one dimension of integration and that integration and out-migration are inversely related (1971:314). Out-migration is less likely when social contacts at a current location are extensive. While Goldscheider considers social ties in the context of the decisions to leave a place, there is other evidence that destination selection is closely and positively linked to the presence of friends or relatives in an area (for a review, see Ritchey, 1976).

The kinds of contacts a potential migrant has at other locations, the sources of these contacts, and the ways in which they actually become translated into direct or indirect influences on migration behavior have not been systematically investigated. That destination selection is a result of a narrowing-down process remains a proposition, and in many cases migrants select destinations before they have become committed to a moving decision. Indeed, Lansing and Mueller have documented the fact that few migrants say they considered more than one destination when asked such a question retrospectively (1967:211).

It is obvious that, from several perspectives, migration scholars have conceded that migration is a decision-making process that often encompasses more than one decision. However, the issue of differing determinants is less well-developed, perhaps because only a handful of researchers have proceeded to allow for separate operational tests of the different decisions.

A recent major analysis of reasons for moving, conducted under the auspices of the U.S. Bureau of the Census, demonstrates the lack of concern for precision in operationalizing migration motivations (Long and Hansen, 1979). The report is based on the very large samples of the 1974, 1975, and 1976 Annual Housing Surveys and is meant to be a major statement on migration motivations. However, in these surveys we find only the question asking for the main reason for moving "from [the] previous residence." This operationalization is oriented toward the reason for out-migration. Yet, the authors of this report consistently refer to their work as an analysis of "reasons for interstate migration," and "reasons for moving." This work reduces the entire process of migration to a process of out-migration. Moreover, the authors suggest as one of their purposes the identification of economic versus noneconomic reasons for moving. On the basis of the literature just reviewed, it is not surprising that in their analysis of "reasons for moving" Long and Hansen find employment reasons overwhelmingly influential since it is in destination selection, not the decision to leave, that social factors are hypothesized to be paramount. Even in caveats, Long and Hansen do not recognize the destination-selection aspect of migration decision making.

The analysis presented here attempts to demonstrate that for many migrants, neither reasons for leaving nor reasons for picking a destination suffice alone as bases for an explanation of "reasons for moving" if the latter phrase is meant as a label for causes of migration. The fundamental thesis is that migration does not involve one decision, but rather includes at least two and, for some migrants, probably several decisions.

Data Sources and Research Design

We will employ an analysis of data from a recent study of in-migrants to rapidly growing nonmetropolitan counties in the Midwest. The next few paragraphs offer a brief description of the relevant aspects of the study design. Further design information is found in Williams and Sofranko (1979) and Sofranko and Williams (1980).

There were 866 nonmetropolitan counties in the 12-state North Central region in November 1975. On the basis of estimates published yearly by the Bureau of the Census, we identified and selected all 75 nonmetropolitan counties that had greater than 10% (1970 base population) net in-migration between 1970 and 1975. This target group contained no counties in Iowa or Kansas, but Missouri and Michigan accounted for 24 and 21 counties, respectively. Forty-eight of the counties contained no urban place in 1970, and 25 of the counties were adjacent to SMSA's.

Within these high net in-migration counties a survey population of 316,430 households with telephones was estimated from 1975 Census estimates of households and 1970 estimates of telephone coverage for the target counties. A systematic sample of households was drawn from telephone directories (for 1976 or 1977), using a sample interval of 1/28 excluding, as much as possible, double and business listings.

In order to maximize the probability of obtaining an in-migrant on any given call, the sample names, addresses, and phone numbers were matched with the appropriate 1970 telephone directory. This matching, performed at the Library of Congress, yielded two strata: (a) expected resident (matched) households; and (b) expected in-migrant (unmatched) households. Problems arising with common surnames, intracounty migrants, and redistricting of telephone exchange areas were handled by treating all ambiguous cases as unmatched and placing them in the expected migrant stratum.

Three respondent types were identified within the survey population

of households, and quotas were established for subsequent disproportionately stratified sampling: (a) continuous residents of the counties
since April 1970; (b) in-migrants since April 1970 who had moved from an
SMSA (metropolitan) county; and (c) in-migrants since April 1970 who
had moved from a non-SMSA county. Resident status and migrant type
were determined from a series of initial screening questions. The various
selection rules and probabilities of selection used in conjunction with
successive subsampling yielded interviews with approximately 502
metropolitan-origin in-migrants and approximately 208 interviews with
nonmetropolitan-origin in-migrants. The present study focuses exclusively on in-migrants, and the resident sample of 425 respondents is
disregarded. Heads of households were primary respondents, although
spouses were interviewed if, after several attempts, interviewers failed
to contact the head. We are studying household migration, not individual migration. Only persons reporting the current location as their
usual place of residence were interviewed; thus, seasonal residents were
excluded.

The two migrant substrata (metropolitan and nonmetropolitan origin)
have been combined in this analysis since subsample differences are not
pertinent here. As the numbers of completed interviews are the result of
complex sampling, the two migrant substrata have been weighted before being combined in order to reflect estimated proportional representation in the population. These population estimates are obtained
from the detailed records kept of screening calls made to potential respondents. Weighting of the two migrant groups has been performed in
such a way as to maintain the actual number of total interviews. The
odds with respect to the metropolitan or nonmetropolitan origin of migrants are altered from the interviewed ratio of about 5:2 to an estimated
4:3 in order to provide a more accurate representation of the proportions
of persons with metropolitan or nonmetropolitan origin in the population. This rather minor adjustment does not, in our opinion, require
extensive alterations in the formulae for significance testing. Our statistical analysis will treat the data as if they were the result of simple
random sampling. Use of weighted data causes slight discrepancies in
table frequencies.

Respondents were asked questions designed to elicit reasons for leaving the place of origin and criteria for destination selection. For the
former, respondents were simply asked why they decided to leave the
city of origin. We elicited up to three reasons, which we recorded ver-
batim. About 26% of respondents gave more than one reason. We asked
these respondents to say which reason they felt was the most important.
An analysis of multiple reasons would usually be superior to one of a

single reason. However, even with probing, the great majority of respondents gave only one reason. The data following refer to one "main" reason for leaving. Reasons related to destination selection are based on a question asking the respondent why she or he picked the place chosen instead of some other place. Again, we report data for only one cited reason.

The open-ended responses to the reason questions were later coded into an initial 62-category scheme that allowed for considerable specificity of responses. In order to assure reliable results, the coding of all reason questions was performed independently three times. Where intercoder discrepancies occurred, differences were arbitrated and necessary changes made.

Reasons for Out-Migration and In-Migration: Differential Causation

The most elementary approach to demonstrating the importance of enumerating each motivation question is simply to examine the marginal distributions in order to observe differences in evaluative dimensions reported by respondents. The distributions of responses to both questions are presented in Table 8.1.

Optimally, one should apply exactly the same classification scheme to both sets of reasons in order to make appropriate comparisons. However, precisely because we are dealing with different behaviors, we must note that it was not reasonable to utilize identical classification schemes. For about 15% of the sample, retirement was given as the reason for leaving the place of origin. In contrast, retirement is not an important response to a question asking why a respondent chose the particular destination. In only three cases was retirement mentioned as the reason for choosing the destination. Perhaps this is due to the highly focused wording of the destination-selection question. These cases have been recoded to the "other–other" response category, eliminating retirement as a basis for destination selection.

It is apparent from the distributions in Table 8.1 that the evaluative dimensions for the two decisions differ. In particular, nearly half (47.6%) of all respondents chose their destination on the basis of pre-existing ties to the destination area, while only about 18% decided to leave for tie-related reasons. The causal bases of in- and out-migration appear to differ.

However, the marginals in Table 8.1 do not tell us about systematic linkages between reasons for leaving and reasons for destination selec-

TABLE 8.1
Detailed Motivations

Reasons	Reasons for leaving			Destination selection criteria		
	Number	Percent of total	Percent of category	Number	Percent of total	Percent of category
All reasons	710	100.0	----	710	100.0	----
Employment	182	25.6	100.0	148	20.8	100.0
Transfer	a 58	8.2	31.9	42	5.9	28.4
Look for new or better jobs	22	3.1	12.1	14	2.0	9.5
Found new or better job	a 63	8.9	34.6	64	9.0	43.2
Unemployment	12	1.7	6.6	0	---	----
Other (incl. military)	27	3.7	14.8	28	3.9	18.9
Ties (location specific capital)	126	17.7	100.0	338	47.6	100.0
Moved closer to business or job	a 33	4.6	26.1	40	5.6	11.8
Owned or received property	a 28	3.9	22.2	70	9.9	20.7
Moved closer to family or friends	a 31	4.4	24.6	97	13.7	28.7
Moved back home; lived in area before	a 23	3.2	18.3	81	11.4	24.0
Vacationed in or visited area before	a 1	0.1	0.8	43	6.1	12.7

Environmental	216	30.4	100.0	176	24.8	100.0
General anti-urban or pro-rural	93	13.1	43.1	45	6.3	25.7
Congestion; wanted a smaller town	31	4.4	14.4	6	0.8	3.4
Pollution; environment	4	0.6	1.9	12	1.7	6.8
Climate	6	0.8	2.7	6	0.8	3.4
Crime	13	1.8	6.0	6	0.8	3.4
Schools	16	2.3	7.4	12	1.7	6.8
Recreational opportunities	5	0.7	2.2	24	3.4	13.6
Cost-of-living; taxes	12	1.7	5.6	15	2.1	8.5
Liked or disliked area in general	22	3.1	10.2	19	2.7	10.8
Other environmental factors	14	2.0	6.5	31	4.4	17.6
Retirement	99	13.9	100.0	—	—	—
Other	83	11.7	100.0	47	6.6	100.0
Family; life cycle	32	4.5	38.6	11	1.5	23.4
Housing	10	1.4	12.0	19	2.7	40.5
Health	20	2.8	24.1	5	0.7	10.6
Other	21	3.0	25.3	12	1.7	25.5

a   See text for explanation.

tion. If there is categorical correspondence between the two reason questions for most respondents, then only one question is needed and there is no loss if only one question is asked. In a statistical sense, we need to ask only one question if answers to one question are of the same type as answers to another question. Such correspondence is illustrated by a person who leaves a place to look for a job and choses a destination because that is where he or she finds a job. This person is an employment migrant; perhaps we need not have known more than the reason for leaving to understand this migrant's causal nexus. From one perspective, we might think of this respondent as answering the reason questions in a consistent push–pull framework.

Some further thought about sources of correspondence in a bivariate table of reasons for leaving and coming, and some reflection on the marginals in Table 8.1 reveals a situation of correspondence that is entirely different from the case of the employment migrant mentioned above. A second source of correspondence results from the situation of making only one decision yet answering two questionnaire items. For some migrants, the basis for initially deciding to leave an origin minimizes the process of search-space formulation so that no destination-selection process can be separated from the decision to leave the area of origin. The prime example is the person who reports having left in order to move "back home." We would expect (and find) that this migrant's basis for selecting a destination is that the place is "home." Thus, for some migrants, the response to the question on leaving determines—rightfully—the response to the question on destination selection and results in a boost in the level of correspondence between the two evaluative-dimension sets of responses. For these migrants, all important information related to the entire decision-making process is contained in the response to why the person left the origin. We find nothing new by asking about destination selection.

To summarize this point, it should be remembered that categorical correspondence between reasons for leaving and reasons for destination selection indicates little statistical need for separate operationalizations. But situations of categorical correspondence can result from entirely different processes. In the employment example, the person who leaves to find a job could select a destination because he or she can stay with family in that location while looking for a job. Or the job could be located in some other fashion. At any rate, the destination-selection response is not necessarily determined. In the example of the person who moves home, correspondence is in the nature of reason for leaving. People who want to move home should not claim that they selected a destination because of good schools.

Figure 8.1 presents the bivariate situation. The relevant significance tests for this and subsequent figures are presented at the bottom of the figure. Drawing on the symbolism and works of Goodman (1978) and his ECTA program, we present likelihood-ratio chi-squares as tests of significance. The advantage of this methodology is that we will be able to test for interaction effects in the data. For Figure 8.1, we have fitted a classic independence model based on the expected frequencies, using the observed marginals of the two-way table underlying Figure 8.1. This model is symbolized as (1) (2). Since the chi-square is large and significant, we know that the cell frequencies generated solely from the marginals do not fit the observed data and thus, there is an association between reasons for leaving and reasons for destination selection.

From Figure 8.1, we observe that much of the associational corre-

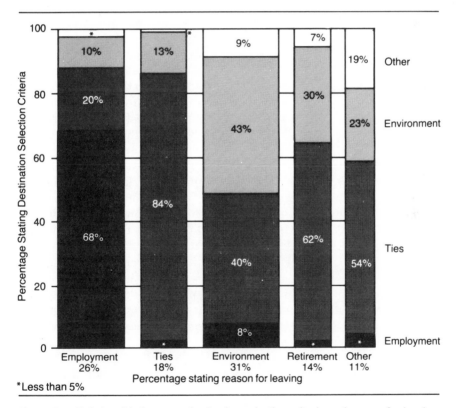

Figure 8.1. Relationship between destination selection criteria and reason for leaving origin. All households. Model fit (1) (2); Liklihood ratio chi-square = 385.49 at 12 d.f., significance at .000.

spondence between the two sets of reasons derives from the influence of the category combinations of "employment–employment" and "ties–ties." Embedded in these cells are both sources of correspondence identified above. The reasons given by these respondents for leaving their origins provide a clue as to whether they appear in identical reason categories because of identical evaluative dimensions in a two-step decision-making process, or whether they simultaneously chose a destination, given a certain reason for leaving.

Consider first, those who report employment-related reasons as the basis for both leaving and choosing a destination. These migrants are moving for relatively traditional reasons. Transfers and searches for new or better employment accounted for nearly half of all leaving decisions among respondents in the U.S. Annual Housing Surveys, 1974–1976 (Long and Hansen, 1979). However, within the employment–employment cell are both sources of the equivalence of responses. The person who is transferred, for instance, is probably quite different in terms of his or her decision-making process than the person who reports leaving to look for better employment. Specifically, the transferee—and for that matter the person who left because of having found a new or better job—has not engaged in any destination-selection process separable from the decision to leave, as operationalized here. Regardless of what process of search-space formulation may precede temporarily the decision to leave, for our purposes we expect a tendency for equivalence in responses among transferees and among those who left because they found other jobs. It would seem that these people knew where they were going when they decided to leave. In contrast, the person who left in order to find a better job engages in what, according to our classification scheme, is a conceptually distinct process of destination selection. This migrant would seem to have a clear need to decide where to look for employment, and this is the destination-selection process we are most interested in for this paper.

Migrants who suggest that they decided initially to leave their origins because of pre-existing ties at the already-chosen destination are conceptually similar to transferees and to those who report having found a better job as the reason for leaving. The destination choice is inseparably linked to the reason for leaving, and it makes little sense to ask separately about destination selection. As a result, we find that about 84% of those who leave for tie reasons also choose their destination for tie reasons, as seen in Figure 8.1.

In an effort to refine Figure 8.1 to include only those who seem to have made more than one decision, we have carefully considered the reasons for leaving (see Table 8.1) in order to identify what we will call *simultaneous decision makers*. The simultaneous decision maker is a migrant who reports a reason for leaving that determines a specific destination. For these migrants, we cannot capture more than one true decision; thus they contribute to the correspondence we see in Figure 8.1. The identified types of reasons for leaving are footnoted in Table 8.1. For all of these, the choice of destination was inseparably linked to the reason for leaving. The categories are those of transfer, new employment was found, and all of the suggestions of leaving to maximize some sort of place specific tie to another location. For these 247 households, or about 35% of the total migrant sample, we cannot argue any empirical need to ask a separate question on destination selection since, in a sense, that element of the process is indicated in the reason for leaving.

The removal of these simultaneous decision makers appreciably reduces the level of correspondence between reasons for the two behaviors. The revised data are presented in Figure 8.2, and the relation-

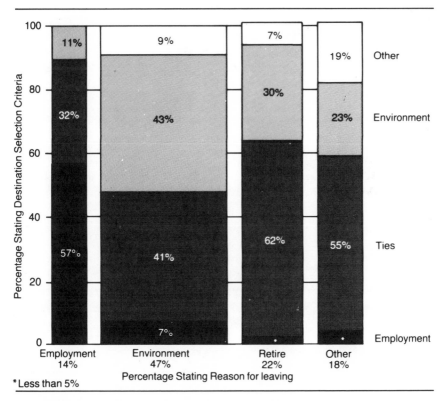

Figure 8.2. Relationship between destination selection criteria and reason for leaving origin. Households in which decisions were not simultaneous. Model fit (1) (2); Liklihood ratio chi-square = 129.48 at 9 d.f., significance at .000.

ship between the two reason responses remains significant. Two types of migrants of further relevance to this paper are left in the analysis: those who have the same bases for both decisions and those with different bases. All have probably made at least two decisions. For 143 cases in Figure 8.2, or for about 32 % of these nonsimultaneous decision makers, we technically need not have asked both questions since we see categorical correspondence (cells employment–employment, environment–environment and other–other). For the rest, the evaluative dimensions, our key to causal bases of the two behaviors, are different with respect to out- and in-migration. Thus, for about 45% of all interviewed migrants, there is empirical justification for asking both questions (those nonsimultaneous decision makers in Figure 8.2 who gave different types of reasons to the two questions).

The patterns in Figure 8.2 reveal that those initially motivated to leave for job reasons tend to choose a destination on the basis of job-related criteria (57%). Thus there is a tendency for more traditionally motivated migrants to make both decisions on the basis of similar evaluative criteria. As a result, there is less statistical need for enumerating the reasons for both behaviors. But among those whose leaving was employment motivated, there remains an additional 43% who selected their destination on the basis of a different criterion—most often, ties (32%).

In contrast to employment-motivated migrants, retirees, especially important to recent patterns of nonmetropolitan in-migration, tend to select their destinations on the basis of a variety of forms of ties including family and friends and prior residence as well as property and vacation experience. Those motivated to leave because of environmental reasons most often suggest destination selection on the basis of environmental reasons (43%), but also draw heavily upon ties (41%).

With the possible exception of those who left for job-related reasons, destination selection is importantly a function of ties in the areas. Furthermore, for the two most important types of in-migrants in terms of reasons for leaving—those who responded with environmental reasons or who cited retirement—we would have grossly underestimated the role of pre-existing ties to an area had we not also asked the basis for destination selection.

Location-Specific Capital and Destination Selection

DaVanzo and Morrison (1978) have recently introduced the phrase *location-specific capital* as a "generic term denoting any or all of the diverse factors that 'tie' a person to a particular place." They find empirical support for the hypothesis that "when a person who has migrated moves again, he or she should favor some former place of residence as the destination because the person has location specific capital there [1978:8]." Thus, it is suggested that location specific capital determines the direction of migration.

As demonstrated in the detailed categorization scheme of Table 8.1, a variety of forms of location-specific capital have been utilized by many migrants. Some have chosen their destination in order to be closer to family or friends. Others simply state that they had experience with the area through previous residence, and many seem to have had or received property in the area. These responses indicate that a migrant need not ever have migrated or have lived in the area before in order to have acquired location-specific capital. For instance, friends or family may have migrated to the area at some earlier time and thus serve as the link to a potential migrant. Vacation contact also need not entail prior migrant status or prior long-term residence. The importance of vacation contact, especially among retirees, in shaping the process of search-space formation has been documented by Sly (1974) in a study of Florida inmigrants. Sly found that nearly three-quarters of the respondents had visited Florida prior to moving there, and most of the visits were in the form of vacations. Many of our sample counties are favored midwestern vacation spots.

These comments simply reinforce the contention that DaVanzo and Morrison's concept of location-specific capital is relevant to the decision-making process of a great variety of types of migrant: those moving for the first time, those who have moved before and do not return to a prior residence in a subsequent move, and return migrants. Their empirical linkage of location-specific capital and return migration tests one route by which an awareness and search space may be shaped by ties to places.

Tie-related responses to the reason questions suggest that respondents have drawn upon some form of location-specific capital in the migration decision-making process. While we are here concentrating on destination selection, it may be noted that those who gave tie responses as their reason for leaving, have, in a sense, "cashed in" on location-specific capital closer to the presumed outset of the decision-making process. The 126 households suggesting ties as a reason for leaving (Table 8.1) plus the 213 households suggesting ties *only* as the basis for destination selection (Figure 8.2) account for about 48 % of all in-migrant households. Although the subsequent analysis could be performed with respect to reasons for leaving, our focus here is on the role of location-specific capital in destination selection.

First, define the level of utilization of location-specific capital as the proportion of respondents suggesting ties as the basis for destination selection. We anticipate that the utilization of location-specific capital presumes the existence of location-specific capital in some form. But location-specific capital need not be cashed in, in the sense of being the reason for selecting a destination. Numerous migrants with friends and relatives in the area, or with prior residence, may have selected their destination because of employment or other non-tie-related reasons. If we can measure the existence of location-specific capital, then we can investigate the relationship between having it and using it in choosing a destination.

Following DaVanzo and Morrison, we have chosen to investigate only one form of location specific capital: prior residence. Among several questionnaire items related to contacts prior to moving, respondents are asked if they had ever lived in the areas they had chosen prior to in-migrating. We form a dummy variable where those who are return-migrating are defined as having one unit of location-specific capital in the form of prior residence. They account for about 30% of the nonsimultaneous-decision-making households in Figure 8.2. We then investigate the relationship between having location-specific capital in the form of prior residence, on the one hand, and using this capital by responding with a tie-related reason for choosing the destination.

The relationship is defined by a slope line that, in this special case, is simply the difference in percentages reporting tie reasons for destination selection between those with and those without prior residential experience in the area. This relationship is graphed in Figure 8.3. The statistical test shows that there is a significant relationship between the two variables. Slightly less than 40% of those who had never before lived in the area gave a tie-related reason for destination selection while 65% of those who had lived in the area before gave a location-specific capital response. The slope of the line, then, is the difference, or about .26 per "unit" of prior residence, per respondent. The 26-percentage-point difference can be thought of as a rate of return to one unit of location-specific capital per 100 respondents, where the return is the specific mention of a tie reason for selecting a specific destination.

Further reflection on the substance of Figure 8.3 suggests the possibility that there is some imprecision in our linking all tie reasons for picking the destination to only one form of location-specific capital: prior residence. Prior residence almost certainly entails the acquisition of location-specific capital in diverse forms. The return-migrant may respond to family or friends left behind in an earlier move, may have housing to return to, a business left behind, or may simply want to "go back home." In further analysis (not detailed here) we find that prior

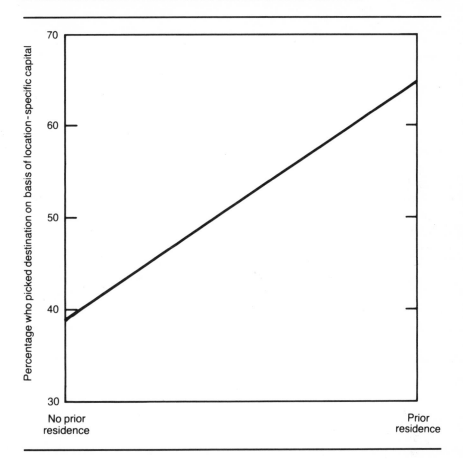

Figure 8.3. Returns to location–specific capital. Non-simultaneous decision makers. Model fit (1) (2); Liklihood ratio chi-square = 26.24 at 1 d.f., significance at .000.

residence is most closely associated with an expressed desire to move back home as the reason for destination selection. It is this linkage that should be pursued—that between having lived in an area before, and wanting to go back and doing so again. Remember, however, that the migrants in this portion of the analysis are those not initially motivated to leave their origin in order to go back home. Rather, they left for non-tie reasons and, to some extent, have drawn explicitly on prior residence in choosing a destination. Thus, we are addressing the question of the salience of a prior place of residence in destination selection for migrants who were initially motivated to migrate because of other reasons.

Our investigation of the linkage between having lived in the area before, and choosing the destination because it is "home," reveals that the constant of the equation linking the two variables is nearly reduced to zero. Only about 3% of those who had not lived in the area before chose the destination because of a desire to go back home. However, these people do have family in the area; and thus, we know that "home" means the location of familial ties and not just a place of prior residence. In contrast, 38% of those who had lived in the area before said they chose the destination because it was home. Hence this respecification yields a rate of return of about .35 per unit of location-specific capital per respondent.

Since we are focusing only on destination selection, we are using only one of the two reason questions. Figure 8.3 involves only a question about why the respondent chose the destination, and a question asking about prior residence. Technically, we have yet to demonstrate the utility of both reason questions for this particular substantive problem of returns to location-specific capital. Statistically, we need to demonstrate an interaction effect between reason for leaving, choosing a destination because of a desire to return home, and the existence of location-specific capital in the form of prior residence.

The interaction effect provides substantive information about variation in the rate of return to prior residence capital for migrants initially motivated to leave their origins for different reasons. For instance, we may determine whether prior residence is more salient for those who are retiring, or for those who left because of employment reasons. However, we have suggested that the person motivated to leave for job-related reasons tends to chose a destination on the basis of job-related criteria. The job-related out-migrant, then, should cash in on location-specific capital in destination areas to a lesser degree than other types of migrants.

The slope lines in Figure 8.4 show that retirees have drawn most heavily upon location-specific capital. To a lesser, but noticeable, extent, environmental, employment, and other types of out-migrants have also drawn upon their previous residential experience in selecting their migration destinations.

Most importantly, the analysis of the significance tests indicates that an interaction term is needed to fit the observed data. The model tested [symbolized (12) (13) (23)] omits the interaction term, and the expected cell frequencies—on the basis only of bivariate relationships—are not close to the observed cell frequencies. Thus, we conclude that the slope lines differ and that knowing the reason for leaving provides additional information about the relationship between having and using location-

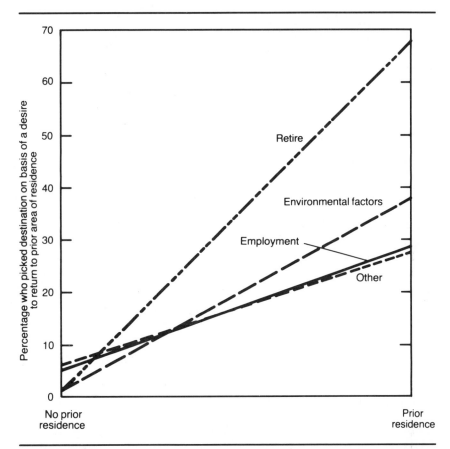

Figure 8.4. Salience of "return" as a form of location-specific capital in relation to prior residence by reason for leaving. Non-simultaneous decision makers. Model fit (12) (13) (23); Liklihood ratio chi-square = 9.32 at 3 d.f., significance at .025.

specific capital in the form of prior residence. Asking respondents about their reasons for leaving *and* their basis for selecting a destination is justified in this investigation.

Summary and Discussion

The analysis could be expanded to incorporate other forms of ties suggested by respondents as important in selecting a destination. For instance, one could generate rates of return for family, friends, prior vacation experience, or property ownership. Rates of return on each of these forms of location specific capital could be compared and inter-preted as to the relative salience of each in destination selection. We have also ignored an analysis of rates of return on location-specific capi-tal in the decision to leave. However, our findings suggest that had we asked only the respondent's reason for leaving the place of origin, we would have seriously underestimated the importance of location-specific capital in migration decision making.

In performing this analysis and others along similar lines, we have been fascinated by the enrichment of our understanding by the inclusion of two questions instead of just one "reason for moving." Yet we still find it necessary to make numerous speculative inferences about the decision-making process of these migrants. It seems regrettable that there is so little process-oriented research in this area. Our efforts here merely raise new questions about *how* people engage in a complex decision-making process. However, we have profited from an examina-tion of some of the *whys*. For example, we cannot say how many deci-sions our migrants made or whether they approached their search spaces positively, by selecting on a desired characteristic, or negatively, by ruling out places on the basis of negative characteristics. But our data do support the hypothesis that where people move is conditioned by sources of information about alternative destinations. Thus, awareness spaces are a good beginning point for predicting where a migrant will be selecting an ultimate destination.

From a more macro perspective, our research raises questions about the broad determinants of migration flows. The importance of informa-tion sources and the varying kinds of ties that are so prevalent among these migrants leads us to wonder about the directional biases, and their sources of large flows. First, our data support the work of others who have used past outflows to predict current inflows in an effort to capture the return-generating effects of prior residence. But there are other translations of information sources. From a probability perspective, any place with a large inflow should see some continuation because people included in that inflow contact others who follow later. And we should not underestimate the possible impact of the media in contributing to the national awareness space. Our own work with areas in the Midwest is an example. Much of the flow to the northern part of Michigan's lower peninsula is derived from the Detroit area, and Detroit papers have been reporting on the migration trends for some time.

The suggestion that survey researchers include two oper-ationalizations of evaluative criteria (reasons) is a conservative approach since it implies a discrete, two-stage, decision-making process. For some migrants we might find a much more continuous decision-making pro-cess involving a narrowing down of the awareness space into a viable search space and, ultimately, to a single destination. Survey researchers, of course, must operationalize on the basis of a discrete process, but we still might benefit greatly from more than two questions.

The importance of disaggregating the migration-decision process into more than a simple move-or-not-move framework implies that the migrant makes choices affecting his or her behavior. That is, separate operationalizations are particularly applicable to the voluntary, relatively unconstrained migrant. This point has important implications.

On the basis of the reasons given for leaving their origins, we must suspect that many in-migrants to high growth areas in nonmetropolitan parts of the Midwest are voluntary migrants and perhaps relatively unconstrained. The modal response category was an environmental reason for leaving the origin. However, further analysis demonstrated that those who left for environmental reasons, as well as because of retirement, drew heavily on location-specific capital in the form of prior residence when selecting their particular destinations. If those leaving their origins for environmental reasons or retirement reasons are a major factor in nonmetropolitan growth nationally, then it is important to ask these migrants about destination-selection criteria. In contrast, we demonstrated that employment-motivated out-migrants tend to choose a destination on the basis of employment criteria. Hence it is probably less important to ask them about destination selection. Because so many in-migrants to nonmetropolitan areas are not moving to seek employment, we conclude that current nonmetropolitan growth is importantly a function of migrants for whom we gain much insight if we disaggregate our operationalization of the migration decision-making process into (a) reasons for moving; and (b) destination-selection criteria.

If voluntary migrants increasingly come to suggest nonemployment bases for migration decision making in the future, then we can expect disaggregated operationalization to be increasingly important in research designs. As yet, we simply do not know the nature of this possible trend. Long and Hansen (1979) attempted a time-series investigation of reasons for migrating but concluded that it is not possible to investigate the matter fruitfully, given currently available data.

In summary, we feel that it is essential that surveys of migrants that focus on nonmetropolitan "amenity" growth areas include separate reason questions for in- and out-migration decisions. This presumption is minimal for an accurate understanding of the total decision-making process. To other migration researchers, we submit that the prudent approach for any survey of migrants attempting to elicit "reasons for moving" is to ask criteria for both leaving and choosing a destination. The potential for added insight would seem to far outweigh the cost of an additional questionnaire item.

Acknowledgments

The authors gratefully acknowledge the support of the North Central Regional Center for Rural Development, Ames, Iowa, and the Agricultural Experiment Station at the University of Illinois. The chapter reflects numerous helpful comments on an earlier draft by John G. Condran and Curtis Roseman.

References

Brown, Lawrence A. and David B. Longbrake
    1970   "Migration flows in intraurban space: Place utility considerations." *Annals of the Association of American Geographers* 60 (2):368–384.
Brown, Lawrence A. and Eric G. Moore
    1970   "The intra-urban migration process: A perspective." *General Systems* 15:109–122.
DaVanzo, Julie and Peter A. Morrison
    1978   "Dynamics of return migration: Descriptive findings from a longitudinal study." Rand Paper P–5913. Palo Alto, Calif.: The Rand Corp.
Goldscheider, Calvin
    1971   *Population, Modernization and Social Structure.* Boston: Little, Brown.
Goodman, Leo
    1978   *Analyzing Qualitative/Categorical Data: Log-Linear Models and Latent Structure Analysis.* Cambridge, Mass.: Abt Books.
Lansing, John G. and Eva Mueller
    1967   *The Geographic Mobility of Labor.* Ann Arbor: University of Michigan, Institute for Social Research, Survey Research Center.
Long, Larry H. and Kristen A. Hansen
    1979   *Reasons for Interstate Migration: Jobs, Retirement, Climate and Other Influences.* Current Population Reports. Special Studies, Series P–23; No. 81. Washington, D.C.: U.S. Government Printing Office.
Quigley, John M. and Daniel H. Weinberg
    1977   "Intra-urban residential mobility: A review and synthesis." *International Regional Science Review,* 2 (1):41–66.
Ritchey, P. Neal
    1976   "Explanations of migration." In A. Inkeles (ed.), *Annual Review of Sociology.* Vol. 2. Palo Alto: Annual Reviews, Inc.
Roseman, Curtis C.
    1977   *Changing Migration Patterns Within the United States.* Resource Papers for College Geography No. 77–2. Washington, D.C.: Association of American Geographers.
Rossi, Peter H.
    1955   *Why Families Move: A Study in the Social Psychology of Urban Residential Mobility.* Glencoe, Ill.: Free Press.
Shaw, R. Paul
    1975   *Migration Theory and Fact.* Bibliography Series Number 5. Philadelphia: Regional Science Research Institute.
Sly, David F.
    1974   "Tourism's role in migration to Florida: Basic tourist–migration relationship." *Governmental Research Bulletin.* Vol. II. Tallahassee: The Florida State Univeristy, Institute for Social Research.

Sofranko, Andrew and James D. Williams
   1980   *Rebirth of Rural America: Rural Migration in the Midwest.* Ames, Iowa: North Central Regional Center for Rural Development.
Speare, Alden, Jr., Sidney Goldstein, and William H. Frey
   1974   *Residential Mobility, Migration, and Metropolitan Change.* Cambridge, Mass.: Ballinger.
Williams, James D. and Andrew J. Sofranko
   1979   "Motivations for the inmigration component of population turnaround in nonmetropolitan areas." *Demography* 16 (2):239–255.
Wolpert, Julian
   1965   "Behavioral aspects of the decision to migrate." *Papers and Proceedings.* Regional Science Association, 15:159–177.
Zelinsky, Wilbur
   1977   "Coping with the migration turnaround: The theoretical challenge." *International Regional Science Review* 2(2):175–178.

9

Retention of Metropolitan-to-Nonmetropolitan Labor-Force Migrants[1]

EDWIN H. CARPENTER

Introduction

The recent occurrence of growth in nonmetropolitan counties at the expense of metropolitan counties is well-documented in this book. However, knowing that there has been an increase in population in nonmetropolitan counties beyond that attributable to natural increase tells one only that for a specified period of time the number of in-migrants has exceeded the number of out-migrants. The dynamics of how the net in-migration occurred are often not specified. Nonmetropolitan areas are growing not only because the flow of in-migrants has increased but also because the flow of out-migrants has declined. Some nonmetropolitan counties are thought to be growing because of short-term retention, that is, because they have received a large influx of migrants, few of whom will be residents for more than a short time. The growth of still other nonmetropolitan counties may result from a moderate influx of migrants who will remain residents for a substantial period of time (long-term retention).

All three of these patterns, and others, are responsible for the recent growth of population in nonmetropolitan America; this chapter will focus attention on the patterns of short- and long-term retention. These two patterns are sufficiently different in their impact on nonmetropoli-

[1]This research was supported by the Arizona Agricultural Experiment Station and is a continuing project to the Western Regional Migration Project W118. It is Arizona Experiment Station Paper No. 344.

New Directions in
Urban–Rural Migration

tan counties that it is important to know which, if either, pattern is dominant. The number of years nonmetropolitan counties will continue to grow could be a function of whether retention patterns are short or long term. The number of people cycled in and out of nonmetropolitan counties over a specified period of time is greater when the short-term retention pattern is dominant than when the long-term pattern is dominant. That being the case, and assuming Fuguitt and Zuiches (1975) are correct in their assessment that there are a limited number of people who may migrate from metropolitan to nonmetropolitan counties, the supply of migrants will be exhausted sooner if the short-term retention pattern is dominant. In turn, this means that nonmetropolitan growth from in-migration will probably continue for fewer years than it would have had the long-term retention pattern been dominant. This will be particularly crucial for rural low-density counties not adjacent to metropolitan counties; it is these rural counties that have grown at the fastest rates since 1970. According to Carpenter (1977), the pool of potential migrants to physically isolated rural communities is one-fifth the size of the pool of potential migrants to rural communities that are more accessible to larger cities.

Short- or long-term retention of in-migrants affects both the socioeconomic development of the community and its potential for future growth. Employers with jobs requiring a lengthy start-up time for training and/or skill development will be negatively affected by the short-term retention pattern. The rapid turnover of employees means that many employees will leave about the time they become highly skilled or trained. Some employers may find it so burdensome to invest time and money in continually replacing employees that they will relocate their facilities elsewhere. For employers who are considering moving their facilities to the community, knowing that the short-term retention pattern is dominant may mean that they will elect to locate in another area where the long-term pattern is dominant.

The dynamics of population growth can make a considerable difference to local public officials and planners. Decisions about whether or not and to what extent public services will be expanded or upgraded should be made in light of the dominant retention pattern. When the retention pattern is short term, the decision may be to expand such facilities as education, health, or welfare by utilizing temporary structures that can be converted to other uses when growth stops. Conversely, if growth is dominated by the long-term retention pattern, new structures of a permanent variety may be more appropriate from a long run cost–benefit standpoint. Local businessmen have to make decisions from a vantage point similar to that of public officials and planners.

Growth in population means increased demands for the goods and services provided by community businesses. Thus it provides businessmen with the expectation that enlarging their operations may result in greater profits. However, if the growth pattern is of the short-term variety, local businessmen who have enlarged their facilities may find themselves overextended at the point when growth is curtailed.

Population growth, regardless of whether it is dominated by the short- or long-term retention pattern, may bring about changes in the way community residents relate to one another. Conflict may arise in communities where new people arrive with ideas or values that are not appreciated by longer-term residents. The more arrivals, of course, the greater the chance that such a set of ideas or values will be brought to the community. That being the case, one might hypothesize that communities with growth dominated by the short-term retention pattern will be more likely to experience interpersonal conflict. Communities that rely on volunteers for various civic programs, such as fire protection, may find it necessary to recruit additional volunteers as the community grows. However, if growth is dominated by the short-term retention pattern, more effort will be expended in training volunteers. This is because turnover will be faster than if growth were dominated by the long-term retention pattern.

The foregoing examples suggest that the socioeconomic development of nonmetropolitan communities will be affected in different ways by the type of retention pattern that dominates growth. However, why would one or the other retention pattern dominate growth? Various conceptual formulations provide a basis for arguing whether or not metropolitan-to-nonmetropolitan migrants will be short- or long-term residents in their nonmetropolitan destinations. The increase in employment opportunities in nonmetropolitan counties argues for long-term retention (Committee on Community Development, 1974). Such growth attracts metropolitan residents and provides them with employment to the extent that the opportunities are not filled by the indigenous nonmetropolitan residents. We cannot be certain that just because the recent inmigrant has a job he or she will not leave the community, but being employed does lessen the chances of such an occurrence.

Research on the size of community that people prefer indicates that a majority of Americans favor small-town living (Dillman, 1973). However, relatively few prefer to live in a small town if it is geographically distant from a metropolitan center (Carpenter, 1977; Fuguitt and Zuiches, 1975). Furthermore, the data on preference for small-town living indicate that some of the metropolitan-to-nonmetropolitan migrants may be disillusioned upon arrival at their nonmetropolitan destination if they find

that the communities' attributes and services are not what they anticipated (Blackwood and Carpenter, 1978). Findings from the preference
research are less than conclusive but suggest that nonmetropolitan
communities that are located near urban centers will be more likely to
experience long-term retention, while the more isolated communities
will more likely experience short-term retention.

Economic factors, such as lower cost of living in nonmetropolitan
counties (U.S. Department of Labor, 1976), increased per capita disposable real income, and greater coverage of both private and federal retirement plans with increased benefits (Carpenter, 1977) make living in
nonmetropolitan counties less taxing financially and thus increase the
likelihood of long-term retention. The nearly completed interstate
highway system and the increasingly sophisticated communication
networks reduce the isolation of many nonmetropolitan areas.

This chapter examines changes in the length of retention of the
metropolitan-to-nonmetropolitan county labor-force migrants during
the period 1965–1975. Data on the length of retention provide information on whether the recent surge in nonmetropolitan growth is due in
part to these migrants having remained longer in their nonmetropolitan
destination. The answer to this question in turn addresses the question
of whether growth is attributable to the short- or to the long-term retention pattern. The size of places of origin and destination and the near-
ness of the latter to an SMSA may play a part in the length of retention.
According to Blackwood and Carpenter (1978), there is a small group of
potential migrants from larger to smaller communities who anticipate
that the quality of all aspects of life is better in nonmetropolitan communities. These potential migrants indicate that the size of population of
the place of destination is an important factor to them, and that smaller
places are more attractive. However, since it is unlikely that the quality
of all aspects of life is in fact better in small, nonmetropolitan communities, these individuals may be disillusioned upon movement to
their preferred destinations. The disillusionment may lead to an early
second migration, thus contributing to a short-term retention pattern.

Data and Methods

Data used in this analysis are from the Social Security Administration's Continuous Work History Sample (CWHS), a national longitudinal data file containing yearly information, including county of
employment, on a 1% sample of individuals in the labor force who are

covered by Social Security.[2] Appended to this file are county characteristics from the fourth-count summary tape of the 1970 Census as adapted by Brown and Hines (Hines *et al.*, 1975). These variables allow for the aggregation of all counties into the seven-class typology of metropolitan–nonmetropolitan county of employment used in the present analysis. These classes are (*a*) large Standard Metropolitan Statistical Area (SMSA), (1 million + population); (*b*) medium SMSA (250,000–999,999); (*c*) small SMSA (50,000–249,999); (*d*) urban nonmetropolitan and adjacent to an SMSA (2500–49,999); (*e*) urban nonmetropolitan and not adjacent to an SMSA (2500–49,999); (*f*) rural nonmetropolitan adjacent to an SMSA (less than 2500); and (*g*) rural nonmetropolitan and not adjacent to an SMSA (less than 2500). Metropolitan and adjacency status are as of the 1970 Census, as defined in 1974.

Since data are for county of employment, not county of residence, labor-force migration is defined as a change in county of employment from one time period to another. All those individuals within the 48 contiguous states and the District of Columbia that changed county of employment at least once from a metropolitan to a nonmetropolitan county between 1965–1975 were identified and selected for analysis.[3] We created seven cohorts, based on the year during which metropolitan to nonmetropolitan change occurred: Thus, the first cohort contains individuals who changed from a metropolitan county in 1965 to a nonmetropolitan county in 1966; the seventh cohort contains people who made the change between 1971–1972. We were concerned with the number of changes ($N = 19,381$) rather than with tracking each individual longitudinally. Therefore, any given individual could be in more than one cohort.

The dependent variable was constructed by dividing each cohort into two groups, according to whether or not a return to *any* metropolitan

[2]Approximately 90% of the labor force is covered by Social Security. Significant omissions from the file include retired persons, some self-employed persons, most agricultural workers, Federal Civil Service employees, and state and local government workers who have discontinued Social Security system coverage. For detailed information on the CWHS file, see Chapter 15, as well as Bureau of Economic Analysis (1976).

[3]No county of employment was reported for the year or years during which an individual was not employed. For cases where there were no more than 3 consecutive years missing, county of employment was "patched in" following the procedures utilized by Morrison (1976): Briefly, they are (*a*) if the missing year or years were bracketed by identical county codes, these codes were substituted for the unknown years; (*b*) if the missing year or years were bracketed by different county codes a single transition was assumed to have occurred at random, and that point of transition was randomly picked within the unknown years.

county had occurred within 3 years after the initial change to a nonmetropolitan county. This cut-off period was necessary in order to compare all cohorts (e.g., there are no 5-year- or 6-year-return figures for the last two cohorts). A 3-year cut-off point for returns was selected because returns to metropolitan counties, if they are going to occur, are more likely to take place within the first few years (DaVanzo and Morrison, 1977). For the 1965–1966 cohort—the one followed the longest (9 years)—51% had returned to some metropolitan county after 3 years, and only an additional 17% returned in the following 6 years. Stated differently, 75% of the returns in a 9-year period occurred within the first 3 years. Thus, for our purposes, the first 3 years are the critical ones. Short-term residents are defined as those in-migrants who returned to a metropolitan county within 3 years.

Log-linear contingency table analysis as developed by Goodman (1972) was used to analyze the data. Based on the likelihood-ratio, chi-square statistic, this technique allows for the multivariate analysis of nominal data and provides a systematic strategy for testing the significance of relationships and establishing estimates of effects. Details of the analysis are presented in abbreviated detail in footnotes, where the findings are expressed as odds and odds–ratios, and so on.

Results

The percentage of each of the seven cohorts that remained in a nonmetropolitan county longer than 3 years is presented in Figure 9.1. Beginning with the 1968–1969 cohort, a distinct increase in the percentage of people remaining longer than 3 years is evident. The timing of this increase coincides roughly with the beginning of the recent growth of population in nonmetropolitan counties. The data indicate that this growth is due in part to longer retention of recent labor-force in-migrants and that the long-term retention pattern increased somewhat. From a statistical standpoint, the only significant difference in percentages occurs between the 1967–1968 and 1968–1969 cohorts. Thus, the only significant contrasts that exist suggest a dichotomy between the first three and the last four cohorts: Individuals in the last four cohorts are more likely to remain beyond 3 years.[4] Dominance of the longer-term reten-

---

[4]Partitioning the logit chi-square value for the two-way table (remain beyond 3 years by cohort) from which Figure 9.1 was constructed supports the importance of the increase in retention that began with the 1968–1969 cohort. At the .01 level, no significant differences were found between the first three and the last four cohorts, suggesting a dichotomy between these two groups. Individuals in the last four cohorts were 1.3 times as likely to remain beyond 3 years as were the first three cohorts.

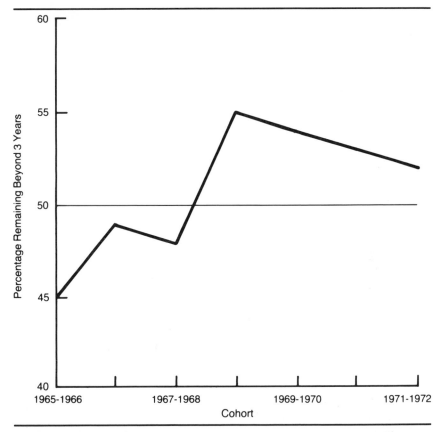

Figure 9.1. Percentage of migrants remaining beyond 3 years in nonmetropolitan area. (Source: Continuous Work History Sample.)

tion pattern could be a result of the recent increase in employment opportunities in the nonmetropolitan counties. This explanation seems reasonable, since these data are for labor-force migrants (individuals who have been employed for the majority of the years in question). However, for some individuals, employment only facilitates retention. It may not be the primary reason for in-migrants remaining beyond 3 years.[5]

[5]Even though differences among the last four cohorts are not statistically significant, there is a consistent decline in the percentage remaining beyond 3 years. If this decline continues, a return to the short-term retention pattern may occur as soon as the early 1980s. The trend toward resumption of a dominance of short-term retention should be regarded with caution. The data from the CWHS for the last 2 years covered, 1974–1975, are preliminary and may contain more errors (see Chapter 15).

Size of Metropolitan County of Origin

The propensity to remain in a nonmetropolitan county may vary by the size of the metropolitan area from which the migrant originated. The residential preferences literature suggests that although the majority of recent metropolitan-to-nonmetropolitan migrants come from larger metropolitan areas (Beale, 1976; Brown, 1980; Wardwell and Gilchrist, 1978), they may also have the highest rates of return migration. They are likely to experience relatively greater cultural shock than other migrants in moving to nonmetropolitan counties (Blackwood and Carpenter, 1978). Alternatively, they may find nonmetropolitan moves particularly rewarding and have lower rates of return because more negative conditions exist in the larger metropolitan areas. From a purely economic standpoint, differences in return rates could occur as a result of var-

TABLE 9.1
Return Status by Cohort and by Size of Metropolitan Area of Origin

Cohort	Size of metropolitan area of origin	Percentage remaining in a nonmetropolitan area beyond 3 years
65–66	large	.43
	medium	.49
	small	.45
66–67	large	.49
	medium	.51
	small	.45
67–68	large	.49
	medium	.47
	small	.47
68–69	large	.54
	medium	.55
	small	.56
69–70	large	.52
	medium	.57
	small	.54
70–71	large	.55
	medium	.52
	small	.51
71–72	large	.51
	medium	.53
	small	.55

iations in rates of industry dispersal from different sizes of metropolitan areas. These possibilities are considered in the analysis of Table 9.1, which cross-classifies metropolitan return-migration status by metropolitan-to-nonmetropolitan cohort and size of metropolitan area of origin.

The data in Table 9.1 indicate that size of place of origin has no significant effect on the percentage of workers remaining in nonmetropolitan counties for longer than 3 years.[6] Blackwood and Carpenter's (1978) suggestion that potential migrants from larger to smaller communities might become disillusioned because their perceptions of the quality of life in smaller places might be overly optimistic implies that as the difference between the sizes of place of origin and of destination increases so will the degree of optimism. How long migrants remain at their destination, then, should also be a function of the difference between the sizes of place of origin and of destination.

However, these findings suggest that the size of place of origin has little effect on how long workers remain. That leaves the size of place of destination as a possible influential factor. In the next section, size of destination along with remoteness of destination will be analyzed to see whether there is substance to Blackwood and Carpenter's thesis.

Size and Remoteness of Nonmetropolitan Destination County

In this analysis, adjacency to a metropolitan county is considered as well as size of the largest place in the nonmetropolitan counties. To this end, the nonmetropolitan destination counties were classed in the follow-

[6]The specifications of the following five models for the log–linear analysis of Table 9.1 delineate all the possible combinations of relationships between the dependent and independent variables in the table: (1) the independence of return migration from both cohort and size of place of origin; (2) an independent effect of cohort but not of size of place of origin; (3) an independent effect of size of place of origin but not of cohort; (4) independent effects of both variables; (5) an interaction or specification effect involving both independent variables. To determine the preferred model for the representation of significant effects of Table 9.1, the fit of each of these models to the observed data was determined, using logit chi-square values. Comparisons of hierarchical models were made by calculating differences in the chi-square values. The .01 level of significance was used both for accepting as adequate a model's fit to the data and for the determination of improvement of fit when comparing hierarchical models. Model 2 ($\chi^2 = 28.39$, $df = 14$), specifying only the cohort effect, was chosen as the preferred model. It was chosen because it improved the fit to the data over the model of independence (Model 1) while Model 3, specifying a single effect of size of place of origin, did not, and because the models specifying independent effects of both variables (Model 4) or an interaction effect (Model 5) provided no further significant improvements to the fit of the data over Model 2.

TABLE 9.2
Return Status by Cohort and by Size and Adjacency Status of Nonmetro
County of Destination

Cohort	Size and adjacency status of nonmetro county	Percentage remaining in a nonmetropolitan area beyond 3 years
65–66	urban, adjacent	.46
	urban, nonadjacent	.44
	rural, adjacent	.40
	rural, nonadjacent	.48
66–67	urban, adjacent	.48
	urban, nonadjacent	.51
	rural, adjacent	.40
	rural, nonadjacent	.55
67–68	urban, adjacent	.47
	urban, nonadjacent	.50
	rural, adjacent	.39
	rural, nonadjacent	.48
68–69	urban, adjacent	.53
	urban, nonadjacent	.58
	rural, adjacent	.50
	rural, nonadjacent	.61
69–70	urban, adjacent	.54
	urban, nonadjacent	.56
	rural, adjacent	.37
	rural, nonadjacent	.62
70–71	urban, adjacent	.50
	urban, nonadjacent	.59
	rural, adjacent	.55
	rural, nonadjacent	.48
71–72	urban, adjacent	.51
	urban, nonadjacent	.54
	rural, adjacent	.43
	rural, nonadjacent	.57

ing four groups: (*a*) urban counties that are adjacent to a metropolitan county; (*b*) urban nonadjacent counties; (*c*) rural, adjacent counties; and (*d*) rural, nonadjacent counties. Table 9.2 presents the distribution of return moves by cohort and size–location of nonmetropolitan county of destination.[7]

[7]The first step in the analysis of Table 9.2 used the same approach as was used for the analysis of Table 9.1, and the model showing separate effects of both independent variables was tentatively selected ($\chi^2 = 29.09$, $df = 18$). However, because partitioning of the

The analysis revealed that both of the independent variables, cohort and nonmetropolitan size–adjacency status, have separate effects on the percentage of people remaining for at least 3 years. The cohort variable was dichotomized into pre– and post–1968 groups. A graph of the percentage remaining in nonmetropolitan counties beyond 3 years by cohort (dichotomized) and size–adjacency status is presented in Figure 9.2.[8] Besides reiterating the earlier finding that those migrants in the last four cohorts were more likely to remain beyond 3 years than migrants in the first three cohorts, Figure 9.2 also shows that workers who moved to rural nonmetropolitan counties adjacent to an SMSA were the least likely to remain beyond 3 years, followed by those in urban nonmetropolitan adjacent counties and urban and rural nonmetropolitan, nonadjacent counties, respectively. Although it may not be apparent from Figure 9.2, the statistical model specifies that the difference by size of place remained constant over time, suggesting that changes that have occurred over time affecting retention in nonmetropolitan counties have affected all four types of nonmetropolitan areas equally. Specifically, across all cohorts, when compared to rural nonadjacent counties (which retained 54% beyond 3 years), the rural adjacent, urban adjacent, and urban nonadjacent counties retained their labor-force migrants beyond 3 years 10%, 4%, and 1% less often, respectively. Furthermore, the analysis showed that the difference between urban and rural nonadjacent counties was only marginally significant; thus, among nonmetropolitan nonadjacent counties size is not an important determinant of retention beyond 3 years.

In brief, for nonmetropolitan counties that are adjacent to metropolitan counties, size is related to retention beyond 3 years, and rural counties have less retention beyond 3 years than more urbanized counties. For nonadjacent nonmetropolitan counties, size makes no difference for retention beyond 3 years. And lastly, the difference between nonmet-

---

earlier data suggested a dichotomy between the first three and the last four cohorts, these two groups of cohorts were analyzed in separate three-way tables to see if the dichotomy persists when cross-classified by destination-county status. (This part of the analysis was not done for Table 9.1 since there was no effect of size of metropolitan county of origin.) No significant effect of cohort was found in either of the two subtables, suggesting that, in the full table, the significant effect of cohort is due only to the contrasts between the pre–1968 and post–1968 cohorts. Thus as before, the cohort variable can be collapsed into a dichotomy without a significant loss of effect, so that a simpler picture of the data emerges.

[8]Re-analysis of the full table with the cohort variable dichotomized produced the final preferred model ($\chi^2 = 5.29$, $df = 3$), again showing independent effects of cohort and nonmetropolitan county characteristics from which estimations of effects of the variables were calculated. Further analysis (partitioning the chi-square on the basis of nonmetropolitan county type) showed that the minor difference in rates of retention beyond 3 years between urban and rural nonadjacent counties was only marginally significant.

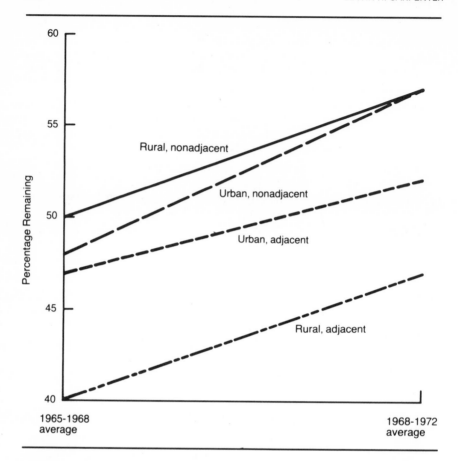

Figure 9.2. Percentage of migrants remaining beyond 3 years in nonmetropolitan area by type of destination county and date of migration. (Source: Continuous Work History Sample.)

ropolitan counties in their retention beyond 3 years did not change for the period studied even though all types of nonmetropolitan counties experienced an absolute increase in retention beyond 3 years.

Several conclusions can be drawn concerning Blackwood and Carpenter's thesis about the relationship between retention beyond 3 years and the difference in sizes of place of origin and of destination. First, size was related to retention beyond 3 years for nonmetropolitan adjacent counties but not for nonmetropolitan nonadjacent counties. Had the reverse been found, it might be tentatively concluded that there is substance to Blackwood and Carpenter's suggestions. That is, it is easier to imagine disillusionment occurring in migrants to small, isolated rural communities than in migrants to small rural communities that are close to metropolitan places. A second conclusion is that Blackwood and Carpenter's suggestion is correct but that it applies to so few people that they went undetected in the present study.

Summary and Implications

The Continuous Work History Sample data base provides yearly information on county of employment for a large national sample of people that are in the labor force and are covered by Social Security. Because county of employment rather than county of residence is the datum provided, migration to counties continguous to SMSAs is understated by the workers who commute from the contiguous counties to places of work in the SMSA counties (see Chapter 2). Even so, the findings derived from this data base are instructive and provide new insights regarding the processes underlying the recent growth that has occurred in nonmetropolitan America. For instance, the long-term retention pattern (beyond 3 years) in nonmetropolitan county growth attributable to net migration was dominant during the 1970s. The change from a short-term retention (3 years or less) to a dominance of long-term retention occurred in the group of people who are employed in a metropolitan county in 1968 and a nonmetropolitan county in 1969; that is, the 1968–1969 cohort. Size of metropolitan area of origin is not related to whether labor-force migrants will be retained beyond 3 years in nonmetropolitan counties of destination. However, the size of a nonmetropolitan destination county and its adjacency to a metropolitan county does make a difference in retention beyond 3 years. Nonmetropolitan counties (either rural or urban) that are not adjacent to metropolitan counties were the ones with a higher percentage of retention beyond 3 years, but there was no difference in retention by size (rural or urban) of the nonadjacent category. Size of county does make a difference for nonmetropolitan adjacent counties, and rural counties have a lower percentage of retention beyond 3 years than urban counties. Interestingly, though, all four types of nonmetropolitan counties have experienced absolute increases in percentage retained beyond 3 years. There is little difference among the four types for the time period studied.

Since the long-term retention pattern is dominant, a limited supply of metropolitan-to-nonmetropolitan migrants will contribute to a more stable growth trend than it would if the short-term retention pattern were dominant. That is, growth would extend for more years into the future. That the long-term retention pattern is dominant could also mean fewer turnover problems for business and, as a result, fewer expenditures for training or skill development. For the same reason, other businesses may be more likely to locate in nonmetropolitan places in order to take advantage of the more recent longer-term retention of residents. Such growth in business should also help to attract new residents.

Another implication of the dominance of the long-term retention pattern is that it reduces, to some degree, the likely incidence of conflict among newcomers to the community and the longer-term residents. That is, fewer people are migrating to the community in any specified period of time than would be the case if the short-term retention pattern were dominant; therefore, there is probably less chance that conflicting ideas will be brought to the community. Additionally, there will likely be less turnover in volunteers for various civic programs in the community; hence less training will be required.

The foregoing implications are set forth more as food for thought than as directives for action at the local community level. However, information on the dominant reasons for growth might assist local communities to attain their goals and objectives.

Acknowledgments

The version of the Continuous Work History Sample used in this research was merged with county characteristics data and accessed through the Center for Social Data Analysis, Montana State University. Grateful acknowledgment of the assistance of Jack Gilchrist and Cel Allard in providing these data and in designing the analysis is made.

References

Beale, Calvin L.
  1976   "A further look at nonmetropolitan population growth since 1970." Paper presented at the annual meetings of the Rural Sociological Society.
Blackwood, Larry G. and Edwin H. Carpenter
  1978   "The importance of anti-urbanism in determining residential preferences and migration patterns." *Rural Sociology* 43:31–47.
Brown, David L.
  1980   "Some spatial patterns of post–1970 work force migration in the United States." *Growth and Change* (In press).
Bureau of Economic Analysis
  1976   *Regional Work Force Characteristics of Migration Data: A Handbook on the Social*

Security Continuous Work History Sample and Its Applications. Washington, D.C.: U.S. Government Printing Office.

Carpenter, Edwin H.
1977   "The potential for population dispersal: A closer look at residential location preference." *Rural Sociology* 42:352–370.

and Larry G. Blackwood
1978   "Rates of return to metropolitan counties among metropolitan to nonmetropolitan migrants 1965–1975." Paper presented at the Annual Meeting of the Rural Sociological Society, San Francisco, August.

Committee on Community Development
1974   *Report on National Growth and Development.* December, Washington, D.C.: U.S. Government Printing Office.

DaVanzo, Julie and Peter A. Morrison
1977   "Migrants who return: Preliminary findings from a longitudinal study." Paper presented at the Annual Meeting of the Western Regional Science Association.

Dillman, Don A.
1973   "Population distribution policy and people's attitudes: Current knowledge and needed research." Paper presented for the Urban Land Institute, U.S. Department of Housing and Urban Development.

Fuguitt, Glenn V. and James J. Zuiches
1975   "Residential preferences and population distribution." *Demography* 12:491–504.

Goodman, Leo A.
1972   "A modified multiple regression approach to the analysis of dichotomous variables." *American Sociological Review* 37:28–46.

Hines, Fred K., David L. Brown, and John M. Zimmer
1975   *Social and Economic Characteristics of the Population in Metropolitan and Nonmetropolitan Counties, 1970.* Economic Research Service Publication AER-272. Washington, D.C.: U.S. Department of Agriculture.

Morrison, Peter A.
1976   "Studying return migration with the Social Security one-percent continuous work history sample." Paper presented to the Social Security Administration's Annual Continuous Work History Sample User's Conference.

U.S. Department of Labor
1976   *Consumer Expenditure Survey Series: Interview Survey 1972 and 1973.* Report 455-3, Washington, D.C.: U.S. Government Printing Office.

Wardwell, John M. and C. Jack Gilchrist
1978   "Metropolitan change and nonmetropolitan growth." Paper presented at the Annual Meeting of the Population Association of America, Atlanta.

MIGRATION TRENDS AND CONSEQUENCES IN RAPIDLY GROWING AREAS

The focus in this part is on nonmetropolitan growth and change in selected regions. The chapters in Part III all share a community and/or individual orientation and an emphasis on the consequences of population and economic growth. The Ozark–Ouachita region was one of the first nonmetropolitan sections of the country to experience a turnaround from decline to growth. This reversal was evidenced in Census Bureau estimates produced in the mid–1960s. Dailey and Campbell (Chapter 10) describe growth trends in the Ozark-Ouachita region and examine their consequences. They indicate that the Ozarks have been transformed from an area of limited resource farming to one in which recreation, retirement, and manufacturing predominate. Demographic, economic, and environmental impacts of new population growth are examined. Changes in population size and composition were shown to be significant for the region's communities. Many new migrants are from large cities. This has created some problems as migrants seek to transfer their urban lifestyles into the rural Ozarks. Migrants to the Ozarks tend to be older than longer-term residents, a factor that contributes to greater need and demand for various goods, services, and facilities. One of the primary reasons for population growth in the Ozarks is the natural beauty of the region's physical environment. However, migration-induced economic development (economic activities, commercial establishments, and residences) may be endangering the very environment that attracted people there in the first place. The authors point out that planners in the Ozarks must face the challenge of maintaining economic prosperity while protecting the amenities of the region.

Colorado, Montana, North Dakota, and Wyoming contain disproportionate shares of the Nation's coal, oil, natural gas, uranium, and other
resources. As the exploitation of these reserves expands, social impacts
will become increasingly important in community growth and expansion. Murdock and his coauthors describe the context and magnitude of
energy-related migration in the northern Great Plains (Chapter 11).
With survey data obtained in five affected communities, they compare
characteristics and perceptions of prior residents and of migrants drawn
to areas by coal developments. They find that migrants drawn by energy
developments have effects on the community that are similar to the
effects of other forms of migration-induced growth. Migrants tend to be
younger, more educated, and more highly skilled, and to have higher
incomes than prior residents. Hence, the authors conclude that community impacts resulting from coal development are not very different from
the impacts resulting from other sources of rapid population growth in
thinly settled areas.

Recent population growth in Maine and other parts of northern New
England seem to be stimulated largely by aesthetic values. For many
northeasterners, northern New England offers rural lifestyles accompanied by an easy proximity to major metropolitan centers. Ploch (Chapter 12) examines the reaction of new in-migrants to the social and physical environment of small Maine communities and the reactions of prior
residents to the new arrivals. He focuses on community participation
and social relationships and describes the revitalization of local newspapers and cultural amenities frequently brought about by the newcomers. He concludes that new in-migrants appear to be adapting quite well
to their new communities even though they are markedly different from
longer-term residents in terms of social and economic characteristics and
life experiences.

Historically, rural communities in Utah have tended to be isolated and
culturally homogeneous. Stinner and Toney (Chapter 13) examine the
consequences of migration to eight nonmetropolitan communities in
Utah to assess the extent to which newcomers differ from prior residents
in socioeconomic and demographic characteristics and in religio-cultural
backgrounds. These researchers link such differences to differing perceptions of the adequacy of community life and services. They attribute
newcomers' higher levels of dissatisfaction with interpersonal relationships and services and facilities to differences in the social backgrounds
of the newcomers and of prior residents. Newcomers view and evaluate
community life from different perspectives and standards largely because they differ from long-time residents in sociocultural background
rather than because they are new to the community.

Zuiches and Price (Chapter 14) discuss recent patterns of population redistribution and industrial dispersal in Michigan and the interaction between these concurrent trends. Using data from the Continuous Work History Sample for 1960–1975, the authors analyze labor-force migration in Michigan's metropolitan and nonmetropolitan sectors prior to and during the "migration turnaround" by origin and destination and by the compositional characteristics of migrants. They show that population redistribution has occurred, in recent years, independently of the relocation of economic activities. Moreover, they show that the recent pattern of economic development in nonmetropolitan Michigan is primarily a response to patterns of population growth. The employment decentralization that has occurred has mostly been in tertiary sectors dominated by workers in service industries.

The nonmetropolitan areas that have been examined in this section and elsewhere in the book demonstrate the diversity in local conditions and in the causes, composition, and consequences of rural and nonmetropolitan population growth. They suggest a continuing need for detailed case studies in these and other regions. Still, the national pervasiveness of the phenomenon suggests more similarities than differences among regions in the underlying processes that shape present and future patterns of population growth in the United States.

10

The Ozark–Ouachita Uplands:
Growth and Consequences[1]

GEORGE H. DAILEY, JR.
REX R. CAMPBELL

Introduction

The key date to remember with respect to the population turnaround in rural America is 1970, yet the reversal from rural decline to growth commenced significantly earlier in certain regions of the country. Population estimates produced by the Census Bureau in 1967 revealed that nonmetropolitan counties in the Ozark–Ouachita uplands of Arkansas, Missouri, and Oklahoma had turned from decline to growth by the mid-1960s. Hence, population growth in this region, considered to be among the most economically depressed and disadvantaged in America, presaged the nationwide turnaround that became evident only several years later. This chapter describes salient aspects of socioeconomic and demographic change in the Ozarks and points out some of the important consequences of these changes.

The resurgence of population growth in nonmetropolitan America is now evident to most people. While there is a continuing need to describe this process and to analyze its determinants, there is also a need to evaluate the impact of growth on the receiving communities. Most reports to date have stressed the reversal in the patterns of population change, the occurrence of population growth in rural areas, the impor-

[1]Data collection was supported by grants from the United States Department of Agriculture, the Ozarks Regional Commission, the United States Army Corps of Engineers, and the Center for Aging Studies, University of Missouri–Columbia. Basic support was provided by the Agricultural Experiment Station, College of Agriculture, University of Missouri–Columbia.

233

New Directions in
Urban–Rural Migration

tance of this growth for balanced population distribution, and the excitement, for some, of seeing the "desert bloom" again. However, before these population shifts are heralded as a solution to rural problems, the ramifications of population change must be understood. Several difficult but key questions must be answered. Are the rural communities structurally adequate to receive these newcomers? What are the community consequences of changes in population characteristics? Is the population revival cost beneficial to nonmetropolitan communities?

This chapter addresses these questions by examining the changes taking place in one region of the country—the Ozark–Ouchita Uplands (herein referred to as the "Ozarks"). This region is a rapidly growing, largely nonmetropolitan area in which the emphasis is on retirement and recreation. Before growth impacts can be discussed, the characteristics of the region and the magnitude and nature of growth and change must be understood.

The Ozark–Ouchita Uplands

The term "Ozarks" has been used to describe a portion of the United States from a variety of points of view—a geographic area, a region of unique cultural heritage, and, more recently, an economic planning region. The Ozarks Economic Development Region is by far the loosest definition of the Ozarks since it includes the entirety of five states, Arkansas, Kansas, Louisiana, Missouri, and Oklahoma. At its inception, the economic development region encompassed a subgrouping of counties closely approximating the Ozark–Ouachita Uplands (Ozarks Regional Commission, 1976). This region is made up of 98 counties in Arkansas, Missouri, and Oklahoma (Figure 10.1). The region tends to represent both a physiographic and—to a lesser extent—a cultural area (Bogue and Beale, 1961; Beale and Fuguitt, 1975).

Physiographically, the 98-county subregion consists of two distinct uplifted areas—the Ozark Plateau and the Ouachita Mountains. Together these highland provinces encompass almost 100,000 square miles. Altitudes and local relief are lower than those seen in the Appalachians (the highest point in the Ozarks is about 2800 feet above sea level), but the valley, ridge, and plateau landforms are similar. Because of the topography and soil types, agricultural pursuits are not extensive. Much of the area is covered with mixed pine and hardwood forests. Several large man-made lakes and productive clearwater trout streams are additional attractions. The region has higher precipitation, warmer summers, and milder winters than most other parts of the mid-

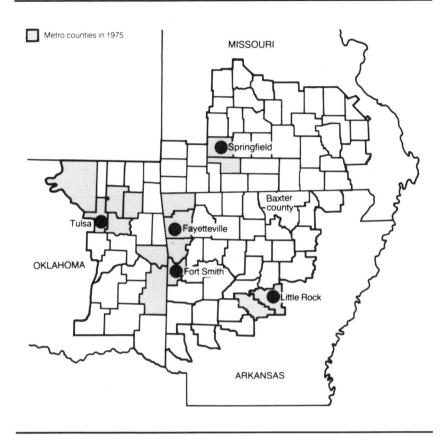

Figure 10.1. The Ozark–Ouachita Uplands.

continent. It is the most extensive elevated area between the Appalachians and the Rockies (Costello, 1975; Hunt, 1974; Rhodes *et al.*, 1974).

The Ozarks before 1950

Major population growth in the Ozarks began in the early nineteenth century. Direct European immigration was an important facet of this development, but the majority of the increase resulted from population movements from southern Appalachia and the southern states (Gerlach, 1976).

The region was and is predominantly rural, with a low population density. In 1950, there were nearly 51 persons per square mile in the continental United States; in the Ozarks there were only about 33 (U.S. Bureau of the Census, 1952). Because of the rugged topography, major road systems and railroads tended to bypass much of the region. The absence of major cities was in part a consequence of inadequate transportation. In 1950, the only major urban places within, or on the fringes of, the region were: Fort Smith, Arkansas; Little Rock, Arkansas; Springfield, Missouri; and Tulsa, Oklahoma. The overwhelming majority of commercial and industrial activity was then concentrated in these growing cities.

Agriculture and related industries were mainstays of employment for the bulk of the population. As late as 1950, over 30% of the labor force in a 115-county Ozark region was employed in agriculture and forestry (Jordan and Bender, 1966). The variation in agriculture was, and is, great. Fertile soils and good crop productivity are found in river bottom areas such as the Arkansas River valley, but in the rougher terrain and even in some plateau areas cereal crop farming is marginal. In marginal areas, cropping has been supplanted by livestock, poultry, and fruit production. Until recently, the average farmer in the Ozarks operated at the subsistence level and often supplemented his income by trapping and hunting. The timber industry, important during the early decades of this century, has gradually been reduced. Today, in most counties, it is a minor industry employing a limited number of people.

Mining is another important source of employment, although it is very localized. An eight-county area of southeast Missouri has been one of the world's major lead-producing districts for over two centuries. Extensive oil fields and refining have been a hallmark of the northeastern Oklahoma section of the Ozarks. Portions of west central Arkansas and eastern Oklahoma contain coal. All of these extractive industries, including agriculture, have experienced substantial employment reductions as a result of technological advances and better employment opportunities elsewhere.

Reduced manpower needs have had severe consequences for the rural Ozarks. Since World War I, incomes and employment opportunities have diminished significantly in the region. General poverty was the rule; subsistence farming was a form of underemployment. Without compensating nonagricultural employment opportunities, many young people moved to major urban centers. Despite low overall levels of educational attainment, this migration represented a loss of human capital because the outbound migration was selective of the region's most capable persons. Aging and depopulation resulted. The region became one of the major economically depressed areas of the nation.

The Ozarks from 1950 to 1970

By 1960 the employment profile of most Ozark counties had changed significantly. Most dramatic was the tremendous drop of employment in agriculture and forestry. From 1950 to 1960 these industries declined by 142,000 employees. This reduced the proportion of the labor force in these jobs to 13.5% (which was still significantly higher than the corresponding proportion for the entire United States). At the same time, the region experienced considerable increases in manufacturing employment (39,945 jobs) and in trade and services (49,745 jobs). However, these gains were not large enough to offset the losses in agricultural and mining jobs. Hence the region showed a net deficit of over 50,000 jobs during the decade (Jordan and Bender, 1966). It is not difficult to understand why the region's median family income was only about 60% of the nation's in 1959. It was undoubtedly much lower in the most rural parts of the region.

Continued heavy out-migration from nonmetropolitan counties between 1950–1960 resulted in a net migration loss of nearly one-quarter of a million persons (Table 10.1). The location of new manufacturing plants in smaller cities and towns in the Ozarks helped to stem the rural outmigration somewhat. However, the majority of these were nonunion, low-wage, and slow-growth plants and employed small labor forces (Jordan and Bender, 1966).

In the midst of general population losses in the region during the 1950s—losses that were greatest in counties with heavy agricultural concentrations—a small number of nonmetropolitan Ozark counties experienced migration gains (Figure 10.2).[2] All of these either had large mineral extraction and refining operations, were adjacent to metropolitan areas, or contained university or military installations.

One exception to this pattern was Camden County, Missouri, a lake and resort area. Camden grew by nearly 1% per year during the 1950s for a total migration gain of over 800 people. Growth in manufacturing employment accounted for a small portion of the increase, but the Lake of the Ozarks, one of the oldest (1931) and largest man-made lakes (59,520 surface acres) in the region, was the major factor. This narrow, winding reservoir, nestled in rugged ridges, became the impetus to new economic and population growth as vacationers and retirees began to visit and remain in the area. County age-specific net migration estimates

[2]For example, in Douglas County, Missouri over 64% of the employed labor force was in agriculture in 1950, and the county had an annual rate of net migration loss of 3.6% between 1950–1960 (Denney, no date; Dailey et al., 1978b).

TABLE 10.1
Components of Population Change in the Ozark-Ouachita Uplands by Metropolitan Status, 1950-1975

Item	Total region number	Annual rate of change	Metropolitan number[a]	Annual rate of change	Nonmetropolitan number	Annual rate of change
Population						
1950	2,334,069		908,542		1,425,527	
1960	2,391,529		1,072,589		1,318,940	
1970	2,718,462		1,283,238		1,435,224	
1975	3,015,300		1,442,100		1,573,200	
Population change						
1950-1960	57,460	0.24	164,047	1.65	-106,587	-0.77
1960-1970	326,933	1.27	210,649	1.78	116,284	0.84
1970-1975 [b]	296,600	1.97	159,000	2.22	137,600	1.74
Net migration						
1950-1960	-231,216	-0.97	13,302	0.13	-244,518	-1.78
1960-1970	138,925	0.54	87,396	0.74	51,529	0.37
1970-1975	218,900	1.45	102,000	1.42	116,900	1.48
Natural increase						
1950-1960	288,676	1.22	150,745	1.52	137,931	1.00
1960-1970	188,008	0.73	123,253	1.04	64,755	0.47
1970-1975	78,000	0.51	56,900	0.79	21,100	0.26

Source: Dailey et al. (1978b).
a The 1975 Standard Metropolitan Statistical Area definitions are used for all time periods.
b Because of rounding, the 1970 to 1975 figures and percents do not always sum.

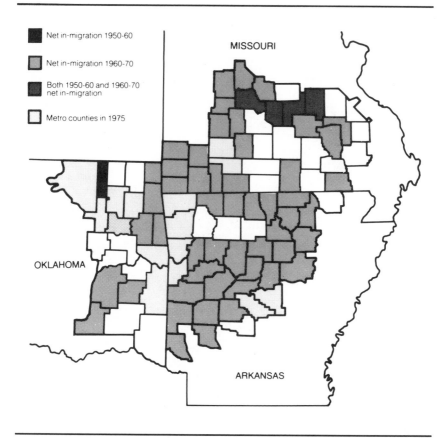

Figure 10.2. Ozark nonmetropolitan counties with net in-migration, 1950–1960 and 1960–1970. (Source: U. S. Bureau of the Census.)

made for the 1950s show this very clearly: The highest positive rates for the county were in the cohorts aged 40–74 (Bowles and Tarver, 1965). Hence Camden County was a forerunner of the recreation and retirement growth now found throughout the region.

Prior to the completion of the Lake of the Ozarks, only one man-made lake existed in the region. Lake Taneycomo (1730 surface acres) was constructed in 1913 in Taney County, Missouri, for electrical power generation. Since World War II there has been a dramatic proliferation of reservoir construction, by the Corps of Engineers and by private concerns, in the drainage basins of the Missouri, Red, White, Ouachita, and Arkansas Rivers.

By 1970, there was a further reduction in the proportion of the labor force in agriculture, and the increase in manufacturing continued. Nonetheless, the region was still substantially above the nation in agriculture and forestry employment (7.9% versus 3.5%) and slightly below it in manufacturing (Table 10.2). In addition, slightly higher proportions of the population were employed in mining and construction in the region. The continued economic depression of the Ozarks relative to other parts of the nation is illustrated by other data. Unemployment rates, the percentage of adults without a high school diploma, and the

TABLE 10.2

Industrial Composition of the United States of the Nonmetropolitan Ozark-Ouachita Uplands, and of Selected Types of Counties, 1970 (in percentages)

Industry	United States	Ozark–Ouachita Uplands			
		Total	Retirement counties	Lake counties	Lake/retirement counties
Agriculture, forestry and fisheries	3.5	7.9	9.3	8.0	8.9
Mining	0.8	1.8	1.1	1.0	0.6
Construction	5.5	7.5	8.3	8.5	9.0
Manufacturing	24.4	23.0	22.7	21.4	20.6
Transportation, communication, and utilities	6.3	5.2	4.8	5.0	4.7
Wholesale and retail trade	18.9	18.9	18.1	18.9	18.6
Finance, insurance, and real estate	4.7	2.6	2.6	2.6	2.7
Business and repair services	2.9	2.0	1.9	2.0	1.9
Personal services	4.3	5.0	5.5	5.7	6.3
Entertainment and recreation services	0.8	0.6	0.7	0.7	0.8
Professional services	16.5	15.5	15.2	15.9	16.0
Public administration	5.2	4.4	3.6	4.8	3.8

Source: Dailey and Campbell (1979a, 1979b).

percentage of families with incomes of less than $5000 were all higher than national levels (Dailey *et al.*, 1978b; U.S. Bureau of the Census, 1972a).

Despite continued economic difficulties, the 1960s were important years for a beginning resurgence of population growth in the nonmetropolitan Ozarks (Table 10.1). With the waning of the baby boom, geographic variations in population growth became increasingly dependent upon migration. Annual rates of natural increase in the Ozarks dropped from 1.22% in the 1950s to .73% in the 1960s. While it was expected that the nonmetropolitan counties would continue their pattern of outmigration and lead to even larger losses, this was not the case. *The nonmetropolitan turnaround, which has become visible on a national basis only since 1970, occurred in much of the Ozark–Ouachita Uplands during the previous decade.* The counties that had lost nearly 250,000 people between 1950 and 1960 gained over 50,000 persons in the 1960s. The number of nonmetropolitan counties with net in-migration increased from only five in the 1950s to over two-thirds of the total in the next decade (Figure 10.2). The age composition of the migration gain also changed to include all ages except young adults (Dailey and Campbell, 1979b). Metropolitan counties also experienced a marked increase in their annual rate of net migration (from .13% in the 1950s to .74% in the 1960s) and had a migration gain of over 87,000 people.

The Ozarks in the 1970s

This pattern of growth continued and intensified during the 1970s (see Table 10.1). Natural increase fell even lower, but the rate of net migration climbed in both metropolitan and nonmetropolitan counties. Through net in-migration in the first half of the decade, the region grew by almost 219,000 persons—an increase that nearly equaled the loss experienced during the 1950s. The gain in nonmetropolitan counties was over two-and-one-fourth times that of the 1960s, and all but three non-SMSA counties had positive net migration rates (Figure 10.3).

Manufacturing, a major factor in nonmetropolitan population growth during the 1960s in the Ozarks, underwent further expansion in the 1970s. Of all new manufacturing plants (463) constructed in the region during 1967–1974, 60% were located in nonmetropolitan counties (Kuehn and Brashler, 1977). Nonetheless, the highest percentage increase in employment in manufacturing establishments between 1970 and 1975 was in metropolitan counties (Table 10.3). Significant differences between rates of change in the metropolitan and nonmetropolitan business patterns were also found in agricultural services, mining,

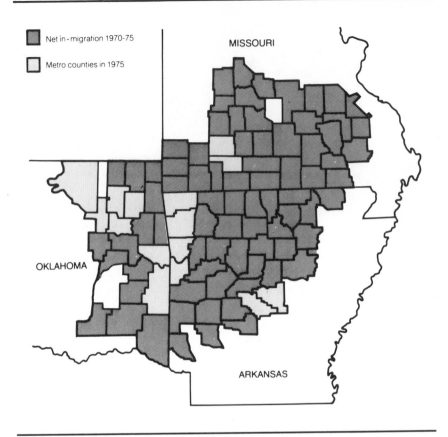

Figure 10.3. Ozark nonmetropolitan counties with net in-migration, 1970–1975. (Source: U.S. Bureau of the Census.)

finance, insurance and real estate, and construction. Only construction had a larger increase in nonmetropolitan counties. This increase was generated by population growth and the resultant need for the construction of housing, business firms, transportation facilities, and so on.

Increases in income were coupled with these changes in employment. In 1969, per capita income in the Ozarks was $2807. By 1974, it had increased to $4241, a 51% change. However, in 1974, the Ozarks per capita income was only 78% of the national figure, a 2% increase above the 1969 proportion.

Overall, the 1975 profile of the Ozarks showed a combination of growth and lag with some dramatic gains since the 1950s. Three major factors account for these changes: (*a*) the continued growth of metropolitan areas and adjacent nonmetropolitan counties; (b) the continued influx of labor-intensive light manufacturing plants; and (c) the development of a recreation–retirement industry. While the region continued to lag behind the national economic maintsream, a self-feeding spiral of regional prosperity had become evident. The trickle of migrants that started in the 1950s heralded the beginning of an economic and demographic boom. Physical and social amenities, in addition to the economic changes described above, are important to nonmetropolitan growth in the Ozarks and in other regions (Biggar, 1979; Campbell et al., 1977; Dailey et al., 1977; Danforth and Voth, 1979; Green et al., 1970; Long and Hansen, 1979; Morrison and Wheeler, 1976; Nolan et al., 1979; Shelley, 1977; Wardwell, 1977; Williams and Sofranko, 1978). Retirees in the Ozark–Ouachita area are particularly drawn by its amenities. As Oliver (1971) noted for one community in southwest Missouri,

> Why aging persons would migrate to this particular region in the Ozarks might be explained by the nature of the environment—both physical and social. Those seeking pure, clean mountain air, pure and uncontaminated

TABLE 10.3
*Percentage Change in the Number of Business Establishments by Industry
in the Ozark-Ouachita Uplands by Metropolitan Status, 1970–1975*

Industry	Total region	Metropolitan counties	Nonmetropolitan counties
Agricultural services	12	20	12
Mining	13	23	11
Contract construction	54	47	55
Manufacturing	27	56	22
Transportation and utilities	26	30	26
Wholesale trade	100	98	100
Retail trade	14	14	14
Finance, insurance, real estate	36	55	33
Services	31	29	32

Source: U.S. Bureau of the Census, County Business Patterns 1972b, 1977c.

water, scenic views of mountains and lakes, desirable climates with changes of season but no extremes, excellent hospital care, modern stores and shopping, low taxes and plenty of churches will find them here [p. 17].

This desirable set of living conditions is important to young as well as older persons. However, younger persons have only recently been able to actualize their preference for the Ozarks because of the lag in growth of economic opportunities.

Return migration is also an important facet of Ozark growth. Many Ozark residents who left the region in past decades have now returned to retire. Living conditions, familial ties, and a sense of coming home are among the determinants of this movement (Campbell et al., 1977; Green et al., 1970). These counterstream migration flows are associated primarily with the older population but are not restricted to this age group. Some younger persons are beginning to come back to the region for a mixture of economic opportunities, amenities, and the social environment (Campbell and Johnson, 1976). Such motivations, for example, were found in a migration study in counties along the Arkansas River navigation system. Although most (56%) new migrants from other states cited economic considerations as the primary motive for their movement, almost as many of them (44%) gave noneconomic reasons. For the other two types of migrants—intrastate and return—social ties and amenities at the point of destination were the major reasons; they constituted 54% of the reasons for intrastate migrants and 69% for returnees (Campbell et al., 1977).

Noneconomic moves do presuppose some measure of economic security regardless of age or occupational status. Although the Ozarks may be a premier example of a high-amenities area, the retired migrant must be able to meet the cost of living, and the young student coming back home requires employment. It is becoming increasingly apparent that the Ozarks region is acquiring a more adequate employment base, which allows many migrants to enjoy the life-style they seek. Furthermore, it appears that some standard of living trade-offs are being made to bring these desires to fruition.

It is probable that persons who moved into the region for employment opportunities will include the amenities of the area in future decisions about whether to remain there. One indicator of this is the response of migrants in the Arkansas River study when they were asked why they were staying in the Ozarks. Nearly equal proportions of migrants cited their jobs (33%) and living conditions (32%) as the factor keeping them in the area. Overall, noneconomic considerations—amenities, family, and home—held sway over purely economic ones. Noneconomic factors were important even among the most mobile and job-oriented group— the younger, interstate migrants (Campbell et al., 1977).

Nonmetropolitan-County Types in the Ozarks

The preceding discussion of growth and change has pointed to the importance of recreational industries and retirement migration as the major impetus to the last 25 years of population increase. The significance of these factors is quite apparent at the regional level, but we need to know whether their relative importance holds for more local areas as well. One way to examine this question is by using a county typology that combines a number of socioeconomic and structural variables (Beale, 1977; Beale and Fuguitt, 1976; Campbell *et al.*, 1978). The typology we used included the following categories:

1. *Retirement:* A county with a net migration rate of 10% or more for persons 60 years of age and over, 1960–1970, as classified by Beale
2. *Lake:* A county containing a lake, man-made or natural, of 1000 surface acres or more and/or a major portion of a lake of 1000 surface acres or more
3. *Senior college:* A county containing a 4-year institution and a college population that was 5% or more of the county's 1975 population (Beale's U.S. figures are for senior state colleges only)
4. *Military base:* A county with an installation as delineated by the Department of Defense, Distribution of Personnel by State by Installation, September, 1975 (Beale's U.S. figures are for counties with a military population)
5. *Controlled access highway:* A county containing at least 25 miles of a highway of four lanes or more, such as an interstate or turnpike as shown on official state highway maps for 1975
6. *High level of agriculture:* A county with 30% or more of its 1970 employed labor force in agriculture
7. *Low level of agriculture:* A county with 4.00 – 9.99 % of its 1970 employed labor force in agriculture
8. *High level of manufacturing:* A county with 30 % or more of its 1970 employed labor force in manufacturing
9. *Intermediate level of manufacturing:* A county with 20.00 – 29.99 % of its 1970 employed labor force in manufacturing
10. *Retirement–lake:* A county classified as both a retirement county and a lake county[3]

As Beale (1976, 1977) noted in his examination of county characteristics, those counties with high levels of older-age migrant populations had the highest total net in-migration rates of any group of counties

[3]The combined classification includes only those counties with an influx of older persons and the presence of a lake, a surrogate for commercial recreation.

(2.52%). At first glance this does not appear to be the case in the Ozark–Ouachita subregion, where the highest 1970–1975 rate was found in counties with high levels of agricultural employment (3.14%) (Table 10.4). The explanation for this discrepancy calls into question the method of single-variable county typifications. The single-characteristic categories are not necessarily mutually exclusive, nor do they necessarily describe the most crucial elements of county growth or decline. In the Ozarks only a small number of counties had high percentages of agricultural employment. One of these, which heavily weighted the total migration rate, is Hickory County, Missouri. In addition to its farm-related employment, Hickory is a major retirement area that contains Pomme De Terre Lake. Hickory gained new migrants from 1970 to 1975 at an annual rate of over 6%. Gauging by national and Ozark regional figures, the county's agricultural practices were not the driving force behind its rapid growth. Thus, caution must be used in interpreting these data. Although the method has limitations, it is still useful. Excluding the anomaly, high level of agricultural employment, the county types in the Ozark–Ouachita subregion compare closely with Beale's national data and the Ozarks regional data.

A closer examination of the Ozark–Ouachita counties shows dramatic changes in rates of growth from the 1960s to the 1970s. With the exception of those counties containing military installations, all had an increased rate of net migration; however, the rates of increase varied greatly. Although these data increasingly suggest a heterogeneous pattern of growth in the Ozarks, retirement counties (2.71%) and retirement–lake counties (2.89%) appear to have grown more rapidly than other types of areas (Figure 10.4). The 26 counties in the second category went from a migration loss of over 88,000 in the 1950s to a gain of nearly 74,000 in the first half of the 1970s. The latter represented almost 63% of the total migration gain in all Ozark–Ouachita nonmetropolitan counties. Not all of this growth was in the older-age cohorts. According to recent estimates, approximately 27% of the total in-migration to retirement–lake counties was among persons aged 55 years and over. An additional 13% was accounted for by the gain in the 25–34 age cohort. Yet, the retirement–lake category absorbed nearly 45% of the Ozark migration gain in the 55-and-over cohort and about 70% of the gain among persons aged 25–34 (Dailey *et al.*, 1978a).

Thus, although older-age migration has made a tremendous contribution to the overall growth of the region, apparently it is not the sole contributor; evidently changes are occurring in the age composition of recent migration to the Ozarks. At the same time retirement and lake counties are still very important in current Ozark population growth.

TABLE 10.4

Average Annual Rates of Net Migration in Nonmetropolitan Counties of the United States, the Five-State Ozarks Region, and the Ozark-Ouachita Uplands by Selected County Characteristics, 1960, 1970-1975

County characteristics [a,b]	United States [c]		Ozarks region [d]		Ozark-Ouachita subregion [e]	
	1960-1970	1970-1975	1960-1970	1970-1975	1960-1970	1970-1975
Retirement	0.90	2.52	0.55	2.21	0.95	2.71
Lake	—	—	-0.50	0.36	0.69	2.12
Senior college	0.11	0.81	0.42	0.65	1.49	2.46
Military base	0.26	-1.37	0.51	-1.21	0.75	-4.06
Controlled access highway	—	—	-0.58	0.33	0.17	0.51
High level of agriculture	-1.89	-0.26	-1.58	-0.16	0.20	3.14
Low level of agriculture	—	—	-0.34	0.56	0.58	2.00
High level of manufacturing	-0.40	0.36	-0.62	0.46	-0.24	1.10
Intermediate level of manufacturing	—	—	-0.69	0.73	0.40	2.03
Retirement-lake	—	—	0.91	2.51	1.17	2.89

a The categories of county characteristics are not mutually exclusive. The average annual net migration rates for each characteristic are expressed as percentages.

b See text for definition of characteristics.

c Data for the United States are from Beale (1977).

d Data for the five-state Ozarks region are from Campbell et al. (1978).

e Data for the Ozark-Ouachita subregion are from the Ozarks Regional Computer File maintained at the University of Missouri-Columbia.

247

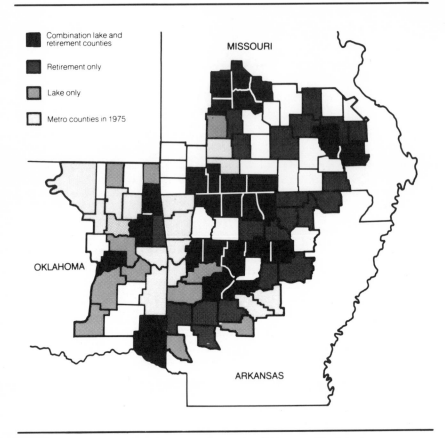

Figure 10.4. Lake and retirement counties in the Ozark–Ouachita Uplands.

Recreation and retirement migration continues to be a clear and major focus of Ozark growth. Hence it is of interest to take a closer look at the impact of recent growth in recreation–retirement areas.

The Effects of Change in the Recreation–Retirement Areas

The Ozarks are in the midst of a prosperous period of economic and demographic expansion, but this optimistic picture must be tempered with some meticulous prying below the surface. Rapid population increase carries with it both positive and negative consequences. Some planners, local government officials, and concerned citizens—natives and newcomers alike—who see both the present growth and the strong probability of future increases, find themselves on the horns of a dilemma. The economic benefits associated with the influx of migrants are widely accepted and appreciated. This is not difficult to comprehend, in view of the impoverished status of the Ozarks in past decades. But people are also beginning to realize that growth can bring too many people. Traffic jams, water pollution, increased crime, and the destruction of natural beauty are some of the possible consequences.

The remainder of this chapter will attempt to sort out some of the effects of growth. Although many of the items discussed have applicability to any area of the Ozarks, the focus of attention is on the retirement and recreation counties because they have had the longest periods of growth and the most rapid rates of increase. Moreover, they are among those Ozark nonmetropolitan counties with the smallest population bases. The effects of growth have been of three major types: demographic, economic, and environmental.

Before discussing these effects, a brief look at one retirement and recreation county will illustrate some of the myriad changes that have taken place. Although this county is not representative of all Ozark recreation–retirement counties, it does embody most of the impacts discussed below.

In 1975, Baxter County was the fastest growing county in Arkansas, with a population of 21,000 people. Its largest town, Mountain Home, increased from 3936 persons in 1970 to 6415 in 1976—an increase of nearly 63%. Two other small towns in the county, Gassville and Lakeview, had equally high rates of change during the 5-year period.

The county's age composition has changed dramatically. In 1950, the age structure was similar to that of the United States overall, with a preponderance of young people. Since then the age structure has skewed in the direction of the older-age cohorts. From 1970 to 1975, the number of persons age 65 and over increased from 3470 to 5428. This cohort comprised almost 26% of the total population in 1975. There was heavy out-migration among younger people in earlier decades, but this pattern reversed in the 1960s and the 1970s.

The economic structure of the county is also changing. In 1950, agricultural employment dominated all other categories. By 1960, farming and related practices were still important facets of the economy, but the construction of Bull Shoals and Norfolk Lakes, in the 1950s, and the influx of retired migrants brought economic changes, especially in the service sector. In 1970, the county's economy consisted of a combination of manufacturing, wholesale and retail trade, construction, and personal and professional services. Consequently, the county's economy is no longer controlled by the waxings and wanings of one industrial component.

Baxter County's growth is not an unmixed blessing. For example, Mountain Home's water treatment facility was built in 1969 with a maximum capacity of 4 million gallons per day. This system must now be enlarged to 8 million gallons a day because of the town's burgeoning population and industrial expansion and because smaller communities in the vicinity, such as Gassville, tap into the system. Traffic tie-ups because of commercial strip development and a general increase in traffic flow along U.S. Highway 62, the principal thoroughfare, have caused the local government to work for a bypass. The demand for rural mass transportation, law enforcement, fire protection, and refuse collection is also increasing. While the demand is high, there is an unwillingness on the part of citizens to vote for tax increases. For example, in the spring of 1978, a bond issue for a new high school comlex was defeated by a two-to-one margin. The large older-age population, who moved to the area partly because of its low taxes, were implied as responsible for this vote. The present difficulties will become more severe if population projections for Mountain Home are accurate. These projections point to a population of between 20,000 and 36,000 by the end of the decade, and to a county population of 45,000 (Dailey and Campbell, 1979a, 1979b).

Demographic Effects

GENERAL POPULATION GROWTH EFFECTS

Regardless of the specific types of changes experienced by an area, some effects do result from sheer numerical growth. During the 1950s, the population of the Ozarks was at its low ebb. Highways were sparsely traveled, and the hills and valleys were virtually deserted. A person could walk in the woods for long distances without encountering other persons. This is rapidly changing, as heavy traffic and even traffic jams are increasingly common. The woods are filled with hunters, hikers, and off-road vehicles.

Young or old, urban or rural migrants, seasonal or permanent populations need certain basic services such as water, housing, food, and so on. The provision of these basic needs is a major challenge in rapidly growing areas. As in the case of Mountain Home, increased size over a short period of time has been significant. Although absolute numerical increases in the nonmetropolitan Ozarks do not compare with those in metropolitan centers, on a proportional basis these increases have a greater impact since most such small places do not have the infrastructure of larger centers.

Basic community services such as law enforcement, fire protection, and refuse collection were not available or were inadequate in many small Ozark communities before the renewed population growth began. Deficiencies still exist, but additional people continue to migrate to these small communities. Subsequent population increases produce still greater strain on the existing infrastructure and still greater demands for additional services. Places like Mountain Home have a hard time coping with present growth, much less anticipating and planning for the future.

One effect of the rapid growth is a considerable lag between the time requests for basic services are made and the time the necessary revenues can provide them. An increase in the number of property owners produces more tax monies, but the increases often come too late to meet the immediacy of some problems. In other cases, augmentation of the tax base is inadequate to meet the growth in needs. Some governments attempt to make up the difference by higher taxes. Although higher taxes are unpopular throughout the nation, this unpopularity may be more intense in the Ozarks because comparatively low taxes have been an important factor in some people's decisions to migrate to the region.

EFFECTS OF COMPOSITIONAL CHANGE

Some consequences are directly tied to the specific nature of population growth such as the place of origin, age, and other characteristics of the migrants.

Place of Origin. Census data show that a significant number of persons moved into the Ozarks from Chicago, Los Angeles, Little Rock, Kansas City, Wichita, and St. Louis (Tables 10.5 and 10.6).[4] Although, movement from these specific metropolitan areas accounts for about one-fifth of the total migration into the two State Economic Areas (SEAs), the importance of these flows should not be underestimated, especially with regard to the point of relocation. For example, a number of community leaders in Arkansas have noted high concentrations of former Chicagoans in their communities—Lakeview, Bull Shoals, Harrison, and Mountain Home. In the latter two places this preponderance is so overwhelming that Dickinson (1978) in *Sunbelt Retirement* calls Harrison "Little Chicago," and a Chicago television station has been added to Mountain Home's cable service.

The influx of metropolitan migrants caused one local leader in southwest Missouri to observe that, "In-migration to the Ozarks is primarily a

---

[4]The analysis is based on data for SEAs. Two areas, SEA-9, northern Arkansas, and SEA-7, southwestern Missouri, are used to indicate one of the major Ozark destination regions.

TABLE 10.5
Migration into Arkansas State Economic Area (SEA-9) by Area of Origin [a]

Migration stream	Number	Percent of total	Percent of interstate in-migrants only
Total from all SEAs	19,359	100.00	
Northeast region	151	0.78	1.06
New England division	27	0.14	0.19
Middle Atlantic division	124	0.64	0.87
North Central region	7,375	38.10	51.64
East North Central division	3,253	16.80	22.78
Illinois	2,267	11.71	15.87
SEA-C "Chicago"	1,445	7.46	10.12
West North Central division	4,122	21.29	28.86
Missouri	2,453	12.67	17.18
SEA-7 "S. Central"	583	3.02	4.08
SEA-A "Kansas City"	575	2.97	4.03
Kansas	996	5.14	6.97
South region	7,846	40.53	19.38
South Atlantic division	519	2.68	3.63
East South Central division	332	1.72	2.32
West South Central division	6,995	36.13	13.42
Arkansas	5,078	26.23	---
SEA-3 "N. Central"	1,165	6.02	---
SEA-8 "Delta"	927	4.79	---
SEA-A "Little Rock"	856	4.42	---
Oklahoma	821	4.24	5.75
Texas	937	4.84	6.56
West region	3,987	20.00	27.92
Mountain division	893	4.61	6.25
Pacific division	3,094	15.98	21.67
California	2,408	12.44	16.86
SEA-F "Los Angeles"	815	4.21	5.71

Source: U.S. Bureau of the Census, 1972c.
[a] SEA-9 consists of: Baxter, Boone, Carroll, Cleburne, Fulton, Izard, Madison, Marion, Newton, Searcy, Stone, and Van Buren Counties.

result of out-migration from urban areas with urban problems." The desire to escape the problems of large cities has been noted in demographic, urban sociological, and historical research (Blackwood and Carpenter, 1978; Biggar, 1979; Gist and Fava, 1974; Jackson, 1973; Wardwell, 1977). However, as residential preference studies point out, the wish to move from metropolitan areas to small towns or open county does not necessarily reflect a preference for the quiet, pastoral Arcadian ideal. It really reflects the hope that Arcadia and urban technology can be melded (Dillman and Dobash, 1972; Fuguitt and Zuiches, 1975; Schmitt, 1973; Wardwell, 1977). A century ago, Frederick Law Olmsted commented,

> The present outward tendency of town population is not so much an ebb as higher rise of the same flood (of urbanization), the end of which must be, not

TABLE 10.6
Migration into Missouri State Economic Area (SEA-7) by Area of Origin [a]

Migration stream	Number	Percent of total	Percent of interstate in-migrants only
Total from all SEAs	26,872	100.00	
Northeast region	349	1.30	2.38
New England division	155	0.58	1.06
Middle Atlantic division	194	0.72	1.32
North Central region	18,186	67.08	40.80
East North Central division	2,817	10.48	19.20
Illinois	1,575	5.86	10.73
SEA-C "Chicago"	653	2.43	4.45
West North Central division	15,369	57.19	21.60
Iowa	790	2.94	5.38
Missouri	12,200	45.40	----
SEA-C "Springfield"	3,731	13.88	----
SEA-A "Kansas City"	1,506	5.60	----
SEA-B "St. Louis"	1,328	4.94	----
SEA-5 "Central"	1,022	3.80	----
Kansas	1,794	6.68	12.23
SEA-A "Wichita"	512	1.91	3.49
SEA-B "Kansas City"	497	1.85	3.39
South region	3,723	13.85	25.37
South Atlantic division	721	2.68	4.91
East South Central division	400	1.49	2.73
West South Central division	2,602	9.68	17.73
Arkansas	1,061	3.95	7.23
SEA-9 "Northwest"	529	1.97	3.61
Oklahoma	679	2.53	4.63
Texas	763	2.84	5.20
West region	4,614	17.17	31.45
Mountain division	1,167	4.34	7.95
Pacific division	3,447	12.83	23.49
California	2,892	10.76	19.71
SEA-F "Los Angeles"	1,091	4.06	7.44

Source: U.S. Bureau of the Census, 1972c.
[a] SEA-7 consists of: Christian, Dallas, Douglas, Howell, Ozark, Polk, Stone, Taney, Texas, Webster, and Wright Counties.

a sacrifice of urban conveniences, but their combination with the special charms and substantial advantages of rural conditions of life [Jackson, 1973: 219–220].

The urban-to-rural migrants are not seeking to escape urbanity. They are looking for the best of both worlds—country living with urban services. This perspective creates difficulties for small Ozark communities in supplying demanded services. As Baxter County's judge pointed out about a small but vocal minority, "Some of these migrants compare Baxter County with Cook County [Illinois] with statements like, 'This is the way we did it in Cicero.'" These former urbanities have linked country living with low taxes. However, they continue to demand services and fail to see the connection between such services and the necessary increase in taxes to provide them.

For the urban-to-rural migrant, one solution is to reside in a purposely developed "second home–retirement village" such as Horseshoe Bend or Cherokee Village in Arkansas, or a major residential housing development such as those in Lakeview, Arkansas. In both settings the newcomer finds, for the most part, paved and lighted streets, water and sewage hookups—basic "urban" amenities—as well as nearby recreational facilities and opportunities. Retirement village developments also include services such as grocery stores, site-specific recreational facilities, and some medical facilities. They are largely self-contained.

High expectations of service are not universal. Many migrants know what to expect in the Ozarks before they move. Prior experience with small communities equips rural-to-rural migrants with a better idea of available services. This is particularly true of previous Ozark residents who are now returning. The director of the Ozark Institute recently observed that returnees have a realistic understanding of the service situation, whereas first-time movers to the region have high expectations. Lower service expectations among recent Ozark migrants have also been evidenced in more indirect ways as a result of their vacationing in the area prior to the actual move to the point of destination or through word-of-mouth. (Campbell *et al.*; Center for Aging Studies, 1978; Shelley, 1977). Finally, regardless of migrant type, origin, or previous associations there is a willingness on the part of some newcomers to make service trade-offs. However, this willingness may last only through a novelty, or enchantment, phase immediately following the move to the region. Dickinson has commented,

> I met some unhappy folks there (Harrison) because they really didn't ever leave Chicago in their hearts and minds. . . . In Arkansas, people say taxes are low and the roads show it. . . . The services of a city such as Chicago couldn't

be achieved without paying higher taxes and insurance rates.... The only way to beat the game is to adapt to the life style of the natives.... Former Chicagoans who do so are happy and adjusted [Davis, no date].

Age of Migrants. With the influx of older-age migrants, there has been a significant alteration in the age structure of the Ozarks population. Because of this, there is a need for more specialized services for older people, such as health care and public transportation. Local agencies dealing with the aging population are working to tackle these problems. But, Peterson (1978) has noted that health planning in some Ozark communities is geared to the age of the retirement migrants at the time of their move into the Ozarks, and not several years later when they start to require increasingly intensive health and social services. Because of inadequate medical services and the lack of sheltered, comprehensive-care retirement centers, Peterson has observed that a small but significant stream of elderly persons who moved to southwest Missouri are leaving.

The concentration of older persons has positive effects as well. In earlier decades the Ozarks lost much human capital; the out-migration pattern of the young was highly selective of the best-educated individuals. This effect has been reversed as talented people have been migrating to the region. However, the practical aspects of this gain are not assured unless older migrants become active in the community. Although a lifetime of occupational and educational talents would appear to be an asset, these skills are frequently unavailable because older migrants are not active participants in community affairs. Not all older migrants remain uninvolved, but the many who do may feel that they have worked for a major part of their lives and that they now want their time for themselves.

The older population, in spite of this low participation rate, does appear to have a major impact on local elections. For example, older persons are more likely to vote than are younger persons (Atchley, 1977). Moreover, older-age citizens (persons 55 and over) make up a numerically significant portion of the population in the nonmetropolitan Ozarks (between 25 and 40% of the population). And perhaps most important, older migrants often do not have the same interests in schools or other services that young families do, and many retirees who have moved to the region because of low taxes do not want to have them raised. These differences can have a dramatic effect on some local elections, such as school bond issues. As a case in point, tax increases for new school facilities were soundly defeated in recent elections in Harrison and Mountain Home. Although not proven, the general feeling in the communities is that retirees' votes defeated the issues.

A variety of reasons explain the need to raise additional monies for schools. One reason is the need to expand existing facilities and staffs, as a direct result of population change. The region is experiencing an increase in school-age children because of the in-migration of young families: School populations have increased in most Ozark counties and even in such retirement areas as Stone and Taney counties in Missouri and Baxter and Marion counties in Arkansas (U.S. Bureau of the Census, 1978).

Economic Consequences

The economic composition of the region, especially that of the nonmetropolitan counties, has changed dramatically in the past several decades. Per capita income increased rather impressively in the Ozarks during the 1970s. This increase resulted from the growth of retirement, recreation, and light manufacturing industries. In turn, shopping centers, fast-food outlets, and all the other accoutrements of growing areas are found in the region. Roadside billboards and other forms of "plastic Americana" are seen everywhere. However, this change in the economic make-up of the nonmetropolitan Ozarks did not occur suddenly. Instead, it was a gradual, staged process directly facilitated by population movements into the region.

EXPORTING THE OZARKS

A modification of export-base theory can be used to explain the transformation of employment in the Ozarks toward correspondence with the national economic structure. The export model was originally developed to explain the settlement structure of underdeveloped regions.

> The assumption is that growth in an unsettled region can be explained in terms of the region's main export commodity or staple.... There is also a superstructure of "residentiary" activities such as retail shops and service centers which are secondary in that they do not export their sales, but which, rather, depend on the staple because they come into existence to serve workers employed in staple industries. The location of residentiary activities is fundamental to a definition of the "impact" region of the staple, because the area affected by growth of the staple comprises the region within which its workers live, together with the region from which these workers obtain their everyday needs.... If the staple industry continues to grow and, if along with it, the residentiary activities of the dependent region expand sufficiently, these secondary activities may, through the internal and external economies of increasing scale of firms and size of agglomerations of industry, become export staples. It is at this point that the region "takes off" into self-sustained growth [Berry and Morton, 1970:96–97].

Manufacturing is generally thought of as a basic industry, or an export staple, and in the 1950s, it began to replace agriculture in the Ozarks.

However, this change is not the real key to understanding how the employment picture in the region is converging with that of the nation. Rather, it was another export that realigned the economy—the Ozark region itself.

Previous research examining the economic base and well-being of urban areas has distinguished between *basic* activities, which bring money into the community by marketing goods and services to people who come from the outside, and *nonbasic* activities, whose goods and services are consumed within the confines of the urban area (Murphy, 1974). Economic and demographic growth is viewed as a function of employment and population multipliers so that an increase in the basic industry results in an increase in nonbasic ones. A college or a military installation can be viewed as a basic industry because it brings dollars into the receiving community. The effect of its presence acts as the stimulus in the development and expansion of secondary, nonbasic employment. This same rationale can be applied to the pattern of growth represented by something as intangible as the *image of the Ozarks as a desirable place of residence.*

THE STAGING OF ECONOMIC DEVELOPMENT IN THE OZARKS

There is a package of physiographic attributes within the region that make it an aesthetically desirable location—topography, forests, climate, spring-fed streams, large lakes, and so on. Recreational opportunities are widely available. With increases in both disposable income and amount of leisure time since World War II, the Ozarks became a popular vacation place for many Midwesterners. In order to service the consumer needs of this temporary population, tertiary-level employment such as retail outlets began to expand in the 1960s. Later, some vacationers decided to combine retirement with recreation. This produced further expansion of service employment as the permanent population began to grow. The increase of the retired population also encouraged the expansion of selected specialized services, for example, health care. Since the older-age newcomers had low levels of labor-force participation, the needed services had to be supplied by younger people. This continued expansion of jobs encouraged an influx of young adult newcomers and increased retention of young natives. Thus, the export—the Ozarks—resulted in the import of people and their monies, and it is this continued population increase that appeared as the recreation and retirement counties first basic industry.

The recent growth is usually welcomed by the local economic community, but it can also create concern. Aware that much of the recent prosperity hinges on service employment, some civic leaders see the need to diversify the community's economy to avoid localized recessions such as those created by gasoline shortages. Attempts have been made to attract more jobs in light manufacturing. One example is the concern of a citizen's organization in the tri-lakes area of Branson, Missouri where in 1970, less than 10% of Taney County's employed labor force was working in manufacturing jobs. Some community organizations have been very aggressive in utilizing the image of the Ozarks to attract economic activities. For example, the development agency in Russellville, Arkansas makes use of photographs of a sunset on Lake Dardanelle in its promotional package for the area. Other factors are obviously important in the final site evaluation, but quality-of-life attributes cannot be dismissed as unimportant.

Although this depiction of staged economic growth has been generalized to the "Ozarks," it does not apply it to every community. Not all areas have followed this pattern. The growth of manufacturing employment can occur at any time. It can develop prior to recreational development—as for example, in Harrison, Arkansas—or without them—as in West Plains, Missouri. Nonetheless, this service-sector staging process with its age-composition ramifications has occurred or is occurring in many Ozark counties. It represents a significant portion of the pattern of growth and change in the region.

Environmental Effects

One of the primary reasons for population growth in the Ozarks is the natural beauty of the physical environment. Whether it be to commune with nature or to escape the built-up form of the city, from the time of Thoreau, writers have pointed to a need for the rural scene, suggesting that it represents something basic to the human condition.[5] Although this idea can be debated, there does seem to be something about the environmental conditions in the Ozarks that is attracting migrants.

Some local leaders and residents feel that too many people are "acting out" their preferences. Such community members fear that the pure air and water and scenic views of mountains and lakes may be in danger of deterioration. Most of the pristine beauty is still there, but it is where the people are not. Although population density has increased throughout the region in total, the nonmetropolitan population is, for the most part, settling in existing small places or creating new residential enclaves. A night flight over the Lake of the Ozarks in Missouri shows most of the lakefront area ringed by lights; this visible density pattern decreases

[5]For examples, see Jensen, 1973; Mumford, 1968; Nash, 1973; Udall, 1963.

rapidly as one moves away from the water's edge. For some places this kind of population increase is creating mini-urban areas with population densities similar to cities.

Because of inadequate zoning, commercial strip developments on major highways and lengthy traffic tie-ups are commonplace. Congestion on major thoroughfares has intensified, especially in the major recreational areas, during the summer months as the tourist season reaches its peak. In Branson, Missouri, home of Silver Dollar City, the Shepherd of the Hills Farm, and many other entertainment establishments, problems on State Highway 76, a three-lane road, are dramatic. These difficulties have been localized to the immediate population centers, but they are spreading outward as existing commercial areas reach capacity.

Subdivision developments carry their own set of problems. Timber loss because of residential construction is evident. Although minimal foliage removal in wooded lots is becoming increasingly apparent, the platting of 22 new subdivisions in outlying areas of Boone County, Arkansas in 1 year has had an impact. Besides the aesthetic loss, the resultant increased run-off and sewage seepage into nearby lakes and streams are combining to threaten the quality of water supplies. In most areas, septic tanks are still the rule because of the high cost of other types of sewage treatment systems even though septic tanks are unsuited to the soil types of the Ozarks. Solid-waste disposal systems have not been successfully established in most small communities and roadsides in many areas are becoming trash dumps.

Some former urbanites are wondering if they really ever left home, as small Ozark places begin to take on the appearance and character of the urban areas left behind. Natives, although appreciative of the economic boom, are sensitive to these changes, and they are becoming concerned over the transfer of unfamiliar urban problems to their once rural communities. What is the threshold point at which environmental deterioration in the Ozarks will become a push factor moving people away in search of yet another area of natural beauty?

The Crisis Orientation to Planning and the Backlash to Growth

In most areas of the Ozarks the reaction to the problems discussed so far appears as after-the-fact planning in response to a crisis. This response involves three factors: First, many areas have a heritage of antiplanning and antizoning attitudes. The "this is my land to do with what I want" attitude is common. Evidence from research in several Arkansas Ozark counties suggests that native Arkansans and people who migrated to these areas before 1960 hold a more negative view of land-use planning and are less aware of community problems than more recent newcomer and returnee groups (Danforth and Voth, 1979). Second, because of the historical nature of population decline in some areas and the rapidity of recent growth, some existing planning bodies have been caught by surprise. And third, some local planning agencies that were once unnecessary have come into existence only after population and economic expansions were well underway. One example is Boone County, Arkansas, where the creation of the county planning board was a reaction to rapid subdivision development outside of Harrison.

Although all of these factors have had a slowing effect on the planning process, agencies are becoming aware that local growth is greater than they had envisioned and that the present unchecked pattern of growth has created problems. Action is being taken out of necessity. Zoning ordinances are being updated or established, and comprehensive plans are being developed.

In some places the damage has been done and the planning response becomes, in effect, the application of a series of Band-Aids to ameliorate immediate symptoms. Emphasis is not placed on "this is where we want to go" but on "how do we solve *this* problem?" In areas where this kind of uphill battle must be fought, both citizen and governmental action groups are forming. In the tri-lakes areas of Branson, Missouri the continued intensification of problems was the impetus behind the formation of an organization fostering "guided growth" whose objectives are (*a*) to improve traffic flow; (*b*) to improve the general appearance of the area's commercial development; (*c*) to preserve the natural beauty of the area; (*d*) to devise ways and means of expanding the economic base; and (*e*) to maintain and improve the quality of the area lakes' water (*Branson Beacon*, 1978).

Civic and governmental bodies in other Ozark localities have benefited from the experiences of sister communities. In Russellville, Arkansas, community leaders are very much aware of what "dirty" industry could mean for their city, and they are attempting to screen potential developments, taking pains to avoid haphazard growth and to maintain a high quality of life.

None of these groups have really tried to check growth. Although these counties and communities are taking a hard look at local expansion, they are still trying to meld continued growth and economic prosperity with the charm of the Ozarks, a combination that may not be possible.

Residents, especially newcomers, may become the driving force behind long-range planning. Many of the recent newcomers are not excited about continuing population increases. In Lakeview, Arkansas, a small number of newcomers have attempted to put a stop to the con-

struction of a sewage treatment plant because they see it as an induce-
ment to continued growth. Although this may be a somewhat extreme
action, the feeling behind it is not uncommon (Biggar, 1979; Graber,
1974; Morrison and Wheeler, 1976). This desire for gate-closing is heard
from migrants wanting to protect the amenities that brought them to the
region. But, the wish to be the last person allowed into the area does not
necessarily bring a halt to requests for more services. The service demand remains high while the wish for a cessation of growth appears to
be associated with population numbers, traffic, strip and industrial developments, and those things that induce future expansion—urban
living without urban problems.

These concerns are also being voiced by natives. As one long-time
Ozark resident stated, "There are Yankees and there are damn Yankees.
A Yankee is someone who comes to the area to visit. A damn Yankee is
someone who stays." Another native noted, "Yankees from Chicago
should stay there; they look down on the natives." Whether they feel the
victims of such snobbery or have a sense of loss, many long-time residents are watching their communities change in ways that they believe
are for the worse. And the problem is two-sided. Natives find that their
communities cannot go back to the way they were before growth, and
they do not necessarily want to lose the socioeconomic benefits of
growth. At the same time, residents do not want the present situation to
worsen. Newcomers are faced with a similar dilemma. As Graber (1974)
observes, "The rural idyll is altered precisely because he (the migrant)
comes [p. 506].

The Future of the Ozarks

Because of economic growth and natural amenities, the Ozark–
Ouachita Uplands has been one of the major growth areas of the United
States during the 1970s. Initially, this growth was associated largely with
the inmigration of older persons. It is now more broadly based and not
specific to any one age cohort. Migration increases are evident in nearly
all of the region's 98 counties. Although growth is found in a variety of
county types, retirement and recreation counties still show the greatest
expansion. If energy supplies do not become overly expensive or restric-
tive, the potential for continued demographic and economic expansion
is likely. The most recent population estimates (1978) show that the
growth around the lake-retirement area is continuing, but that other
areas may have slowed down and in some cases may have had minor
population losses. The cost and availability of energy and capital will be
two major factors influencing future growth.

This pattern of population increase brings dramatic benefits but equally dramatic costs. Overall, income levels are increasing, employment opportunities are expanding, and community services are improving. Given the small population size of the majority of nonmetropolitan counties, the speed of change, and limited community infrastructures, the Ozarks will continue to have growing pains. In order to adequately meet stepped up demands for services, to combat the adverse effects of change and to maintain the high quality of life, these areas need to immediately come to grips with this new-found growth. In some communities, the immediacy of addressing these problems has become urgent. To prepare for present and future growth and the attendant effects of population increase, considerable thought must be given to the types of demographic and economic growth occurring and to the needs of the population. If the ultimate goal of planning is to maintain economic prosperity and the amenities of the region, Ozark planners must face the major challenge of long-range planning as well as concern over immediate effects.

References

Atchley, Robert C.
  1977   *The Social Forces in Later Life.* 2nd ed. Belmont, Calif.: Wadsworth Publishing Company, Inc.
Beale, Calvin L.
  1976   "A further look at nonmetropolitan population growth since 1970." *American Journal of Agricultural Economics,* 58 (December):953–958.
  1977   "Current status of the shift of U.S. population to smaller communities." Paper presented at the Annual Meeting of the Population Association of America, St. Louis, Missouri, April 22.
Beale, Calvin L. and Glenn V. Fuguitt
  1975   "Population trends of nonmetropolitan cities and villages in subregions of the United States." Center for Demography and Ecology Working Paper 75-30. Madison: University of Wisconsin, September.
  1976   "The new pattern of nonmetropolitan population change." Center for Demography and Ecology Working Paper 75-22. rev. Madison: University of Wisconsin, July.
Berry, Brian J. L. and Frank E. Norton
  1970   "Theories and techniques for studying urban and regional growth." Chapter 4 in *Geographic Perspectives on Urban Systems: With Integrated Readings.* Englewood Cliffs, N.J.: Prentice-Hall, Inc.
Biggar, Jeanne C.
  1979   "The sunning of America: Migration to the Sunbelt." *Population Bulletin* 34 (March).
Blackwood, Larry G. and Edwin H. Carpenter
  1978   "The importance of anti-urbanism in determining residential preferences and migration patterns." *Rural Sociology* 43 (Spring):31–47.
Bogue, Donald J. and Calvin L. Beale
  1961   *Economic Areas of the United States.* New York: The Free Press of Glencoe, Inc.

Bowles, Gladys K. and James D. Tarver
  1965   *Net Migration of the Population 1950-60, By Age, Sex and Color.* Volume I "states, counties, economic areas, and metropolitan areas." U.S. Department of Agriculture, Economic Research Service; Oklahoma State University, Research Foundation; and U.S. Department of Commerce, Area Redevelopment Administration; May.
Branson Beacon
  1978   April 13.
Campbell, Rex R. and Daniel M. Johnson
  1976   "Prospositions on counterstream migration." *Rural Sociology* 41 (Spring): 127–145.
Campbell, Rex R., Gary J. Stangler, George H. Dailey, Jr., and Robert L. McNamara
  1977   *Population Change, Migration and Displacement Along the McClellan-Kerr Arkansas River Navigation System.* IWR Contract Report 77-5, Fort Belvoir, Virginia: U.S. Army Engineer Institute for Water Resources, December.
Campbell, Rex R., George H. Dailey, Jr., and Robert L. McNamara
  1978   *Population Change in the Ozarks Region: 1970–1975.* A Report to the Ozarks Regional Commission. Columbia: University of Missouri, Department of Rural Sociology, September.
Center for Aging Studies
  1978   "A general profile of lakes country retirement." Kansas City: University of Missouri.
Costello, David F.
  1975   *The Mountain World.* New York: Thomas L. Crowell Company.
Dailey, George H., Jr. and Rex R. Campbell
  1978   *Age-Specific Net Migration in the Ozarks Region, 1950–1970: A Chartbook.* Columbia: University of Missouri, Department of Rural Sociology, September.
  1979a   "Consequences of retirement migration in the Ozark–Ouachita Uplands: An exploratory research." Columbia: University of Missouri, Department of Rural Sociology, May.
  1979b   "Consequences of retirement migration in the Ozark–Ouachita Uplands: An exploratory research, appendix tables and figures." Columbia: University of Missouri, Department of Rural Sociology, May.
Dailey, George H., Jr., Thomas E. Jokerst, Robert L. McNamara, and Rex R. Campbell
  1978a   *Age-Specific Population and Net Migration Estimates for the Ozarks Region, 1970–1975.* Columbia: University of Missouri, Department of Rural Sociology, September.
  1978b   *A Quarter Century of Population Change in the Ozarks, 1950–1975.* Columbia: University of Missouri, Department of Rural Sociology, September.
Dailey, George H., Jr., Gary J. Stangler, and Rex R. Campbell
  1977   "Migration to the Ozarks: The aging migrant." Paper presented at the Annual Meeting of the Rural Sociological Society, Madison, Wisconsin, September 1–4.
Danforth, Diana M. and Donald E. Voth
  1979   "Consequences of migration into Arkansas for population change." Paper presented at the Conference on Regional Migration Trends, St. Louis, Missouri, October 17–19.
Davis, Jerry C.
  n.d.   "Best bargains in retirement." Reprint of a *Chicago Sun–Times* Interview.
Denney, Hugh (editor)
  n.d.   *South Central Ozark Regional Profile.* Extension Division Report MP364. Columbia: University of Missouri.

Dickinson, Peter A.
   1978   *Sunbelt Retirement: The Complete State by State Guide to Retiring in the South and West of the United States.* New York: Dutton Publishers.
Dillman, Don A. and Russell P. Dobash
   1972   *Preferences for Community Living and Their Implication for Population Redistribution.* Agricultural Experiment Station Bulletin 764. Pullman: Washington State University, November.
Fuguitt, Glenn V. and James J. Zuiches
   1975   "Residential preferences and population distribution." *Demography* 12 (August):491–504.
Gerlach, Russel L.
   1976   *Immigrants to the Ozarks.* Columbia: University of Missouri Press.
Gist, Noel P. and Sylvia Fleis Fava
   1974   *Urban Society.* 6th ed. New York: Thomas Y. Crowell Company.
Graber, Edith E.
   1974   "Newcomers and old timers: Growth and change in a mountain town." *Rural Sociology* 39 (Winter):504–513.
Green, Bernal L., Lloyd D. Bender, and Rex R. Campbell
   1970   *Migration into Four Communities in the Ozarks Region.* Agricultural Experiment Station Bulletin 756. Fayetteville: University of Arkansas.
Hunt, Charles B.
   1974   *Natural Regions of the United States and Canada.* San Francisco: W. H. Freeman and Company.
Jackson, Kenneth T.
   1973   "The crabgrass frontier: 150 years of suburban growth in America." Pp. 196–221 In Raymond A. Mohl and James F. Richardson (eds.), *The Urban Experience: Themes in American History.* Belmont, Calif.: Wadsworth Publishing Company, Inc.
Jensen, Clayne R.
   1973   *Outdoor Recreation in America: Trends, Problems, and Opportunities.* Minneapolis: Burgess Publishing Company.
Jordan, Max F. and Lloyd D. Bender
   1966   *An Economic Survey of the Ozark Region.* Agricultural Experiment Station Report 97, Fayetteville: University of Arkansas, July.
Kuehn, John and Curtis Brashler
   1977   *New Manufacturing Plants in the Nonmetropolitan Ozarks.* Economic Research Service AER 384. Washington, D.C.: U.S. Department of Agriculture, September.
Long, Larry H. and Kristen A. Hansen
   1979   "Reasons for interstate migration: Jobs, retirement, climate and other influences." Current Population Reports Series P–23, No. 81. Washington, D.C.: U.S. Bureau of the Census, March.
Morrison, Peter A. with Judith P. Wheeler
   1976   "Rural renaissance in America? The revival of population growth in remote areas." *Population Bulletin* 31 (October):3.
Mumford, Lewis
   1968   *The Urban Prospect.* New York: Harcourt, Brace and World, Inc.
Murphy, Raymond E.
   1974   *The American city: An urban geography.* 2nd ed. New York: McGraw-Hill.
Nash, Roderick
   1973   *Wilderness and the American Mind.* rev. ed. New Haven, Conn.: Yale University Press.

Nolan, Michael, Paul Lasley, Gary Green, and William Heffernan
  1979   "Rural residents in the Ozarks: A comparison of migrants and non-migrants."
          Paper presented at the Annual Meeting of the Rural Sociological Society, Bur-
          lington, Vermont, August.
Oliver, David Busch
  1971   "Career and leisure patterns of middle-aged metropolitan outmigrants." *The
          Gerontologist* Part II (Winter):13–20.
Ozarks Regional Commission
  1976   *Economic Development Action Plan.* Little Rock, Arkansas, July.
Peterson, Warren
  1978   Interview conducted at the University of Missouri-Kansas City, Center for
          Aging Studies, October.
Rhodes, Richards and The Editors of Time–Life Books
  1974   *The Ozarks.* The American Wilderness Series. New York: Time–Life Books, Inc.
Shelley, Fred M.
  1977   "Search behavior and place utility of recent migrants to the Arkansas Ozarks."
          Paper presented at the Annual Meeting of the Association of American Geog-
          raphers, Salt Lake City, Utah, April.
Schmitt, Peter J.
  1973   "Back to nature." Pp. 454–468 In Alexander B. Callow, Jr. (ed.), *American Urban
          History: An Interpretive Reader with Commentaries.* 2nd ed. New York: Oxford
          University Press.
Udall, Stewart L.
  1963   *The Quiet Crisis.* New York: Avon Books.
United States Bureau of the Census
  1952   *Number of Inhabitants.* United States Census of Population: 1950, vol. I.
          Washington, D.C.: U.S. Government Printing Office.
  1972a   *General Social and Economic Characteristics.* Census of Population: 1970, Final Re-
          port PC(1)–C1 United States Summary. Washington, D.C.: U.S. Government
          Printing Office.
  1972b   *County Business Patterns 1970.* Washington, D.C.: U.S. Government Printing
          Office.
  1972c   *Migration Between State Economic Areas.* Census of Population: 1970, Subject Re-
          ports PC(2)–2E. Washington, D.C.: U.S. Government Printing Office.
  1977a   *Statistical Abstract of the United States 1977.* 98th ann. ed. Washington, D.C.: U.S.
          Government Printing Office.
  1977b   *State and County Data.* 1974 Census of Agriculture, vol. 1, parts 4, 25, and 36,
          Arkansas, Missouri, and Oklahoma. Washington, D.C.: U.S. Government Print-
          ing Office.
  1977c   *County Business Patterns 1975.* Washington, D.C.: U.S. Government Printing
          Office.
  1978   *County and City Data Book, 1977.* Washington, D.C.: U.S. Government Printing
          Office, May.
Wardwell, John M.
  1977   "Equilibrium and change in nonmetropolitan growth." *Rural Sociology* 42
          (Summer): 156–179.
Williams, James D. and Andrew J. Sofranko
  1978   "Migration motivations for population turnaround in nonmetropolitan areas."
          Agricultural Economics Staff Paper No. 78 5-4. Urbana: University of Illinois,
          March.

Migration and Energy Developments: Implications for Rural Areas in the Great Plains

STEVE H. MURDOCK
F. LARRY LEISTRITZ
ELDON C. SCHRINER

Introduction

The magnitude and causes of the renewed growth of nonmetropolitan areas in the United States have received extensive analysis (Beale, 1976; Fuguitt and Zuiches, 1975; Hansen, 1973; Keuhn, 1978; McCarthy and Morrison, 1978; Wardwell, 1977). Despite such analyses we lack sufficient information about the characteristics and perceptions of migrants to many types of nonmetropolitan areas and about the effects of migration on destination communities and their residents (Schwarzweller, 1979).

We particularly lack information about those migrants entering rural areas in the Great Plains as a result of energy developments. Except for occasional inclusions in case study analyses of individual impacted communities (Gilmore and Duff, 1974; Watts *et al.*, 1977), the characteristics of persons migrating to rural areas due to increased development in the energy industry and their effects on local community structure have not been systematically examined. This chapter proposes to fill part of the gap by examining the nature and effects of migration to energy development areas in the Great Plains.[1]

---

[1]Table 11.1 lists the states included in the Great Plains.

New Directions in
Urban–Rural Migration

TABLE 11.1
Energy Reserves, Production, and Planned Production in the Great Plains

State	Coal reserve base (million tons)		Coal production (million tons)		Additional production capacity from planned new coal mines and mine expansions, 1976–1980 (cumulative; in million tons)
	Total coal reserves (1)	Strippable coal reserves (2)	1969 (3)	1977 (4)	(5)
Colorado	14,869	870	5.5	12.0	65.6
Kansas	1,388	1,388	1.3	0.6	0.4
Montana	108,396	42,562	1.0	30.4	90.7
Nebraska	---	---	---	---	---
New Mexico	4,395	2,258	4.5	10.8	70.8
North Dakota	16,003	16,003	4.7	12.2	67.4
Oklahoma	1,294	434	1.8	5.0	2.4
South Dakota	428	428	---	---	---
Texas	3,272	3,272	---	14.3	72.1
Wyoming	53,336	23,845	4.6	40.7	296.8
Total for Great Plains[a]	203,381	91,060	23.5	126.0	666.2
Great Plains as a percentage of U.S.	46.6	66.5	4.1	18.4	66.9

Source: Columns (1) and (2): U.S. Department of the Interior (1974); columns (3), (8), and (9): U.S. Department of the Interior (1970); column (4): Wilkinson (1978); column (5): Nielsen (1978); and columns (6) and (7): U.S. Department of the Interior (1978).
[a] Because of independent rounding, columns may not add up precisely to total figures.

Dimensions and Implications of Energy-Related Migration

A look at energy-related migration offers the opportunity to examine several key issues: the social, economic, and ecological differences between this and other forms of migration; the effects of this migration on the future of many rural areas, such as the Great Plains; and the significance of a number of often controversial issues related to the effects of growth.

Renewed growth of rural areas is based on a number of different social, demographic, and economic changes (Wardwell, 1977). From a human ecological perspective (Hawley, 1950; Sly, 1972; Sly and Tayman, 1977), many recent types of migration turnaround may be seen as resulting from an interaction of technological (such as improved transporta-

Additional electric generation capacity of planned new coal-fired power plants		Crude petroleum (including lease condensate) production, 1974 (thousands of barrels)	Natural gas marketed, 1974 (millions of cubic feet)
No. of plants (6)	Total capacity (megawatts) (7)	(8)	(9)
6	5,295	37,508	144,629
3	2,686	61,691	886,782
4	2,650	34,554	54,873
4	2,475	6,611	2,538
4	3,684	98,695	1,244,779
3	2,680	19,697	31,206
5	4,335	177,785	1,638,942
5	1,240	494	---
17	18,503	1,262,126	8,170,798
5	3,490	139,997	326,657
56	47,038	1,839,158	12,501,204
---	---	57.4	57.9

tion) and social organizational (such as better retirement systems) factors. In particular, energy-related migration results from an interaction of technological (energy development technologies) and environmental resource (energy resource bases) dimensions and thus may have effects on rural areas that are similar to the effects of initial frontier settlement patterns of migration (Murdock, 1979). These developments may serve less to diversify the economic bases of rural areas than simply to alter their emphases. They may shift but not lessen the extent of control that single industries exert in the Plains. The investigation of energy-related migration offers an opportunity to reexamine the implications of resource-based migration for rural areas (United Nations, 1973).

Energy-related migration is significant because it is likely to affect many areas in the Great Plains. The Great Plains states contain 46.6% of the nation's coal reserves and over 66% of the strippable reserves (Table 11.1). Coal production increased fivefold from 1969 to 1977, and over 66% of the increase in coal production anticipated for 1976–1986 is expected to come from the development of Great Plains coal. As many as 56 new coal-fired power plants and numerous coal gasification and liquefaction plants may be built in the area (Federal Energy Administration, 1977; Murdock and Leistritz, 1979). The area contains over 50% of the nation's present oil and natural gas production, it has a majority of the nation's uranium deposits, and it is likely to be of major importance in the development of future resources such as wind and solar energy. Colorado, Montana, North Dakota, and Wyoming are the major resource centers, but all areas in the Plains, with the possible exception of Nebraska and South Dakota, will experience substantial energy-related developments.

Energy developments are likely to have particularly profound effects on the characteristics of the Plains population. Although their impact on total regional population increase is likely to be relatively small, estimates indicate substantial population growth may occur in some local areas (Gilmore et al., 1976). For example, a single Lurgi-process coal gasification plant—many of which are proposed for the area—may employ 3000 construction workers and 1000 operating workers after the construction is completed. These persons plus the induced employment required to service them and their families may add up to more than 10,000 persons settling in a local impact area during the construction phase and over 5000 persons arriving during the 30–50-year operational life of a project (Northern Great Plains Resources Program, 1974). Although many of the newly created jobs can be filled by local persons, present estimates indicate that more than 60% of the construction work force and roughly 40% of the operational workers will be in-migrants (Mountain West Research, 1975; Wieland et al., 1977). As a result, relatively sparsely populated areas of the Plains, such as Western North Dakota, may experience an influx of as many as 50,000 new residents by the year 2000, and areas in Wyoming and Montana may experience even more rapid growth (Northern Great Plains Resources Program, 1974).

Much of the expected growth is problematic, not because of its absolute magnitude, but because of the likely timing of that growth and the characteristics of the local areas in which the growth will occur. Energy developments involve at least three major stages. The construction stage, which lasts roughly 3–7 years for most projects, involves significant employment growth. Employees tend to be young adult males who may live some distance from the plant site. Generally they do not bring their families with them to the area. They often choose to live in rented or temporary forms of housing such as mobile homes. They put intensive strains on local service structures and sometimes show little concern for local cultures. The second major stage, the operational stage, which lasts for 30–50 years, involves fewer employees who tend to settle permanently in the area. They are likely to be married and to have moderate-size households (Wieland et al., 1977). The final stage of such projects involves the closing of the facility. Unless the community has developed alternative forms of employment, this stage may mark the end of economic prosperity and a return to the previous pattern of population decline. Migration-induced population increases in areas affected by energy development projects may produce severe uncertainties and planning difficulties for local communities, particularly during the construction phase.

The effects of such migration are further accentuated by the sparse settlement structure of the Plains, and by the history of decades of population decline. For example, in 1970 the Plains states contained over 31% of the total land area of the nation, but only 11% of the population. Population density was less than 10 persons per square mile in such development states as Montana, North Dakota, and Wyoming. The Northern Great Plains production area (Western North Dakota, Eastern Montana, and Northeastern Wyoming) contained only eight cities with more than 9500 people in 1970 (Murdock and Leistritz, 1979). Even a small energy project involving a few hundred employees may have a relatively great impact on such areas.

Because a majority of these areas have experienced many decades of population decline (Beale, 1974), they possess service infrastructures that are poorly equipped to deal with population increase. In such areas, in-migration related to energy development may lead to increased business activity and employment but also to increased costs for public services and large investments in community infrastructure.

In sum, the magnitude of energy development in the Plains is likely to be sustantial, and population growth resulting from extensive in-migration is likely to have profound effects on rural communities and their residents. Because of the small population bases and historical patterns of population decline, local communities may not be prepared to deal with the economic impacts and social costs of such in-migration.

An analysis of energy-related migration is important also because it is often suggested that energy-related migrants are quite different from migrants in general and that their impact on rural communities is particularly acute (Gilmore and Duff, 1974; Gold, 1974). They are perceived as being highly transient, relatively unconcerned about the community and its welfare, and more critical of its service base than longtime residents (Cortese and Jones, 1977). In turn, longtime residents are often thought to gain few economic or employment benefits from energy developments (Little and Lovejoy, 1977), to be resentful of migrants, and to disapprove of the overall effects of developments (Gilmore and Duff, 1974). However, such conclusions are based on limited analyses, and it is far from clear whether migrant–longtime resident characteristics and perceptions either are as different as suggested or are unlike those of residents in other destination areas. Such issues require additional exploration.

Scope and Methodology of Research

The analysis presented here addresses three key dimensions bearing on migration issues. These are (a) The characteristics of persons migrating to energy development areas; (b) the effects of such migrants on the social, demographic, and economic structure of affected areas; and (c) the effects of energy-related developments on the social and economic conditions and perceptions of migrants and longtime residents in affected communities.

The data presented are derived from household surveys conducted in western coal development communities. These communities are Colstrip and Forsyth, Montana; Green River and Rock Springs, Wyoming; and Center, North Dakota. All are experiencing significant new exploitation of their coal resources. Admittedly they are at somewhat different stages of the development process, but all are feeling its effects.[2] These data were collected under the auspices of the Old West Regional Commission by Mountain West Research, Incorporated (1975) and were made available for our use by these agencies. The samples in each community were selected by a two-stage process. Communities were first divided into clusters and a small random survey was conducted to determine the prevalence of migrant (referred to as *newcomer*) households in each cluster. Having obtained this information, samples of migrant and longtime residents were selected by redrawing clusters equal to the number of respondents desired and then randomly choosing a household from each cluster. Data were obtained for all members of the household from the one member interviewed. Data used in the present analysis are based on data for household heads only. Sample size was determined by using a 95% level of confidence estimate of the parameter of family size. Of the 1147 households selected, 1069, or 93% were interviewed. Of the 1069 completed interviews, 708, or 66% were migrant households, defined as households that had moved to the com-

[2]More exact matching of communities was not possible (see Mountain West Research, 1975), but data for migrant groups seem likely to reflect conditions in communities experiencing a major impact because a large proportion of the migrants (477, or 67%) included in this analysis were from the heavily impacted communities of Rock Springs and Green River.

TABLE 11.2
Selected Characteristics of Study Communities and Related County and State Areas

Geographic area	1960 population	1970 population	1975 population	Percent of population change		Net migration rate	
				1960–1970	1970–1975	1960–1970	1970–1975
Montana	674,767	694,409	746,244	2.9	7.5	- 8.6	3.7
Rosebud County	6,187	6,032	9,253	- 2.5	53.4	-14.5	33.9
Colstrip	---	160	a 3,000	---	1,775.0	---	---
Forsyth	2,032	1,873	2,396	- 7.8	27.9	---	---
North Dakota	632,446	617,761	642,888	- 2.3	4.1	-14.9	-0.8
Oliver County	2,610	2,331	2,408	-11.0	3.7	-22.1	0.6
Center	476	610	812	30.0	31.2	---	---
Wyoming	332,416	335,719	376,309	1.0	13.2	-11.9	7.4
Sweetwater County	17,920	18,391	30,144	2.6	63.9	-8.0	59.0
Green River	3,497	4,196	7,423	20.0	76.9	---	---
Rock Springs	10,371	11,657	17,773	12.4	52.5	---	---

Source: U.S. Bureau of the Census.
a Population estimate by Mountain West Research, Inc., 1975.

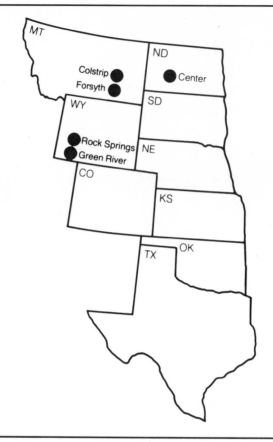

Figure 11.1. Location of study communities in the Great Plains.

munity since the beginning of the construction of the energy project.[3] These data provide extensive information on the characteristics and perceptions of both longtime residents and migrants in these impact communities and thus allow comparisons to be made between the responses of the two groups.

The communities under study are located in typical Northern Great Plains areas. The data in Table 11.2 show recent population changes in each community and for the counties and state in which each community is located. Figure 11.1 is a map of the location of these communities

---

[3]This definition did not employ an areal dimension normally included in definitions of migration. However, given the extensive commuting in such areas, it is unlikely that those who had moved to take employment in the area had not crossed a county boundary.

within the Great Plains region. As the data in Table 11.2 indicate, Montana, North Dakota, and Wyoming have had recent histories of small overall population change and net out-migration. The counties in which the study communities are located also experienced small population decreases from 1960 to 1970 (Sweetwater County had a small increase during that period). However, in each of the county areas there was extensive out-migration (−14.5 %, −22.1 %, and −8.0 %) from 1960 to 1970.

The boom experienced in each community during the early 1970s can also be seen in Table 11.2. Each community experienced more growth in the first 5 years of the present decade than in the entire period from 1960 to 1970. In communities like Colstrip, which was essentially created by the coal developer, all growth has been energy-related growth, and in all other communities rates of growth exceed those in other areas of the state. It is apparent that near-boomtown conditions characterize several of these areas and that migration is playing a significant role in this recent growth.

Analysis

Differentials in Energy-Related Migration

The data in Table 11.3 reveal that the sociodemographic characteristics of energy migrants are typical of other migrating populations as well. The migrants to energy-development areas tend to be young adults with at least a high school education. They have relatively high incomes and, like many other new nonmetropolitan residents, they tend to live in mobile homes. However, they are less highly educated than the majority of metropolitan-to-nonmetropolitan migrants have been shown to be by previous national-level research (Bowles, 1978). This is true of both migrating construction workers and other migrants.

Many of the migrants have been attracted to the Plains by the construction activities. More than 54% of the migrants but only 22% of the longtime residents were employed in construction-related jobs (Table 11.4).

The data in Table 11.4 also indicate the extent to which migrants are concentrated in particular occupations and the kinds of jobs obtained by migrants as compared with longtime residents in the construction and nonconstruction labor markets. A majority of construction-related migrants are craftsmen; those in nonconstruction-related employment tend to be professionals, managers, craftsmen, and laborers. These characteristics are similar to other economics-induced migrants (Lansing and Mueller, 1967; Shaw, 1975). In contrast, longtime residents are less likely to be employed in construction than migrants, but they are not disproportionately concentrated in the low-skill laborer categories as is sometimes maintained (Little and Lovejoy, 1977). These data suggest that migrants to energy developments are typical of migrants in general, and that their employment opportunities have not been obtained at the expense of opportunities for longtime residents.

The area of origin of migrants to the impact areas is shown in Table 11.5. In this table, impact communities are analyzed according to the state in which they are located. An examination of these data reveals that it is only in Wyoming that a substantial number of migrants from outside the state or from adjacent states are found. In most cases, energy migrants are persons familiar with the Plains and with communities similar to the impact communities.

Migrants have characteristics that differ significantly from those of longtime residents and that will affect overall community demographic and social patterns (see next section). There are indications that new

TABLE 11.3
Characteristics of Migrant and Longtime Resident Households in Energy-Impact Communities

Characteristic	Longtime residents	Migrant construction workers	Other migrants	Total community
Number of households	361	385	323	1,069
Average household size	3.8	3.6	3.6	3.7
Percent married	81.5	76.7	80.2	79.3
Median age of house- hold head	46	33	31	37
Average annual household income (dollars)	12,467	19,168	16,569	16,992
Educational attainments of household heads (percent)				
Less than high school	28.4	13.5	11.0	17.8
High school	42.7	43.8	29.5	39.1
Some college or vocational	15.4	32.2	29.8	25.7
College or more	13.5	10.4	29.5	17.4
Dwelling type (percent)				
Single family unit	76.0	19.1	43.7	45.6
Duplex, condominium, apartment	5.4	11.9	21.0	12.5
Mobile home	17.7	53.4	31.9	34.9
Other	0.9	15.6	3.3	7.0

TABLE 11.4
*Occupational and Industrial Characteristics of Migrant and Longtime
Resident Household Heads in Energy-Impact Communities (in percentages)*

Occupation	Longtime resident	Migrant
Energy-related construction		
Employment	22.7	54.2
Professional, technical,		
supervisory	4.8	6.4
Craftsman, operative, transport	14.8	37.9
Laborers	3.1	9.9
Non-construction employment	77.4	45.7
Professional, technical,		
managerial	23.0	16.6
Sales, clerical	5.6	3.1
Craftsman, operatives, transport	13.4	11.4
Laborers	5.0	5.8
Farm, farm foreman	2.0	0.3
Service	7.6	3.7
Retired	18.8	2.6
Unemployed	2.0	2.2
Total number	361	708

Source: Mountain West Research, 1975.

employment opportunities (for example, in construction of new facilities) have been shared by migrants and longtime residents. Despite differentials in characteristics that favor migrant groups, longtime residents appear to be competing effectively for newly created job opportunities.

TABLE 11.5
Origin Areas of Migrants for Energy-Impact Communities

State	Number of inmigrant workers	Percent of in-migrant workers from		
		Same state	Surrounding state	Other areas
North Dakota	20	75.0	10.0	15.0
Wyoming	492	20.3	35.0	44.7
Montana	211	53.6	10.0	36.4

Source: Mountain West Research, 1975.

Effects on Community Structure

Energy developments and the associated population growth change the demographic, social, and economic patterns of many communities. Some indication of the effects of energy-induced migration on the demographic structures of local communities can be ascertained by comparing the last column in Table 11.3, which presents total sample characteristics for the communities, with the first column, which shows the characteristics of longtime residents.

TABLE 11.6
Occupational and Industrial Structures of Longtime Resident Population and Total Population in Energy Impact Communities (in percentages)

Occupation/industry	Longtime residents' predevelopment status	Total population's present status
Occupation:		
Profession-managerial	24.9	25.8
White collar	8.0	4.5
Skilled labor	17.9	30.0
Semi-skilled	10.9	12.3
Unskilled	12.8	13.5
Service	12.1	5.6
Farmers	3.2	0.9
Retired	6.7	6.9
Housewife	1.3	0.2
Student	0.0	0.3
Armed Services	2.2	0.0
N	313	921
Index of dissimilarity	15.9[a]	
Industry:		
Agriculture-forestry	4.6	1.6
Mining	17.4	18.4
Construction	16.8	35.7
Manufacturing	3.6	3.0
Transportation	18.4	13.9
Wholesale	0.3	0.3
Retail	10.2	5.4
Services	19.4	12.5
Armed Forces	0.7	0.0
Student	2.0	0.2
Retired	6.6	6.5
Unemployed	0.0	2.5
N	304	934
Index of dissimilarity	22.4[a]	

Source: Murdock and Schriner, 1978
[a] Because of problems in reporting, retired persons are excluded from the indices for comparisons of predevelopment and present distributions within community types.

This comparison reveals that the migrants will tend to decrease household size, lower the average age, and to increase education, income levels, and the incidence of mobile home residency in impacted areas. The effects will be greatest in terms of age, education, and housing; migrants tend to reverse age and educational trends in such areas and to accentuate a strong overall tendency toward mobile home housing in rural areas. These are communities whose predevelopment population characteristics reflect those of many rural areas (Zuiches and Brown, 1978) and whose demographic structures are likely to be markedly affected by energy developments.

A second type of community change is found in the occupational and industrial structures of rural communities. The data in Table 11.6 describe longtime residents' occupations and industries of employment before energy developments were initiated as well as occupations and industries of employment for migrants and longtime residents at the time of the survey. Assuming that predevelopment structures approximate nondevelopment structures, these data may be used to examine migration-induced changes in the occupational and industrial structures of the local economy.

The data in Table 11.6 reveal that the major effect of migration on occupational structure has been to increase the number of skilled workers in the impacted areas (from 17.9% to 30.0%). Although increased industrialization is often believed to lead to increased economic diversity in rural areas, the data in Table 11.6 tend to show a change in industrial concentration (from transportation, services, and agriculture to mining and construction) rather than a diversification in industrial employment.[4]

Relative Effects on Migrants and Longtime Residents

SOCIODEMOGRAPHIC CHARACTERISTICS

The effects of energy developments on the occupational mobility of migrants and longtime residents are shown in Table 11.7. Occupational mobility was measured by comparing respondents' occupational changes, if any, in the last 5 years to their occupations at the time of the survey (see Murdock and Schriner, 1978). Those who had changed from a lower- to a higher-status occupation were considered to be upwardly

---

[4]The lack of such diversification may, of course, result from the relative newness of these developments. As the overall level of development in the region increases, the development of secondary and induced employment may also increase. On the other hand, in several analyses of rural industrialization, diversification has not been evident (Lonsdale and Seyler, 1979).

TABLE 11.7
Occupational Mobility of Household Heads in Energy Impacted Communities by Migration Status (in percentages)

Item	Longtime residents			Migrants		
	Upward	Stability	Downward	Upward	Stability	Downward
Total	15.6	63.7	20.7	28.6	57.1	14.3
Age						
< 25	46.4	35.7	17.9	39.6	44.6	15.8
26–40	21.5	66.4	12.2	28.3	60.3	11.4
41–64	10.1	73.2	16.7	14.2	69.0	16.8
65+	1.8	49.1	49.1	9.1	45.5	45.5
		Gamma = −0.49			Gamma = −0.24	
Years of education						
< 12	13.4	55.7	30.9	22.1	55.8	22.1
12	15.2	64.5	20.3	22.4	61.8	15.8
13–15	23.8	66.7	9.5	34.0	50.9	15.1
16+	13.7	74.5	11.8	35.5	57.2	7.2
		Gamma = 0.22			Gamma = 0.21	
Weekly income						
< 100	9.6	53.9	36.5	40.7	33.3	25.9
100–199	18.1	58.5	23.4	39.6	37.7	22.6
200–299	17.9	65.9	16.3	29.6	59.6	10.8
300+	11.9	76.3	11.9	21.0	66.1	12.9
		Gamma = 0.20			Gamma = −0.11	

Source: Murdock and Schriner, 1978.

mobile. Those moving from a higher- to a lower-status occupation were classed as downwardly mobile, and those remaining in similar-status occupations were placed in a stable occupational category.

The data in Table 11.7 reveal that, due to migration and employment at the development site, migrants have increased their occupational mobility more than have longtime residents. Whereas 28.6% of all migrants experienced upward mobility, only 15.6% of longtime residents experienced upward mobility. Moreover, rates of downward mobility were higher for longtime residents than for migrants. These results tend to confirm Ritchey's (1976) finding that migration tends to contribute to the socioeconomic advancement of migrants.

Table 11.7 presents the levels of occupational mobility of longtime residents and migrants controlling for selected characteristics. These data allow one to examine not only overall levels of occuptaional mobility, but also the extent to which respondents with certain characteristics may be particularly negatively or positively affected by the developments. It is often assumed that the oldest, least well educated, and poorest longtime residents are most negatively affected, and that migrants benefit more than others (in part, because of characteristics such as younger age and higher educational levels [Little, 1977]).

However, the data show several unexpected patterns. Age does tend to inhibit mobility for longtime residents more than for migrants. In contrast, education and income are not related to mobility. Except for age, these data fail to point to migrant's characteristics as the source of their higher occupational mobility or to longtime resident's characteristics as the underlying factor in their lower occupational mobility. As with the data on occupational and industrial structure, the data on occupational mobility point to gains for migrants, but not at the expense of longtime residents.

ATTITUDES AND PERCEPTIONS

Migrants' attitudes toward the community and their intentions to remain there are displayed in Table 11.8. The first panel in this table presents the categorized responses to an open-ended question in which migrants were asked to indicate the first and second word or phrase that best described the community. These responses have been categorized according to whether they are positive or negative in tone.

The responses reveal that more migrants are dissatisfied than satisfied with their new communities. More than 66% of the first phrases listed and over 70% of the second phrases listed are negative. However, the most frequently mentioned area of dissatisfaction—expenses—stems from the development situation, not from the community in general.

TABLE 11.8

Migrants' Perceptions of Impacted Communities (in percentages)

Item	First choice	Second choice
Phrases describing community		
Positive	33.5	29.9
Easy	4.3	3.2
Happy	5.9	3.3
Modern	1.2	0.4
Exciting	1.0	1.8
Rewarding	2.1	3.2
Friendly	16.4	12.7
Relaxed	2.6	5.3
Negative	66.5	70.1
Lonely	5.5	2.5
Competitive	1.7	1.6
Impersonal	3.1	4.9
Dull	8.1	6.3
Conservative	1.9	4.4
Unfriendly	3.3	1.6
Isolated	8.7	7.6
Slow moving	4.3	5.8
Difficult	2.2	3.2
Expensive	18.7	17.2
Dirty	9.0	15.0
Number of responses	518	569
Aspects of community most liked and disliked		
Most liked		
Economic–employment related	22.8	19.9
Social–familial	31.0	24.8
Environmental and community context	39.7	48.3
Community services	5.3	5.3
Other	1.9	2.5
Number of responses	560	202
Most disliked		
Economic–employment related	8.2	7.7
Social–familial	12.3	12.4
Environmental and community context	41.5	32.5
Community services	38.5	47.8
Other	0.0	0.0
Number of responses	597	324

Source: Derived from Mountain West Research data, 1975.

Similarly, the second most frequently mentioned item is dirt, which in boomtowns tends to result from project-related activities. Other negative comments reflect dissatisfaction with certain aspects of a rural social environment, such as greater isolation (8.7%).

The positive perceptions indicate that the "friendly" nature of a community is its most attractive feature, followed by "happy" and "easy," or "easy going," characteristics. Overall, the data reveal more negative than positive perceptions, but they also indicate that many of the negative perceptions may result from the development rather than from community characteristics. If development-related comments are ignored, both the areas of positive and negative perceptions appear to reflect differential evaluations of rural settings and ways of life.

The second panel of Table 11.8 describes those aspects of the communities that migrants most liked and disliked. Again, this table shows categorized responses to open-ended questions. These items indicate that in terms of both liked and disliked aspects, the general community context was most often mentioned. The items mentioned next most frequently under negative aspects are community services, while under positive aspects, the social characteristics of the community and the opportunities to be closer to family members are frequently mentioned.

The data in Table 11.9 provide an additional indicator of overall community satisfaction—whether or not migrants want to remain in communities. For many of these migrants, the mining communities represent only temporary stopping places. Over 38% indicate that they will remain only as long as their present employment continues and 4% want to leave immediately. On the other hand, 45% plan to remain in the communities throughout their working lives (22% expect to remain for an indefinite period, and 23% until retirement). Evidently, the eco-

TABLE 11.9
Migrants' Intentions to Remain in Community

Intention	Percent
Remain and settle	21.7
Remain until retirement	23.8
Remain until employment ends	38.3
Leave as soon as possible	4.4
Uncertain	11.8
Number of responses	613

Source: Derived from Mountain West Research data, 1975.

nomic opportunities that brought many migrants to the communities have been satisfactory and many migrants have found the communities attractive as settlement locations. Although respondents are quite dissatisfied with aspects of their new community, if faced with a choice of remaining or leaving the area, many would choose to remain.

Many migrants are dissatisfied with many aspects of their new communities, but much of this dissatisfaction relates to the development rather than to the community itself. For some, the rural way of life is attractive; for others it is distressing. Nearly equal porportions want to leave as want to remain in the communities. These data point to dissatisfaction, but not to extreme dissatisfaction among migrants as has been shown in other reserach (Gilmore and Duff, 1974).

Table 11.10 presents data on the perceptions of longtime residents of the development of their communities. These data provide some evidence of the acceptance of migrants by longer-term residents. Over 65% of the longtime residents think the project has been more positive than negative. The data in Table 11.10 suggest that this evaluation is based on the project's economic benefits. Inadequate services are the most often mentioned negative factor. Finally, other data not presented here indicate that over 77% of respondents said they had made friends among the migrants. Overall these data point to quite positive perceptions of development and to little outright rejection of migrants by longtime residents.

TABLE 11.10
Longtime Residents' Perceptions of Effects of Developments and Migrants (in percentages)

Types of effects	First	Second
Positive effects	64.9	58.5
Economic	39.8	15.9
Community-social	12.3	9.8
Service increases	5.6	20.4
Migrants beneficial	7.2	12.4
Negative effects	35.0	41.5
Economic	6.7	6.2
Community-social	5.4	13.1
Service inadequacies	15.8	12.4
Migrants detrimental	7.1	9.8
Number of responses	292	113

Source: Derived from Mountain West Research data, 1975.
Note: Question was asked in the following way, "List ways in which this community has been affected by development."

TABLE 11.11
*Means and Standard Deviations of Satisfaction with Community Services
in Five Western Communities by Migration Status* [a]

Services	Longtime residents		Migrants	
	Mean	Std. dev.	Mean	Std. dev.
	(N=328)		(N=615)	
Law enforcement	1.5	1.3	3.2	1.6
Fire protection	2.8	1.1	2.9	1.1
Water supply	2.1	0.7	2.5	0.8
Sewer supply	2.4	0.9	2.5	1.0
Garbage collection	2.5	1.0	2.4	0.9
Streets and sewers	2.5	1.0	2.8	1.2
Medical services	3.4	1.2	3.8	1.2
Outdoor recreation	2.7	1.0	2.7	1.2
Indoor recreation	2.9	1.0	3.1	1.0
Other amusements	3.3	1.1	3.4	1.2
Shopping	2.8	1.1	3.0	1.2
City government	2.8	1.0	2.9	0.9
Clubs and organizations	2.4	0.7	2.6	0.7
Schools	2.4	0.9	2.6	0.9
Mental health services	2.8	0.8	2.9	0.6
Housing availability	3.7	1.1	4.0	1.1
Housing quality	3.2	1.1	3.6	1.2

Source: Murdock and Schriner, 1979.
[a] Responses in the table indicate mean values of satisfaction on
a five-point scale in which responses were scored (1) for a very
satisfied, (2) for a satisfied, (3) for a neither satisfied nor
dissatisfied, (4) for a dissatisfied, and (5) for a very dissatisfied
rating of each service.

Migrants are more dissatisfied with almost all community services
than are longtime residents, but the differences are very small (Table
11.11). Also, there is general agreement among migrants and longtime
residents concerning services that are most problematic. For both
groups, housing, medical services, and recreation are areas of dissatisfaction.

Conclusions

Increased development of the energy resources of the Great Plains
promises to affect many of the social, economic, and demographic aspects of the region. Much of this impact is a direct result of the movement of large numbers of migrants into sparsely settled areas. These
migrants represent sources of change for many rural communities. They
will constitute new customers and consumers for local businesses, but

they may also place additional strain on local public services and may bring values and ways of life that conflict with those of longtime residents.

Although the data discussed in this paper are not sufficient for making broad generalizations about effects on other areas, they do support some tentative observations about migrants in energy-impacted areas and their effects on impacted areas in the rural Plains.

Energy-related migrants to the Plains are relatively young, well educated, and highly skilled, and have high incomes. They are younger, better educated, more skilled, and have much higher incomes than longtime residents in the area. They have migrated to the impacted communities from other parts of the same state or from adjoining states. In general, migrants occupy highly skilled positions at the developments and experience increased occupational mobility as a result of the move. They are dissatisfied with many aspects of their new communities, especially public services, but in many cases likely will remain in the communities.

For the impacted areas and their longtime residents, the developments and migrants have created economic opportunities that have benefited longtime residents as well as migrants. Migrants have gained more from such developments, but not at the expense of longtime residents or disadvantaged groups in the communities. However, communities have not experienced extensive economic diversification as a result of the energy developments. Longtime residents share migrants' concerns about the quality and quantity of public services. Longtime residents feel the developments have been positive overall and express little antipathy toward migrants.

These profiles suggest that many of the common assumptions about energy developments require more extensive analysis. Data presented here do not support the common assumptions that energy migrants are vastly different in sociodemographic characteristics from longer-term residents, that migrants are likely to be from distant areas and unfamiliar with the Plains, that they are likely to obtain the best of the energy-related jobs at the expense of local residents, that they are not likely to want to remain in rural areas, and that they arouse the antipathy of many longtime residents, who come to regret the existence of the energy development. In fact, the data suggest that the impact of migration in energy-development areas may be little different from that of migration in other rural areas that do not have new energy-extractive activities.

For students of migration, these findings suggest that additional analyses of energy-related migration may provide results applicable to the general questions that surround the phenomena of renewed rural growth and its implication for rural areas. The phenomenon of energy-related migration is thus not only a phenomenon of value to those interested in rural industrialization and rural development but also an area of conceptual and pragmatic importance for understanding the complex phenomena of migration in general.

For the people and the communities in the Plains, energy-related migration and the energy developments themselves are best viewed with cautious optimism. On the one hand, these developments are creating a younger, better educated population base and some renewed economic growth in areas that have long desired such growth. Moreover, these new migrants do not, at present, appear to be the focus of concern, antipathy, or resentment for longtime area residents. Rather, these new residents appear to be adapting quite well to many aspects of their new communities, and longtime residents appear to be adapting well to the presence of new persons in their communities. On the other hand, the level of projected development far exceeds the present level, and as development increases many problems not evident in this analysis may appear.

The possibility that much of the furor over energy development may prove unwarranted because the level of such development may remain small should also be considered. Although all projections point to substantial growth, the slow evolution of a national energy policy favoring increased use of coal from the Plains, the powerful lobbying efforts of nonwestern coal areas, and the large distances between major energy-consuming areas and western coal deposits may lead to less development than anticipated. If so, then the present energy developments in the Plains may simply be part of yet another boom and bust cycle (Murdock and Leistritz, 1979).

Even if the expected levels of growth materialize, difficult choices may lie ahead for the people and communities in the Plains. Energy development is in potential conflict with agriculture and the environment. The attractiveness of the area for recreation and continued agricultural productivity could be threatened in some areas if the level of energy development is high.

Equally significant, the lack of diversification in the economies of many impacted areas may make growth less desirable and pervasive than sometimes thought (Lonsdale and Seyler, 1979). If energy developments simply replace agriculture as the dominant industry, the results may be much different from what populations in the Plains expect or desire. In addition, because energy developments are likely to be controlled by private developers based outside the Plains and by the federal government through its large ownership of federal lands, these developments may decrease the level of control that local people can exercise over their economic well-being.

The issues faced by rural communities as the result of energy-related migration and growth are not unique; they are similar to issues being faced by other rural turnaround areas (Schwarzweller, 1979). Whether renewed demographic and economic change offsets fiscal and other costs of adapting to growth is a critical question that must remain a central focus in future research on the rural migration turnaround.

References

Beale, Calvin L.
   1974   "Quantitative dimensions of decline and stability among rural communities." In Larry R. Whiting (ed.), *Communities Left Behind: Alternatives for Development*. Ames: The Iowa State University Press.
   1976   "A further look at nonmetropolitan population growth since 1970." *American Journal of Agricultural Economics* 5 (5):953–958.
Bowles, Gladys K.
   1978   *Contributions of Recent Metro/Nonmetro Migrants to the Nonmetro Population and Labor Force*. Athens: The University of Georgia.
Cortese, Charles and Bernie Jones
   1977   "The sociological analysis of boom towns." *Western Sociological Review* 8:76–90.
Federal Energy Administration
   1977   *Regional Profile of Energy Impacted Communities*. Denver: Federal Energy Administration.
Fuguitt, Glenn V. and James J. Zuiches
   1975   "Residential preferences and population distribution." *Demography* 12 (3):491–504.
Gilmore, John S. and Mary K. Duff
   1974   *The Sweetwater County Boom: A Challenge to Growth Management*. Denver, Colorado: University of Denver Research Institute.
Gilmore, John S., Keith D. Moore, Diane M. Hammond, and Dean C. Coddington
   1976   *Analysis of Financial Problems in Coal and Oil Shale Boomtowns*. Washington, D.C.: Federal Energy Administration.
Gold, Raymond L.
   1974   *A Comparative Case Study of the Impact of Coal Development in the Way of Life of People in the Coal Areas of Eastern Montana and Northeastern Wyoming*. Denver: Northern Great Plains Resources Program.
Hansen, Niles M.
   1973   *The Future of Nonmetropolitan America: Studies in the Reversal of Rural Small Town Population Decline*. Lexington, Mass.: D.C. Heath.
Hawley, Amos H.
   1950   *Human Ecology: A Theory of Community Structure*. New York: The Ronald Press Company.
Kuehn, John A.
   1978   "Rural industrialization and migration." Paper presented at the Annual Meeting of the Association of American Geographers.

Lansing, John B. and Eva Mueller
  1967   *The Geographic Mobility of Labor.* Ann Arbor: University of Michigan, Institute for Social Research, Survey Research Center.
Little, Ronald L.
  1977   *Some Social Consequences of Boomtowns.* Lake Powell Research Project Bulletin No. 57. Logan: Utah State University.
Little, Ronald L. and Stephen E. Lovejoy
  1977   *Employment Benefits from Rural Industrialization.* Lake Powell Research Project Bulletin No. 56. Logan: Utah State University.
Lonsdale, Richard E. and H. L. Seyler (eds.)
  1979   *Nonmetropolitan Industrialization.* New York: John Wiley & Sons.
McCarthy, Kevin F. and Peter A. Morrison
  1978   *Demographic Structure and Implications of Nonmetropolitan Growth Since 1970.* Santa Monica, Calif.: Rand Corporation.
Mountain West Research, Inc.
  1975   *Construction Worker Profile.* Washington, D.C.: The Old West Regional Commission.
Murdock, Steve H.
  1979   "The potential role of the ecological framework in impact analysis." *Rural Sociology* 44 (3):543–565.
Murdock, Steve, H. and F. Larry Leistritz
  1979   *Energy Development in the Western United States: Impact on Rural Areas.* New York: Praeger Publishers.
Murdock, Steve H. and Eldon C. Schriner
  1978   "Structural and distributional factors in community development." *Rural Sociology* 43:426–449.
  1979   "Community service satisfaction and stages of community development: An examination of evidence from impacted communities." *Journal of Community Development* 10 (1):109–124.
Nielson, G. F.
  1978   "Keystone forecasts 765 million tons of new coal capacity by 1987." *Coal Age* 83 (2):113–134.
Northern Great Plains Resources Program
  1974   *Socioeconomic and Cultural Aspects.* Work Group Report. Denver: Northern Great Plains Resources Program.
Ritchey, R. Neal
  1976   "Explanations of migration." Pp. 363–404 In *The Annual Review of Sociology,* Vol. II. Palo Alto, Calif.: Annual Review.
Schwarzweller, Harry K.
  1979   "Migration and the changing rural scene." *Rural Sociology* 44:7–23.
Shaw, R. P.
  1975   *Migration Theory and Fact: A Review and Bibliography of Current Literature.* Philadelphia: Regional Science Research Institute.
Sly, David F.
  1972   "Migration and the ecological complex." *American Sociological Review* 37:615–628.
Sly, David F. and Jeff Tayman
  1977   "Ecological approach to migration reexamined." *American Sociological Review* 42:783–795.
United Nations
  1973   "The determinants and consequences of population trends." *Population Studies,* Vol. 1, No. 50, New York: United Nations.

U.S. Department of the Interior
1970   *Minerals Yearbook,* Vol. I, various issues. Washington, D.C.: U.S. Government Printing Office.
1974   *Demonstrated Coal Reserve Base of the United States, by Sulfur Category, on January 1, 1974.* Washington, D.C.: U.S. Government Printing Office.
1978   *Projects to Expand Energy Sources in the Western States.* Bureau of Mines Information Circular 8772. Washington, D.C.: U.S. Government Printing Office.
Wardwell, John M.
1977   "Equilibrium and change in nonmetropolitan growth." *Rural Sociology* 42 (2):156–179.
Watts, Gary, James Thompson, and Audie Blevins
1977   *First Year Progress Report of a Socioeconomic Longitudinal Monitoring Project.* Laramie: University of Wyoming, Center for Urban and Regional Analysis.
Wieland, James S., F. Larry Leistritz, and Steve H. Murdock
1977   *Characteristics and Settlement Patterns of Energy Related Operating Workers in the Northern Great Plains.* Fargo, North Dakota: North Dakota State University, Department of Agricultural Economics.
Wilkinson, J. F.
1978   "The outlook for 1978: Some good news, some bad news." *Coal Age* 83 (2):59–63.
Zuiches, James J. and David L. Brown
1978   "Changing character of the nonmetropolitan population, 1950–1975." In Thomas R. Ford (ed.), *Rural U.S.A.: Persistence and Change.* Ames: Iowa State University Press.

12

Effects of Turnaround Migration on Community Structure in Maine

LOUIS A. PLOCH

Introduction

The turnaround migration phenomenon of the 1970s has been pervasive. This chapter continues the discussion of this phenomenon, focusing on the effects of renewed population growth on the smaller towns and rural areas of Maine.[1]

Since at least the late 1960s, Maine, particularly in its rural areas, has been sharing in the movement of people into northern New England. Largely as a result of net in-migration, Maine, New Hampshire, and Vermont have been gaining population in recent years at significant rates. Since 1970, New Hampshire has been the most rapidly growing state north of Virginia and east of Colorado (Figure 12.1). In this geographical area, Maine ranks second and Vermont third in rate of population growth. The increased rate of population growth in Maine can be seen clearly by comparing the varying lengths of time it has taken to add an additional 100,000 people to the state over recent years. It took 17 years, from 1931 to 1948, for Maine's population to increase from 800,000

---

[1]Major sources of data include an ongoing observational study of four Maine rural communities; an empirical study of in-migrants to Maine; monitoring of the Maine press, particularly weekly newspapers; and systematic analyses of other information sources, particularly data from the Maine State Planning Office and the U.S. Bureau of the Census. The four Maine rural communities are Bradford (1976 population, 684) and Greenbush (1976 population, 832) in Penobscot County, and Lincolnville (1976 population, 1192) and Troy (1976 population, 675) in Waldo County.

New Directions in
Urban–Rural Migration

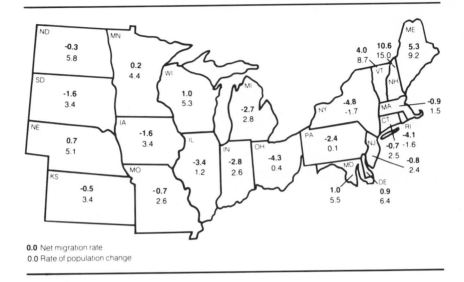

Figure 12.1. Percentage net migration and population change 1970–1977, for Northeastern and North Central states. (Source: U.S. Bureau of the Census.)

to 900,000. The next 100,000 increase took longer; 23 years, from 1948 to 1971. And the next 100,000 was gained in just 7 years, from 1971 to 1978. Approximately one-half of this last increase can be attributed to net in-migration (Ploch and Dearborn, 1978).

The recent increase in Maine's population has been concentrated outside of major urban areas, and much of it has taken place in areas that had previously experienced slow growth or actual decline. The southern area of the state, closest to the Boston and Hartford metropolitan areas, has experienced rapid growth through in-migration. But the western coastal counties (Figure 12.2) have also been the sites of significant population gains since 1970. Gains in population have not been confined to the coastal counties. During the decade from 1960 to 1970, 12 of Maine's 16 counties had net out-migration; 5 suffered absolute population losses. During the 1970–1975 period, all 16 counties gained population; only Aroostook, the most northern and isolated of the counties, still experienced net out-migration (Dearborn, 1976). Much of the loss in Aroostook County was attributed to reductions in the military establishments in the county. In the 1960–1970 period, 225 of Maine's 498 organized cities, towns, and plantations—45% of the total—lost population. Since 1970, Bureau of the Census estimates indicate that only 76 organized places (15%) experienced population declines.

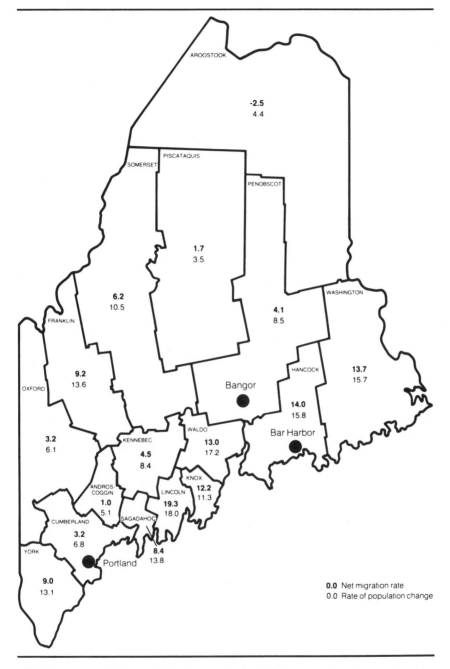

AROOSTOOK

-2.5
4.4

PISCATAQUIS

SOMERSET

PENOBSCOT

1.7
3.5

WASHINGTON

6.2
10.5

FRANKLIN

4.1
8.5

9.2
13.6

HANCOCK

13.7
15.7

OXFORD

Bangor

14.0
15.8

WALDO

3.2
6.1

KENNEBEC

13.0
17.2

Bar Harbor

4.5
8.4

KNOX

12.2
11.3

ANDROS-
COGGIN

LINCOLN

1.0
5.1

19.3
18.0

CUMBERLAND

SAGADAHOC

3.2
6.8

YORK

8.4
13.8

9.0
13.1

Portland

0.0 Net migration rate
0.0 Rate of population change

Figure 12.2. Percentage net migration and population change 1970–1977 for Maine counties. (Source: U.S. Bureau of the Census.)

Migration to Maine

As can be seen from Figure 12.1, northern New England is a convenient, proximate, and perhaps familiar territory for people from the urban areas of southern New England, New Jersey, and eastern areas of New York and Pennsylvania who are seeking a rural residence and perhaps a rural lifestyle. The hill-and-valley country of northern New England is similar in physical configuration and climate to other parts of the Northeast and shares a common cultural history with the entire region. Thus, migrants to the area from other parts of the Northeast should in general have less difficulty adjusting to its geographic and cultural conditions than to other sections of the United States.[2] It is not surprising that the bulk of recent migrants to Maine and northern New England have come from the Northeast (Forbush, 1978; Luloff, 1979; Ploch, 1977a, 1977b). In Maine, 45% of household-head informants were from New England and 24% were from other states in the Northeast. Approximately 70% had migrated from relatively large counties (200,000 or more population). The average county in Maine contains 67,750 people (1978 estimate), and all but one of the 16 counties are below the 200,000-size threshold. The New York City and Boston areas account for two-thirds of the net migration to the New Hampshire and Vermont counties studied by Forbush (1978).

The data for this analysis of new migration trends are derived primarily from a study of migration to Maine conducted in 1976 (Ploch, 1977a, 1977b). The major sample consists of 1373 self-designated household heads who moved to Maine between 1970 and 1975. The data were obtained by sending questionnaires to a sample of 2100 persons who exchanged their previous driver's licenses for Maine licenses in 1975. Because the respondents had to be licensed drivers, the data may be biased toward the middle-class. There may also be an age bias because fewer older migrants probably chose to renew licenses they had held in their previous states of residence. Similarly, our data may somewhat underenumerate migrants with alternative lifestyles, particularly those who may live in larger-than-average-size, multi-adult households and be dependent upon a single vehicle.

The original sample, randomly stratified by county, consisted of approximately one-sixth of all in-migrant applicants for a Maine driver's license in 1975. The rate of return, when deaths, invalid addresses, and other contingencies are accounted for, was approximately 70%.[3]

---

[2]For the role played by former residence in Maine and visits to the state in recent in-migration, see Brewerton (1978).

[3]If a questionnaire was not returned within 10 days after the original mailing, a follow-up letter and a second questionnaire were sent. The first mailing produced approximately

In the decades prior to the 1970s, the population distribution of most rural communities exhibited gross distortions in the young adult categories. Part of this imbalance can be attributed to the lower birth rates of the 1930s and the early 1940s. Most of the "missing" young adults were the result of out-migration to urban areas in search of economic and educational opportunities. Their departure had the twin effects of retarding rural community population growth and of preserving or reserving important community-status roles for their remaining siblings. Copp (1961) has speculated that those who were left behind were the more conservative and less innovative.

National studies (Zuiches and Brown, 1978) indicate that at least until 1970 older-age groupings predominated among rural adults. Recent in-migration to Connecticut (Steahr, 1978), New Hampshire (Luloff, 1979), and Maine (Ploch, 1977a) indicate that this trend has been reversed for New England. In these three states, the turnaround migration flows have been overrepresentative of young adults (Figure 12.3). This reversal has been a mechanism that, in effect, has helped to fill in the gaps in the population distribution of many rural communities.

In a sense then, in-migration has helped to normalize the age distribution of the northern New England population. There are now relatively more young persons to take positions of community leadership and to provide continuity in age groupings. In many communities the addition of young adults could restore a positive attitude toward change and progress that had been lost through heavy out-migration. The data in Figure 12.3 indicate that just over one-half (51%) of the in-migrant household heads sampled in Maine in 1976 were under 35 years of age, whereas only 7% were 65 years of age or older. Over two-fifths (43%) of these household heads had completed 4 or more years of college, and two-thirds (66%) had completed at least 1 year of college.[4] By contrast, in 1970 (the next-most-recent year for which comparable information is available), only 8% of Maine males 25 years of age or older had completed at least 4 years of college.

Selected aspects of household composition are also shown in Figure 12.3. Unlike the large-family pattern that was traditionally characteristic of rural areas, the Maine in-migrant sample tends to consist of small families. Two-thirds of the households contained no children of school age—there were approximately seven school-age children for every ten in-migrant households.

In 1970 in Maine, approximately 21% of the males active in the labor force held white-collar occupations. In contrast, approximately 54% of

two-thirds of the total response. See Dillman (1978) for details on returns to mailed questionnaires.

[4]For a similar example for a Colorado community, see Santopolo et al. (1979).

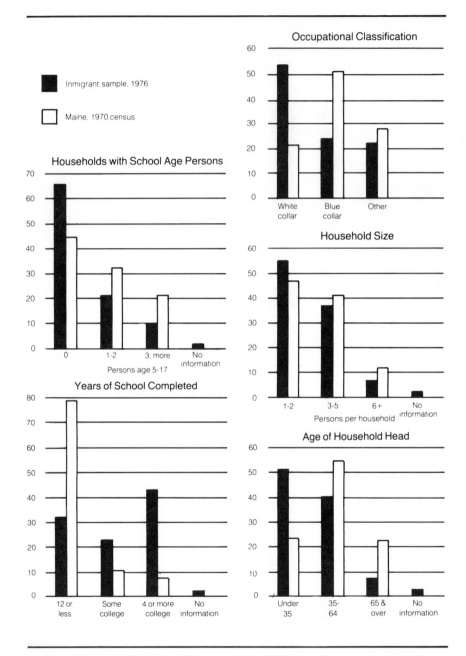

Figure 12.3. Selected characteristics of 1976 Maine in-migrant sample compared with entire state of Maine in 1970 Census.

the household heads in the in-migrant sample identified themselves as white-collar workers. In 1970, 51% of Maine males in the labor force were blue-collar workers, but among the in-migrant household heads only 24 % so identified themselves. Not only is the population composition of rural Maine communities changing, but the structure of communities and the patterns of interrelationships are undergoing significant change. Examples of these changes are presented later in this chapter.

The Impact of Population Growth

The sociological significance of the reversal in net urban–rural migration is found in the impact of change on the stability of community and individual life, and in the adequacy of community institutions to cope with the changing social needs and characteristics of the resident population. "In short, the significance of population change lies in how it affects the community life and the lives of the residents of the community [Klietsch *et al.*, 1964:5.]"

In the foregoing quotation, Klietsch and his associates refer primarily to the effects of rural-to-urban migrations. It is likely that the urban-to-rural migrations of the 1970s have (or will have) at least as much impact as did the earlier migrations in the opposite direction. One basis for this assumption is that rural communities are smaller than their urban counterparts. In rural communities, as compared with urban areas, a larger proportion of relationships are personalized and primary. Although the compositional and interactional differences between rural and urban locales may be overdrawn, major differences still exist (Taylor and Jones, 1964). In this chapter the primariness and personalization of interactions, the high social visibility of individuals, and the *Gemeinschaftness* (Loomis and Beegle, 1975) of rural areas are construed to be major explanatory factors of the impact of the new migration on rural Maine.

In Maine, the typical nonsuburban rural community reached its population peak between 1850 and 1890. With few exceptions, most rural towns experienced net out-migration until the 1950s. Only a relatively high birth rate kept population levels near stability.[5]

Newcomers were a rarity in these communities. New residents were most often the spouses of natives who married out of the community but, unlike their brothers, sisters, aunts, and uncles, chose to remain

---

[5]See Holbrook (1950) for a documentation of the nineteenth-century depopulation of northern New England, and Mitchell (1978) for a detailed picture of the effects of population decline on a single community.

within their home area. A definitive pattern of social relationships and services developed in which the past was glorified, the present was grumblingly accepted, and the future ignored (Copp, 1961). If changes in the structure of social relationships in government, education, or religion were made, they were usually the result of outside forces, as exemplified in Warren's (1978) analysis of the impact of vertical ties on local communities. The state legislature or bureaucrats made decisions that modified local governmental forms and regulations; the same forces decreed changes in educational policy and delivery (Davis, 1976).

Federal decision makers also decreed changes in local practices that local communities have been powerless to resist. Even people's religious orientations and traditions were affected—headquarters of major denominations, located hundreds of miles away, made decisions affecting local churches. Local communities and individuals often resented these actions, but they usually lacked the resources or the organization to resist them effectively.

In the late 1960s and early 1970s, most rural Maine communities were confronted with a new and unexpected situation to which they could react directly. Significant numbers of strangers began to appear. Unlike rules, regulations, and other changes promulgated by higher levels of government and other sources, the in-migrants were a force that could be reacted to on a personal, day-to-day basis.

The newcomers were ready targets for reaction—many were strangers in every sense of the word. They differed in appearance, education, life-style and behavior from longer-term residents. Counterculture refugees from the turmoil of the cities and the college campuses in the late 1960s were particularly vulnerable to the reactions of traditional rural residents. The men typically wore beards and long hair; the women had their hair in braids and wore long dresses. Many of the couples were not married. Some of them were explicitly seeking a form of agrarian life style that many earlier out-migrants from Maine had defined as oppressive and sought to escape.

By local definition, if some of these new migrants fitted the counterculture stereotype, they all did. In local discussions the numbers of these odd strangers were often exaggerated. There may have been some conscious action in this exaggeration—if numbers were magnified, perhaps enough negative community reactions could be created to induce some of the counter culturalists to leave; perhaps the flow of similar in-migrants might be stemmed.[6] Thus, in the early years of the turnaround

---

[6]These conclusions are based primarily on the author's field experience in four Maine rural communities; see also Mills (1972).

migration, it was not only the number of in-migrants that was perceived as a threat to community and individual stability, but also the composition of the in-migrant streams. Strange as the counterculture arrivals seemed, they were at least accorded a unique status outside of the usual value framework of the community.

Paradoxically, the more conventional and somewhat older migrants presented the greatest enigma to many longer-term residents of stable or declining rural communities. Residents raised questions about their intentions and motivations: Why were college educated, obviously successful city people choosing to live out here? Why were they moving into these old, tumble-down places when they could build or buy the best houses in town? Why did they want to farm when they could buy all the food they needed?

In-Migrants and Community Change

Communities are networks of relationships. Although these networks are constantly evolving in any community, there are strong and pervasive forces at work to maintain the status quo. Loomis and Beegle describe this action as *boundary maintenance*, defined as the process by which members of the system (community) retain their identity and interaction pattern (Loomis and Beegle, 1975). In Maine, numerous examples of boundary maintenance can be observed in places where both in-migrants and longtime residents are present at discussions of local affairs. In recent years, during vestibule discussions at town meetings, the author has heard local people remark that the in-migrants have come to the community to take over its functions. However, the majority of local people are not ready to permit relative strangers to take over town government, schools, or other institutions.[7]

Community Involvement of In-Migrants

The average native or longtime settler gives little thought to the fact that most of the new migrants have moved voluntarily, value rural life, and wish to maintain their perceptions of it. In-migrants are generally attracted to participation in those types of community institutions in which they have had previous experience and have particular expertise

[7]Unless otherwise indicated, statements in this section attributed to community residents are paraphrases of quotations recorded by the author in meetings or interview situations during the 1977–1979 period in one of the four communities designated in footnote 1.

or vested interests. An example is the involvement of parents of school-age children in educational activities. As long as this form of participation is not perceived as threatening to existing situations, the newcomers are likely to encounter little resistance, and may, in fact, be gratified at the welcome they receive.

On the other hand, seeking membership on the school board is more likely to generate suspicion among longtime residents. They wonder what the in-migrants are up to; they accuse them of wishing to citify rural schools by bringing in new programs and thus raising local taxes. Although our research in Maine does indicate that there is opposition to in-migrants seeking positions as school committee members, the barriers are not as impenetrable as we first expected. One of our studies analyzed membership on three local policymaking or regulating bodies, and found that in-migrants were most likely to become planning board members, and least likely to become selectmen; membership on school committees was intermediate (Kelly, 1976).[8]

The mere fact that new migrants from urban origins seek positions on official community boards and membership in community organizations may strain existing relationships. Once achieved, such positions may pose another source of strain through the relatively rapid advancement of the newcomers. Their generally superior education, past leadership and managerial experience, ability to assess local situations without the encumbrance of past history, and orientations that are often creative and innovative are likely to hasten their movement into leadership positions.

The rapid assumption of leadership positions by newcomers has created social and psychological dilemmas. On the one hand, many in the community welcome the fact that new people are breathing new life into local activities. Conversely, some traditional leaders, members of old families, and relatively younger prior residents, are suspicious of the motivations of the new leadership. Although many of these prior residents will admit, often grudgingly, that the new people are making community contributions, they still harbor fears and frustrations. The longer-time residents have difficulty in assessing the motivations of the newcomers. The older settlers may recognize (again grudgingly) that the suggested change may have merit, but they tend to worry about who will pay for it. Fears of potential tax increases are expressed.

In general, these fears relate to the possibility that newcomers will take over too much too quickly. Paradoxically, the opposite situation

[8]The difficulty of newcomers assuming official positions of leadership, particularly that of county commissioner in rural Michigan, is described by Beegle et al. (1979).

also raises questions in the minds of some community-oriented residents. They wonder why such obviously qualified persons do not do "their share." The newcomers should make use of their experience and skills. Similarly, some longer-time residents feel that some of the newcomers waste too much time with arts and crafts when they could be contributing to the good of the community.

Revival of Local Newspapers

The effects of new migration to Maine of talented, creative, and motivated persons go beyond their involvement in pre-existing community organizations. There are numerous examples of newcomers making efforts to provide themselves and their neighbors with cultural, social, and intellectual experiences and opportunities. Some of these take the form of hobbies or avocations; others are business ventures. One of the concomitants of the economic and population revival of rural communities in Maine has been a renewed interest in local newspapers, primarily weekly papers. Local papers are particularly important to rural people. The local newspaper is generally the major, if not the only, source of community news. In its "local" columns, a small town paper "serves as a communicator of important social facts for the rural readership [Vidich and Bensmen, 1968:145]". In addition, in small communities the owner–editors of local newspapers tend to be highly visible. Through their multiple roles of communicator, political evaluator–watchdog, and independent entrepreneur they often become significant community decision makers. Thus, the assuming of control of a vital local service by newcomers becomes doubly important.

At the present time, it appears that the papers that are being bought, published, and usually edited by one or two private individuals are having the greatest local impact.[9] Rather than urbanizing the format and content of the papers, a concerted effort is usually made to retain or regain their rural image. Features on local personalities are regularly presented, particularly if there is some idealized rural role relationship involved. The "can you identify this historical photograph," usually with some local traditional significance, is a popular feature.

The rejuvenated papers, to increase reader acceptance, tend to hire well-qualified feature writers and competent, creative photographers. Thus, the owner–publishers and the professional staffs tend dispropor-

---

[9]Outstanding examples are the *Ellsworth American* (Ellsworth, Maine) and the *Republican Journal* (Belfast, Maine).

tionately to be newcomers. Many of them admit to working for much less than they could earn (or have earned) on metropolitan dailies such as the *Washington Post, Boston Globe,* and *Manchester Union Leader.* Through these actions, rural residents enjoy a preservation of nostalgic traditionalism and an increase in the quality of the journalism available to them.

In a few smaller Maine communities, recent migrants, sometimes with the assistance of longer-term residents, have established another type of publication. These papers can be described as regularly circulated, informal chronicles of local events. In Bradford, Maine (1976 population, 684) an in-migrant woman established a monthly paper (*The Bradford Chronicle*) that has become a chronicle of local events and a sounding board for local opinion. In 3 years it has reached an intown circulation of 190 copies and a total circulation of 225. Subscribers are located in six states.

Publications of this type exemplify the community orientations of many of the in-migrants and their active participation in community building and maintenance. They have moved to a rural community in part because they value what they perceive to be its inherently superior quality of life. They want to maintain and foster this quality. And these newspapers not only may serve to satisfy the creative energies of their founders but may function as community-building forces. They feature and encourage community activities and orientations. However, long-time residents tend to be suspicious of the editors' motivations. This is particularly true if the paper supports a particular cause such as local land-use planning or increased taxes.

Revival in the Arts

Newspapers are only one of the institutional activities that attract the interest and participation of in-migrants. Within the last 10 years in Maine, at least a dozen musical–dance–theatre companies have been founded in rural communities and small cities, largely through the work of newcomers (Guptill, 1977). It was not unusual in the middle- and late-1800s for Maine rural communities to have musical and dramatic presentations. Many organizations, such as the Grange, the Odd Fellows, and the Masons, regularly presented entertainment. Comparatively well-to-do families, farmers and nonfarmers, had parlors with pianos, melodeons, or organs. Older residents whose families have lived in the area for three or more generations recall that it was not uncommon for rural youngsters to receive music lessons.

Much of this orientation was lost in the ensuing years of depopulation, loss of services, and general community decline. In the 1950s and 1960s, few children in the more remote rural communities ever experienced a live dramatic or musical performance. Now such groups as the Incredible Happy Time Theatre, in Athens (1975 population, 592), and the Cornville Players (1975 population, 623) give local performances and also travel through a wide area of the state. Other forms of live theatre and music have been started and/or supported by newcomers. These include the Robert Coller Chorale, Belfast (1975 population, 5957); the Bagaduce Chorale of Brooksville (1975 population, 673), which presents classical-to-modern music; and the Haydn Festival of LaMoine (1975 population, 615), which features the music of Haydn and other composers.

Largely through the efforts of recent migrants, Maine residents are sharing in artistic and cultural activities that had long been absent from rural and small-community life. It is difficult to say what the total impact of these experiences will be on communities and individuals. At minimum, many persons will have opportunities to widen their cultural horizons through opportunities that were not locally available to the immediately preceding generations.

In-migrant Effects on Land Values and Housing

A prominent factor in the nonmetropolitan population turnaround is the declining importance of economic motivations in migration, and the increasing importance of residential preferences and other quality-of-life considerations. But the process is not without its economic consequences. One such effect is on land and housing values. Just as in any case of population increase in a local area, land and housing values have risen as the flow of migration has increased. For example, in Maine, as rates of in-migration and population growth increased in coastal areas, there was increased migration to inland communities where housing and land prices were generally lower.[10]

Where property is locally owned, the profit from land and housing sales has usually stayed in the community. However, where the supply of land and housing is definitely limited, as it is on some of the islands off Maine's coast, property becomes so expensive that local people can-

[10]This information was obtained through personal interviews with realtors and in-migrants, 1976–1979. For a Michigan example see Beegle *et al.* (1979).

not afford to buy home sites.[11] Continuing out-migration of local young people can then result from the processes of new household formation and natural population growth. Rising land values can often result in higher taxes which make it more difficult for low-income persons and the fixed-income elderly to continue living in the community.

Improvements in Health Services

The middle-class nature of a large proportion of in-migration contributes other service-related consequences. In our Maine study (Ploch, 1977a), 21% of the in-migrant household heads were professionals. Although some of these people moved to Maine to retire, reduce their workloads, or locate their professional activity in larger places while establishing their residences in smaller towns, a large number of them moved both their residences and their professional activities into rural areas. These people provide services that had been lost through the decades of population stagnation or decline. For example, Hancock County, which experienced both population loss and net migration loss for decades, is now growing. The county had a 1960 population of 32,293 and approximately five dentists. In 1978, the population increased by 25% to approximately 40,000, but the number of dentists more than tripled, to 18 (Maine Board of Dental Examiners, 1978). Most of the new dentists were recent in-migrants. The growth of professional manpower in the smaller communities is being complemented by an increase in professionals in the urban areas. Interestingly, many urban professionals choose to establish their residences in nearby rural communities.

The medical staffs of the two largest hospitals in the state (in Portland and Bangor) have both more than doubled in a 5-year period during the 1970s. But the growth in hospital staffs and related services is not restricted to the larger cities. The Waldo County Hospital (the only hospital in the county; the county's 1976 population was 26,821) had severe staffing problems during the 1960s. The resident staff declined to five physicians. During the 1970s the hospital increased its roster to 17 full-time members. Thirty additional persons are on the consulting staff and six of the full-time staff were added during a 15-month period in 1978–1979. Of the six, two were from Massachusetts and one each from Rhode Island, Pennsylvania, Michigan, and New Mexico. Many of the new physicians are board-certified specialists.

In Blue Hill (1976 population, 1638), an attractive, residential Hancock County coastal town, the staff of the local hospital has more than dou-

---

[11]For a similar albeit nineteenth-century example, see Mitchell (1978).

bled in the last 5 years. Changes taking place on the hospital's board of trustees are also important. The board now numbers among its members a former senior vice-president of First National City Bank of New York, a senior vice-president of Litton Industries, and a senior executive of a large Canadian paper manufacturing firm.[12] Persons with such experiences and abilities will no doubt contribute to strengthening the board and thus help to assure a high level of health care in this small community.

Changes in Interpersonal Relationships

The patterns of interrelationships in most rural communities are definite, traditional, and class-based (Vidich and Bensman, 1968). The intrusion of migrants into a local system is not taken lightly; newcomers must earn the right of acceptance. It is not always the old-timers, nor the parental generation, who are most resistant to the in-migrants' overtures for recognition. Rather, it is often the younger persons, the son-and-daughter generation, who tend to be the most suspicious of the newcomers.[13] One explanation for this anomaly is that the younger generation has the most to lose as a result of the arrival of talented newcomers. They may lose economically, in terms of employment opportunities; they may lose socially, in terms of accession to positions of community and organizational leadership. In the normal course of events, the sons and daughters would replace their parents in positions of power and prestige. This situation has suddenly changed because of the appearance in town of strangers who have educational, occupational, and organizational experiences that qualify them for a wide range of important community roles. The fear that the migrants will want to take over and the negative self-evaluation that may result from comparing themselves to the newcomers are likely sources of the younger generation's resistance to accepting the new in-migrants into the community.

In Maine, the town meeting is a major forum for native and longer-term residents to express their displeasure toward newcomers. Although at town meetings (and other public gatherings) in-migrants are directly accused of being aggressive, opposition to them as potential

[12]These data were supplied in an interview with the treasurer, Blue Hill Memorial Hospital, 1979.

[13]This situation has been noted specifically in the four Maine rural communities in which the author and a research associate have conducted systematic observations. Corroboration of these findings has been communicated to the author by observers in at least 10 additional Maine communities.

leadership threats is often more subtle. General remarks and innuendos about newcomers wanting to urbanize the town and bring city-style services ranging from garbage collection to a full-time paid police force, seem to be aimed more at discrediting the newcomers than toward rejecting the services per se. The motivation for much of this negative behavior toward in-migrants appears aimed at reducing their viability as candidates for elected or appointed offices, or for organizational leadership posts. [14]

In the four communities we are currently observing, we are noticing a polarization of factions similar to that described by Colfer and Colfer (1978). The most obvious factions are the son–daughter group of younger residents and the relatively young-to-younger middle-aged in-migrants. But the factionalism is complex. Some of the older members of the resident population are sympathetic to the interests and motivations of the son–daughter generation and identify with them. In other cases, the older generation tends to identify with the newcomers.

These older people, particularly those who were or are small-scale or traditional farmers, tend to see a kind of reincarnation of their own agrarian values in many of the in-migrants. In many cases they view their own children as *migrants in place*—persons who remain in the local community but who assume many of the values and ways of urban life. Material goods have become important in their lives, participation in the credit-based modern life-style is enthusiastic and active. They seem more attuned to the values and norms of urban America than toward traditional local culture. In contrast, many of the in-migrants prefer a much simpler, more old-fashioned, style of life.

The older generation can readily identify with the in-migrant who comes to them for information on topping off the bee hive or pruning old apple trees. Paradoxically, many of the older residents and new in-migrants find themselves in agreement over tax and service issues. Contrary to the perceptions of them held by the younger resident population, many of the in-migrants do not want to see their chosen rural locations urbanized. They came to the rural community to experience new values in new settings; they see a worthiness in rurality and want to preserve it. In-migrants with these orientations express attitudes toward the community that are directed more toward preservation than toward change. Thus, in one of the rural Maine communities that we have studied (Greenbush), one alternative life-style in-migrant who sought to

---

[14]These observations were made at town meetings in Bradford, Greenbush, Troy, Starks, Maine, between 1976 and 1979. For an account of interactions at a Maine town meeting see Ploch (1979b).

preserve the ruralness, even the primitiveness, of his section of the community was elected as selectman; largely by the votes of the older natives. They identified with his old-fashioned community-related values even though they did not condone his specific life-style.

In summary, because the in-migrants do differ in demographic characteristics from the modal rural resident, and because these in-migrants are perceived and reacted to differentially by different segments of the resident population, the new growth through the turnaround migration pattern is likely to become a major factor in reshaping the social class system and the system of social relationship in many rural communities.

Conclusions

Beale (1978) has spoken to the difficulty of inferring the social consequences of the nonmetropolitan turnaround migration from the knowledge of its demographic aspects:

> There is an unrealistic assumption that knowledge of the demography of the event makes one an authority on its implications. I wish that I did know what it means for residential and automotive use, for health services, for municipal and other local financing, for water and sewer needs, for schools, for gross national product, for land use issues, for U.S. economic policy, for rural law enforcement [p. 13].

One of the reasons for this difficulty is the diversity of migration streams. Even within a very specific flow such as that to rural Maine, there are important substrata among the migrants. The stream may be described in modal terms as basically middle class as measured by educational background, prior income levels, and occupational pursuits. But there are major differences between the counterculture migrants, the environmentalists, and the young executives seeking a relatively stress-free economic venture in a more rural locale (Ploch, 1978). Each of these subtypes tends to react differently toward community structure, services, and values. In turn, the community reacts differently toward each definable subgroup among the new in-migrants.

Even the terms subgroup and substrata may be too global. A given individual or individuals in a given household may be identified by a combination of characteristics that cut across the boundaries of several definable subgroups. For example, two recent in-migrants may be known to the community as environmentalists, antihunter bird watchers, and organic gardeners. But one may be a reclusive member of a counterculture group who lives in a multi-adult household in a primitive cabin lacking modern conveniences. The other person may be a relatively young, semiretired executive who has bought the best farm in the area and who has ambitions to be on the local school board.

Thus, while the impacts of migration streams upon rural communities might be superficially greater (and would certainly be more readily identifiable) if those migration streams were more homogenous, the actual complexities of the population flows create greater problems of adjustment for both the longtime residents and for the newcomers. For example, it is difficult to know how to react to a person who embodies characteristics normally possessed by several different types of persons. On what basis would residents of a small, Downeast, Maine town place within the existing local status system the college-educated newcomer who, on the one hand, holds a responsible position in a government agency with a salary double or more the community average and who, on the other hand, chooses to dress in unconventional style and to live in an isolated cabin lacking most modern conveniences?

If taken out of context, some of the incidents and situations cited in the preceding paragraphs might lead one to conclude that turnaround migration has fostered widespread conflict in rural Maine. Some incidents of conflict have occurred, but in general, adjustment to turnaround migration is proceeding relatively smoothly.

There appear to be a number of contributing factors in the general acceptance of newcomers. One of the most important is that in contrast with some other areas of the country, and with a few local exceptions, communities in Maine have not been inundated with a flood of newcomers. Even in the coastal areas where the most rapid rates of population growth are occurring, typical rates for the 1970–1975 period were in the 15–25% range.

Another important reason why oldtimer–newtimer conflict may be at a minimum in rural Maine is that the in-migrants do not tend to represent a single, identifiable type or group of persons toward which the community could react uniformly. There are significant proportions of retired persons in the in-migrant stream to Maine but there is no major concentration as in many sunbelt communities. And many of the retirees to Maine are in their forties and fifties. They seem to fit relatively easily into the fabric of the community.

A probable third underlying reason is that the ethnic and racial backgrounds of in-migrants are generally similar to the modal rural Maine resident; most in-migrants are white Anglo-Saxons.

Perhaps the major exception to the lack of concentration of homogeneous groups among the in-migrants to Maine has been the alternative life-style settlers. As indicated above, this type of in-migrant was fairly common in Maine in the late 1960s. The reactions of local people to alternative life-stylers was often less than hospitable. By the late 1970s, the situation had changed dramatically. Most of these in-migrants had disappeared in one of two ways. Many soon realized that making a living off the land where the soil was shallow, the growing season short, and the winters long and cold was not for them. They left for more welcome climates—both physically and socially. Those that remained have been acclimatized. Some have done it by conquering the adverse conditions of their original settlement; larger numbers have stayed in Maine but have moved to better land and/or are leading more conventional life-styles.

Many of the former counterculturalists and other in-migrants have adopted a pattern of acculturation that rests on mutual avoidance. They interact with the old settlers only when necessary. Many of the settled people also find this pattern to their liking. But, in general, there is increasing contact between the migrants and nonmigrants without obvious conflict. Overall there appears to be a mutual desire upon the part of both the migrants and nonmigrants to get on with the business of making their communities better places in which to live.

The uncertainties (fuel shortage, inflation, changes in preferences, etc.) related to the turnaround's continuation, and the lack of fully relevant precedents, particularly for the declining or stable communities of the Northeast, make it difficult to predict the long-run effects of the phenomenon for Maine and comparable states. This situation thus invites not only additional research but research that is coordinated at both the regional and national levels. By such an approach, the variances that exist among turnaround population streams and in local ecological and cultural conditions can be evaluated and analyzed by appropriate, standardized methodologies (Ploch, 1979a).

Acknowledgment

Grateful acknowledgment is made of Vance E. Dearborn's help in providing statistical and other pertinent information and insights. Acknowledgment is also accorded to Mrs. Joan Bouchard for her assistance in the preparation of the manuscript.

References

Beale, Calvin L.
   1978   "Population trends in the Northeast." Paper presented at 1978 annual meeting of the Northeast Agricultural Economics Council, Durham, New Hampshire.

Beegle, J. A., Richard Rathge, and Fred Frankena
  1979 "Impacts of population growth on social institutions in a nonmetropolitan county of Michigan." Paper presented at the U.S.D.A. Conference on Recent Migration Trends, St. Louis, Missouri, October.
Brewerton, Lawrence O.
  1978 "In-migration to Maine: Selected aspects." Masters thesis, Orono: University of Maine.
Colfer, Carol J. and A. Michael Colfer
  1978 "Inside Bushler Bay: Life-style in counter point." *Rural Sociology* 43 (Summer):204–220.
Copp, James H.
  1961 "The people in stable and declining town–country communities." Paper presented at Northeast Conference on the Rural Nonfarm Population, Gettysburg, Penn.
Davis, Jay
  1976 "Freedom Fighters." *Yankee* (March):80–84.
Dearborn, Vance E.
  1976 "Maine at mid-decade, facts and figures." ARE 280. Mimeographed. Orono: The University of Maine at Orono.
Dillman, Don A.
  1978 *Mail Telephone Surveys: The Total Design Method.* New York: Wiley.
Forbush, Dascomb R.
  1978 "The New In-migration to the north countries of New England and New York." Unpublished. Potsdam: Clarkson College.
Guptill, Michael
  1977 "In-migrants and the Maine performing arts." Unpublished. Orono: University of Maine.
Holbrook, Stewart A.
  1950 *The Yankee Exodus, An Account of Migration from New England.* New York: MacMillan.
Kelley, Ethan A.
  1976 "Census of board members." Unpublished. Orono: University of Maine.
Klietsch, R. G., W. H. Andrews, W. W. Bauder, J. A. Beegle, J. A. Doerflinger, D. G. Marshall, M. I. Taves, and M. P. Riley
  1964 *Social Response to Population Change and Migration.* Special Report No. 40. Ames: Iowa State Agricultural and Home Economics Experiment Station.
Loomis, Charles P. and J. Allan Beegle
  1975 *A Strategy for Rural Change.* New York: John Wiley and Sons.
Luloff, Albert E.
  1979 "Migration to New Hampshire. Preliminary findings." Pp. 29–33 in *New Hampshire Situations and Trends: A Basis for Program Development.* Durham: University of New Hampshire, Cooperative Extension Service.
Maine Board of Dental Examiners
  1978 *Directory of Dentists and Dental Hygienists Registered in Maine.* Augusta: Maine Board of Dental Examiners.
Mills, Dennis
  1972 "New settlers–townspeople battle it out over roads." *Bangor Daily News,* January 29/30:1.
Mitchell, Robert
  1978 "Tradition and change in rural New England—Case study of Brooksville, Maine, 1850–1870." *Maine Historical Society Quarterly* 18:87–100.

Ploch, Louis A.

1977a   "The in-migrants are coming." Update 5. Orono: Maine Life Sciences and Agriculture Experiment Station, July.

1977b   "The in-migrants are coming, part II." Update 6. Orono: Maine Life Sciences and Agriculture Experiment Station, October.

1978   "The reversal in in-migration patterns—Some rural development consequences." *Rural Sociology* 43 (Summer):293–303.

1979a   "Turnaround migration—A research challenge." ARE 324. Mimeographed. Orono: University of Maine at Orono.

1979b   "Town meeting time in Crafton." ARE 325. Mimeographed. Orono: University of Maine at Orono.

Ploch, Louis A. and Vance E. Dearborn

1978   "Implications of demographic trends for Maine schools." ARE 312. Mimeographed. Orono: University of Maine at Orono.

Santopolo, F. R., Gary Williams, and Dennis S. Mileti

1979   "Perception of growth impacts in nonmetropolitan Colorado." Paper presented at the U.S.D.A. Conference of Recent Migration Trends, St. Louis, Missouri, October.

Steahr, Thomas E.

1978   "An analysis of in-migrants to rural Connecticut since 1970." Paper presented at annual meeting of the Population Association of America, Atlanta, Georgia.

Taylor, Lee and Arthur R. Jones, Jr.

1964   *Rural Life in Urbanized Society.* New York: Oxford University Press.

Vidich, Arthur J. and Joseph Bensman

1968   *Small Town in Mass Society; Class, Power, and Religion in a Rural Community.* Rev. Ed. Princeton, N.J.: Princeton University Press.

Warren, Roland L.

1978   *The Community in America.* 3rd ed. Chicago: Rand McNally Publishing Company.

Zuiches, James J. and David L. Brown

1978   "The changing character of the nonmetropolitan population, 1950–75." Pp. 55–72 In Thomas R. Ford (ed.), *Rural U.S.A.: Persistence and Change.* Ames: The Iowa State University Press.

Migrant–Native Differences in Social Background and Community Satisfaction in Nonmetropolitan Utah Communities[1]

WILLIAM F. STINNER
MICHAEL B. TONEY

Introduction

The nonmetropolitan migration turnaround is widespread, but few detailed analyses have been conducted of factors associated with the turnaround in specific settings. Because of their unique socioreligious setting, the nonmetropolitan Utah communities on which this research focuses provide ideal laboratory settings for such an analysis.

Preferences for rural living have long been a part of the American cultural heritage (see DeJong, 1977; Fuguitt and Zuiches, 1975). Historically, however, employment opportunities, transportation and communication technology, and recreational opportunities divorced from natural habitat were concentrated in the cities and militated against rural development. As a result, a large-scale exodus from rural areas to urban centers occurred. Thus, despite higher levels of natural increase, rural areas initially grew at a slower pace than urban areas, and subsequently many actually suffered population decline. Recent developments have enabled people to act on long-established preferences favoring nonmetropolitan life. As a result, nonmetropolitan communities have exhibited a greater ability to retain their native born and to attract a greater number of in-migrants or newcomers (Tucker, 1976).

The increasing volume of in-migration to small, homogeneous nonmetropolitan communities has produced in its wake impacts on mi-

[1]This research was supported by Utah State University Agricultural Experiment Station Projects 835 and 836.

313

New Directions in
Urban–Rural Migration

grants, longer-term residents (natives), and overall community life as strains on social, economic, and service delivery systems have become exacerbated. However, this is only part of the picture. An additional dimension is the tendency for newcomers to differ from long-established residents in socioeconomic, demographic, and cultural background, which, in turn, yields differing perceptions regarding community life and the desirability of various community functions. This knowledge is relevant because differences between newcomers and long-time residents along the above dimensions could contribute to potential conflict in the determination of community priorities (see for example, Cortese and Jones, 1977; DeJong, 1974; DeJong and Humphrey, 1976; Morrison, 1977). Alternatively, newcomers may voice their discontent by moving from the community. In fact, this possibility has already been raised (see Chapter 9; Zuiches, 1977). On the other hand, this latter alternative may be a less viable option for long-settled residents (Cortese and Jones, 1977).

Assessments of the volume of recent nonmetropolitan-directed migration flows and its correlates are accumulating. Most investigations have focused on aggregate-level relationships between socioeconomic characteristics of counties and county population growth. This body of research has made a substantial contribution to our understanding of the migration turnaround at the community level. However, micro-level analyses (individual or household) addressed to the specific consequences of the turnaround on local rural community life, migrants, and natives are needed to complement aggregate-level studies. A prime focus for research in this respect is the degree to which newcomers differ from long-established residents in background attributes and attitudes toward community life.

In the research reported in this chapter we aimed to articulate the interplay between migrant–native differences in social background and community satisfaction in eight nonmetropolitan Utah communities. Specifically we wished to ascertain

1. The extent to which newcomers differ from settled migrants and natives in family life-cycle stage, educational attainment, and religious affiliation
2. The degree to which newcomers differ from settled migrants and natives regarding satisfaction with selected aspects of community life
3. The strength of the relationship between migrant status and satisfaction with selected features of community life relative to that obtained for family life-cycle stage, educational attainment, and religious affilitation.

Setting

The state of Utah provides the focal point for the Mormon culture area (see Meinig, 1965; Thompson, 1935; Zelinsky, 1961). Approximately 70% of the state's population is Mormon (Bureau of Economic and Business Research, 1976). The basis for this numerical dominance was the collective movement of Mormon pioneers to Utah in the mid-nineteenth century—the largest volume of singularly coordinated migrants in United States history. Despite a continuing inflow of non-Mormons that began in the 1870s, Mormon numerical dominance has prevailed given relatively higher Mormon in-migration and fertility levels. (For more extensive discussion of Mormon fertility see Pitcher, Kunz, and Peterson, 1974; Skolnick et al., 1978.; Smith and Kunz, 1976; Spicer and Gustavus, 1974.)

Relationships between Mormons and the larger national society have been extremely antagonistic. In fact, the initial movement to Utah was spurred by open and bloody conflict in Missouri and Illinois. Indeed, at that time an important consideration in selecting Utah for settlement was its relative isolation from and inaccessibility to the rest of the nation. For example, the Salt Lake Valley, site of initial settlement, was located a great distance south of the Oregon Trail and north of trails to southern California. Although increasing contact with the broader society and accompanying secularization can be traced as far back as 1870–1880, with the discovery of silver and other important minerals (see Skolnick et al., 1978), contemporary Utah still remains an enclave for Mormon adherents.

The Mormon population of nonmetropolitan Utah communities has exhibited an especially high degree of cohesion, which can be linked to numerical dominance, geographic isolation, a well-established belief system, and a life style oriented largely around church-related activities. Homogeneity in population composition tends to be coupled with a pervasive and highly integrated social structure containing close knit social networks. However, recent socioeconomic developments— including energy exploitation, industrial decentralization, recreational opportunities, and expanding transportation networks—have linked these formerly remote communities into economic, social, and cultural networks on state, regional, and national levels. These factors have spurred in-migration into nonmetropolitan Utah and to some extent restricted out-migration, thereby paralleling the nonmetropolitan reversal found in other areas of the country. These changing migration patterns, as they affect the demographic, social, and cultural homogeneity of these communities, create ideal conditions for heightened social conflict.

The data in Table 13.1 show that between 1970 and 1974 nonmetropolitan counties in Utah reversed the net pattern of out-migration of the 1950s and 1960s. Moreover, the annual rate of net in-migration for nonmetropolitan counties between 1970 and 1974 was more than three times that of the state's metropolitan counties. Finally, the net migration data indicate a process of population deconcentration between 1970 and 1974 within the nonmetropolitan sector itself. An overwhelming share of 1970–1974 nonmetropolitan net in-migration was attributable to movement into counties not adjacent to SMSAs.

The eight communities included in this research are all situated at some distance from the major metropolitan complexes (see Figure 13.1). Geographical distance is buttressed by the intervening Wasatch mountain range. Hence, for the majority of the communities, developments other than access to an SMSA have spurred recent population growth. Duchesne, Roosevelt, and Vernal, all situated between 120 and 180 miles east of Salt Lake City, lie in the energy-rich Uintah Basin in the northeast corner of the State. Duchesne and Vernal also function as county seats for Duchesne and Uintah Counties, respectively. Vernal is near Dinosaur National Monument. Both Duchesne and Uintah Counties reversed the out-migration patterns of the 1950s and 1960s during the first half of the 1970s. Although net migration estimates are not available for the communities, it can be noted that Roosevelt and Duchesne virtually doubled their populations while Vernal increased by about 40% between 1970 and 1975.

TABLE 13.1
Net Migration Trends for Utah: 1950–1975

Time period	Utah total	Metropolitan	Nonmetropolitan Total	Nonmetropolitan Adjacent	Nonmetropolitan Nonadjacent
			Net migration		
1950–60	10,105	52,019	−41,914	−16,213	−25,701
1960–70	−10,483	13,305	−23,788	− 4,501	−19,287
1970–74	28,879	15,496	13,383	441	12,942
			Annual rate of net migration		
1950–60	.13	.89	−2.04	−1.82	−2.21
1960–70	−.11	.17	−1.12	− .47	−1.67
1970–74	.61	.41	1.37	.10	2.44
Number of counties	29	5	24	7	17

Source: Fuguitt (1977:65).

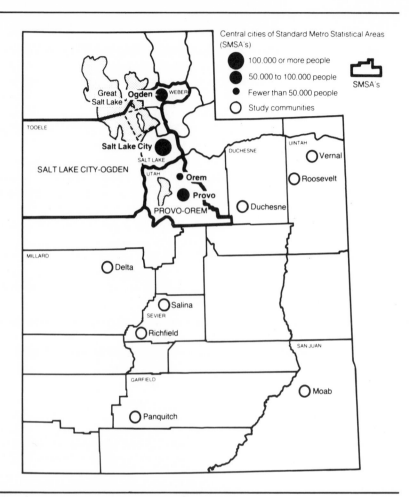

Figure 13.1. Location of study communities in Utah.

Salina, Delta, and Richfield lie in the central portion of the State between 140 and 160 miles south of Salt Lake City. Salina lies close to
Interstate Highway routes 15 and 70 (I–15 and I–70) and has benefited
from developments in coal exploration and agribusiness. Richfield, also
located close to I–70, functions as the county seat for Sevier County.
Delta, located in Millard, County, has been the site of mining operations
as well as agribusiness. Both Sevier and Millard Counties have witnessed recent reversals of the net out-migration trends of the 1950s and
1960s. Salina and Richfield grew by 13% 11% respectively between 1970
and 1975, while Delta grew by 25% during the same interval.

The communities of Moab and Panguitch are the most remotely situated with regard to existing metropolitan complexes. Moab lies about 235 miles southeast of Salt Lake City, and Panguitch lies due south at the same distance. Moab and Panguitch are the county seats of Grand and Garfield Counties, respectively. Moab serves as the gateway point for Arches and Canyonlands National Parks. Panguitch lies about 22 miles from Bryce Canyon National Park. Moab's economy is based on uranium mining, textiles, government, and tourism. Panguitch's economic base relies heavily on sawmill products, textiles, and government. Grand County has exhibited continuous net out-migration since 1960, following a population boom in the 1950s associated with extensive uranium exploration. Garfield County has undergone net out-migration on a continuous basis since 1950, although the rate of net out-migration has consistently diminished over time. Moab and Panguitch were the only communities in the investigation to have sustained population loss in the first half of the 1970s (-6.1 and $-.3\%$, respectively).

Despite their remote locations, six of these eight communities have grown during the first half of the 1970s. This growth has occurred within the context of initially small, homogeneous population bases and rudimentary service delivery systems. Reinforcing the impact of overall growth are the effects of increasing diversity in socioeconomic, demographic, and cultural backgrounds and of an accompanying heterogenity in life styles, values, and interests. The degree of this diversity and corresponding differences in community satisfaction are the subjects of this investigation.

Rationale

A longstanding proposition in the sociology of migration is that inmigration entails consequences for both the arriving migrant and the community (see, for example, Mangalam and Schwarzweller, 1970). For the migrant, movement to a new community entails a potential change in interaction systems (Mangalam and Schwarzweller, 1970). Broadly defined, the sphere of interaction includes both social and economic exchanges. Migrants evaluate the quality of these exchanges within the context of expectations based partly on past experience and partly on what is usually incomplete information about the community itself. To the extent that migrants perceive discrepancies between their evaluation standards and their actual experiences, they may be dissatisfied.

Previous research has tended to show that migrants are more dissatisfied with the communities to which they move than are long-term residents of those communities, whether their destination is urban or rural (Speare *et al.*, 1974). Nevertheless, a basic question emerges. To what extent does the relative community satisfaction of newly arrived migrants reflect the fact of their newness as opposed to their possession of personal attributes different from those who have lived in the community for much lengthier periods of time? Stated somewhat differently, would a relatively lower degree of expressed community satisfaction among recent migrants compared to long-term community residents reflect a temporary period of readjustment as opposed to the possession of a set of attributes which themselves are linked to relatively lower levels of satisfaction?

Recent systemic models of community attachment have been focused on length of residence as the key exogenous factor influencing community behavior and attitudes (Berry and Kasarda, 1977; Kasarda and Janowitz, 1974). According to this line of reasoning, the longer a person resides in a given community, the stronger are his social and economic bonds to the community. It is argued that the stronger these social and economic ties, the greater will be the level of community satisfaction. In a national quality-of-life study, length of residence was found to be positively related to community satisfaction; however, the magnitude of the association was the lowest of the six attributes under consideration (Campbell *et al.*, 1976; Marans and Rodgers, 1975). Rojek *et al.* (1975) found that length of residence was positively associated with satisfaction with a set of community services, and Speare (1974) showed that length of residence was similarly associated.

The mixed support for the length-of-residence argument suggests an alternative model in which individual attributes or characteristics are controlled. Research into the selectivity of recent nonmetropolitan-bound migration streams has yielded evidence indicating that at destination migrants do differ from nonmigrants along a number of important dimensions (Lichter *et al.*, 1979; Wardwell, 1977; Zuiches and Brown, 1978). Two characteristics usually stressed are life-cycle stage (generally indexed by age) and educational attainment. For example, Zuiches and Brown (1978) found that in-migrants to nonmetropolitan counties between 1970 and 1975 were substantially younger and had completed more years of formal schooling than persons who, in both 1970 and 1975, had been residing in nonmetroplitan counties.

Life-cycle stage and educational attainment have also been linked to community satisfaction (Campbell *et al.*, 1976; Marans and Rodgers, 1975; Rojek *et al.*, 1975; Speare, 1974). In their national quality of life study, Campbell *et al.* (1976) found life-cycle stage to have the strongest relationship with community satisfaction among six personal attributes—community satisfaction was expressed more frequently at later than at earlier stages in the life cycle (see also Marans and Rodgers, 1975). Speare (1974) found a positive association between age and community satisfaction and suggested that this was due to income and seniority privileges associated with advanced age and higher levels of home ownership. Rojek *et al.* (1975) also demonstrated statistically significant positive relationships between age and satisfaction with community services.

The relationship between educational attainment and community satisfaction has generally been found to be inverse and relatively weak. In the national quality-of-life study, persons with low levels of formal education were most satisfied with their community (Campbell *et al.*, 1976; Marans and Rodgers, 1975). Speare (1974) also noted a weak inverse association between educational attainment and community satisfaction. Similarly, Rojek *et al.* (1975) found nonsignificant relationships between educational attainment and satisfaction with selected community services. (In one exception, educational attainment and satisfaction with commercial services were inversely related.)

A personal attribute of particular saliency in the Utah context is religious affiliation. It can be argued that the high degree of group identity and cohesion among Mormons produces a greater degree of integration into the community hence higher levels of community satisfaction than are found among non-Mormons. On the other hand, non-Mormons residing in long-settled Mormon communities may be less satisfied with community life because of incompatibilities between their values and life-styles and those of the predominant Mormon population. Although the violence of the past has subsided, contemporary relationships between Mormons and non-Mormons are often characterized by animosity and suspicion (Meinig, 1965).

Returning to our initial argument, we reason that in small nonmetropolitan communities currently undergoing rapid change, unrealized expectations and relatively lower levels of community satisfaction will be found among newly arrived migrants. These phenomena could reflect difficulties associated with the impermeability and resilience of well-established social networks in the community and/or the incapacities of extant service delivery systems and facilities. Therefore, newcomers would be expected to be relatively less satisfied with interpersonal relationships and the quality of community services. However, it remains problematic whether this hypothesized relatively lower level of satisfaction could be attributed to newness or to the possession of attributes that differ from those of residents who have been present in the community

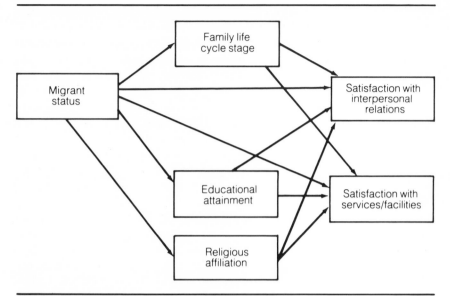

Figure 13.2. Expected relationships between demographic variables and community satisfaction.

for a longer period of time. In approaching the problem, we have made a further distinction among long-established residents. We divided them into two groups: settled migrants and natives. We anticipated that the level of satisfaction of settled migrants would fall between that of recent migrants and natives. Figure 13.2 diagrams the relationships examined in this study.

Data and Methods

This study is based on secondary analysis of data obtained from a quality-of-life survey conducted in 1975 in the eight communities under investigation. The sample for the present analysis consists of 751 respondents who were married at the time of the survey. The questionnaire elicited information on a variety of social, economic, and demographic characteristics of the respondents, as well as on the respondents' perceived satisfaction with various aspects of the community. Information was also secured on respondents' residential histories; reasons for past moves; future migration intentions; reasons for intending to move; and, where intention to move was expressed, preferred destinations.

Residential histories were used to develop a three-category typology of migrant status, the major independent variable in this study. *Natives* consist of respondents who were born in the community in which they were residing at the time of the survey and who listed no other residence in the migration history. *Settled migrants* include those respondents who moved into their current community before 1970. *Recent migrants* are persons who moved into the community after 1970. We selected 1970 as our cutoff point since this date corresponds closely to the starting point for the population turnaround in nonmetropolitan America.

The other explanatory variables in the analysis included educational attainment, religious affiliation, and family life-cycle stage. Education was measured by four categories ranging from "less than high school" to "college graduate or higher." Religious affiliation was measured by a dichotomous classification, that is, Mormon and non-Mormon. Family life-cycle stage was a composite variable based on age of the household head, presence of children, and age of youngest child. The categories for this variable are as follows:

1. *Prechildbearing:* Household head less than 45 years of age; no children present.
2. *Childbearing:* Household head less than 45 years of age; one or more children present; youngest child less than 6 years of age
3. *Child launching:* Household head less than 45 years of age; one or more children present; youngest child 6–17 years of age
4. *Middle age with children:* Household head 45–64 years of age; one or more children present
5. *Middle age/empty nest:* Household head 45–64 years of age; no children present
6. *Elderly:* Household head 65 years of age or older

Respondents were asked to give their relative evaluation of 40 aspects of the community setting on a 7-point scale ranging from "exceptional" (1) to "badly needs improvement" (7). "Satisfactory" was coded 4. Thirty-nine of these items were subjected to principal components (with iteration) factor analysis with varimax rotation. Factor analysis was used to reduce the large set of items to a small set of independent analytical factors based on the extent of interitem clustering. This reduced set of factors, therefore, accounts for the variance common to indicators that are strongly intercorrelated. Varimax rotation provides a more readily interpretable structure.

Our earlier discussion suggested that interpersonal relationships and community services and facilities are two salient domains in community satisfaction. In our factor analysis we found these two domains to be the first two factors extracted, accounting for three-quarters of the variance

TABLE 13.2
Factors of Community Satisfaction [a]

Factors and variables	Factor loadings	Variance	% Cumulative variance
I. Interpersonal relations		64.2	64.2
1. Friendliness and concern of neighbors	.72		
2. Place to raise a family	.51		
3. Community spirit and cooperation	.53		
4. Equal opportunity for all to take part in community life	.52		
5. Friendly groups of common age and interest	.57		
6. Making newcomers feel welcome	.59		
7. Quality of religious life	.51		
8. Help from others in time of need	.71		
9. Chance to develop close relationships with others	.70		
II. Community services and facilities		10.8	75.0
1. Housing for new families	.51		
2. Shopping facilities	.59		
3. Restaurants and entertainments	.55		
4. Child day-care and baby-sitting	.52		
5. Facilities for youth	.65		
6. Opportunities for cultural activities	.54		
7. Public parks and playgrounds	.54		
8. Recreational opportunities	.55		

[a] Principal components solution (with iteration), orthogonal (varimax) rotation.

in the factor matrix (Table 13.2). Additional factors were extracted, but since they accounted for such a small portion of the variance and provided little information in trial analyses they were dropped. Composite scales for the two factors based on items with factor loadings of .45 or above were computed by weighting standardized scores by their respective factor scores and summing over all items subsumed under each factor.

The analysis comprised two phases. In the first phase we related migrant status to family life-cycle stage, education, and religious affiliation. These relationships were tested through the use of chi-square and gamma. In the second segment of the analysis, migrant status and the three individual attributes (family life-cycle stage, education, and religious affiliation) were related to each of the two satisfaction scales. Multiple classification analysis (MCA) was employed in this latter phase. MCA is a multivariate technique for examining the relationships between a number of independent variables and a dependent variable (see Andrews *et al.*, 1967). The independent variables can be at less than interval level of measurement. Category effects are expressed in terms of deviations from the sample grand mean.[2]

Findings

Figure 13.3 shows the relationship between migrant status and family life-cycle stage, education, and religious affiliation. The relationship between migrant status and each of the three background variables is statistically significant at the .001 level of probability. The degree of association is low to moderate. Recent migrants to these nonmetropolitan communities are concentrated at the early stages of the family life cycle. Approximately 60% of recent migrants have preschool children, compared with only about 20% of natives and settled migrants. Conversely, 56% of natives and 62% of settled migrants are middle-aged or elderly, whereas only 17% of recent migrants are. Recent migrants tend to have higher levels of educational attainment than both natives and settled migrants ($\gamma = -.19$). Over 62% of recent migrants have had some college education, compared with 46% of settled migrants and 41% of the native population. Finally, over 36% of recent migrants are non-Mormon, compared to 21% of the settled migrants and less than 10% of natives ($\gamma = .46$). In summary, recent migrants to

---

[2]MCA does assume additivity. Preliminary investigation revealed no statistically significant interactions.

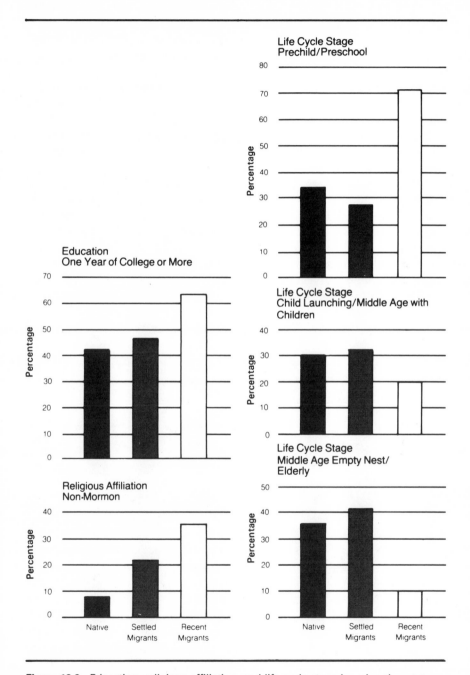

Figure 13.3. Education, religious affiliation, and life-cycle stage by migration status.

these nonmetropolitan Utah communities do differ noticeably from natives and earlier migrants. They tend to be at earlier points in their family life-cycle and higher in socioeconomic status, and they are less likely to claim membership in the dominant community religion.

Next we turn our attention to the relationship between migrant status and the two domains of satisfaction (Figure 13.4). An initial bivariate analysis revealed that recent migrants were less likely to be satisfied with interpersonal relationships in these communities than were settled migrants and, especially, natives ($\eta = .16$). However, what influence migrant status had on satisfaction with interpersonal relationships was reduced by nearly one-half when the three background variables—age, education, and religion—were included in the analysis ($\beta = .09$) and the relationship was not statistically significant. Religious affiliation and level of educational attainment are the best predictors of satisfaction. Specifically, affiliation with the Mormon religion and high levels of educational attainment are linked with higher levels of satisfaction with interpersonal relationships in the community.

Satisfaction with community services and facilities was analyzed next. As in the domain just discussed, recent migrants were less likely to be satisfied with community services and facilities than were settled mi-

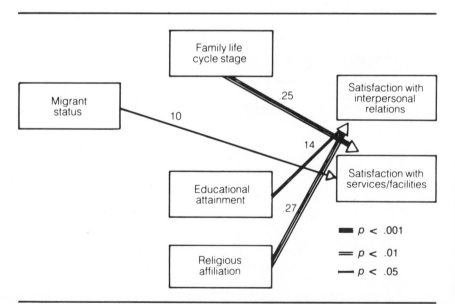

Figure 13.4. Statistically significant relationships between demographic variables and community satisfaction.

grants and natives (η = .18). In contrast, however, the relationship, although reduced, remained statistically significant when the three background variables were included (β = .10; $p <$ .05). Nevertheless, the dominant explanatory variable for this dimension appears to be family life-cycle stage (β = .25; $p <$ .001). More concretely, middle-aged and elderly community residents are more satisfied with community services and facilities than are residents in the prechild, preschool, or child-launching phases of the family life cycle.

In summary, we find that migrant status is related to satisfaction with interpersonal relationships and community services and facilities. Recent migrants are less satisfied with interpersonal relationships and community services and facilities than are settled migrants and natives. Nonetheless, there is strong support for the "characteristics" argument. Specifically, in both satisfaction domains the bivariate relationships between migrant status and satisfaction were reduced considerably when the personal attributes were entered into the analysis. However, even though the magnitude of the differences is reduced, satisfaction with community services and facilities remains significantly related to migrant status.

Discussion

The repopulation of nonmetropolitan communities after decades of population loss has raised many questions about the extent to which other changes are accompanying the resurgent growth. Nonmetropolitan Utah, given its unique sociocultural heritage amidst recent socioeconomic developments that have expanded its socioeconomic and cultural exchange networks, provides an interesting laboratory for examining the impacts generated by renewed growth. Furthermore, the net migration reversals that have accompanied the above developments in even the more remote nonmetropolitan areas parallel those found in other areas of the nation. Thus, despite its unique socioreligious history, nonmetropolitan Utah has been experiencing a migration reversal similar to that found in other nonmetropolitan areas of the United States. Recent developments and the accompanying migration currents have had a significant impact on these small, isolated, and relatively homogeneous nonmetropolitan communities. The effects of recent migration are both quantitative (increasing numbers) and qualitative (increasing diversity). This research was directed to the latter aspect.

Recent migrants were found to be at earlier stages of their family life cycle and to possess higher levels of education, and they were less likely to be Mormon than were both settled migrants and natives. Settled migrants and natives were quite similar in these background characteristics. Newcomers tended to be less satisfied with interpersonal relationships and community services and facilities than were long-established residents. However, these differences were attributable largely to the fact that recent migrants differed from established community residents in social background rather than in recency of the move per se. The greatest impact on the two domains of community satisfaction was attributable to background characteristics, not migration status.

The mediating role of educational attainment is of particular interest. Unlike the other two social background variables, the direction of its relationship with community satisfaction runs counter to expectation. Specifically, prior research led us to expect an inverse relationship between educational attainment and community satisfaction; however, we uncovered a positive relationship. Since recent migrants tend to be better educated than long-established residents, we must conclude that the lower levels of community satisfaction among recent migrants are primarily a function of being at earlier stages in their life cycles and non-Mormon. The influence through educational attainment mediates this negative effect to some extent. Regarding interpersonal relationships, a higher level of educational attainment among recent migrants offsets to some degree the dissatisfaction associated with not being Mormon. Respecting community services, a higher level of educational attainment offsets to some extent newcomer dissatisfaction associated with being in an earlier stage of the life cycle.

Historically, selective migration altered the composition and socioeconomic conditions of American cities. Pivotal axes for this increasing differentiation included life-cycle stage, socioeconomic status, and ethnicity. Similar alterations are now occurring in contemporary nonmetropolitan communities. Traditionally, these communities were small and homogeneous. Now their populations are not only growing but diversifying as well.

Newcomers view and evaluate community life from different perspectives and standards than those of long-term residents, largely because they are different from them in background and not merely because they happen to be new to the community. Were the latter to be the case, we might anticipate that after a period of adjustment migrants would resemble long-term residents in their attitudes and behaviors. However, since they differ in basic sociodemographic attributes, such a smooth assimilation process is questionable. Nonetheless, our finding regarding the mediating role of education tends to suggest that the higher levels of education among newcomers may act as a lubricant to an otherwise friction-laden atmosphere produced by dissimilarities along other dimensions such as religion or life-cycle stage. On the other hand, long-term residents face the necessity of re-evaluation as the friendliness, security, harmony, and relaxed atmosphere provided by smallness and homogeneity come under assault. For example, Cortese and Jones (1977) found that longtime residents in three energy-impacted communities felt their communities had "become *less* relaxed, friendly, traditional, isolated, harmonious, and rundown; and . . . *more* expensive, difficult, progressive, and competitive [Pp. 84–85]."

When the number of in-migrants is large relative to the destination's base population and dissimilar in composition, conflicts may result from the adjustments the two groups must make in respect to one another. Migrants in larger streams may react to differences between themselves and settled residents by segregating themselves in neighborhoods, thereby forming long-term boundaries that inhibit social integration. Whether this generalization, which may be derived partly from the historical movement of ethnic groups to urban areas, applies to nonmetropolitan areas is questionable. Such segregation may require separate facilities that no one group can provide. The small size of total population may not be conducive to the segregation, impersonal relationships, and tensions associated with the large-scale movement of diverse groups to cities. On the other hand, lower levels of migration flows may be temporarily disruptive but socially integrative over an extended period of time. Moreover, smaller numbers of migrants, even if dissimilar, may be viewed more positively because they are not as likely to threaten the receiving community's social system.

Even though Utah's general metropolitan–nonmetropjlitan migration pattern parallels the national pattern, some of the relationships obtained in this study may not apply to other settings. The state is atypical with respect to other demographic processes. Life expectancy is very high and the state's fertility level is higher than that found in any other state. The high fertility rate exists despite the fact that the state's population also has the highest level of educational attainment in the nation. This provides a clear example of the difficulty of making generalizations when studying a unique culture setting. Such a situation may exist with some of the findings obtained from the survey data. Therefore, the results may be more important for documenting the relationships in a peculiar setting than for generalizing findings to other settings. Nevertheless, the evidence of the migration reversal and its effects in Utah suggests how widespread the phenomenon is.

In summary, increasing diversification presents opportunities for community invigoration and intercultural stimulation, but it also presents challenges. Nonmetropolitan communities are becoming less isolated and provincial as new and different kinds of people with different ideas, values, and life-styles arrive. But the changes wrought by increasing diversity are not cost free for either the natives, the migrants, or the community as a whole. Nevertheless, it need not be a zero–sum game. Imaginative leadership will be required in the reassessment and redefinition of community institutions and priorities and the pooling of resources within a context of increasingly variegated interests, values, needs, and aspirations.

References

Andrews, Frank, James Morgan, and John Sonquist
    1967   *Multiple Classification Analysis*. Ann Arbor: University of Michigan, Institute for Social Research.
Berry, Brian J. L. and John D. Kasarda
    1977   *Contemporary Urban Ecology*. New York: MacMillan Publishing Co., Inc.
Bureau of Economic and Business Research
    1976   *Utah Facts*. Salt Lake City, Utah: University of Utah Press.
Campbell, Angus, P. E. Converse, and W. L. Rodgers
    1976   *The Quality of American Life: Perceptions, Evaluations, and Satisfactions*. New York: Russell Sage Foundation.
Cortese, Charles F. and Bernie Jones
    1977   "The sociological analysis of boom towns." *Western Sociological Review* 8 (1):76–90.
DeJong, Gordon F.
    1974   "Residential preference patterns and population redistribution." Pp. 270–313 In Wilbur Zelinsky, C. Humphrey, E. E. Raphael, P. D. Simkins, and G. F. DeJong (eds.), *Population Change and Redistribution in Nonmetropolitan Pennsylvania, 1940–1970*. Report submitted to the Center for Population Research, National Institutes of Health, Department of Health, Education and Welfare, Washington, D.C.
    1977   "Residential preferences and migration." *Demography* 14 (2):169–178.
DeJong, Gordon F. and Craig R. Humphrey
    1976   "Selected characteristics of metropolitan-to-nonmetropolitan area migrants: A study of population redistribution in pennsylvania." *Rural Sociology* 41 (4):526–538.
Fuguitt, Glenn V.
    1977   *Reference Tables: Population Trends and Net Migration for the States and Regions of the United States, 1950-74*. Population Series 70-8, Applied Population Laboratory, Department of Rural Sociology, College of Agricultural and Life Sciences. Madison: University of Wisconsin–Extension, University of Wisconsin–Madison, February.
Fuguitt, Glenn V. and James J. Zuiches
    1975   "Residential preferences and population distribution." *Demography* 12 (August):491–504.
Kasarda, John D. and Morris Janowitz
    1974   "Community attachments in mass society." *American Sociological Review* 39 (3):328–339.
Lichter, Daniel, Tim B. Heaton, and Glenn V. Fuguitt
    1979   "Trends in selectivity of migration between metropolitan and nonmetropolitan areas: 1955–1975." *Rural Sociology* 44 (4): 645–667.

Mangalam, J. J. and Harry K. Schwarzweller
  1970 "Some theoretical guidelines toward a sociology of migration." *International Migration Review* 4 (2):5–20.
Marans, Robert W. and Willard Rodgers
  1975 "Toward An understanding of community satisfaction." Pp. 299–352 In Amos H. Hawley and Vincent P. Rock (eds.), *Metropolitan America in Contemporary Perspective*. New York: John Wiley.
Meinig, D. W.
  1965 "The Mormon culture region: Strategies and patterns in the geography of the American West, 1847–1964." *Annals of the Association of American Geographers* 55 (2):191–220.
Morrison, Peter
  1977 *Migration and access: New public concerns of the 1970s*. Santa Monica, California: The Rand Corporation.
Pitcher, Brian, Phillip R. Kunz, and Evan T. Peterson
  1974 "Residency differentials in Mormon fertility." *Population Studies* 28 (1):143–151.
Rojek, Dean G., Frank Clemente, and Gene Summers
  1975 "Community satisfaction: A study of contentment with local services." *Rural Sociology* 40:177–192.
Skolnick, M., L. Bean, D. May, V. Arbon, K. DeNevers, and P. Cartwright
  1978 "Mormon demographic history. I. Nuptiality and fertility of once-married couples." *Population Studies* 32 (1):5–19.
Smith, James E. and Phillip R. Kunz
  1976 "Polygyny and fertility in nineteenth-century America." *Population Studies* 30 (3):465–480.
Speare, Alden, Jr.
  1974 "Residential satisfaction as an intervening variable in residential mobility." *Demography* 11 (2):173–188.
Speare, Alden, Jr., Sidney Goldstein, and William H. Frey
  1974 *Residential Mobility, Migration and Metropolitan Change*. Cambridge, Mass: Ballinger Publishing Co.
Spicer, Judith C. and Susan O. Gustavus
  1974 "Mormon fertility through half a century: Another test of the Americanization hypothesis." *Social Biology* 21 (1):70–76.
Thompson, W. S.
  1935 *Ratio of Women to Children*. Washington, D.C.: Bureau of the Census, U.S. Government Printing Office.
Tucker, C. Jack
  1976 "Changing patterns of migration between metropolitan and nonmetropolitan areas in the United States: Recent evidence." *Demography* 13 (4):435–444.
Zelinsky, Wilbur
  1961 "An approach to the religious geography of the United States: Patterns of church membership in 1952." *Annals of the Association of American Geographers* 51:139–193.
Zuiches, James J.
  1977 "Mobility and preferences: A review." Paper presented at the annual meetings of the American Association for the Advancement of Science, Denver, February.
Zuiches, James J. and David L. Brown
  1978 "The changing character of the nonmetropolitan population, 1950–1975." Chapter 4 in Thomas R. Ford (ed.), *Rural Society in the United States—Current Trends and Issues*. Ames: Iowa State University Press.

Industrial Dispersal and Labor-Force Migration: Employment Dimensions of the Population Turnaround in Michigan[1]

JAMES J. ZUICHES
MICHAEL L. PRICE

Introduction

Theories of development often link the location of economic activities with population distribution. As the economies of agglomeration in metropolitan centers and the geographical concentration of industry, capital, and population occurred, metropolitan and nonmetropolitan sectors began to experience uneven rates of growth. Moreover, when technological developments in traditional rural industries such as agriculture and mining displaced nonmetropolitan workers, many rural locales were beset with large-scale out-migration, high levels of unemployment, and generally depressed economies.

In recent years, however, two changes have indicated improvement in the nonmetropolitan situation. First, the balance of migration streams between metropolitan and nonmetropolitan areas has shifted in favor of the nonmetropolitan sector. This dispersal of population is pervasive throughout regions of the United States (Beale and Fuguitt, 1975), and in most, if not all, advanced industrial societies (Vining and Kontuly, 1977). Second, technological advances in production processes and in transportation and communication systems have lessened constraints on location for manufacturers and other industries, and, in fact, many industries have penetrated the nonmetropolitan sector (Hansen, 1978; Summers *et al.*, 1976). Since both population and industry are being

[1]This work has been supported by the Michigan Agricultural Experiment Station (Journal Article No. 9174), Project 1160, a contributing project to Western Regional Project W–118.

333

New Directions in
Urban–Rural Migration

attracted to nonmetropolitan locations, it is important to understand the linkage between these concurrent trends. Yet, "in pondering the multifaceted demographic implications of industrial dispersal," Lonsdale and Seyler (1979) have observed that, "it is remarkable how little we really know. [p. 185]."

By monitoring the mobile labor force over an extended time period and by analyzing changes in the compositional characteristics of labor-force migration streams, we hope to reveal some of the underlying dynamics and their contribution to more general patterns of population distribution. Specifically, the research reported here focuses on patterns of labor-force change from 1960 to 1975, emphasizing the role of migration in metropolitan and nonmetropolitan Michigan.

In the North Central region, population growth rates are now closer and moving more rapidly than in the nation as a whole toward zero population growth (Morrison, 1979). Moreover, recent population redistribution in the region is characterized by decentralization: Nonmetropolitan areas are growing more rapidly than metropolitan, and smaller rural nonmetropolitan areas are growing more rapidly than those including larger centers (Fuguitt, 1978). Michigan, in particular, offers an interesting case in which to assess the turnaround. The state is highly industrialized—a national leader in automobile manufacture and in other heavy industries. Industrial location within Michigan has concentrated in its metropolitan belt, cutting across the southern tier of the Lower Peninsula (see Figure 14.1). In many ways, this metropolitan region represents the "older industrial heartland" associated with high levels of unionization and a wide range of social and welfare services. On the other hand, many nonmetropolitan areas of the state, especially to the north, offer a bounty of natural and environmental amenities. Michigan's lakes, shorelines, and forests have been a longtime haven for vacationers and seasonal migrants. Recent settlement patterns in these areas, often characterized by retirement migration, are marked by their quality-of-life orientation (Marans and Wellman, 1978). Thus, the character of the turnaround in Michigan may represent some of the more salient dimensions of the national turnaround.

Changing Industrial Mix of Nonmetropolitan Areas

Agriculture no longer provides the economic foundation for many nonmetropolitan areas. By decreasing the need for manpower, high productivity in agriculture has substantially reduced farm employment

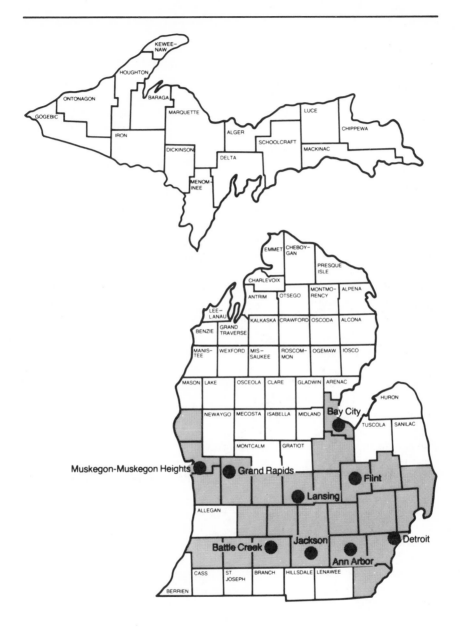

Figure 14.1. Standard metropolitan statistical areas and nonmetropolitan counties in Michigan, 1975.

to the extent that in more than 1000 nonmetropolitan counties less than 10% of employment is in farming and farm-related jobs. Moreover, only 5.2% of recent migrants to nonmetropolitan areas are employed in the agricultural sector (Beale, 1978; see also Chapter 2 of this book). In contrast to these losses in agricultural employment, nonmetropolitan areas have made substantial gains in diversifying their industrial mix.

Manufacturing Growth

Many rural regions have been successful at reviving their economies by attracting manufacturing firms to locate in their communities. On this point, Haren and Holling (1979) note, "The addition of nearly two million manufacturing jobs in rural and other smaller communities between 1962 and 1978 raised manufacturing employment from 3.9 to 5.7 million workers, for an increase of almost 50 percent. The share of the Nation's manufacturing found in nonmetropolitan areas increased from 23.5 to 28.8 percent [p. 43]."

The early decentralization of manufacturing industries into rural areas had been perceived as filtering down through the hierarchy of cities and places (Thompson, 1967). From this perspective, new industries are born and nurtured in large metropolitan areas where innovations are welcomed and labor is highly skilled. As production processes become more efficient and routinized, firms seek new environments of comparative fiscal advantage and of less skilled, nonorganized labor pools. However, recent evidence shows that nonmetropolitan areas are receiving a favorable mix of both high-growth and slow-growth industries, indicating that rural settings are also suitable for newer innovative industries (Petrulis, 1979). Concomitantly, branch–plant location appears to have little connection with innovativeness, and new firms are more likely to seek less urbanized settings and to prefer small-town environments (Erickson, 1976).

Service Sector Growth

Concurrent with the decentralization of manufacturing has been a nationwide expansion of the service sector. Bell (1973) argues that the "post-industrial society deals primarily with changes in the social structure, the way in which the economy is being transformed and the occupational system reworked [p. 13]." This transformation has had major impacts upon the economic structure of both metropolitan and nonmetropolitan areas. Since 1973, nonmanufacturing employment has accounted for practically all nonmetropolitan employment gains (Haren and Holling, 1979). The increased demand for leisure activities indicated by trends toward early retirement, a shorter work week, and longer vacation time stimulated the development of recreational industries in rural wilderness and shoreline settings. The settlement of retired persons contributes to population growth and stimulates the growth of services in many nonmetropolitan areas (Wang and Beegle, 1978). In fact, counties experiencing relatively high rates of elderly in-migration during the 1960s are by far the most rapidly growing class of nonmetropolitan counties in the 1970s (Beale, 1975). Government influences, the location of state universities and military installations, and state and local governments are among other factors associated with recent nonmetropolitan population growth. As McCarthy and Morrison observe, a common feature of these circumstances is that they provide the bases for expansion of nonmetropolitan service employment (McCarthy and Morrison 1978: 6–7). The presence of either permanent or temporary migrants increases the demand for services, encouraging economic development in many nonmetropolitan communities.

The industrial expansion into nonmetropolitan areas is viewed by some as the latest phase in the modernization process in economically advanced industrial societies (Lonsdale and Seyler, 1979; Summers *et al.*, 1976). As expansion of communication and transportation systems lessens the friction of distance, as production processes become routinized, and as the occupational structure is transformed, inequalities between metropolitan and nonmetropolitan sectors in the standard of living that evolved during the initial phases of the development process are being reduced. Moreover, the educational and occupational skill levels of recent migrants to nonmetropolitan areas have enhanced the sophistication of the local labor pools in the receiving communities (Ploch, 1978; Zuiches and Brown, 1978). As a result of these technological, organizational, and demographic changes, many nonmetropolitan areas once dependent on extractive industries for their economic base have developed more diversified economies that provide a variety of occupational opportunities.

Employment and Population Dispersal

As previously noted, little is known about the demographic implications of employment dispersal. This fact stems from the inconstant nature of the interaction between migration and economic development. Analytically, migration may be viewed as either a cause or a consequence of economic growth. Considering the relationship between migration and economic development from a macrolevel of analysis, Goldscheider (1971) comments

> Under some conditions, for example in the early stage of industrialization, when rural–urban migration or international movement takes place, population movement may stimulate economic development in the areas of destination. In these cases, migration may be viewed analytically as the *independent* variable and economic growth as the *dependent* variable. Under other conditions, for example, movement between metropolitan areas in mature or developed stages of industrialization, migration may be a response to economic growth and labor demands. Therefore, migration in these situations may be viewed as a *consequence* of economic growth. Moreover, it is likely that the particular role of migration as a determinant or as a consequence of economic changes is unclear empirically. In fact, migration may be viewed as an integral part and a necessary condition for economic developmental processes, that is, migration and population redistribution are important components in the evolution of industrial societies. Its particular cause–effect relationship may be impossible to isolate empirically and unrealistic to predict theoretically. In broadest perspective, migration and economic development should be treated as a circular interdependent probability process wherein mobility changes may stimulate economic growth, which in turn may further stimulate mobility, and so on [p. 73].

Thus, migration and economic development may be viewed as reciprocal processes by which population and economic activities are distributed through both time and space. In advanced industrial societies, economic growth involves the movement of factors of production, including labor, to adjust to changes in opportunities related either to improving the efficiency of production processes or to taking advantage of new markets established by previous population movements. The recent nonmetropolitan experience reflects both of these opportunities. The economic advantage once maintained by metropolitan industrial centers has waned due, in part, to their "overspecialization of structures" and the "stiffening of arteries," that is, their high levels of unionization, age dependency, and welfare dependency (Sternlieb and Hughes, 1975: 2–3). On the other hand, many nonmetropolitan areas have attracted industry as a result of labor costs and availability, environmental considerations, and energy availability (Kale and Lonsdale, 1979). However, other nonmetropolitan areas have attracted population independently of industrial location, therefore establishing ready markets for trade and service businesses.

This industrialization of nonmetropolitan America has created labor demands, thus stimulating migration into many nonmetropolitan areas. Manufacturing firms that expand from the metropolitan setting do not always have to rely on the indigenous labor pools of the area in which they intend to relocate. As Thompson (1975) observes, "Relocating manufacturers contend that they do not have to depend on workers already in town. They simply announce in, say, the Baltimore newspapers that they are headed for, say, Lynchburg, and the native sons return with Northern-acquired skills [p. 190]." Thompson's observation emphasizes the return migration of former rural residents, but it is certainly the case that many workers other than "native sons" are encouraged to leave the city when opportunities in rural settings occur. When an aluminum plant located in a nonmetropolitan community in West Virginia, over 85% of the 4000 new jobs went to commuters or in-migrants (Gray, 1969). However, recent patterns of population movement into nonmetropolitan areas may have little connection with industrialization. Doubting the role of industrial expansion as a panacea to population decline in nonmetropolitan locales, Heaton and Fuguitt (1979) note "that manufacturing may have received more attention than it merits. . . . Nonmetropolitan centers enjoying industrial expansion can no longer be assured of a more favorable balance between in- and out-migration on the whole than other nonmetropolitan areas [p. 134]."

As many factors have contributed to the outward movement of the population, the recent "migration turnaround" is more than a demographic response to employment dispersal. Some of the recent in-migration into nonmetropolitan areas has occurred independently of the industrial relocation. National and state surveys show that residential preferences of urbanites favor a rural habitat as long as ties to the metropolis are not severed (Fuguitt and Zuiches, 1975). In fact, many nonmetropolitan in-migrants have combined the "best of both worlds" by taking up residence in a rural setting within commuting range to the city (Graber, 1974). In addition, the movement of the elderly into rural areas, which is predominant in the Upper Great Lakes and Ozarks regions, has established a regular stream of "retirement migration" into nonmetropolitan areas. These settlement patterns are distinguished by their quality-of-life orientation, that is, migrants are basing locational decisions, at least in part, on the natural and social amenities associated with rural or small-town living. Nevertheless, these normative patterns are resulting in population growth in many nonmetropolitan areas subsequently creating demands for certain trade and service industries. The size, composition, and income of the population are important determinants of the mix of goods and services desired. For example, a retirement community will demand more health-related and personal services than will a younger population. It is doubtful that the indigenous labor pools in many of these nonmetropolitan areas will have the required levels of education and skills to meet the demand for new services and enterprises. Labor demands therefore should stimulate the influx of even more in-migrants.

Since the migration turnaround may be viewed as either a consequence of employment dispersal or as one of its causes, the interaction between population and employment dispersal may be conceptualized as taking two basic forms. First, the relocation of secondary industries into nonmetropolitan areas usually has attracted labor for employment in manufacturing and, through multiplier effects, has attracted other workers to meet the demands of the larger population and complementary industries. And second, the outward movement of population, motivated by quality-of-life considerations, attracts certain industries, usually services and light manufacturing, to meet the demands for support services in growing communities. These processes overlap in time and space. However, these two forms of interaction are qualitatively different, and the selectivity of either migrants or industries will differ accordingly.

For example, Brown (1980, in press) demonstrates the effects of net out-movement of workers from large metropolitan areas to nonmetropolitan areas and the increased retention of the workforce in nonmetropolitan counties. Although his analysis focuses on volume rather than composition of migration streams, Brown discusses two explanations of the turnaround pertinent to our analysis: The first of these is that the economic basis of rural life has become increasingly diversified; the second is that the integration of rural areas by highway, telephone, television, and centralized water and sewer systems has lowered the social and economic disadvantages of rural areas. These effects are particularly noticeable in Michigan and the Upper Great Lakes Region where recent settlement patterns are distinctly nonurban (Fuguitt and Beale, 1978). Growth in this region is characterized by dispersed settlement in unincorporated territory, primarily in resort and retirement areas.

Based on residential preference surveys, nonmetropolitan population growth is expected to continue, but industrial growth is expected to continue only for some industries. Specifically, manufacturing growth in nonmetropolitan areas is expected to level off, whereas service-related activities are expected to grow. As rising energy prices increase the costs of transportation, manufacturers may be forced to locate closer to primary markets, back near the cities. Furthermore, the attractiveness of nonmetropolitan areas to management, stemming from their nonorganized labor pools, will diminish if unions begin to organize in nonmetropolitan labor markets. On the other hand, the outward movement of population motivated by quality-of-life concerns will continue to increase the demand for services in nonmetropolitan areas.

Given the recent trends of population and employment dispersal, the patterns of change in the work force prior to and during the general migration turnaround ought to reflect the changing distribution of economic activities and, specifically, the employment dimensions of the nonmetropolitan revival. Although the specific nature of the interaction between population migration and economic development is not directly assessed in this analysis, it is assumed that the migration of workers in secondary industries is a response to industrial location, whereas the migration of tertiary workers is a response to the demand for services associated with recent population growth.

To test these ideas here, we trace the patterns of labor-force change in Michigan over the three quinquennia between 1960 and 1975, emphasizing the role of migration. The labor-force migration streams into and out of Michigan's metropolitan and nonmetropolitan sectors are compared to migration patterns of the general population and analyzed by age and industrial sector. Changes in the composition of migration streams should reflect some of the economic and demographic dimensions of the turnaround. The streams themselves are analyzed by their origins and destinations. And finally, the overall patterns of labor-force change are disaggregated into two basic components, that is, net worker migration and worker turnover. Turnover is defined as the difference between those workers entering and leaving the active work force during a specific time period. Changes in the overall structure of the work force indicate the flexibility of the industrial sector to absorb or shed workers as geographical and organizational shifts in employment demands occur.

Data

Labor-force data are from the Social Security Administration's 1% First Quarter Continuous Work History Sample (CWHS). These data are available for the first quarter of the year for the 1960–1965 quinquennium, and annually from 1965 through 1975. Although the data set includes only those workers covered by the Social Security system, they account for about 90% of the work force in Michigan. The data do not include the self-employed, farm workers, certain groups of railroad and government workers, nor nonprofit workers who are not covered by Social Security.[2]

[2]For further information concerning the utility and caveats of these data, consult U.S. Department of Commerce, Bureau of Economic Analysis (1976); see also Chapter 15 of this book.

The issue of coverage of the labor force and the impact of misreporting or misclassification remains difficult to resolve. However, for Michigan, we have an independent estimate of the size and industrial composition of the labor force through the Michigan Employment Security Commission, (MESC) which monitors the labor force covered by unemployment insurance. Each of the two sources have different definitions of the educational sector: MESC classifies all public education workers in the government sector, whereas CWHS classifies them in the service sector; thus, these categories are noncomparable. However, for the manufacturing, trade (retail, wholesale), and financial sectors, comparisons are possible. The annual estimate of the manufacturing labor force is slightly greater in the CWHS than in the MESC from 1965 through 1973. At the highest point, CWHS shows 12% more workers than MESC, and it averages 6% higher during this period. From 1973 through 1975, years for which the First Quarter files have not been corrected, the CWHS estimates are consistently lower than the MESC. A similar pattern is revealed for the trade and finance sector. From 1965 through 1971, very close similarities in coverage are observed. In 1972, CWHS coverage decreases relative to the MESC; and during 1973–1975, CWHS coverage is 10% less than MESC. Although coverage slips significantly for these sectors and for construction, transportation, and utilities, we have no way to discern if there are differentials for migrating workers and non-migrants.

We have proceeded on the assumption that the CWHS's quality of coverage declines rather consistently during the 1973–1975 period, but since this decline is magnified by detailed tabulations or annualized analysis, we have maintained a 5-year level and aggregaged industrial sectors.

Since employer reports on the CWHS labor force are based on the county of employment, complete congruence between county of residence and work is not expected. Some shifts in location of workplace may actually bring jobs into the same county as incumbent workers; similarly, commuting patterns are undetectable through CWHS alone.

Other limitations of the CWHS files are discussed in the BEA Handbook on the Social Security Continuous Work History Sample (U.S. Department of Commerce, Bureau of Economic Analysis, 1976). Rather than be overwhelmed by the problems of the CWHS data, Wardwell and Gilchrist (1978) compared the CWHS migration findings with Current Population Report results. They showed that while the CWHS data overstated the migration of the employed labor force relative to census statistics, the pattern of change in out-migration is the same for 1965–1970 and 1970–1975 periods.

For our purposes, the crucial value of this data set lies in its ability to identify compositional characteristics of workers and their location of employment at designated points in time. For example, it is possible to select those workers who are employed in Michigan's metropolitan counties in 1965 and in Michigan's nonmetropolitan counties in 1970; thus, migrants are operationally defined as those workers employed at a specific location at the beginning of a 5-year period and who are employed at another location at the end of the period. Estimates of labor-force turnover are obtained by subtracting numbers of workers entering from those leaving the active work force. *Exits* are operationally defined as those workers who are employed at a specific location at the beginning of a time interval and who are no longer in the work force at the end of the interval. Similarly, *entrants* are those not in the work force at the beginning of the interval but employed at the end of the interval. Some migration of workers is masked by the turnover estimates, since the location of workers not in the work force cannot be determined.

Michigan's metropolitan sector is defined by using the Census Bureau's most recent definition of Standard Metropolitan Statistical Areas (SMSAs) (see Figure 14.1). The definition of a county's status is then held constant from 1960 to 1975.

Analysis

Population and Labor-Force Migration

Michigan's migration turnaround has been quite dramatic. It became evident during the 1960s, as several nonmetropolitan counties in the northern Lower Peninsula experienced net in-migration (Beegle, 1971). By 1975, the turnaround had spread to almost all nonmetropolitan areas of the state, as all but one county in the historically depressed Upper Peninsula gained population through migration, and at least 12 counties in the northern part of the Lower Peninsula sustained net in-migration rates in excess of 20% (O'Hare *et al.*, 1977). Of interest to our study is how these patterns of demographic redistribution coincide with the distributional patterns of economic activities as indicated by the migration of the work force. The data in Table 14.1 show that the direction of net migration patterns for the general population and for the labor force is consistent over each quinquennium in Michigan. In the early 1960s, metropolitan and nonmetropolitan sectors lost both population and jobs through migration. Metropolitan areas lost nearly 37,000 persons and nonmetropolitan areas lost over 28,000 persons; however, nonmet-

TABLE 14.1
Net Migration of the General Population and of the Labor Force for Michigan, 1960-1975 (in thousands)

Area	1960–1965		1965–1970		1970–1975	
	General population	Labor force	General population	Labor force	General population	Labor force
Michigan	−65.0	−21.9	96.9	24.3	−104.0	−41.9
Metropolitan areas	−36.9	− 9.9	66.6	22.6	−198.2	−51.3
Nonmetropolitan areas	−28.1	−12.0	30.3	1.7	94.2	9.4

Sources: For labor force: Continuous Work History Sample; for general population, 1960–1970: U.S. Department of Agriculture, University of Georgia, and National Science Foundation, 1975. "Net Migration of the Population, 1960–1970, by Age, Sex and Color," Population-Migration Report 1960–1970, Part 2; U.S. Bureau of the Census, Current Population Reports, Series P–25, No. 701 (1977); for general population, 1970–1975: U.S. Bureau of the Census, Current Popuation Reports, Series P–26, No. 75–22 (1976).

ropolitan Michigan lost 2100 more workers than the metropolitan sector. With the economic revival of the late 1960s, both geographical sectors gained population and work force. While the nonmetropolitan net migration gain in population was nearly half that of metropolitan areas, labor-force gain in nonmetropolitan areas was less than 8% of that experienced in metropolitan areas. In the early 1970s, labor-force migration paralleled the population turnaround: Metropolitan Michigan lost over 51,000 workers and over 198,000 population, while nonmetropolitan areas accelerated the pattern established in the late 1960s by gaining 9400 workers and 94,200 population.[3]

Earlier, we noted that in the outward movement of the population, many were not in the labor force. In turn, we pointed out that this is expected to affect the employment growth of the service sector. A comparison of quinquennial net migration for the labor force and for the total population may verify the "nonemployment" dimensions of recent development patterns.

Examining the ratio of labor-force net migration to population net migration (see Figure 14.2) reveals two quite different patterns for Michigan's geographical sectors. Metropolitan areas had a fairly consistent pattern over the three quinquennia, as the labor force–population net migration ratios were approximately .27, .34, and .26, respectively. However, for nonmetropolitan areas from 1960 to 1965, this ratio was nearly .43, indicating a considerably higher labor-force loss than in metropolitan areas. As nonmetropolitan areas began to turn around in the late 1960s, the ratio shifted dramatically to .06, and finally, in the early 1970s the ratio increased to approximately .10. The relatively low ratios for nonmetropolitan Michigan during the quinquennia associated with the turnaround imply that the recent dispersal of population has occurred, for the most part, independently of the relocation of the work force. The further growth of bedroom communities or the migration of

[3]To obtain net migration estimates of the population for the 1960–1965 and 1965–1970 periods required the combination of two data sources. From the Census Bureau's Current Population Reports (Series P–25, No. 701), we obtained the county net migration estimates for the population 5 years old and over from 1965 to 1970 (Table 14.1). Since the Population–Migration Report 1960–1970 (U.S. Department of Agriculture, University of Georgia, and National Science Foundation, 1975) provides county net migration figures by age, we were able to obtain the net migration estimates from 1960 to 1970 for the population 0–4 years old in 1970. By summing the latter estimates and the CPR estimates, we acquired reasonable estimates of net migration of the total population for the 1965–1970 period. Then these figures were subtracted from the 1960–1970 net-migration estimates for the total population (Population–Migration Report 1960–1970) to provide county estimates of net migration for the 1960–1965 period. County estimates were aggregated by metropolitan–nonmetropolitan status (1975). This imperfect procedure is useful for illustrative purposes only.

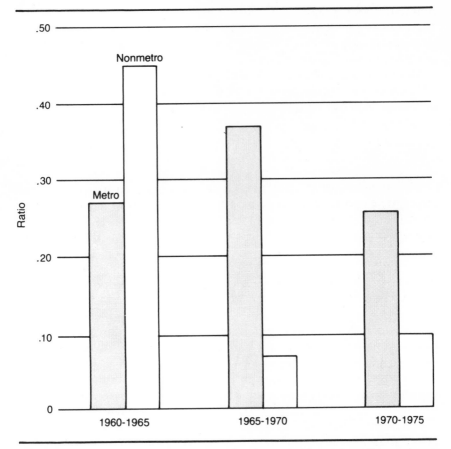

Figure 14.2. Labor force–population net migration ratios for metropolitan and non-metropolitan Michigan, 1960–1965, 1965–1970, 1970–1975. (Source: Continuous Work History Sample.)

segments of the population who are not active in the work force—namely, retired persons or college-age students—may account for these patterns.

We would caution the reader to consider these ratios with care and as illustrative of the point. Since they have been calculated on the basis of multiple data sources, they cannot be interpreted as proportions. Under-reporting in the 1970–1975 CWHS may vary for metropolitan and nonmetropolitan areas, resulting in lower ratios for the last 5-year period. Similarly, the residential error of our estimates of the 1960–1965 total net migration may have increased the denominator and lowered the ratio for that period. However, even with these caveats, the consistent pattern for metropolitan areas in all three periods and for nonmetropolitan areas in the preturnaround period across two independent data sources, the Current Population Survey (CPS) and the 1970 Census, strengthens the inference.

Moreover, independent estimates by the Census Bureau (U.S. Bureau of the Census, 1970: Table 7) for Michigan corroborate the 1960–1965 estimates of net migration and increase our confidence in the use of these ratios.

Origins and Destinations of Migrants

Although we have emphasized the migration volumes of the general population in contrast to the work force, many workers have recently migrated for employment in nonmetropolitan Michigan. The economy of any state is vulnerable to fluctuations in the national economy or to regional shifts in labor demand. For example, declining employment opportunities in Michigan's metropolitan region are indicative of the overall employment condition in America's "older industrial heartland." The nonmetropolitan revival in Michigan may have resulted, in part, from a dispersal of work force within the state and/or from national patterns of labor-force movement. An assessment of the origins and destinations of the mobile work force will characterize Michigan's turnaround in a national context.

The origin-destination matrix in Table 14.2 provides data on all mobile workers, total in-migrants to each location, total out-migrants, and net migration for each sector. Comparisons can be made between the in-migrant and out-migrant streams by looking at the statistics above and below the diagonals indicated by dashes. For example, the labor-force in-migration to nonmetropolitan Michigan during 1960–1965 was 31,900 workers, and the majority (17,000) of these workers came from metropolitan areas within the state. However, in the early 1960s, Michigan's nonmetropolitan counties lost 43,900 workers to metropolitan areas and to other states, for a net loss of 12,000 workers. Of the 12,000 net loss, 8000 went to metropolitan areas and 4000 left the state.

Between 1965 and 1970, Michigan's nonmetropolitan areas improved upon their interchange of interstate migrants. Yet, as many workers were lost as were gained, resulting in an even exchange. Within the state, early evidence of the turnaround was observed as a net of 1700 workers dispersed from the metropolitan sector, even though this was a period of economic expansion and overall labor in-migration into metropolitan Michigan. As the general population turnaround accelerated in the early 1970s, Michigan's nonmetropolitan areas overcame a net loss

TABLE 14.2
Migration Origin and Destination Matrix for Michigan Labor Force, 1960–1975 (in thousands of workers)

| Origin | Destination | | | | |
	Metropolitan Michigan	Nonmetropolitan Michigan	Out of state	Total out-migrants	Net migration
1960 to 1965					
Metropolitan Michigan	---	17.0	112.4	129.4	− 9.9
Nonmetropolitan Michigan	25.0	---	18.9	43.9	−12.0
Out of state	94.5	14.9	---	109.4	21.9
Total inmigrants	119.5	31.9	131.3	---	---
1965 to 1970					
Metropolitan Michigan	---	31.1	123.5	154.6	22.6
Nonmetropolitan Michigan	29.4	---	25.2	54.6	1.7
Out of state	147.8	25.2	---	173.0	−24.3
Total inmigrants	177.2	56.3	148.7	---	---
1970 to 1975					
Metropolitan Michigan	---	34.5	152.4	186.9	−51.3
Nonmetropolitan Michigan	23.9	---	26.5	50.4	9.4
Out of state	111.7	25.3	---	137.0	41.9
Total inmigrants	135.6	59.8	178.9	---	---

Source: Continuous Work History Sample.

of 1200 interstate labor force migrants by gaining a net of over 10,000 workers from metropolitan areas within the state. During this last quinquennium, Michigan's metropolitan areas were devastated by a net out-migration of 51,300 workers.

While nonmetropolitan counties fail to show a net increase in migrating interstate workers since 1960, the interstate exchange of labor consistently grew in its share of the total migration activity in nonmetropolitan Michigan. From the early 1960s to the early 1970s, gross migration between nonmetropolitan Michigan and other states increased from nearly 34,000 to nearly 52,000 workers, improving its share of total migration activity from roughly 45% to 47%. This trend may indicate that Michigan's nonmetropolitan sector is becoming more susceptible to national labor flows as it becomes more integrated into the national economy.

Age Selectivity of Migration

The selectivity of migration has resulted in dramatic consequences for places of origin and destination. Historical patterns of rural-to-urban migration have left many rural communities without valuable human resources, as the young and more educated typically have migrated out. The selectivity of workers entering and leaving various geographical sectors also reflects the structural dynamics of the recent nonmetropolitan revival. As the data in Table 14.3 show, the age selectivity of migration in metropolitan Michigan varied greatly during the three 5-year periods under examination. In the early 1960s, metropolitan areas gained workers from the youngest cohort (less than 30 years old) while they lost workers from the two older groups; thus overall, these areas lost workers. Later in the decade, younger worker in-migration increased in both volume and rate, and there was a net gain of 4700 middle-age workers. However, older workers (more than 54 years old) continued to leave metropolitan areas, and in the early 1970s workers were lost from all age cohorts, with the heaviest losses occurring in the middle working years.

In nonmetropolitan Michigan, age-specific migration was quite different from that experienced in metropolitan areas. The youngest cohort lost workers in each quinquennium, but in the early 1970s the rate of net out-migration was reduced to one-third of the rate in the early 1960s. The two older age groups lost workers from 1960 to 1965, but this pattern was reversed in the late 1960s and continued into the early 1970s with rising rates. Thus, recent labor-force migration indicates a diminishing of the historical patterns of age selectivity that often have acted to the detriment of many nonmetropolitan locales.

TABLE 14.3
Labor-Force Migration for Metropolitan and Nonmetropolitan Michigan by Age, 1960-1975 (in thousands of workers)

Area and age	1960-1965				1965-1970				1970-1975			
	In	Out	Net	Rate a	In	Out	Net	Rate a	In	Out	Net	Rate a
Metropolitan area												
Less than 30	31.7	28.0	3.7	19.0	58.3	39.0	19.3	69.3	51.4	58.9	- 7.5	-21.8
Between 30-54	77.2	88.9	-11.7	-11.6	102.2	96.5	5.7	5.5	70.6	106.9	-36.3	-35.7
Greater than 54	10.6	12.5	- 1.9	- 6.0	16.7	19.1	- 2.4	- 6.7	13.6	21.1	- 7.5	-22.9
Total	119.5	129.4	- 9.9	- 6.5	177.2	154.6	22.6	13.6	135.6	186.9	-51.3	-30.4
Nonmetropolitan area												
Less than 30	8.8	12.2	- 3.4	-110.7	15.8	17.8	- 2.0	-48.3	19.0	20.6	- 1.6	-31.1
Between 30-54	19.9	28.1	- 8.2	- 57.9	33.9	31.2	2.7	18.5	33.2	25.1	8.1	54.3
Greater than 54	3.2	3.6	- 0.4	- 8.8	6.6	5.6	1.0	19.2	7.6	4.7	2.9	53.1
Total	31.9	43.9	-12.0	- 55.1	56.3	54.6	1.7	7.1	59.8	50.4	9.4	36.8

Source: Continuous Work History Sample.
a Labor-force migration rates are calculated per thousand workers at the beginning of the 5-year period (in Tables 14.3 and 14.4). Age and industry classification are specified at the end of each 5-year period.

Selectivity by Industrial Sector

The economic underpinnings of the turnaround are reflected in the selectivity of work-force migration by industrial sector (see Table 14.4). During the first half of the 1960s, while Michigan incurred substantial out-migration of its work force, metropolitan areas experienced slight net gains of migrants in secondary industries, but all service-related industries lost workers. The bulk of this loss was from the trade and finance sector, which lost a net of 6700 workers at a rate of over 22 per 1000. Transportation and utility industries and the government sector also lost employees at relatively high rates. In the same period, nonmetropolitan Michigan lost workers from all industrial sectors except extractive industries. High rates of loss were incurred in manufacturing, transportation and utilities, trade and finance, and government.

From 1965 to 1970, metropolitan areas recovered as the trade and finance sector and the services sector showed net gains of 3500 and 4600 workers, respectively. However, the largest portion of labor-force increase was in manufacturing, which accelerated from 1600 net migrants in 1960–1965 to 19,400 in the next 5 years. Despite the general pattern of growth, metropolitan areas lost workers from the construction, transportation, and utility sectors. In nonmetropolitan areas, manufacturing accounted for most of the overall growth (2400 net growth) while the trade and finance, government, and construction sectors continued to lose workers. The gross flows of service workers doubled in the latter half of the decade, but the net gain was zero.

In the early 1970s, metropolitan areas lost workers from every industrial sector except government, as a net of 18,000 service workers left the area and over one in ten employees in transportation and utility industries were lost. In contrast, nonmetropolitan areas experienced gains in extractive, manufacturing, and transportation and utility industries. Services showed the highest increase in migrants, as 7000 workers were gained at a rate of over 116 per 1000.

Overall Patterns of Labor-Force Change

Although data on migration activity are essential for understanding labor-force growth, migration's effect is often eclipsed by turnover in the work force (Table 14.5).[4] For example, the net out-migration of workers

---

[4]Some migration is included in the turnover estimates. Moreover, entrants may be new participants in the labor force, other workers not previously covered by CWHS, or others newly counted by reason of changes in employer-reporting procedures. Exits can be characterized by similar causes of error; nevertheless, turnover demonstrates better than any other indicator the complexity of labor-force dynamics.

TABLE 14.4
Labor Force Migration for Metropolitan and Nonmetropolitan Michigan by Industry, 1960-1975 (in thousands of workers)

Area and Industry	1960-1965				1965-1970				1970-1975			
	In	Out	Net	Rate [a]	In	Out	Net	Rate [a]	In	Out	Net	Rate [a]
Metropolitan area												
Extractive	0.8	0.6	0.2	55.6	0.6	1.7	- 1.1	-239.1	0.4	3.6	- 3.2	-470.6
Construction	7.8	7.6	0.2	3.1	9.8	11.3	- 1.5	- 19.8	8.7	12.5	- 3.8	- 54.4
Manufacturing	51.7	50.1	1.6	2.1	78.1	58.7	19.4	24.7	49.6	51.9	- 2.3	- 3.2
Transportation and utilities	6.4	8.3	- 1.9	- 22.7	9.1	10.8	- 1.7	- 18.8	3.9	11.2	- 7.3	-107.2
Trade and finance	29.8	36.5	- 6.7	- 22.3	42.2	38.7	3.5	10.7	35.5	50.9	-15.4	- 44.3
Services	20.7	22.0	- 1.3	- 5.5	32.6	28.0	4.6	15.6	29.2	47.2	-18.0	- 48.1
Government	2.0	3.4	- 1.4	- 19.7	3.8	3.8	0.0	0.0	7.8	7.0	0.8	7.9
Other	0.3	0.9	- 0.6	-187.4	1.0	1.6	- 0.6	-100.0	0.5	2.6	- 2.1	-375.0
Total	119.5	129.4	- 9.9	- 6.5	177.2	154.6	22.6	13.6	135.6	186.9	-51.3	- 30.4
Nonmetropolitan area												
Extractive	1.6	0.9	0.7	74.5	0.6	0.3	0.3	50.0	1.0	0.7	0.3	45.5
Construction	2.1	2.4	- 0.3	- 33.7	3.3	4.1	- 0.8	- 72.7	3.1	3.7	- 0.6	- 50.4
Manufacturing	13.4	19.5	- 6.1	- 60.0	24.5	22.1	2.4	22.1	20.2	15.9	4.3	42.9
Transportation and utilities	2.0	2.7	- 0.7	- 83.3	3.2	2.5	0.7	69.3	2.2	1.6	0.6	63.2
Trade and finance	5.1	10.2	- 5.1	-120.9	11.5	11.8	- 0.3	- 6.9	10.8	12.8	- 2.0	- 38.0
Services	7.1	6.5	0.6	16.9	11.5	11.5	0.0	0.0	19.1	12.1	7.0	116.1
Government	0.6	1.6	- 1.0	-102.0	1.6	2.2	- 0.6	- 50.4	1.9	3.1	- 1.2	- 96.0
Other	0.0	0.1	- 0.1	-500.0	0.1	0.1	0.0	0.0	1.5	0.5	1.0	588.2
Total	31.9	43.9	-12.0	- 55.1	56.3	54.6	1.7	7.1	59.8	50.4	9.4	36.8

Source: Continuous Work History Sample.
[a] Labor-force migration rates are calculated per thousand workers at the beginning of the 5-year period (in Tables 14.3 and 14.4). Age and industry classification are specified at the end of each 5-year period.

TABLE 14.5

Change in the Labor Force through Migration and Turnover, Metropolitan and Nonmetropolitan Michigan, by Industry; 1960-1975 (in thousands of workers)

Area and industry	1960-1965			1965-1970			1970-1975		
	Net migration	Turnover	Total change	Net migration	Turnover	Total change	Net migration	Turnover	Total change
Metropolitan area									
Extractive	0.2	1.5	1.7	- 1.1	1.6	0.5	- 3.2	- 1.5	- 4.7
Construction	0.2	7.6	7.8	- 1.5	3.8	2.3	- 3.8	- 17.2	- 21.0
Manufacturing	1.6	20.6	22.2	19.4	27.2	46.6	- 2.3	-157.1	-159.4
Transportation and utilities	- 1.9	0.0	- 1.9	- 1.7	1.5	- 0.2	- 7.3	- 17.3	- 24.6
Trade and finance	- 6.7	94.3	87.6	3.5	155.8	159.3	-15.4	19.5	4.1
Services	- 1.3	66.6	65.3	4.6	122.7	127.3	-18.0	40.1	22.1
Government	- 1.4	- 1.7	- 3.1	0.0	20.9	20.9	0.8	0.7	1.5
Other	- 0.6	0.0	- 0.6	- 0.6	0.9	0.3	- 2.1	0.6	- 1.5
Total	- 9.9	188.9	179.0	22.6	334.4	357.0	-51.3	-132.2	-183.5
Nonmetropolitan area									
Extractive	0.7	- 1.0	- 0.3	0.3	- 2.2	- 1.9	- 0.3	0.4	0.1
Construction	- 0.3	1.9	1.6	- 0.8	1.1	0.3	- 0.6	- 2.2	- 2.8
Manufacturing	- 6.1	8.5	2.4	2.4	20.2	22.6	4.3	20.4	16.1
Transportation and utilities	- 0.7	- 1.2	- 1.9	0.7	0.7	1.4	0.6	- 0.1	0.5
Trade and finance	- 5.1	22.2	17.1	- 0.3	25.8	25.5	- 2.0	13.5	11.5
Services	0.6	10.6	11.2	0.0	19.5	19.5	7.0	12.8	19.8
Government	- 1.0	- 0.9	- 1.9	- 0.6	2.4	1.8	- 1.2	0.6	- 1.8
Other	- 0.1	0.1	0.0	0.0	0.1	0.1	1.0	1.4	2.4
Total	-12.0	40.2	28.2	1.7	67.6	69.3	9.4	4.0	13.4

Source: Continuous Work History Sample.

experienced by both the metropolitan and nonmetropolitan sectors in the early 1960s was compensated for by an increase of workers through turnover. Entrants outnumbered exits by nearly 189,000 workers in metropolitan areas and by over 40,000 in nonmetropolitan areas. In both metropolitan and nonmetropolitan areas, all industrial sectors, except transportation and utilities and government, showed overall gains in employment. Between 1965 and 1970, manufacturing posted employment gains in both geographical sectors. More important, however, service-related industries accounted for most of the employment increases. In metropolitan areas, the trade and finance and the services sectors combined to increase employment by 286,000 workers. Employment gains in the tertiary sector accounted for nearly 70% of the total increase of workers in nonmetropolitan Michigan. In the early 1970s, when Michigan's metropolitan centers were devastated by employment decline, both migration and turnover contributed to this loss, but turnover did show overall gains in some service-related sectors. As the turnaround progressed, nonmetropolitan Michigan demonstrated overall employment gains, but, in this case, migration accounted for most of the change. Similar to the experience of metropolitan areas, service-related industries accounted for all the increase in workers compensating for the fact that manufacturing lost over 16,000 workers through turnover in nonmetropolitan areas.

Discussion

As we argued in the introduction, the interaction of population and labor-force redistribution creates an analytic situation in which the results are neither simple nor straightforward. Using Michigan as an example, a number of aspects of the relationship have been clarified; even as simultaneously more questions were raised. First, the parallel cycles of population migration and labor-force migration for both metropolitan and nonmetropolitan areas provide confirmation of the general expectation. However, the comparison of labor force/population ratios reveals significant differences between geographical sectors: The metropolitan areas show relative constancy, but nonmetropolitan areas experience nearly twice the population growth per worker. It is this indicator of a large noneconomically related in-migration to rural areas that could be interpreted as the stimulus for concurrent or later tertiary sector growth. We shall return to this issue.

The second aspect of labor-force migration to nonmetropolitan areas is its source. During the 1960s, Michigan's metropolitan and nonmetropolitan areas gained or lost population in concert. But metropolitan areas gained from the national labor market and lost to other states.

Nonmetropolitan areas were linked primarily to metropolitan areas within the state. All this changed in the early 1970s, as metropolitan areas lost work force both to other states and to nonmetropolitan areas and the nonmetropolitan areas gained work force from the within-state metropolitan areas. We would argue that a partial explanation for this shift lifes in the dispersal of manufacturing jobs during the late 1960s. The manufacturing sector continued to experience a net migration gain into the early 1970s in nonmetropolitan areas. A complementary explanation lies in the continued expansion of the trade and service sector, resulting from the increased demand for services due to recent nonmetropolitan growth of the population not in the labor force.

The third aspect of labor-force migration to nonmetropolitan areas, which makes these conclusions more tentative, is the effective role of entrants to and exits from the labor force in contributing to restructuring the labor force in each geographical sector. Net turnover and net migration do not necessarily operate in the same direction in changing the labor-force mix. For example, both migration and turnover contributed to manufacturing growth in metropolitan areas during the 1960s, but in nonmetropolitan areas net migration was negative and turnover positive in the early 1960s, and both were positive in the 1965–1970 period. Nonmetropolitan net in-migration continued in the 1970s but was counterbalanced by heavy losses due to turnover. During this period in metropolitan areas, the net loss due to migration was accelerated by turnover. Looking at manufacturing employment in nonmetropolitan areas, it is clear that a significant growth did occur in the 1965–1970 period. The sector continued to attract in-migrants in the early 1970s, but overall, the manufacturing sector did not sustain the larger work force.

The character of tertiary sector growth differs from that of manufacturing. Growth occurred primarily through a net increase by turnover. Only in the expansion years of 1965–1970 did both migration and turnover contribute to trade, finance, and service sector growth in metropolitan areas. In the early 1970s, the service sector provided a source of growth through turnover but loss through out-migration. However, in the nonmetropolitan areas we see a gradual shift over the three quinquennia with an increasing contribution to service sector growth through net in-migration. It is this pattern that indicates the importance of population growth for further labor-force growth in the service sector. Similar research focusing on the distributive lag between employment growth and population growth in metropolitan areas demonstrates that growth in service employment is independent of the expansion of manufacturing in all but the largest of cities. Overall, income growth has been shown to be a consistent determinant of service employment growth (Moriarty, 1976:209). Thus, as population dispersal raises the income levels of nonmetropolitan areas, we expect further growth in the tertiary sector, which will, in turn, attract more workers to nonmetropolitan areas.

A consideration of the shifts over time in the age selectivity of labor-force migrants adds another ingredient in predictions of the next stage of the turnaround. The shift from a net in-migration of young workers into metropolitan areas to a net loss of such workers, in comparison with workers of older ages, completely reverses the earlier migration pattern. Although the shift is primarily the result of net interstate out-migration, a decline in the volume and the rate of net out-migration for nonmetropolitan areas is also apparent. In the 1970–1975 period, the net out-migration was only 1600 workers under the age of 30, and the total labor force grew through both net in-migration and turnover. Unfortunately, we cannot separate out entrants by age and prior location from the turn-over. However, we may speculate that overall labor growth is a function of younger new entrants.

In summary, the Michigan experience reveals two important dimensions of the turnaround. First, the volume of population migration into nonmetropolitan areas exceeded the expected level of job relocation during the late 1960s and early 1970s. Population redistribution and the relocation of economic activities are somewhat independent of each other. Second, the migration of service workers and the overall growth of the tertiary sector increasingly dominated the employment dimensions of the turnaround in Michigan. Thus, in the interaction between migration and economic development in Michigan, economic development is a response to recent population growth in nonmetropolitan areas. We therefore conclude that noneconomic reasons are contributing significantly to Michigan's nonmetropolitan revival and may serve as a foundation for future economic and demographic growth.

Acknowledgments

The authors thank C. Jack Gilchrist and Celia Allard at the Center for Social Data Analysis, Montana State University, Bozeman, Montana, for their assistance in data preparation.

References

Beale, Calvin L.
　　1975　"The revival of population growth in nonmetropolitan America." ERS–605. Washington, D.C.: U.S. Department of Agriculture, Economic Research Service.
　　1978　"Making a living in rural- and small-town America." *Rural Development Perspectives* 1 (November): 1–5.

Beale, Calvin L. and Glenn V. Fuguitt
   1975   "The new pattern of nonmetropolitan population change." CDE Working Paper
          75-22. Madison: University of Wisconsin, Center for Demography and Ecology.
Beegle, J. Allan
   1971   "Population growth and redistribution." East Lansing: Michigan State University
          Agricultural Experiment Station, Research Report No. 150.
Bell, Daniel
   1973   *The Coming of Post-Industrial Society: A Venture in Social Forecasting.* New York:
          Basic Books.
Brown, David L.
   1980   "Some spatial aspects of post–1970 Work Force Migration in the United States."
          Growth and Change in press.
Erickson, Rodney A.
   1976   "The filtering-down process: Industrial location in a nonmetropolitan area." *The
          Professional Geographer,* (August): 254–260.
Fuguitt, Glenn V.
   1978   "Population trends of cities and villages in the North-Central States. In J. Allan
          Beegle and Robert L. McNamara (eds.), *"Patterns of migration and population change
          in Americas Heartland.* East Lansing: Michigan State University Agricultural Exper-
          iment Station, Research Report No. 344, and North-Central Regional Research
          Publication 238.
Fuguitt, Glenn V. and Calvin L. Beale
   1978   "Population trends of nonmetropolitan cities and villages in subregions of the
          United States." *Demography* 15, 4:605–620.
Fuguitt, Glenn V. and James J. Zuiches
   1975   "Residential preferences and population distribution," *Demography* 12 (3):491–
          504.
Goldscheider, Calvin
   1971   *Population, Modernization, and Social Structure.* Boston: Little, Brown and Com-
          pany.
Graber, Edith E.
   1974   "Newcomers and oldtimers: Growth and change in a mountain town." *Rural
          Sociology* 39 (4):502–513.
Gray, Irwin
   1969   "Employment effects of a new industry in rural areas." *Monthly Labor Review* 92
          (June):26–30.
Hansen, Niles M.
   1978   *The Future of Nonmetropolitan America.* Lexington: D. C. Heath and Company.
Haren, Claude C. and Ronald W. Holling
   1979   "Industrial development in nonmetropolitan America: A locational perspective."
          In Richard E. Lonsdale and H. L. Seyler, *Nonmetropolitan Industrialization.*
          Washington, D.C.: V. H. Winston & Sons.
Heaton, Tim and Glenn V. Fuguitt
   1979   "Nonmetropolitan industrial growth and net migration." In Richard E. Lonsdale
          and H. L. Seyler, *Nonmetropolitan Industrialization.* Washington, D.C.: V. H.
          Winston & Sons.
Kale, Steven R. and Richard E. Lonsdale
   1979   "Factors encouraging and discouraging plant locations in nonmetropolitan
          areas." In Richard E. Lonsdale and H. L. Seyler, *Nonmetropolitan Industrialization.*
          Washington, D.C.: V. H. Winston & Sons.

McCarthy, Kevin F. and Peter A. Morrison
  1978   *The Changing Demographic and Economic Structure of Nonmetropolitan Areas in the 1970s.* Santa Monica: The Rand Corporation, P–6062.
Marans, Robert W. and John D. Wellman
  1978   *The Quality of Nonmetropolitan Living: Evaluations, Behavior, and Expectations of Northern Michigan Residents.* Ann Arbor: The University of Michigan, Survey Research Center, Institute of Social Research.
Moriarty, Barry M.
  1976   "The distributed lag between metropolitan-area employment and population growth." *Journal of Regional Science* 16, 2:195–212.
Morrison, Peter A.
  1979   *The Transition to Zero Population Growth in the Midwest.* N–1167–NICHD/EDA. Santa Monica: The Rand Corporation.
O'Hare, William, J. Allan Beegle, and Jim Leonard
  1977   "Michigan population: Growth and Distribution Changes." East Lansing: Michigan State University Agricultural Experiment Station, Research Report No. 331.
Petrulis, M. F.
  1979   "Growth patterns in nonmetropolitan–metropolitan manufacturing employment." Rural Development Research Report No. 7. Washington, D.C.: U.S. Department of Agriculture, Economic, Statistics, and Cooperative Service, Economic Development Division.
Ploch, Louis A.
  1978   "The reversal in migration patterns—Some rural development consequences." *Rural Sociology* 43 (Summer):293–303.
Seyler, H. L. and Richard E. Lonsdale
  1979   "Implications for nonmetropolitan development policy." In Richard E. Lonsdale and H. L. Seyler, *Nonmetropolitan Industrialization.* Washington, D.C.: V. H. Winston & Sons.
Sternlieb, George and James W. Hughes (eds.)
  1975   *Post-Industrial America: Metropolitan Decline and Inter-Regional Job Shifts.* New Brunswick: Rutgers University, The Center for Urban Policy Research.
Summers, Gene F., Sharon D. Evans, Frank Clemente, E. M. Beck, and Jon Minkoff
  1976   *Industrial Invasion of Nonmetropolitan America: A Quarter Century of Experience.* New York: Praeger Publishers.
Thompson, Wilbur R.
  1967   "Toward an urban economics." In Leo F. Schnore and Henry Fagen (eds.), *Urban Research and Policy Planning.* Beverly Hills: Sage Publications.
  1975   "Economic processes and employment problems in declining metropolitan areas." In George Sternlieb and James W. Hughes (eds.), *Post-Industrial America: Metropolitan Decline and Inter-Regional Job Shifts.* New Brunswick: Rutgers University, The Center for Urban Policy Research.
U.S. Bureau of the Census
  1970   "Use of Social Security's Continuous Work History Sample for Population estimation." *Current Population Reports,* Series P–23, No. 31. Washington, D.C.: U.S. Government Printing Office.
  1976   "Estimates of the Population of Michigan Counties and Metropolitan Areas: July 1, 1974 and 1975." *Current Population Reports,* Series P–26, No. 75-22. Washington, D.C.: U.S. Government Printing Office.
  1977   "Gross migration by county: 1965–1970." *Current Population Reports,* Series P–25, N–. 701. Washington, D.C.: U.S. Government Printing Office.

U.S. Department of Agriculture, University of Georgia, and National Science Foundation
   1975   "Net migration of the population, 1960–70, by age, sex, and color." *Population–Migration Report 1960–70*, Part 2. Athens: University of Georgia Printing Department.
U.S. Department of Commerce, Bureau of Economic Analysis
   1976   *Regional Work Force Characteristics and Migration Data: A Handbook on the Social Security Continuous Work History Sample and Its Application*. Washington, D.C.: U.S. Government Printing Office.
Vining, D. R. and T. Kontuly
   1977   "Increasing returns to city size in face of an impending decline in the sizes of large cities: Which is the bogus fact?" *Environment and Planning A* 9:59–62.
Wang, Ching-li and J. Allan Beegle
   1978   "Retirement function and community growth in Michigan nonmetropolitan areas." Paper presented at the Annual Meeting of the Rural Sociological Society, San Francisco, August.
Wardwell, John M. and C. Jack Gilchrist
   1978   "External validation of migration findings from the Continuous Work History Sample." Paper presented at National Bureau of Economic Research Workshop on Policy Analysis with Social Security Files, Williamsburg, Virginia.
Zuiches, James J. and David L. Brown
   1978   "The changing character of the nonmetropolitan population, 1950–1975." In Thomas R. Ford (ed.), *Rural U.S.A.: Persistence and Change*. Ames: Iowa State University Press.

DATA RESOURCES FOR POPULATION DISTRIBUTION RESEARCH

The decade of the 1970s has witnessed a proliferation of data resources for the study of population mobility. Existing data-gathering programs have been expanded and systematized, and new data sets have been initiated. For example, annual estimates of county population and net migration are now available (the County Net Migration Estimates, or CNME); the Current Population Survey (CPS) provides a wealth of data on migrant characteristics for fixed intercensal time periods, and the Continuous Work History Sample (CWHS) provides longitudinal data on labor mobility by county of employment and a limited range of migrant characteristics.

Two problems face the researcher who wishes to make effective use of these new data resources. The first concerns validity and reliability of the information. Many of the new data resources were gathered for administrative rather than statistical reasons. Consequently, they may vary in population coverage, definitions of units and items, accuracy and processing procedures. The researcher must proceed cautiously and must get to know the data set intimately, becoming familiar with its limitations and other unique characteristics, in order to make effective and appropriate use of the data.

The second problem is the cost of maintaining access to the resulting data systems. Information management strategies must be developed to bring the data resources within the reach of the researcher working within a small-to-medium data analysis budget, as well as to his or her more prosperous counterparts.

The two chapters in this final section address these two problems.

361

Renshaw (Chapter 15) systematically compares the county net migration estimates data and the Continuous Work History Sample to Current Population Survey mobility data, noting the stengths and weaknesses of each. Gilchrist and Allard (Chapter 16) present a new approach to information management and data analysis that solves many of the problems inherent in traditional approaches.

Renshaw discusses the three major data sets from the standpoints of population coverage, size of sample, time spans covered, and migrant characteristics included. When combined with contextual characteristics obtained from other sources, the net migration estimates provide great flexibility in analyzing population and migration change by types of counties. As Renshaw notes, most of the early work on the discovery of the nonmetropolitan migration turnaround was done with these data. The county estimates are considered weakest for young adults and other highly mobile segments of the population—the same groups least well covered by the CPS. Hence the CNME and CPS may both overstate the relative growth of nonmetropolitan areas in the 1970s.

The larger sample size and flexible analysis periods of the Continuous Work History Sample make it ideal for studying labor mobility changes that are associated with the general migration turnaround. However, reporting and processing errors in the CWHS tend to overstate migration rates relative to the CPS. The degree of systematic bias with respect to geographic areas in other groupings of counties is not well known (see Chapters 9 and 14).

The traditional approach to accessing very large data sets places several obstacles between the researcher and the data. These include the necessity for an intervening individual or unit to provide the requisite programming expertise and the cost premium attached to gaining all desired information on a single pass through the data file. Lengthly waits for results are taken for granted, and significant time and cost penalties result from incomplete or incorrect specification. For these and other reasons, the use of large data sets is frequently monopolized by the agency that originates the data or by a small number of very large data-analysis agencies. The small researcher is frequently forced to be content with the secondary use of published data.

Gilchrist and Allard propose an alternative strategy that removes most of these obstacles and also facilitates solution to some of the technical problems of merging different data sets that are discussed by Renshaw. Their alternative strategy, already implemented and operating on a number of data sets, makes use of three key ideas to improve access, reduce costs, and shorten the interval between formulating an analysis request and receiving the desired information. These ideas include variable rather than case orientation of data storage, the use of dichotomous variables for sample definition, and matrix formation for data analysis. The professional implications for expanded research with large administrative and statistical data sets are particularly pertinent to the 1980 Census products, which will soon become available.

Renshaw points out that the combination of high costs of survey research and federal restrictions on new information-gathering efforts will cause existing administrative record systems to increase in value for scientific research. He notes that there is a great deal of scope for making more effective use of administrative records for migration analyses. Gilchrist and Allard contribute a software strategy that will enable migration researchers to enlarge that scope through cost-effective access to and use of large data sets. Both of these developments define a data analysis context within which the mobility data for the 1980 Census will be received.

Using Administrative Records for Migration Analysis: Potential and Pitfalls

VERNON RENSHAW

Introduction

This chapter focuses on two major existing sources of intercensal migration data that are based largely on information from administrative records. These are (*a*) the cooperative program that enables the U.S. Census Bureau and state agencies to make annual intercensal estimates of county-level population and net migration (County Net Migration Estimates or CNME)[1]; and (*b*) the Continuous Work History Sample (CWHS) program of the Social Security Administration (SSA).[2] Administrative records are compared with statistical surveys in the first section. The CNME and CWHS programs are discussed in the next sections, and the final section discusses the potential for improving migration data from administrative sources.

Administrative Records Compared with Statistical Surveys

Administrative records are collected by federal, state, and local governments for direct use in operating governmental programs. Because

[1]These estimates, along with brief methodological descriptions, are published in the U.S. Bureau of the Census's *Current Population Reports,* Series P–25 Population Estimates and Projects, and Series P–26 Federal–State Cooperative Program for Population Estimates.

[2]A general documentation of CWHS files and their uses and limitations for migration analysis can be found in U.S. Department of Commerce (1976b).

365

administrative records are collected for specific program purposes, they usually do not contain information about all of the population groups and individual characteristics that interest statistical analysts in the social sciences. To some extent, population coverage and detail relating to individual characteristics can be expanded by merging information from more than one administrative source. But the difficulty of coordinating information collection among separate administrative programs and the need to prevent inappropriate use of confidential administrative records often severely limit the scope for merging information from different administrative sources in statistically satisfactory ways. Therefore, social scientists have generally preferred survey data collected specifically for statistical applications to information available from administrative sources, even though the volume of socioeconomic data collected in administrative programs is often far greater than that collected by survey methods.

Although migration analysts and other social scientists naturally prefer information that has been collected with their needs specifically in mind, a number of factors suggest that administrative records will become increasingly important sources of intercensal socioeconomic data for geographic areas in the future. Therefore, it is important for those concerned with migration and regional analysis to increase their awareness of the processes whereby administrative records can be used and improved as sources of socioeconomic data.

The clearest advantage associated with the use of existing administrative records rather than surveys relates to cost. Designing and conducting surveys is much more costly than processing records that have already been collected, and the cost of surveys rises rapidly as the frequency of data collection and the number of geographic areas for which data are needed increase. The high costs of survey data can be seen, for example, in estimates made by the National Commission on Employment and Unemployment Statistics of the costs that would be involved in expanding the Current Population Survey (CPS) to obtain the regular unemployment estimates required for distributing federal funds to state and local areas under such programs as the Comprehensive Employment and Training Act (CETA). The Commission's estimate of the costs of using the CPS for making monthly unemployment estimates for 4200 areas involved in the CETA program is $2.3 billion annually (National Commission on Employment and Unemployment Statistics, 1979). This cost estimate assumes a cost of $25 per household interview, and a requirement that 1850 households be interviewed to obtain a statistically reliable estimate of unemployment in a particular area for a single time period.

As in the case of survey unemployment estimates, survey estimates of gross—and especially net—migration for individual areas require relatively large numbers of household interviews. Therefore, the costs of using a CPS-type survey to obtain estimates of, say, annual migration by county would be very expensive (nearly $150 million, assuming $25 per interview and 1850 interviews per county). In fact, the sampling proportions required for small counties are so great that even the sample 5-year migration question asked in the decennial census cannot be used to estimate net migration reliably for most of the counties in the country. Clearly, then, in an era of tight budgets, survey estimates of net migration are not likely to be considered a cost-effective substitute for the CNME program for making annual county-level estimates of net population migration.

In addition to being a very costly source of reliable migration estimates for small geographic areas, household surveys are generally inadequate for conducting detailed longitudinal analysis of migration. The CPS and most other household surveys monitor migration via questions concerning the location of residence of current members of a household as of a particular point of time in the past. Such retrospective migration questions introduce the possibility of recall bias in survey migration data and severely restrict the scope for tracing individual movements over several periods or for varying the time periods of analysis after a survey has been conducted. In the CWHS, by contrast, migration is not determined by asking retrospective questions, but rather by directly linking work records of individuals for different time periods to determine which workers moved (changed work location) during the time interval being considered. Work records for all individuals in the CWHS sample are updated annually, and migration can be measured for periods of varying length (chosen at the researcher's discretion). Individuals can be traced through several periods to measure such phenomena as multiple sequential moves.

The relatively low cost and longitudinal features of some record sets are important advantages in using administrative records for migration analysis rather than relying on expansions of surveys such as the CPS to provide frequent and geographically detailed migration data. Perhaps even more important than the high direct costs and limited longitudinal capability of large-scale household surveys, however, is the high response burden placed on the individuals called on to answer detailed questions relating to migration and other socioeconomic characteristics of themselves and their families. In fact, the burdens of federally imposed information requests have become a matter of national concern, and detailed voluntary household surveys such as the CPS are particularly vulnerable to the frustrations of both individuals and politicians seeking to stem or cope with escalating paperwork burdens. Not only are increasing numbers of individuals refusing to respond (or responding carelessly) to elaborate statistical surveys, but the President's "Guidelines for Reducing the Burden of Public Reporting to Federal Agencies" as reported in the *Statistical Reporter*, have been formulated explicitly to limit the expansion of surveys to provide geographically detailed data. The Guidelines for 1978 state

> No statistics program which collects information annually or more frequently shall be designed to produce geographic detail below national totals for the United States unless: (1) the information is required by law more frequently than would be provided by a census and (2) cannot be obtained from existing administrative records or (3) the data collection is an integral part of a specific Federal–State cooperative program or (4) the survey is designed to produce statistical information for only a defined portion of the United States and not for the Nation as a whole [U.S. Department of Commerce, 1978].

With the increasing use of regional data for such purposes as allocating federal funds to state and local governments, in addition to growing data needs for research, it may seem somewhat unfair or inappropriate to single out regional survey data in efforts to stem reporting burdens to the federal government. However, the large surveys required to obtain detailed regional data are very expensive in terms of both reporting burdens and direct costs to the government. And there is a great deal of scope for making more effective use of administrative records to supply migration data and other regional data needs. Therefore, statisticians and researchers would be well advised to examine carefully the potential for making statistical use of administrative records. Not only may it be unrealistic to hope for substantially expanded statistical surveys, but the quality of responses in existing surveys as well as new or expanded surveys may deteriorate significantly if major efforts are not made to stem the rising burden placed on the public by government requests for information.

In developing and using migration and related data from administrative records, it is important to be aware of both the potential and the problems associated with the statistical use of administrative records. Table 15.1 briefly summarizes the major features of administrative-based CNME and CWHS migration data and compares these features with those of CPS migration data. Subsequent sections of this chapter discuss in more detail the features of CNME and CWHS data and indicate some of the steps that need to be taken to improve administrative sources of migration data.

TABLE 15.1
Features of Alternative Intercensal Migration Data Sources

Data sources	Population coverage	Features			
		Sample size and geographic detail	Time spans covered	Demographic characteristics of migrants	Economic characteristics of migrants
Current Population Survey	Civilian population (noninstitutional)	Less than .1% sample of all households Census regions	Any annual or longer period during the 1970s	Sex Age Race Family status Marital status	Income Employment status Occupation Industry
County Net Migration Estimates	Total resident population	Not based on a sample All counties	Any annual or longer period during the 1970s	None	None
Continuous Work History Sample	Social Security covered work force	1% sample of individual workers Data can be tabulated for states, SMSA's, and large counties	Any annual or longer period during the 1970s	Sex Age Race	Wage earnings Industry

Annual County Net Migration Estimates (CNME)

The U.S. Census Bureau, in cooperation with designated state agencies, has made annual estimates of population change and net migration throughout the 1970s for each county in the country. These estimates make use of information from a variety of administrative sources. Thus far, only net migration estimates have been published, and important population coverage gaps and other problems with many of the administrative data sources used raise complex questions concerning possible errors and biases in the population estimates. However, tests of the estimating methodologies generally suggest that reasonably reliable population and migration estimates can be made from available administrative data for most counties.

The introduction of the annual CNME series during the 1970s has proven to be a very important factor in documenting the extent and characteristics of the post-1970 reversal of the historical trend of net migration from nonmetropolitan to metropolitan parts of the nation. Beale relied primarily on CNME data to make perhaps the first thorough documentation of the widespread nature of post-1970 net in-migration flows for nonmetropolitan areas. Moreover, Beale and others have continued to make extensive use of CNME data to document the persistence of the new trends and to indicate the types of areas that have been involved in the reversal of past migration trends (Beale, 1975). Although the CNME data alone do not indicate the characteristics of migrants involved in the new migration patterns of the 1970s, migration analysts have been able to shed a great deal of light on the new patterns by relating the CNME data to a wide variety of information on county characteristics taken from census and other sources.

The CNME data are based primarily on county data derived from administrative sources, but the county estimates also take advantage of superior data for population and migration estimates at the state and national levels. The published county population estimates for each state are controlled to independently derived state estimates, which are in turn controlled to an independently derived national population total. The published state and county estimates represent an average of estimates derived from three different basic methods—an *administrative records* method, *Component Method II*, and a *ratio–correlation* method. The administrative-record-method migration estimates are based largely on Internal Revenue Service (IRS) individual income tax records, while the Component Method II migration estimates are based largely on school enrollment data, and the ratio–correlation migration estimates are derived as a residual by subtracting natural increase in the population (births minus deaths) from population change estimates based on a variety of symptomatic indicators (obtained largely from administrative sources). Separate population estimates are made for special population groups, such as the military and elderly, for which the standard estimating series are weak and independent population counts or indicators are available.

The greatest weakness in each of the standard population estimation methods is an absence of reliable indicators of the migration patterns of single young adults and other mobile individuals. These persons generally do not develop strong attachments to the communities they move to and are frequently missing from administrative record files pertaining to those communities. Single young adults will generally not have children in school, for example, and therefore their migration patterns will not be reflected in changes in school enrollment data. Component Method II adjusts for historical differences among areas in the relationship of school-age migration to adult migration, but such relationships could change in unexpected ways and distort estimates of total migration. Young adults are generally reflected in the IRS tax records used to estimate migration for the administrative records method or in indicators such as automobile registrations, which are commonly used in ratio-correlation methods. But young adults are not uniform in their tax-filing and driving habits, and highly mobile young people do not always update their address information for administrative record systems reliably enough to ensure that their migration patterns will be accurately captured in the available data.

In general, it is likely that the population groups that are most difficult to monitor reliably with available administrative data are the same poor and/or transient populations that are most frequently missed or misrepresented in censuses and surveys. Therefore, biases in migration data based on current county population estimates could be similar to any biases in major surveys such as the CPS. In particular, if the post-1970 turnaround in the pattern of net migration between metropolitan and nonmetropolitan areas has been primarily a product of changing migration flows for persons in stable family units and other individuals who are reliably monitored in surveys and administrative systems, then both surveys and administrative data could be overstating the extent of the metropolitan–nonmetropolitan migration turnaround. Moreover, the significance of any migration estimate biases along these lines could have been rising during the 1970s because of such factors as the rapid growth of the young adult population, falling birth rates, rising divorce rates, and possible growth of illegal immigration. Such factors tend to increase the relative importance of people who traditionally have chosen to live disproportionately in central cities of large metropolitan areas and who have also traditionally been hardest to monitor reliably with existing survey and estimation techniques. Indeed, it has been a chronic complaint of large cities that available population data underestimate their size, overestimate their population decline, and generally deprive them of their fair share of federal and state funds distributed to municipalities on the basis of population data.

Geographic biases in population and migration data resulting from incomplete and unreliable data for particular groups are, of course, not always clear in terms of directions. While incomplete administrative records could, for example, understate the movement of young adults from nonmetropolitan to metropolitan areas, the same record sets would also understate the return and reverse flows; without good data, it can be highly speculative to suggest the direction of net bias. Therefore, it is unlikely that controversy concerning bias in current county population estimates will be resolved prior to the 1980 Census. Even then, questions related to census undercount and other measurement problems are likely to keep the controversy alive. Nevertheless, it may be possible to shed substantial additional light on migration questions through more effective use of administrative records.

In general, administrative records have been used as aggregate symptomatic indicators of migration in most population estimation methods. There have been relatively few comprehensive efforts to trace administrative records for individuals in order to monitor migration directly. The major exception to the use of aggregate records in the current county estimates program is the administrative records method, which traces changes in address information supplied by the same individuals on income tax returns for different years. This matching of individual records permits estimates of both gross and net migration and permits the merging of information from more than one administrative file in order to fill information gaps in single files. It also permits cross-classification of migration flows by those characteristics of individual migrants that are available in the files used.

Thus far, gross migration estimates based on the administrative record method have not been prepared for publication, and efforts to extend administrative record linkages beyond the basic IRS files have been limited in scope. However, testing and evaluation of the current migration estimates as well as possible extensions are under way. The tests reveal both promise and pitfalls, and a great deal of work remains to be done to achieve a full evaluation of the potential of administrative records for developing reliable gross migration data (U.S. Bureau of the Census, 1973, 1980). Some idea of the nature of the potential and the pitfalls can be obtained by reviewing SSAs Continuous Work History Sample. For many years, the CWHS has been the only major administrative data set in general use for tracing individual migration patterns over time.

The Continuous Work History Sample (CWHS)

The CWHS merges a variety of SSA records for a sample (usually 1 percent) of workers in employment covered by Social Security. Individual demographic characteristics (sex, age, and race) are obtained from worker applications for Social Security numbers; wages and work experience information are obtained from regular employer wage reports to SSA; and location and industry of employment are obtained from SSA's files of employer information. Several distinct CWHS files are assembled or updated annually, and annual files can be linked longitudinally to monitor migration in terms of geographic changes in place of work (U.S. Department of Commerce, 1976a).

As with the CNME data, CWHS migration data have played an important role in documenting recent changes in metropolitan–nonmetropolitan migration patterns. In particular, the CWHS has shown that increased net migration to nonmetropolitan areas has been associated with substantial worker migration and dispersion of job opportunities out of metropolitan areas. In addition, the CWHS has been very helpful for determining the timing of shifting metropolitan–nonmetropolitan migration patterns during the 1960s and 1970s and for determining the characteristics of the workers involved in these changing patterns.[3]

The CWHS has a number of distinct advantages for use in studying migration. It is a public-use file of records for individual workers (in which precautions are taken to ensure individual anonymity) that can be used to study either individual or aggregate migration behavior. The data are coded by county, and the sample size is large enough to tabulate migration estimates for many geographic areas for which no intercensal survey data are available. Most important, however, the annual records can be linked longitudinally as far back as 1957 so that migration studies can be designed to cover any time periods of interest from 1957 to the date of the most recently available file. Such longitudinal records permit the tracing of workers both before and after moves, and through

---

[3]For an illustration of CWHS metropolitan–nonmetropolitan studies contrasting different time periods during the 1960s and 1970s, see Wardwell and Gilchrist (1980), Brown (1980), or U.S. Department of Commerce (1976a).

series of moves, without danger of recall bias. This longitudinal tracing process can provide a much more detailed picture of individual migration behavior than can nonlongitudinal surveys such as the CPS. There are a few national longitudinal surveys, but none comes close to matching the sample size or length of time covered by the CWHS.

Although there are significant advantages to using the CWHS to study migration, there are also some important limitations. Most important, the files cover workers only for periods in which they are employed in jobs covered by Social Security (about 90% of all employment). The migration behavior of individuals is not reflected in the CWHS for periods during which they are not in the work force or in cases in which individuals do not earn at least $50 in a covered job at both the origin and destination of a move. Moreover, CWHS migration data reflect migration in terms of change in place of work and are therefore not strictly comparable to household-survey migration measures, which reflect changes in place of residence. And, while the CWHS does contain information on the sex, age, and race of workers as well as the wage earnings and industry of employment for each covered job a worker holds, the CWHS does not contain information for such important characteristics as family status, education, and occupation.

For a limited number of years, linkages between CWHS files and IRS taxpayer address files were made in order to add information on place of residence to the CWHS files. This new information permits analysis of migration by place of residence in addition to migration by place of work and it also permits comparison of work and residence locations for purposes of studying commuting patterns. However, confidentiality provisions in the Tax Reform Act of 1976 have at least temporarily halted linkages of IRS and SSA records as a part of the CWHS program. Use of residence information in the CWHS has thus far been limited largely to testing, evaluation, and selected efforts to develop worker commuting estimates. Nevertheless, the IRS residence data used in conjunction with the SSA data on place of work have added important insights into the limitations of the geographic information available in administrative data files.

It has been known for some time that errors in employer reports of employees by place of work can lead to spurious indications of migration in CWHS files. The availability of information on worker place of residence has added an important tool for identifying possible errors in work location information in the CWHS as well as possible errors in residence location information in IRS files. Indeed, analysis of inconsistencies in reported work and residence locations suggest that reporting, coding, and clerical errors in the CWHS may be contributing to more misrepresentations of migration than most CWHS users have suspected (Cartwright, 1978).

The most readily identified problems in CWHS migration data arise out of the failure of large employers with employees at several distinct geographic locations to report those employees in a manner consistent with the guidelines for SSA's voluntary establishment reporting plan. Occasionally, inconsistencies in reporting from year to year will result in spurious transfers of large groups of employees between different geographic locations of the same employer. In addition, a number of large employers do not report their employee groups in as fine (county-level) geographic detail as requested by SSA. This tendency to report geographically dispersed employees from centralized or regional headquarters locations tends to overstate employment in central (usually metropolitan) locations relative to peripheral (often nonmetropolitan) locations. When branch plants of major employers in nonmetropolitan areas are erroneously reported from metropolitan locations, there can be spurious net migration from nonmetropolitan to metropolitan areas when the branch plants expand rapidly or when they pay relatively high wages that attract experienced workers away from smaller, local employers. In fact, comparisons of CWHS and census migration data for the 1965–1970 period do suggest a tendency for the CWHS to overstate net migration out of nonmetropolitan areas, particularly in the South, and to overestimate net migration into metropolitan areas, particularly in the Northeast (U.S. Department of Commerce, 1976a).

Since most of the migration research with the CWHS has been financed by federal and state government funding, it is somewhat paradixoical that these government units appear to make the least effort of any group of employers to report employees in compliance with the SSA establishment reporting plan. At the federal level, most civilian employees are not covered by Social Security, but temporary employees and other civilian workers for whom Social Security taxes are paid are reported as if they were working at the central location where the payroll records for their agency are kept, whether or not they actually work at that location. For members of the military, who are generally covered by Social Security, all workers are reported in a single reporting unit and are placed in a special *military* category with no geographic location codes in the CWHS.

At the state level, Social Security coverage of government workers is at the option of the individual states. Most state governments have chosen coverage for their workers, but, as in the case of the few covered federal workers, reporting tends to be in terms of agency payroll locations rather than actual work locations. A few states, such as New York, for example, report all state government workers in a single reporting unit, which is coded in the CWHS to the county containing the state capitol. And even states that distinguish several or even a large number of separate reporting units generally appear to be reporting workers from the locations where payroll records are kept without indicating which workers actually are working in the counties where their paychecks originate. Hence considerable caution should be exercised when interpreting the intrastate distribution and migration of state government employees in CWHS data.

In general, incorrect geographic reporting of workers to SSA tends to bias CWHS estimates of gross migration rates upward, but a tendency for large employers to report management workers centrally could lead to an understatement of migration for highly paid managers who tend to be transferred frequently. If there is a single reporting location for an employer's management personnel, no migration would be recorded in the CWHS unless a managerial employee in the sample changed employers, even though the employee may have experienced a number of geographic transfers while working for the same employer.

Not all errors in the CWHS result from unreliable employer reporting. Coding and clerical errors at SSA can also lead to spurious indications of migration in the CWHS. In general, individual clerical errors in the CWHS are likely to be small, and distortions in migration data stemming from clerical errors are likely to be difficult to detect. However, in a few CWHS files some substantial overstatements of employment in Alaska appear to have arisen as the result of clerical problems. These problems have greatly distorted CWHS estimates of migration for Alaska for much of the late 1960s and early 1970s.

It is likely that the number of errors originating at SSA has been rising during the 1970s as tighter administrative budgets have cut back the resources available for monitoring the reporting, coding, and clerical operations necessary to ensure that workers are assigned correct geographic locations in the CWHS. This decline in resources for maintaining and improving the quality of geographic information in the CWHS is regrettable from a statistical point of view, but it is understandable from an administrative one. It does not really matter, from the point of view of collecting payroll taxes, exactly where individual employees do their work, so long as employers report their wages correctly. In fact, geographic reporting of employees is requested from multilocation employers entirely for statistical purposes. Hence administrators may be understandably reluctant to devote large amounts of resources to monitoring geographic information or pressing employers to comply with voluntary geographic reporting guidelines in an era of tight budgets and business resistance to what appear to be unnecessary reporting burdens.

Resources have not been available to make a full evaluation, let alone to correct, problems of spurious migration in the CWHS. However, some biases in CWHS migration rates are reasonably clear, and migration analysts should be very careful to consider these as well as other potential biases when they examine CWHS migration data. The most obvious effect of the erroneous reporting of migration is a general upward bias in CWHS gross migration rates for nearly all geographic areas. Estimates of annual interstate gross worker migration based on CWHS records, for example, have been as high as 10% of the working population at risk. Work-force migration rates measured by place of work are not strictly comparable to population migration rates by place of residence, and survey population migration rates may be biased downward because of difficulties in surveying highly mobile young adults. Nevertheless, CWHS interstate work-force migration rates seem to be out of sync with CPS annual interstate population migration rates to the extent of 3–4%. Moreover, CWHS migration rates show a general upward drift since 1970 that is not apparent in CPS rates. This upward drift in CWHS gross migration rates seems to correspond reasonably closely with the decline in resources devoted to maintaining the CWHS and to other indications of rising errors in CWHS files.

The effect of errors on CWHS migration rates is not uniform geographically, but it is difficult to identify systematic regional differences in the upward bias in gross migration rates. Nevertheless, certain types of analysis of gross migration using the CWHS could be very misleading because of the nature of CWHS errors. For example, it would probably be inappropriate to use the CWHS to try to determine the extent to which return migration of workers to nonmetropolitan areas has been a factor in the metropolitan–nonmetropolitan migration reversal of the 1970s. This is because spurious out-migration in the CWHS is very often associated with spurious return migration in subsequent years and because the apparent general rise in spurious migration in the 1970s could be increasing spurious return migration as a proportion of estimated total migration or return migration. Large amounts of spurious out-migration followed by spurious return migration can arise, for example, when large business establishments are misreported or miscoded in one (or several) of the annual CWHS files but handled correctly in other years. Employees who work continuously at such establishments will appear as out-migrants for the year in which the error first occurs and as return migrants when the error is corrected. And even when establishments are continuously reported or coded in the wrong location, some local workers will erroneously appear as out-migrants as long as they remain with the affected establishments and as returnees when they leave those jobs for other local jobs. Therefore, with apparently large and growing numbers of spurious migrants in the CWHS files, inferences about return migration based on the CWHS could be particularly hazardous. With the possibility of spuriously rising gross migration rates in general, it would also be inappropriate to use the CWHS to suggest, for example, that it is rising in-migration rates rather than falling out-migration rates that have made the greatest contribution to the post-1970 nonmetropolitan net migration turnaround.

While systematic regional differences in the upward bias of gross migration rates are difficult to detect in the CWHS, it was suggested earlier that erroneous centralized reporting by some large employers could contribute to spurious net migration from nonmetropolitan areas to metropolitan areas that serve as regional or national headquarters for multi-establishment employers. This bias seemed reasonably clear in the late 1960s and may be continuing during the 1970s, but increasing problems with coding and clerical errors at SSA could be tending to offset or obscure the bias pattern of the 1960s. Whatever the net migration biases resulting from spurious migration, users should be aware that, in addition, the CWHS does not capture net migration of people outside the work force or net migration associated with entry into and exit from the work force. The entry and exit problem with the data can be particularly severe if CWHS files are used to measure migration over a period of several years without monitoring migration behavior in years between the beginning and ending periods of concern. Many young people and women have entered the work force in recent years, and the chances of capturing their migration behavior over long periods in the CWHS decline rapidly if their job experience is not monitored continuously back to their initial entry into the work force.

Although there are a large number of problems and some clear data biases that restrict the value of the CWHS for some types of migration analysis, CWHS data for the most part reveal migration patterns that are consistent with data from other sources (Wardwell and Gilchrist, 1978). The quality of most of the earnings and demographic data on the CWHS is likely to be very good because of the importance of such information for administering Social Security programs. Therefore, the CWHS could prove to be particularly useful in isolating certain kinds of demographic and wage developments related to migration that other sources of intercensal migration data cannot reveal or would not reveal reliably. For example, since 1970 CWHS data suggest that the metropolitan–nonmetropolitan reversal in net migration patterns has been stronger among working males than among working females (Renshaw *et al.*, 1978). This trend suggests a number of possible hypotheses concerning the nature of nonmetropolitan job growth, the types of individuals and families choosing to leave metropolitan areas, and/or the effectiveness of affirmative action programs in nonmetropolitan versus metropolitan areas. And the CWHS, particularly when supplemented with information from other sources, could probably be used to shed a great deal of additional light on hypotheses related to female job prospects in nonmetropolitan areas.

In summary, the CWHS has many attractive features for the study of migration, but also some important limitations. In principle, many of the coverage limitations of the CWHS could be overcome by linking the CWHS with other major federal administrative record files. Increased resources for monitoring reporting and clerical operations could improve the accuracy of the information in the CWHS. In a number of instances, however, confidentiality restrictions on linking administrative files for statistical use have been becoming tighter and resources for maintaining the quality of geographic information in the CWHS have been declining. Nevertheless, demands have been rising sharply for the kinds of intercensal socioeconomic data for geographic areas that can only be supplied by administrative records. Much has been learned about the kinds of technical problems that must be solved to provide high quality general data from administrative records. And a number of projects are planned or under way that could lead to much improved statistical use of administrative records, provided the projects do not fall victim to growing problems of access and funding.

Potential Improvements in Administrative Migration Data

The key to improving the migration data that can be obtained from administrative files such as the CWHS lies in linking together information on individuals from various different record files. Linking of record files helps both to overcome the coverage limitations of single files and to evaluate the quality of the information in the separate files when there is overlapping coverage. A high degree of population coverage could be obtained through links of IRS individual income tax files with the CWHS and other SSA files covering such groups as Social Security beneficiaries and Supplemental Security Income recipients. Even greater population coverage and more information on individual and family characteristics could be obtained by extending linkages beyond IRS and SSA records to records of other Federal (e.g., Veterans Administration, or VA) and federal–state cooperative (e.g., Aid to Families with Dependent Children, or AFDC) administrative programs. However, both the technical problems of linkage and questions related to maintaining confidentiality become more complex as the scope of record linkages is expanded.

The technical problems of linking most major federal administrative record systems for statistical purposes do not appear to pose insurmountable barriers. However, in federal–state programs inconsistencies in recordkeeping procedures from state to state often give rise to very serious technical problems that would have to be overcome if such records were to be included in large-scale statistical linkage projects. There is a project associated with the federal–state Unemployment Insurance (UI) program to use state-level UI administrative records in the construction of a statistical "Continuous Wage Benefit History" (CWBH) sample file.[4] The CWBH is to be based on sampling procedures that would eventually permit linkage to statistical files of federal administrative records. Thus, a precedent is being established for federal–state cooperation in developing linked microrecord administrative data files for statistical use.

Probably the greatest barriers at the federal level to comprehensive statistical record linkage projects involve confidentiality constraints limiting interagency transfers of records pertaining to individuals. These barriers have not always proven to be insurmountable, and some very important linkage studies have been made. Of particular importance have been record-linking studies involving matches of individual records from IRS, SSA, and Census Bureau sources (Kliss and Scheuren, 1978). These studies have involved the CPS as well as IRS and SSA administrative records and have, therefore, permitted a direct comparison of administrative information with related information collected by survey techniques. Thus far, linkage projects involving several agencies and record sets have been carried out on a small scale and have not involved large enough samples or sufficient longitudinal information to prove particularly useful for migration analysis. The Federal Statistical System Project of the President's Reorganization Project has recommended that the process of developing statistical samples from administrative record systems should be integrated so that the full potential of general-purpose files such as the CWHS and the IRS Statistics of Income (SOI) file can be realized (Federal Statistical Systems Project, 1978).

---

[4]The CWBH is being developed through cooperative arrangements between individual states and the Employment and Training Administration (ETA) of the U.S. Department of Labor. Planning and development efforts undertaken thus far are described in unpublished papers available from ETA.

There has been planning and discussion concerning the possibility of coordinating the sampling procedures for the CWHS and SOI data. Linking of CWHS and SOI records would begin on a small sample basis, but with adequate resources the samples could be enlarged and information could be added from other accessible administrative sources. Such an integrated statistical file could potentially have a very high rate of population coverage and contain a great deal of information on the demographic characteristics and income, work experience, and other socioeconomic characteristics of the population. Through linkage to currently available CWHS files, the much-expanded integrated files would have obvious benefits for migration analysis; with longitudinal extensions and adequate sample sizes, integrated administrative record samples could provide a powerful tool for analyzing population and work-force migration in the 1980s.

Detailed geographic analysis would require larger samples than are currently available from either the SOI program of IRS or from the 1% CWHS files. In anticipation of the need for more detailed geographic analysis, SSA has had a limited program of drawing 10% CWHS files for selected periods. Three 10% CWHS files have already been linked to the IRS Individual Master File records that were used in developing the migration estimates for the Census Bureau's administrative records program of population estimation. Thus far, the linked 10% IRS–CWHS samples have been used principally for analyzing place-of-residence (IRS) by place-of-work (CWHS) information to develop intercensal work-force commuting estimates (Galdi and Knott, 1978). But such large-sample linked files also offer considerable promise for migration analysis, and they can provide invaluable information for evaluating the problems and potential for ultimately developing large-scale samples with the more detailed socioeconomic information that could be obtained by integrating and expanding the regular SOI and CWHS small sample statistical programs.

References

Beale, Calvin L.
    1975   *The Revival of Population Growth in Nonmetropolitan America.* ERS 605. Washington, D.C.: U.S. Department of Agriculture, Economic Research Service.
Brown, David L.
    1980   "Some spatial aspects of post–1970 work-force migration in the United States," *Growth and Change* (in press).
Cartwright, David
    1978   "Major limitations of CWHS files and prospects for improvement." Pp. 577–593 in *Policy Analysis with Social Security Research Files.* Proceedings of a work-

shop at Williamsburg, Virginia, March 1978. HEW Publication No. (SSA) 79-11808. Washington, D.C.: U.S. Government Printing Office.

Federal Statistical System Project
  1978   "Issues and options." Draft report. Washington, D.C.: President's Reorganization Project, November.

Galdi, David and Joseph J. Knott
  1978   "The use of administrative records in updating journey to work data." Paper presented at the American Statistical Association Annual Meetings, San Diego, California.

Kliss, Beth A. and Frederick J. Scheuren
  1978   "The 1973 CPS–IRS–SSA Exact Match Study." *Social Security Bulletin* 41 (October):14–22.

National Commission on Employment and Unemployment Statistics
  1979   *Counting the Labor Force.* Washington, D.C.: U.S. Government Printing Office.

Renshaw, Vernon, Howard Friedenberg, and Bruce Levine
  1978   "Work force migration patterns, 1970–76." *Survey of Current Business* 58 (February):17–20.

U.S. Bureau of the Census
  1973   "Federal–State cooperative program for population estimates: test results— April 1970." *Current Population Reports* Series P–26, No. 21. Washington D.C.: U.S. Government Printing Office.

U.S. Department of Commerce
  1976a   "Work-force migration patterns, 1960–73." *Survey of Current Business* 56 (October):23–26.
  1976b   *Regional Work Force Characteristics and Migration Data: A Handbook of the Social Security Continuous Work History Sample and its Application.* Bureau of Economic Analysis. Washington, D.C.: U.S. Government Printing Office.
  1978   *Statistical Reporter* 78 (April):243.
  1980   "Population and Per Capita Money Income Estimates for Local Areas: Detailed Methodology and Evaluation." *Current Population Reports*, Series P.-25, No. 699. Washington, D.C.: U.S. Government Printing Office (in press).

Wardwell, John M. and C. Jack Gilchrist
  1978   "External validation of migration findings from the continuous work history sample." Pp. 333–343 in *Policy Analysis with Social Security Research Files.* Proceedings of a workshop at Williamsburg, Virginia, March 1978. HEW Publication No. (SSA) 79–11808. Washington, D.C.: U.S. Government Printing Office.

Wardwell, John M. and C. Jack Gilchrist
  1980   "Employment deconcentration in the nonmetropolitan migration turnaround." *Demography* 17 (May):145–158.

16

New Strategies for Processing Large Data Files in Migration Research[1]

C. JACK GILCHRIST
CELIA A. ALLARD

Introduction

Interest in the study of migration has increased in recent years. Relatively stable death rates combined with declining birth rates have resulted in declining rates of natural increase throughout the United States and in most developed countries. In this demographic context, migration patterns take on added importance in accounting for variations in the growth of regions within the nation (Goldstein, 1976). Regional redistribution trends have been accompanied by a decline rather than an increase in the efficiency with which migration is redistributing the national population (Long and Hansen, 1977). That is, more gross migration is taking place than would be inferred from net redistribution. Net migration rates give little clue as to the total volume of movement that is producing the net population shifts. Primary analyses of gross migration streams are needed to identify the changes responsible for the net shifts. Similarly, the changes that are responsible for and attendant upon the turnaround in metropolitan–nonmetropolitan migration streams generate increasing needs for gross migration data combined with detailed characteristics of sending and receiving areas (Beale, 1975; Schwarzweller, 1979).

The need for a flexible, cost-efficient mode of access to large data sets grows concurrently with the need to perform detailed primary analyses

[1]The Agricultural Experiment Station and the Office of the Vice-President for Research at Montana State University have provided financial support for this research.

New Directions in
Urban–Rural Migration

of gross migration data. The types of migration data range from longitudinal migration histories constructed from the University of Michigan Panel Study of Income Dynamics (PSID) (DaVanzo and Morrison, 1978) through Current Population Surveys and the decennial census mobility data, to such administrative data sources as the annual county net migration estimates and the Social Security's Continuous Work History Sample (CWHS). The larger the data set, the greater the likelihood that a majority of the research is done from hard copy published by the agency responsible for gathering and disseminating the data. Examples from 1970 Census and Current Population Survey mobility include Tucker (1976), Wardwell (1977), and Zuiches and Brown (1978). Many researchers outside of the data-generating agencies do not have the computer and financial resources necessary to do other than work from published reports. Direct analysis of census or other tapes, when undertaken, is usually carried out without reference to nondemographic data from other sources. Resulting analyses tend to be restricted to those few nondemographic characteristics, such as labor-force status of migrant or metropolitan–nonmetropolitan classification of place, that are available in the particular mobility data set being used. The difficulties associated with merging several large data files on a common unit of observation restrict the researcher's ability to complement migration data with any desired contextual properties of sending and receiving geographical units. They also restrict the researcher's ability to compare migration trends observed in one type of mobility data with those observed in another data type. Thus, for example, it is both difficult and uncommon for the single researcher to make the direct comparison of (*a*) gross migration patterns from one data source with (*b*) net migration estimates from another source by (*c*) detailed characteristics of counties from a third source. Similarly, it is difficult to compare mobility patterns for the labor force from the Continuous Work History Sample with those observed in 1970 Census and later Current Population Survey mobility data within a single data analysis system.

The purpose of this chapter is twofold: to acquaint migration researchers with a set of computer software strategies particularly applicable to the analysis of large data files, and to discuss the implications of these strategies for overcoming some of the barriers to research that are associated with traditional modes of data access. The traditional modes are invariably costly, regardless of whether cost is measured in terms of dollars, time, inconvenience, constraints on analyses, or a combination of these considerations. The ideas presented in this chapter address the technical sources of these costs and provide the basis for a major reorientation toward the analysis of large data sets. The potential scope of this reorientation becomes apparent in the discussion of research implications, since the full power of these strategies is realized only when they are efficiently combined. Later discussion focuses on a software package that successfully implements these and other strategies.

The Traditional Approach

Although the traditional approach to managing large data sets has minor variations for specific computer installations, the arrangement of data files by case is common to all applications. The traditional data file, be it large or small, is always case-oriented. Case orientation is essentially a carry-over from precomputer days, when data were stored on cards and analyzed by tabulating machines.

A case-oriented data file consists of all case records in sequential order, with each case occupying one record. The record for each case contains values for the specific variables or characteristics associated with that case. In Table 16.1, information concerning the characteristics sex, race, socioeconomic status, and education are attached to each of five cases.

Table 16.1 merely illustrates the record structure; a typical data set contains far more than four variables and five cases. The data sets we refer to as "large" contain many thousands or even millions of cases, each having a hundred or more variables. But regardless of the number of cases or variables in a data set, the traditional storage approach arranges cases consecutively: The first case with all attached variables is stored, followed by the second with all its values, followed by the third, and so on. Since the data in most data sets are arranged by case, most

TABLE 16.1
A Case-Oriented Data File

		Sex	Race	Socioeconomic status	Education
First record:	Case 1	1	1	4	20
Second record:	Case 2	2	3	4	16
Third record:	Case 3	1	1	5	18
Fourth record:	Case 4	1	3	2	8
Fifth record:	Case 5	2	2	1	6

analytical programs designed to provide access to data are also case-oriented. This is particularly true of most canned packages, such as SPSS, BMD, OSIRIS, and SAS. These packages were developed to analyze data files of small or moderate size, and when the number of cases for analysis is not large, the inefficiencies inherent in case-oriented programs are not significant. However, when a very large data set is analyzed using such programs, those same inefficient mechanisms result in prohibitively high expenditures of time and money.

The mode of data storage is also a factor in the management of large data sets. Although disc storage provides fast data access, tape storage is generally preferred because large data files require considerable storage space and tape storage is less expensive. Access to data at the time of program execution is usually from tape, and this may contribute significantly to the amount of turnaround time required to pass through a data set.

Consequently, researchers have developed a "one pass" philosophy toward the analysis of large data files. Each pass through the data tends to be expensive, since passing through a case-oriented file containing a million or more cases requires a sizeable amount of computer time. The researcher endeavors to save as much data as possible from each case record at the time it is read by the computer. As a result, researchers using large case-oriented files usually make complete, extensive data analysis requests through canned programs in order to glean as much information as they can from a single, expensive pass through the entire data file. Their requests tend to be global in nature and thus lack provisions of exploring relationships in the data contingent upon other relationships or on specification of subsamples in the data set. Sample counts and test runs, while commonplace with small data sets, are possible with large data files only when time and money are not at issue. A misspecification of the data required may not only negate the usefulness of a substantial part of the analysis, but may result in considerable cost if a rerun is necessary.

The situation often arises in which only a subset of a large data file is required for analysis. To facilitate multiple passes through this subset, a subfile may be created. For example, a subfile consisting of the data for one state could be formed from a national file, and all subsequent analyses would draw from this subfile rather than from the total data set. While the savings achieved by utilizing subfiles may be considerable, there are two disadvantages to this strategy. First, all subfiles must be stored and documented in the same manner as the original data file; this requirement increases both storage and labor charges. Second, the analysis of a subfile is confined to the cases present within the subfile; it cannot refer back to the main data set. If a particular analysis requires cases not present within the subfile, the subfile must be reformed, necessitating yet another pass through the total data set.

The traditional data file is costly both to maintain and to analyze. As a result, the maintenance and analysis of such files are often left to software experts. The inevitable consequence of this management strategy is the emergence of a hierarchy of experts who intervene between researchers and their data. The average researcher rarely has the opportunity simply to sit at a terminal and interactively analyze a large data file. A simple request for analysis often involves negotiations with a data support staff and sometimes with a programming staff as well. Thus, researchers have learned to associate large data sets with large computers and the bureaucracies developed to maintain them.

Bureaucratic maintenance of large data sets leads, in turn, to the monopolization of those data sets by the agencies maintaining them. As a result, data sets containing related information fall under the varied jurisdictions of an assortment of government bureaus and agencies. In order to obtain analyses from related data sets, a researcher is forced to tailor his analysis requests to the specifications of various agencies, coordinate his research efforts around the responses of those agencies, and integrate the disparate analyses once they are received. A considerable time gap frequently exists between the researcher's expectations and an agency's response, and this gap tends to be a function of competing demands made upon the agency. Data analysis is usually only one of many duties assigned to an agency housing a large data file; the diversification of responsibilities is ultimately reflected in the lengthy turnaround time required to obtain even simple analyses.

In summary, the traditional approach to management of large data bases has been characterized by case-oriented computer programs and packages; dependence upon magnetic tapes for both program execution and data storage; the development of a one-pass analysis philosophy that precludes exploration of alternative strategies; significant time and cost penalties attached to misspecification; the proliferation of data subfiles; the emergence of software experts separating the researcher from the data; and monopolization of large data sets by certain agencies.

A Viable Alternative

Future computer hardware developments may well lessen the impact of some of these problems. For example, reliance upon magnetic tapes for data storage will diminish as disc storage becomes cheaper and more readily available. But hardware improvements are unnecessary for solving the research problems associated with the traditional approach. Most of the problems discussed above can be circumvented effectively by the use of current software developments. Considerations of data security will continue to necessitate existing monopolies of certain data sets, but the improvement in access capability that can result from the implementation of the three ideas detailed below should allow for a substantial enhancement of the services these agencies can provide to researchers.

Although the ideas presented here are not new, their particular combination in the development of GRASP (Generalized Rapid Access Software Package) may well be. The basic ideas discussed here are (*a*) *variable orientation* as a mode of data storage; (*b*) *dichotomous variables* as a means of sample definition; and (*c*) *matrix formation* as an analytical approach. It is not our intent to provide exhaustive documentation of systems containing some of these elements, but rather to convince the reader that these elements can, indeed, be successfully combined into a flexible, cost-efficient research system that eliminates the necessity of most practices traditionally associated with the management of large data bases.

Variable Orientation

This first strategy involves a simple modification in data storage. Rather than arranging the data by case, as in the traditional approach, we arranged the data by variable. Compare the structure of the variable-oriented file in Table 16.2 with the case-oriented file in Table 16.1. Both files contain the same data.

Obviously, only four records instead of five are required to store the

TABLE 16.2
A Variable-Oriented Data File

		Case 1	Case 2	Case 3	Case 4	Case 5
First record:	Sex	1	2	1	1	2
Second record:	Race	1	3	1	3	2
Third record:	Socioeconomic status	4	4	5	2	1
Fourth record:	Education	20	16	18	8	6

data for Table 16.2. The implications of this data transformation are more obvious when a slightly larger file is examined. Consider, for example, a file of 200 cases, each having values for 20 variables. In the traditional case orientation, this file would consist of 200 records with 20 entries per record. If a researcher needed all of the information for one particular characteristic present in the file, he would have to read that information from each of the 200 records in the case-oriented file. Arranging this same file by variable rather than by case would result in a file consisting of 20 records with 200 entries per record. A researcher could then obtain all the information for one characteristic in that file by reading only one record.

The variable-oriented file is practical because data analysis usually focuses selectively on particular variables or attributes of cases rather than on the cases themselves. With a variable-oriented file, only the variables that are going to be used in analysis need to be read by the computer; variables not used can be ignored. Since reading data is not one of the operations a computer performs most efficiently, using this strategy to reduce the number of readings required results in considerable savings of time and money when doing analytical work with standard survey research data. For example, the amount of computer time required to analyze the National Opinion Research Center (NORC) General Social Survey data (Davis *et al.*, 1978) has been reduced by approximately 95 % by implementing this change in storage strategy.

Rather than create one large variable-oriented file from a large case-oriented one, the more practical approach is to reduce the large file to many small ones containing a few variables each. Then these small files can be stored on magnetic tapes. Since only those variables required for an analysis need be accessible by the program, and since variable-oriented files contain information for all cases, the small files containing necessary data can be transferred to disc immediately prior to program execution and deleted thereafter. In this manner, all variables or selected groups of variables can be maintained as independent files on tape and transferred to disc as needed. As new variables are added to the file, they are created as additional independent files and also stored on tape.

As an example, consider a hypothetical variable-oriented data file containing demographic information on 1 million cases (for example, workers, persons, or households). Frequency distributions by sex, race, and age for those cases residing in the Western region could be computed by reading only those records containing sex, race, age, and location, leaving the rest of the data set undisturbed. Obtaining these same frequency distributions from a case-oriented file would necessitate reading all 1 million records just to obtain the sex, race, age, and location information from each one. Although the variable-oriented records are longer than the case-oriented ones, the fact that unnecessary information need not be read greatly reduces the computer time required to produce the frequency tables. Since only four variables are utilized in this analysis, the data can easily be stored on disc rather than tape during program execution, thus taking advantage of rapid disc access. The prohibitive cost of storing the entire million-case file on disc virtually rules out this mode of data access for analysis of the case-oriented file.

Dichotomous Variables

The second basic strategy involves forming special variables that increase the storage efficiency of variable-oriented records and, more important, play a crucial role in the rapid identification of subsamples in large data bases. Using such variables, it is possible, in less than a minute, to define a subsample of specific interest from a file containing several million cases. This rapid sampling capability makes the exploration of large data sets cost efficient, both in terms of computer expense and the researcher's time.

These special variables are dichotomous variables, or variables with only two possible codes: 0 and 1. Dichotomization of variables is similar to the creation of dummy variables, as dichotomization requires that a new variable be created for each category of the original. For example, if the original variable were census region having four codes—Northeast, North Central, South, and West—four new variables would be created. For each of the new variables, code 0 would indicate absence from that region and code 1 would indicate presence in that region. Each case would have a code 1 for one of the new variables and code 0 for the other three, since the case could be present in only one of the census regions.

Dichotomous variables that indicate some combination of characteristics from an original variable may be created. For example, a variable grouping counties might have the following nine codes:

1 = large metropolitan county
2 = medium metropolitan county
3 = small metropolitan county
4 = urbanized nonmetropolitan county adjacent to an SMSA
5 = urbanized nonmetropolitan county not adjacent to an SMSA
6 = less urbanized nonmetropolitan county adjacent to an SMSA
7 = less urbanized nonmetropolitan county not adjacent to an SMSA
8 = thinly population nonmetropolitan county adjacent to an SMSA
9 = thinly populated nonmetropolitan county not adjacent to
    an SMSA

A new dichotomous variable, "metropolitan," could be created from the first three codes of the new county-grouping variable; all counties coded 1, 2, or 3 in the original variable would be coded 1 in the new metropolitan variable, and original codes 4–9 would be coded 0. Or a researcher might want to create a "nonmetropolitan adjacent" variable in which code 1 represented codes 4, 6, and 8 of the original variable and code 0 represented all other codes. In a similar manner, dichotomous variables based on characteristics or attributes from several different variables can also be created.

Although savings in storage space and computer time may not be the expected results of creating even more variables, storage space can be minimized and analysis time maximized by packing the dichotomous variables efficiently in computer storage space. However, the most important reason for creating dichotomous variables has nothing to do with storage considerations; the real power of these variables comes through their use in defining subsamples rapidly. Dichotomous variables are an extremely efficient mechanism for sample definition. A sample can be defined merely for the purpose of counting the number of cases included in just a fraction of a minute of computer time.

A sample may be defined using one or several dichotomous variables. The logical operators 'and', 'or', and 'eor' (exclusive or) serve to combine dichotomous variables, and variables can be negated with the operator 'not'. Cases coded 1 for specified variables are included in the sample, and cases coded 0 are omitted. The size of any sample can be quickly determined by counting the number of 1s. Logical operators define samples according to the following rules:

X AND Y: Sample includes cases coded 1 for both variables
X OR Y: Sample includes cases coded 1 for one or both variables
X EOR Y: Sample includes cases coded 1 for either variable but not both
NOT X: Sample includes cases not coded 1

The samples considered in Table 16.4 can be defined with these two variables and the different logical operators.

TABLE 16.3
Sample Dichotomous Variables

| Variable | Values | | | |
	Case 1	Case 2	Case 3	Case 4
Male	1	1	0	0
White	1	0	0	1

TABLE 16.4
Logical Combinations of Dichotomous Variables

Sample definition	Cases included in sample	Sample size
Male and white	Case 1	1
Male or white	Cases 1,2,4	3
Male eor white	Cases 2,4	2
Not male	Cases 3,4	2
Not white	Cases 2,3	2

Many dichotomous variables strung together define samples with great precision. If a researcher wanted to determine how many white males migrated from the Northeastern region to the Southern region between 1965 and 1970, he or she would specify the following set of dichotomous variables:

MALE AND WHITE AND NER65 AND SR70

This sample definition can be modified to include all white males in the Northeastern region in 1960 or 1965 and in the Southern region in 1970 or 1975:

MALE AND WHITE AND (NER60 OR NER65) AND (SR70 OR SR75)

Since samples can be so rapidly defined with dichotomous variables, the researcher could continue to modify this definition and explore the size implications of various samples quite inexpensively. The sample definition utilizes six variables; to define that sample, a variable-oriented program reads only the records containing the information for those six variables. In contrast, a case-oriented program must read each case record in the entire data set. Determining the sizes of various samples in a million-case file using a conventional case-oriented program is a major proposition. The task is trivial with a variable-oriented program.

The computer central processing unit (CPU) time required to define a sample is dependent less on the number of cases included in the sample than on the number of variables required to define it. Still, there is no significant limitation on the number of dichotomous variables that can be combined in this manner. The logical operators work very rapidly; several samples can be generated in less than 1 minute of CPU time.

In practice, a dichotomous variable should be created from an attribute with multiple codes when the same specification of that attribute will be used many times to define samples. The basic sample can be defined with dichotomous variables and then further refined with variables that are not dichotomous. Such a strategy allows a large data set to be repeatedly sampled without incurring the penalties normally attached to reading a large file.

Matrix Formation

The last basic strategy to be presented is not restricted to variable-oriented files, but provides an increase in analytical efficiency comparable with that achieved by transforming files from case- to variable-oriented data storage. This strategy involves the formation of an n-dimensional matrix consisting of all possible values or codes for all variables as an intermediate step between reading the raw data and executing the data analysis. Such a matrix occupies relatively little computer disc space and permits a large number of analyses to be accomplished with incredible speed. Although this strategy has many possible applications, we will restrict our discussion to its role in tabular analysis.

Consider the following example: A researcher wishes to explore the sex, race, and age characteristics of migrants to and from the census

TABLE 16.5
Four Demographic Variables

Variable	Codes
Sexrace	1 = white male
	2 = nonwhite male
	3 = white female
	4 = nonwhite female
Age	1 = 1 to 20
	2 = 21 to 45
	3 = 46 to 65
	4 = 66 to 99
Region 65	1 = Northeast
	2 = North Central
	3 = Southern
	4 = Western
Region 70	1 = Northeast
	2 = North Central
	3 = Southern
	4 = Western

regions for the years 1965 and 1970. He or she could accomplish such analysis with the four variables shown in Table 16.5. These four variables could be incorporated into a four-dimensional matrix—a table containing cells for all possible combinations of codes. This matrix is illustrated in Table 16.6. Each of the rows in Table 16.6 represents one cell. Each cell contains the number of cases that meet the code criteria for that cell. For example, the first cell in Table 16.6 contains the number of white males 1–20 years of age in the Northeast region in 1965 and 1970. Since each of the variables has four codes, the resulting matrix consists of 256 cells (4 × 4 × 4 × 4). It is important to note that the amount of computer space required to store this matrix is independent of the number of cells the matrix contains; a 100,000-case matrix will require the same amount of storage space that a 100-case matrix occupies.

This matrix can be developed from case or variable information as it is presented to the program and then saved as a small file to be retrieved repeatedly for future analysis. The importance of this strategy lies in the flexibility and speed with which data in this small file can be analyzed. Frequency distributions and cross-tabulations can easily be accomplished in a simple series of executions, without returning to the raw

TABLE 16.6
Cells of a Four-Variable Matrix

Cell	Sexrace	Age	Region 65	Region 70
1	1	1	1	1
2	1	1	1	2
3	1	1	1	3
4	1	1	1	4
5	1	1	2	1
6	1	1	2	2
7	1	1	2	3
8	1	1	2	4
9	1	1	3	1
.	.	.	.	.
.	.	.	.	.
.	.	.	.	.
248	4	4	2	4
249	4	4	3	1
250	4	4	3	2
251	4	4	3	3
252	4	4	3	4
253	4	4	4	1
254	4	4	4	2
255	4	4	4	3
256	4	4	4	4

data. The initial analysis may suggest others—particularly, what codes of variables should be controlled. It is a simple matter to analyze selected variables while controlling codes on others.

A typical analysis using this matrix would probably begin with frequency distributions on each of the individual variables and a cross-tabulation showing regional migration. The next step might involve generating frequency distributions or cross-tabulations of certain variables while restricting the sample to particular code ranges of other variables. For example, the region migration cross-tabulation can be further refined as follows:

1. REGION 65 by REGION 70 for each category of SEXRACE
   (4 cross-tabulations)
2. REGION 65 by REGION 70 for each category of AGE
   (4 cross-tabulations)
3. REGION 65 by REGION 70 for each unique category of SEXRACE and AGE
   (16 cross-tabulations)

This analysis could also be performed using any two variables in the matrix and refined in terms of the other two. The frequency distribution for any one variable can be similarly refined in terms of the other three variables.

Once the cells of the data matrix have been defined, the cases within those cells cannot be further differentiated. For example, the age category 21–45 cannot be broken down into the categories 21–35 and 36–45. However, categories can be collapsed for ease of analysis. The sex–race variable could be collapsed into male–female or white–nonwhite categories. Although categories from an existing table can always be collapsed by the researcher this is a tedious and time consuming process better left to the computer.

None of the analyses need be performed at the time the matrix is developed; once the matrix exists as a small file it is accessible for later analysis. The amount of computer time required for these analyses is trivial, and turnaround time is extremely rapid because the data are aggregated in a relatively small number of cells rather than arranged in terms of thousands of individual cases.

Implementation of the Alternative Strategy

We have reviewed major characteristics of the traditional approach to the management of large data bases and have presented three key ideas that can minimize most of the constraints and disadvantages of the traditional approach. These ideas are the use of variable orientation as a mode of data storage, the use of dichotomous variables to facilitate rapid sample definition, and the retrieval of data in an n-dimensional matrix to facilitate rapid tabular analysis.

These ideas must be embedded in an operational system before the benefits can be derived from their use. Although each of these ideas is useful individually, the greater benefits are achieved when they are combined in a single system. Several alternative designs could be proposed to accomplish this implementation, but not all of these designs would necessarily produce systems with comparable advantages over the traditional approach. Furthermore, the benefits of these implementations are difficult to measure in terms of time and cost because of variations among computers and differences in management policies at computer installations. The optimum strategy at one installation might be much less efficient at another.

A comparative discussion of the merits of various software implementation is beyond the scope of this chapter. Our purpose here is to present the research implications of an optimum implementation, which we will refer to as the *alternative strategy*. After discussing these research implications in general, we will discuss our experience with an actual implementation of the alternative strategy called GRASP.

General Research Implications

The disadvantages of the traditional mode of data access and analysis can ultimately be traced to the large amounts of time and money consumed in that approach. The alternative strategy—an optimum implementation of our three key ideas—overcomes these disadvantages by providing both faster access and faster analysis of data stored in large files. Furthermore, the alternative strategy has research implications that extend beyond the obvious savings of time and money.

Converting files to variable orientation makes possible a file-merging capability that gives a flexibility in file content. Small files containing only the variables required for a particular project can be created from the main data set, and since the case structure of the main file is preserved, additional variables can be moved to the small file if the project definition is changed. Two files sharing a common unit of observation can easily be merged into a single file, or selected variables from one file can be integrated into another.

Variable orientation also makes possible the creation of efficiently packed dichotomous variables, which in turn permit rapid sample definition. Sample definition with the alternative strategy is sufficiently rapid to encourage researchers to pursue an exploratory, stepwise approach to analysis rather than the comprehensive type of analysis associated with the traditional mode. Both dichotomous variable sampling and data matrix retrieval are factors that lower turnaround time. The short turnaround time associated with the alternative strategy makes feasible a remote data-access network with the prospect of cost-efficient analysis of large data files a viable possibility for an ever-increasing number of researchers.

The Research Potential of the Alternative Strategy

The general implications of the alternative strategy can best be understood in the context of a few specific examples of the analytic advantages accruing from an optimal implementation. These examples serve to illustrate the capability to merge data sets, the generation of a stepwise research strategy, the sampling alternative to the formation of data subfiles, and the determination of who will access large data sets with what degree of flexibility.

DATA-MERGING CAPABILITY

Rapid data access requires a file converted to variable format and a data directory index to the variables in the file. When data are available in variable orientation, only those variables needed for a particular analysis need be moved from tape to disc. Variables isolated from the main data set can exist as separate files, because the variables receive their organizational structure from the data directory. Since the data directory is the structural key to a variable-oriented file, any variables added to the directory also become incorporated into the structure of the larger file. In this manner, the alternative strategy permits a type of data merging that bypasses the need for physical movement of files. The time and space requirements of the physical merging process have traditionally been obstacles to the merging of large data files; with the alternative strategy, data merging becomes a trivial operation for files sharing a common unit of observation. This merging capability allows considerable flexibility in file structure; data from different files can be merged to create a new file with the cumulative data of both originals, and variables can be extracted from a large file to form a small file containing only a subset of the data. Thus, a researcher desiring to incoroporate his own data into a large file can send it to be merged with that file and analyzed in conjunction with it. Similarly, a researcher requiring a unique set of variables for analysis can order a custom file from an organization maintaining a large file that contains those variables.

The fact that only those variables needed for a current request need be present on disc to execute the analysis combined with the fact that these variables can be obtained from tape without manipulating the entire data set means that large data bases can be maintained and managed on a medium-size computer with resources that are relatively limited by modern standards. Given this degree of flexibility, the available disc storage can be used to set up data simultaneously from several different large data sets.

RAPID SAMPLING AND THE STEPWISE RESEARCH STRATEGY

A variety of questions concerning the migration turnaround phenomenon discussed in this book would lead a researcher to consider the use of a large data file such as the Continuous Work History Sample (U.S. Department of Commerce, 1976). However, research with a case-oriented CWHS file is extremely expensive. But if a variable-oriented file and a compatible software implementation are available, considerably more research can be accomplished with considerably less money.

Once the decision has been made to utilize a large file like the CWHS, on the basis of the researcher's general area of interests, specific research questions must be developed. Technically, the case or variable orientation of a data set has no influence on the types of questions that can be answered. Practically, however, resources are a major consideration. In the traditional mode it is almost imperative that a research request be of a comprehensive rather than of an exploratory nature. Exploratory requests require reading the entire case-oriented data set several times; only one reading is required to gather the data for a comprehensive request.

Nothing inherent in the alternative strategy precludes a one-pass data analysis, and the latter may be the method of choice for a researcher who has become familiar with a data set through extensive work with it. But for the researcher whose hypotheses are very tentative or who is working with a data set for the first time, the alternative strategy offers the capability of a stepwise approach to data analysis. This stepwise approach affords the researcher some protection against unforeseen problems with a hypothesis or peculiarities of a data set that might render a one-pass analysis virtually worthless. To obtain a one-pass analysis on a large data set, the researcher must submit a detiled description of his sample and of all the analyses to be performed on that sample. If the results run counter to expectations, the researcher has two options: redefine and resubmit the request, or make the best of the results obtained. Either option represents a waste of the researcher's time, money, and effort.

A researcher using the alternative strategy need not plan an entire analysis in advance. The researcher can take advantage of the savings in time and cost to plan the analysis as it proceeds. Initially, several samples can be defined in order to ascertain the number of cases present in each. Once a working sample is chosen, the researcher can examine the implications that recoding may have for some of the analytic variables. Finally, the researcher can proceed with his statistical analysis in serial fashion, basing each step of the analysis upon previously obtained results. If the analysis yields unexpected results, the researcher has the opportunity to rethink the hypothesis before continuing. If the analysis seems to be leading nowhere, the researcher can reexamine the direction of his or her work.

Most researchers are familiar with this stepwise approach through analysis of small data sets; the alternative strategy makes a stepwise approach possible for large data sets as well. The savings are most apparent with very large data sets containing tens of thousands or millions of cases.

As an example, if a researcher wished to discover which industries were principally responsible for leading the deconcentration of the labor force currently going on in the United States, he or she would have to make decisions concerning the precise industry categorization and geographic classifications required to design the analysis for a case-oriented CWHS file. To a large extent, of course, these decisions must be made from theoretical rather than data-base considerations. But with the alternative strategy, the sample-size, or cell-size, implications of all these decisions can be explored prior to attaching the specifications of additional attributes ultimately desired in the analysis. When a particular sample is revealed to be of insufficient size, it can be discarded before further analysis costs are incurred. In the context of our example, a fruitful approach might be to examine the implications of a new recategorization of the industry variable from the original two-digit SIC classification to an arbitrary grouping of these entries into seven categories by obtaining answers to the following questions: (a) "How many persons were in each of the new industry groupings at specific points in time?"; (b) "How many persons changed or did not change industry status during a given period?"; (c) "For persons employed in a particular industry grouping at the start of a time period, in which industries are they employed at the end of the period?" If the answers to these questions yield groups large enough to merit further study, then several additional questions can be pursued: (*a*) "What proportion of the industry switchers also changed county of employment during the period?"; (*b*) "For those industry switchers identified as migrants, what proportion changed from a metropolitan county of employment to a nonmetropolitan county?"

In addition, given a particular migration stream—for example, metropolitan to nonmetropolitan—the proportions of workers who were industry switchers and industry stayers could be readily obtained. Without belaboring the point, the samples could be further explored with additional specifications giving regional answers to all of the above questions or identifying migration streams more precisely by county type or by patterns of wage change. This sequence of questions cannot be answered by means of a single pass through a case-oriented data set, but obtaining the answers is a trivial problem with a variable-oriented file and an appropriate software system. Obviously, the latter approach gives the researcher considerable flexibility in conducting any analysis.

The important point is that these questions can be answered quickly and at very low cost. The time necessary to complete a request is a function more of scheduling staff time than computer time. The actual computer time necessary to process any of the above requests would not exceed more than 10 minutes of central processing unit (CPU) time. In short, the rapid turnaround time and low cost associated with the alternative strategy allow a researcher to develop a stepwise approach for addressing a data set and then utilizing the information generated at each step to plan subsequent analyses. It is not necessary that a comprehensive request of the data be generated without the benefit of initial, direct examination of samples of interest.

Given the ease with which a stepwise strategy can be executed, it is obvious that the costs associated with making specification errors with the alternative strategy are far less than they would be for similar errors in the traditional mode. Repeating an analysis step because of specification error is analogous in scope to asking for another computer run for any other reason. The implications for project completion time and cost are generally trivial.

A SAMPLING ALTERNATIVE TO SUBFILE FORMATION

A researcher working with a large case-oriented data file frequently forms a subfile containing only data for cases included in the sample of interest. A typical subfile formed from the CWHS might include all cases in a particular state or region. Analysis of this case-oriented subfile could be accomplished at substantially lower cost than an analysis of the entire file, but once a set of cases has been isolated in a subfile those cases can no longer be analyzed in conjunction with the main file. With the alternative approach developed in this paper, the identification, documentation, and storage procedures necessary to maintain subfiles are eliminated. The process of sample definition is so rapid with this system that the desired sample can be redefined hundreds of times at less cost than that required to form a traditional case-oriented subfile. Furthermore, this is accomplished without severing the ties of those cases to the main data base.

As an example, the researcher may define a sample of nonmigrants for the western region from 1965 to 1970. All variables used to define this sample and to describe the nonmigrants contain information for all cases in the country, not just the western region. Thus, any change in definition of the region to be studied can be implemented immediately. Similarly, another region can be defined and a comparative analysis conducted. If characteristics or variables are not present for immediate use, they can be quickly retrieved from tape to complement the existing set of variables residing on disc.

Data Access for Researchers

The research implications of rapid data access cannot be separated from those of rapid analytic capability, since it is the interrelationship of these aspects of the alternative strategy that results in a truly powerful system. This linkage has been essential to the advantages identified with the stepwise research strategy and the elimination of the subfile structure by means of a sampling alternative. The implications of the alternative software strategy for the general improvement of access to large data sets are a function of this linkage as well. The most important implications of the alternative strategy emerge when the strategy is considered as a whole, and these implications are predominantly a function of lowering costs.

As the costs incurred in analyzing larger data files diminish, more researchers will begin to use these files. Many of these researchers will be persons unable to afford an analysis in the traditional mode, including faculty and students associated with academic institutions, data analysts in planning agencies, policy analysts in government and industry, and others with limited resources. As the number of persons analyzing larger data files increases, so will the amount, variety, and complexity of the research undertaken. The rapid turnaround time between submission of a request for data analysis and receipt of the results has a twofold implication: More research can be accomplished in a given period of time, and projects can be completed more quickly. Rapid access coupled with rapid analysis could lead to the most exciting research implication of all—the formation of national and regional data-access networks. Large files of related data could be merged and maintained in these centers, with remote-access service available for interactive analysis and with provisions for more conventional data-analysis services. The greatest advantage of such centers lies in the sheer amount of data that could be assembled in a few locations, permitting cost-efficient analysis of data previously unavailable in combination.

The small amount of computer time required for most work based on the alternative strategy makes direct interactive analysis by long distance phone not only feasible, but practical. With a long distance line, a telephone coupler, a computer terminal, and some training in the alternative approach, a researcher can in many instances bypass the middleman who usually mediates acess to large data files.

Thus, the alternative strategy gives researchers the option to choose the extent to which they will participate in their own work. A researcher can submit a well-defined request for data analysis to personnel trained in the strategy and let them plan the details of the analysis. The researcher can proceed with a stepwise strategy through a middleman, submitting requests serially. Or the researcher can learn to use an alternative program personally and to interact directly with the data base. At the very least, the alternative strategy can save the researcher substantial amounts of money. At most, it can give the researcher a kind of control over the analysis of large data sets that is impractical for most persons with conventional programs.

GRASP—An Illustrative Implementation

All of our experiences in data access and analysis with the alternative strategy have been with GRASP, a program developed at Montana State University by the Center for Social Data Analysis. Generally speaking, the benefits of GRASP can be attributed to the three key ideas presented earlier; however, GRASP is a system that utilizes many software strategies, and power of the system is a function of the successful meshing of many ideas rather than the obvious superiority of a few. GRASP optimizes the ideas detailed earlier by using a variety of software strategies. The interrelationship of these strategies will become more apparent as we discuss our application of GRASP to migration research with our own version of the Continuous Work History Sample.

Our CWHS file contains data for the years 1960 and 1965–1975 with Social Security numbers removed; it is a 1% first-quarter sample, representing 1,317,484 cases (see Chapter 15 for a full discussion of these data). We have arranged this file for our own purposes using GRASP, and by so doing we have overcome some of the disadvantages associated with analyzing the CWHS. The sample size and work-force composition are, of course, considerations beyond our control, but the limited number of characteristics available and the expenses associated with data analysis are aspects we have altered with GRASP.

The expense associated with analyzing the CWHS is largely a function of case orientation. Every pass through a large case-oriented file is expensive, because all of the data must be read whether or not they are required for the analysis. We used GRASP to convert the CWHS file to a variable-oriented format, and the expense of this conversion was quickly offset by the savings in analysis costs subsequently achieved with GRASP. Our experience with the CWHS file is applicable to any other large data file: The greatest single expense is incurred in converting the file to variable orientation. Once converted, all the efficient access and analytic capabilities of GRASP can be brought to bear on the data.

Since our CWHS file has a variable-oriented format, we need move from magnetic tape to disc only those variables required for the analysis in progress. The variable orientation also facilitates formation of dichotomous variables from existing characteristics or combinations of characteristics in the file. Once our dichotomous variables are formed, we can take advantage of the rapid sampling approach discussed earlier. We have expanded the basic data in our original CWHS file to over 1000 variables, many of which are dichotomous for sampling purposes.

Many of the variables we have added to the CWHS file are transformations or combinations of existing variables; we have made these changes in variable structure to simplify and expedite data analysis. Of more interest from a substantive point of view are variables we have added as contextual properties from other data sources. The variable orientation of the GRASP software in combination with the directory system providing access to the data has enabled us to merge data from other files with the CWHS when both files share a common unit of observation. For example, we have attached a variable from the 1970 Census Fourth Count County Summary Tape categorizing county size and adjacency status to each case (worker) in the CWHS file having a valid county location code (some cases in the CWHS have only valid state location codes). We accomplished this by first adding the Federal Information Processing Standards (FIPS) location code equivalent of each Social Security location code to the CWHS file and then using the FIPS code as a common index between files. The result is a new variable in our CWHS file that indicates the size–adjacency status of the county in which each worker is employed.

Since GRASP does allow new variables to be formed as recoded versions of existing ones, we could have added this variable to the CWHS file by assembling the size–adjacency information for all counties and then recoding the counties by type. In this particular instance, however, the process is labor intensive, both in gathering the necessary information and in specifying recodes for each county in the country. The merging procedure we elected to use required little staff work and less than 2 minutes of CPU time.

This size–adjacency status variable has made possible CWHS-based migration research oriented by county type, such as studies of the characteristics of migrants from metropolitan to nonmetropolitan areas. The fact that so little effort was required to add this variable to our file means that the cost of this operation is relatively low. The low costs provide one incentive to explore other characteristics that could be integrated to allow for greater freedom in conceptualizing points of origin and destination of migration streams or to describe those migration streams in greater detail. For example, the percentage of persons in each county employed in a given industry could be merged from the Bureau of Economic Analysis (BEA) employment tapes to answer questions concerning the influence of industrial base on migration. Similarly, environmental information on climate, elevation, water area, shore line, and rivers could be merged from the Area Resource File and the Area Measurement File in order to explore the relationship between migration and recreational development. Finally, population centroids merged from the Area Measurement File would permit better estimates of distances involved in county-to-county moves.

Just as we can use GRASP to merge data at an aggregate level into a large file of individual cases, so can we merge data sets at the same level having a common unit of analysis. We have used GRASP's merging procedure to create the National County Data Base (NCDB), a county-level data file consisting of social, economic, and demographic information on each county unit in the nation. Because data-base merging is accomplished by means of a logical process centering on the design of the data directory system, none of an existing data base need be disturbed to accomplish its merger with another data set. For example, when we merged data from the Area Resource File with our existing county data set, we first converted the data from the Area Resource File to a variable orientation and then updated our county directory to achieve the merger. No reading or writing of the existing county file was necessary to accomplish this merger. The NCDB becomes more valuable with each such addition, since any variable in the file can be analyzed in terms of any other variable. The collation of variables in the NCDB allows us to prepare detailed profiles of counties or collections of counties of interest as well as cross-county comparisons.

During the past 3 years a number of researchers have taken advantage of the GRASP software and variable-oriented CWHS and NCDB files to further their migration-oriented investigations.

These investigations begin to tap the potential uses of the system. With the existing data base, longitudinal analysis of changes in rural, social, economic, and demographic structure can be obtained with a breadth that was heretofore impossible at such low cost and speed. Comparison counties matched on a number of characteristics to a county or group of counties of interest can be examined for social impact analysis and other quasi-experimental designs of change effects. Baseline levels of health resources and other human services can be determined in growing rural areas to examine the impact of recent migration-induced growth. Retirement migration can be compared to general population mobility and to labor-force mobility by industry. Indices of recreation growth can be constructed and related to the locations of counties with respect to proximate and distant large metropolitan centers of population.

Although the NCDB is not a large file in terms of the number of cases it contains (all counties in the United States), the 7000 variables attached to those cases make the file large enough to be analyzed much more efficiently with GRASP than with a conventional software package. Given the rapid access capabilities of GRASP, users far removed from Montana find it cost-efficient to dial direct to the Montana State University computer to analyze both the CWHS and the NCDB. Work with the CWHS file is especially facilitated by access through the matrix mode illustrated earlier. Typically, a researcher chooses a sample of the file and a few variables for analysis. A data matrix is created according to the researcher's specifications, and the researcher analyzes the matrix using GRASP and long-distance phone. GRASP and our variable-oriented data files allow us to operate a small-scale national data-access network. Our success in providing rapid cost-efficient access to the CWHS and the NCDB is testimony to the utility of the ideas involved in the alternative strategy. Our ability to provide this access with limited core and disc resources demonstrates that large data bases need not be inextricably bound to giant computers.

Conclusions

This chapter represents one of the first formal attempts to disseminate information about the technology that is utilized in GRASP. Our aim has been to stimulate readers to examine potential benefits that could derive from widespread usage of a GRASP-like software implementation. We have shown that three key ideas, when optimally implemented in a software system, provide for radical changes in the opportunity afforded researchers to access a large data base. The professional advantages that have accrued thus far to researchers through their activities with GRASP and the data bases available at Montana State University represent only a tiny fraction of what we think is possible if more persons had ready access to centers or agencies with this combination of resources.

What we have accomplished on a small scale could be profitably repeated on a larger scale to create regional data centers to provide access to integrated data bases. Each of these centers could develop data bases that expand disciplinary coverage to include data from the physical and biological sciences, while keeping to a minimum unnecessary duplication. Although several institutional arrangements are undoubtedly workable, the USDA-affiliated regional rural-development centers provide an existing structure that could serve as a network of viable data depositories. In addition to the regional centers, it would be necessary to have at least one federal agency maintaining data bases of a confidential nature and serving as a conduit for updating the data bases at the regional centers. Federal work on large data bases would also be greatly facilitated by the GRASP approach. Of course, an appropriate substantive commitment to management of the data and maintenance of the software is essential to ensure the ongoing success of such an endeavor. Adequate, low-cost communication linkage to these centers must also be provided so that the effectiveness of remote national access capability is not diminished.

In short, the ideas presented here provide an opportunity to greatly expand the ability to do effective research with large data bases. What the future will bring is in large part a function of the professional response generated by the realization of the advantages so far accrued and a recognition of what is indeed possible.

Acknowledgments

We would like to take this opportunity to acknowledge the contributions of several persons and agencies who have been involved in one way or another in the development of GRASP. Major credit goes to Edward O. Moe for his continued moral support and for his efforts on our behalf with Cooperative Research to provide the funding necessary to develop GRASP. The Computing Center at Montana State University has provided technical support and, for 2 years, the Office of the Vice-President for Research of that University has provided a needed institutional base.

Our thanks go to Bob Motsch for providing the initial stimulus to utilize several of the ideas on which GRASP is based. We owe a debt of gratitude to Tom Klindt and Bob

Hunter, programmers in the Center for Social Data Analysis. They have contributed many ideas toward the development of GRASP and have been fully responsible for its coding. We give special thanks to Lloyd Bender, who provided our initial version of the CWHS file and who has been an important supporter of the system ever since. The Economic Development Division of ESCS–USDA helped support the development of the National County Data Base. Thanks are also given to all users of the system.

We would like to thank Fred Halley for painstakingly reviewing the initial part of the chapter and Dorothy Jorgensen for patiently typing the seemingly endless drafts.

References

Beale, Calvin L.
  1975 "The revival of population growth in nonmetropolitan America." ERS–605. Washington, D.C.: U.S. Department of Agriculture, Economic Research Service.
Da Vanzo, Julie and Peter A. Morrison
  1978 "Dynamics of return migration: Descriptive findings from a longitudinal study." The Rand Corporation.
Davis, James A., Tom W. Smith, and C. Bruce Stephenson
  1978 *General Social Surveys, 1972–1978: Cumulative Codebook.* Chicago: University of Chicago, National Opinion Research Center.
Goldstein, Sydney
  1976 "Facts of redistribution: Research challenges and opportunities." *Demography* 13 (November): 423–434.
Long, Larry H. and Kristin A. Hansen
  1977 "Migration trends in the United States." Washington, D.C.: U.S. Bureau of the Census. Unpublished.
Schwarzweller, Harry K.
  1979 "Migration and the changing rural scene." *Rural Sociology* 44: 7–23.
Tucker, C. Jack
  1976 "Changing patterns of migration between metropolitan and nonmetropolitan areas in the United States: Recent evidence." *Demography* 13 (November): 435–443.
U.S. Department of Commerce
  1976 *Regional Work Force Characteristics and Migration Data.* Bureau of Economic Analysis. Washington, D.C.: U.S. Government Printing Office.
Wardwell, John M.
  1977 "Equilibrium and change in nonmetropolitan growth." *Rural Sociology* 42 (2):156–179.
Wardwell, John M., C. Jack Gilchrist, and Celia A. Allard
  1978 "Regional variation in nonmetropolitan migration." Paper presented at the Southern Sociological Society Annual Meetings, New Orleans.
Zuiches, James J. and David L. Brown
  1978 "The changing character of the nonmetropolitan population, 1950–75." Chapter 4 in Thomas R. Ford (ed.), *Rural Society in the United States—Current Trends and Issues.* Ames: Iowa State University Press.

Index